D1357754

Berlin's Black Market: 1939–1950

Worlds of Consumption

Published in association with the German Historical Institute, Washington, DC

Series Editors: Hartmut Berghoff and Uwe Spiekermann

Worlds of Consumption is a peer-reviewed venue for the history of consumption and consumerism in the modern era, especially the twentieth century, with a particular focus on comparative and transnational studies. It aims to make research available in English from an increasingly internationalized and inter-disciplinary field. The history of consumption offers a vital link among diverse fields of history and other social sciences, because modern societies are consumer societies whose political, cultural, social, and economic structures and practices are bound up with the history of consumption. *Worlds of Consumption* highlights and explores these linkages, which deserve wide attention, since they shape who we are as individuals and societies.

Published by Palgrave Macmillan:

Decoding Modern Consumer Societies
Edited by Hartmut Berghoff and Uwe Spiekerman

The Development of Consumer Credit in Global Perspective: Business, Regulation, and Culture
Edited by Jan Logemann

The Rise of Marketing and Market Research
Edited by Hartmut Berghoff, Philip Scranton, and Uwe Spiekermann

The Science of Beauty: Culture and Cosmetics in Modern Germany, 1750–1930
By Annelie Ramsbrock

Berlin's Black Market: 1939–1950
By Malte Zierenberg

Berlin's Black Market: 1939–1950

Malte Zierenberg

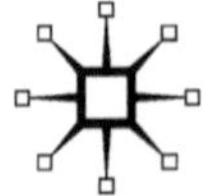

BERLIN'S BLACK MARKET: 1939–1950

First published 2015 by
PALGRAVE MACMILLAN

The author has asserted his right to be identified as the author of this work in accordance with the Copyright, Designs and Patents Act 1988.

Palgrave Macmillan in the UK is an imprint of Macmillan Publishers Limited, registered in England, company number 785998, of Houndmills, Basingstoke, Hampshire, RG21 6XS.

Palgrave Macmillan in the US is a division of Nature America, Inc., One New York Plaza, Suite 4500, New York, NY 10004-1562.

Palgrave Macmillan is the global academic imprint of the above companies and has companies and representatives throughout the world.

Hardback ISBN: 978–1–137–01774–1
E-PUB ISBN: 978–1–137–01776–5
E-PDF ISBN: 978–1–137–01775–8
DOI: 10.1057/978–1–137–01775–8

Distribution in the UK, Europe and the rest of the world is by Palgrave Macmillan®, a division of Macmillan Publishers Limited, registered in England, company number 785998, of Houndmills, Basingstoke, Hampshire RG21 6XS.

Library of Congress Cataloging-in-Publication Data

Zierenberg, Malte.
[Stadt der Schieber. English]
Black market Berlin : profiteers, illegal networds, and urban space in the German capital, 1939–1950 / Malte Zierenberg.
pages cm. — (Worlds of consumption)
Includes bibliographical references and index.
Summary: "This is a social history of Berlin's black market during World War II and the post-war period, looking at both its participants and their practices, the macroeconomic context in which the market operated and the everyday strategies that were deployed by individuals to navigate the market. Malte Zierenberg reveals the black market to be a complex structure, which is on the one hand a geographical space but on the other hand represents a conceptual category within an economy" — Provided by publisher.
Summary: "This book puts the illegal economy of the German capital during and after World War II into context and provides a new interpretation of Germany's postwar history. The black market, it argues, served as a reference point for the beginnings of the two new German states" — Provided by publisher.
ISBN 978–1–137–01774–1 (hardcover : alkaline paper)
1. Black market—Germany—Berlin—History—20th century. I. Title.
HF5482.65.G3Z5413 2015
381—dc23 2015014745

A catalogue record for the book is available from the British Library.

Contents

Figures

Acknowledgments

This book may have one author, but it certainly also has many facilitators. I would like to thank Hartmut Berghoff and Uwe Spiekermann of the German Historical Institute, Washington, DC, who kindly accepted this book into their *Worlds of Consumption* series. Hans-Peter Ullmann tremendously supported me as I launched into my research and, together with Margit Szöllösi-Janze, reviewed the original German manuscript. That manuscript, however, would neither exist nor have been able to see the light of day without the generous support of the Fritz Thyssen Foundation. My thanks also go to the German Historical Institute in London and the Schmoelders Foundation for much needed assistance during the final writing stage—the most critical for any research project.

I am indebted to Danuta Kneipp, Annelie Ramsbrock, Felizitas Schaub, Molly Loberg, and Thomas Mergel for their help and steady encouragement. I would furthermore like to thank Jeffrey Verhey for taking on the challenge of translating the sometimes awkwardly academic German text into readable English. Mark Stoneman and Patricia Sutcliffe superbly edited the English text. Barbara Schaeche of the Landesarchiv Berlin proved to be the most helpful and generous archivist I had the privilege of working with. Thanks to you all.

Introduction

The true war is a celebration of markets. Organic markets, carefully styled "black" by the professionals, spring up everywhere. Scrip, Sterling, Reichsmarks continue to move, severe as classical ballet, inside their antiseptic marble chambers. But out here, down here among the people, the truer currencies come into being.

Thomas Pynchon, *Gravity's Rainbow*[1]

1 2 4 3 5 6
b a t r e r

A Berlin woman using numbers to correct a mistyped word in her memoir manuscript[2]

The opinion of broad circles—and there are indeed many indicators of this—is that black marketeers should, as a rule, go to hell in the end.

Max Brinkmann, *Little Handbook for Black Marketeers*[3]

Yet another November 9. A less important one perhaps, certainly a different one. On November 9, 1944, Martha Rebbien, a black marketeer, was arrested in her Berlin apartment. For four years, she had participated in the black market, had found partners with whom to exchange goods, had learned the rules of the market, and had built up a distribution system. The present study uses Martha Rebbien's exchange network as a thread to hold the story together. Because the history of these networks is embedded in their historical context, this is more than the history of an illegal trader. It is also the history of a market, the participants in this market, their practices and methods, the macroeconomic context, and how individuals adapted to everyday conditions. Finally, this is also the history of a city and its inhabitants during the transition from war to postwar. By following our protagonist Martha Rebbien and her companions, as well as the traders of Berlin's illegal public marketplaces after 1945, we get a clearer picture of the black market as a radical market experience. It was this radical experience, this book argues, that shaped the discourses on postwar economies in both East and West Germany as key concepts for establishing the legitimacy of the new states.

This undertaking requires us to broaden our horizons. Up to now, historians have largely focused on those seemingly anachronistic black market activities that took place after the war ended. Yet unlawful trading was already visible in the middle of the 1930s, and it became a mass phenomenon when the war began, changing shape in the following years. Until the winter of 1944–45, black market trading mainly took place indoors with a limited number of participants. Martha Rebbien's story evinces this trend. Starting in November 1944 at the very latest, there were black markets in Berlin's streets and public squares. As a result, prerequisites for participation in this forbidden form of trade changed. Since it was no longer necessary to make arrangements to meet and trade, building up a complex network to exchange goods was also superfluous. Whoever wanted to trade something on the black market merely had to visit one of the illegal public markets located throughout the city.

Berlin's postwar black markets are well known and frequently visited sites of memory. Pictures of Germans and Allied soldiers exchanging goods in front of the Brandenburg Gate or the ruins of the Reichstag constitute an essential part of Germans' collective memory; they are a recurring theme in the stories and reports of life among the ruins. Yet historians have generally avoided these sites and paid little attention to the wartime history of the conditions favorable to their emergence. It is not that the black markets do not appear in the historiography, but they are usually only mentioned in passing, as if they were not worth an in-depth examination because of their fleeting, ephemeral nature.[4] With only a few exceptions, the markets have remained well known but largely uninvestigated sites of contemporary history.[5] This is due only in part to their peculiar character, which seems to lie somewhere between the immoral and something worthy of a Hollywood adventure. For the most part, one must explain this lack of attention with reference to a general historiographical trend. For a long time, the history of the immediate postwar years was largely neglected, especially for questions that lay outside conventional political or economic history. Indeed, macroeconomic questions long predominated in debates about the founding period of the Federal Republic. Looking for answers, researchers ended up replicating a central contemporary obsession with the paradigm of an economic upswing, thus diverting attention away from the cultural history of the transition period between Nazi Germany at war and the establishment of a new (divided) postwar order.[6]

To be sure, one can apprehend "the wild, reckless conditions" of this mad "epochal break" in German history by examining economic activity, but the usual concepts and categories of economic history are not adequate for such an undertaking. Instead, one must turn to the economics of everyday life, understood as a comprehensive process of negotiation and reevaluation of relationships among people, goods, city spaces, and societal norms. Martin Broszat, Klaus-Dietmar Henke, and Hans Woller emphasize quite rightly that the transition from war to postwar was not merely an "episode," even taking into account the exceptional situation.[7] For contemporaries, the experiences of the 1940s were intertwined with those of the previous years. Above all, World War I and the interwar period provided a set of experiences that shaped practices, perceptions, and attitudes in the years that followed. When the West Berlin government asked older citizens in the 1970s to write down their memories of the postwar years for a contest, the response was substantial. Alongside other themes, the black market played a central role in numerous accounts.[8] And in 1989, when "illegal trading" (*wilder Handel*) appeared in the form of the so-called Polish markets that occupied the empty spaces left by the Berlin Wall's collapse, public authorities and the authors of letters to the editor discussed the new markets in conceptual terms whose relationship to the black markets of the 1940s could not be denied.[9]

Research by Broszat, Henke, Woller, and their collaborators broke new ground in 1988 by focusing on the myriad changes that the Wehrmacht's defeat in Stalingrad and the "total" war that ensued brought about in German society in 1942–43. The deepening war not only produced massive social changes but also affected the population's experiences and expectations. This transformation, these historians argued, only came to an end in 1948 with the West German currency reform and the beginning of a normalization on almost every level of society.[10] In recent years, a fresh impetus to study the transitional wartime and postwar years has come primarily from scholars in the United States. These authors are interested in a cultural history of the transition period that breaks open established narratives and lends more weight to individual groups of actors and their actions and perceptions, while keeping an eye on the economic, legal, and political structures of this historical process. The present study takes up this task by focusing on the Berliners' illegal trading in cultural terms, that is, by understanding the economic history of the Berlin black market as a cultural history.[11]

This book focuses on the Berlin black market between 1939 and 1950. As early as 1936, the political decision to steer the movement of goods through extensive regulations according to the needs of the National Socialist war economy limited consumers' room to maneuver. Then the rationing system installed at the beginning of the war radicalized this development.[12] The imposed constraints had a leveling effect inasmuch as they divided everyone who received goods into certain groups without regard for reputation or class. In fact, many experienced this development as a form of social humiliation. They were indignant at being subsumed under the category of "normal consumer." Furthermore, the establishment of the rationing system was followed by a phenomenon that Rainer Gries has called a "comparing mentality."[13] From that point on, people kept a wary eye on each other, and denunciations became daily occurrences. Pursuing a prophylactic policy to secure their authority and power, decision makers in the political and justice systems formulated an extensive catalog of new criminal offenses. Circumventing rationing regulations became a "war economy crime," a "price violation," or an offense against the Penal Code for Consumer Regulations. At the same time, those responsible for organizing an adequate supply of food and goods took into account the experiences of World War I, when the expectations of "women of lesser means" in particular had presented state officials with new challenges and made adequate provisioning an essential item on the political agenda for a long time thereafter.[14] This tension between consumer expectations and efforts to stabilize government authority was reflected in the definitions and regulations formulated at the beginning of World War II. Having established the framework for further discussions about everything that fell under the generic "black market" heading, these definitions remained in place—in a slightly modified form—until 1950.[15] In tandem, efforts to sustain a broad and "just" provisioning of goods, on the one hand, and the prosecution of violations, on the other, were supposed to keep the home front stable and make possible the return to "normal" economic life after the war.

Considerable numbers of urban dwellers, "foreign workers," and members of the Allied armies, however, broke the laws and regulations. They exchanged all sorts of goods outside of the existing allocation system and thus created a growing informal economy. No one knows the exact size of the illegal markets, but they must have been large. Contemporary estimates assumed that there were times when at least a third of all goods and services in Berlin were traded on the black market—and as much as half of some kinds of merchandise.[16] In terms of the quantity of merchandise and transactions alone, such numbers illustrated the profound significance of the black market, yet its importance went beyond such quantitative parameters.

The newly established market had its own rules. In contrast to life in peacetime, a system of managing the individual household economy arose that replaced customary shopping rituals and forced market participants to learn new practices. Bartering replaced shopping in stores. It became an everyday activity and at the same time created a new social divide by privileging those who possessed objects in demand. Consequently, a specific form of bartering culture emerged in 1940s Berlin that came to characterize everyday life there. This book examines this phenomenon and its location within the context of the general history of the transitional wartime and postwar years. In so doing, it seeks to cover new ground in three ways: by offering a perspective on contemporary history inspired by an "ethnographic gaze"; by focusing on an area of urban consumption and everyday life during the war and the postwar period; and by bringing both facets together in a comprehensive "bartering culture" concept, thereby contributing to a cultural history of household economic management. Here the term "bartering culture" encompasses the economic, political, and cultural processes of negotiation that occurred among market participants during their bartering.

Berlin's bartering culture manifested itself on several different levels and in a variety of contexts. The practice of bartering changed how Berliners experienced time and space, it led to alternative consumption practices, it shaped new personal relationships and networks, and it transformed the relationship between goods and currencies. Economic practice changed in response to political circumstances and political developments, it formed a benchmark in the encounters between losers and victors, and it shaped much of the public sphere that characterized everyday life during and immediately after the war. In connection with bartering and its side effects, Berliners also negotiated questions of loyalty and disloyalty, gender roles, and economic systems. Discussions during this period about the black market reflected a whole series of discourses about crisis.

The primary goal of this study is to trace Berlin's everyday bartering culture in what was the most "unmodern" span of German history in the twentieth century. Never before, and never again, were the inhabitants of German cities so quickly catapulted out of modern civilization into what many contemporaries termed "a state of nature," in which people behaved like wolves toward their fellow human beings. Against this turbulent background, one interpretation of the 1950s emphasizes contemporaries' longing for normality, and another sees the Germany of these years as a site of economic growth that can only adequately be described with the word "miracle." Although we have to differentiate, especially in terms of periodization and the decade's ambivalences, strong arguments can be made for both interpretations.[17] But we need to know more about the experiences that led to such perceptions. What exactly did this unmodern, insecure, and abnormal phase of German history look like? Analysis of the black market as part of the continuum of everyday life in Berlin during the war years and early postwar period can provide some answers.

In order to examine both the microphenomenon of everyday bartering in Berlin and the cultural and interpretive framework that Berliners developed around this activity, the present study interweaves two perspectives. On the one hand, it offers a "thick description" of everyday black marketeering in that city during the war and the early postwar period, albeit with gaps determined by the availability of sources. The activities of Martha Rebbien and the circle of traders around her form the starting point for a close analysis of black marketeering during the entire period under consideration, both the initially more clandestine dealmaking and the later trading in public squares. On the other hand, the study draws on these findings to reflect systematically on the political, economic, and cultural contexts of Berlin's black marketeering. At the microlevel, this book concentrates on the lives of small-time and big-time black marketeers alike, that is, on their business practices, self-images, everyday circumstances, and coping strategies. At the macrolevel, the book's attention to ethnographic details helps tease out the unfamiliar in Berlin's bartering society, that is, its utter strangeness to observers otherwise at home in a modern consumer society. The anachronistic circumstances of bartering—under the open sky at Alexanderplatz, for instance, or in bars, apartments, or the workplace—become clear when one contrasts this practice with fin-de-siècle department store palaces or the conditions of urban shopping in the age of the retail store.[18] This apparent disjunction forms the starting point for analysis of the bartering society. It helps us to approach this part of German history "not as intimate prior history . . . but instead . . . as something alien."[19] A primary concern of this study thus entails a historical turn to the culturally foreign.

Details can say a great deal about the whole. Likewise, this work discusses what the everyday world of the Berlin black market tells us about German society during and after World War II. In so doing, it takes up the approaches of urban histories of World War I and the inflationary period that ensued as well as of regional studies of Germany in the 1940s. At the same time, the present study attends to developments after 1945 that were specific to Berlin, such as the city's special legal situation, the postwar trade between its different sectors, the blockade, and the experience of a currency reform in a divided city.[20]

Describing bartering between two or more trading partners initially reveals a process, including, for example, establishing contacts, agreeing to meet again, and making an initial offer that might still be misunderstood. The resulting transaction turns out to be a praxis that is always embedded in economic, social, political, and cultural contexts. Analyzing these contexts entails apprehending conditions and events at both the meso- and microlevels, which expands the boundaries of the description. The motives of those participating in the black market become the focus of attention—along with their socioeconomic position; their occupation, which perhaps gave them access to sought-after goods or interested buyers; and political discussions about the boundaries between legal and illegal activities, boundaries reflected in discursively negotiated descriptions of the black market.

Markets illustrate how different facets of reality overlap because, in their concrete form, they are not only spaces in which people trade but also sites of complex interactions and social communication. Next to the market as an economic phenomenon, there is the market as a social and cultural event; next to the site of business transactions is the site of politically or religiously "imposed order."[21] Not only economic and social anthropology but also more recent economic theories—especially new institutional economics (NIE)—comprehend economic processes in terms of stakeholder actions that are embedded in other social processes.[22] In the empirical analysis of concrete (historical) markets, the "pure" economic paradigm—with its premise that a subject will maximize his or her utility and an equilibrium will be achieved—has proven deficient. More important is to account for what Jens Beckert calls "nonmarket coordination mechanisms," that is, "embeddedness," to borrow Mark Granovetter's influential concept.[23] Harrison White has summed up this perspective in his characterization of "market activity" as a praxis that can be "as social as kinship."[24] These assumptions are useful for analyzing the illegal Berlin markets because they make it possible to account for factors beyond mere utility maximization, including the "moral costs" of participating in the black markets, the political implications of the illicit public markets' presence, and the bartering customs that obtained in them. Such an approach enhances our economic perspective by incorporating relevant cultural conditions during and after the war.

Here we can see a reflection of what Marcel Mauss called a "total social fact." Mauss used the concept in connection with his analysis of the gift-giving cultures of tribal societies, but it applies to the Berlin black market insofar as participants there not only bartered with other people but also negotiated legal, political, and cultural issues.[25] The very fact that bartering existed amounted to a break with the legal and ideological consensus propagated by the National Socialist concept of the *Volksgemeinschaft* or "people's community" (with "people" defined racially as the collectivity of "Aryan" Germans). Bartering negated the claim of the primacy of politics in shaping society and furthermore established the foundation for a culture of individual household economic management that responded to everyday situations. This experience shaped mentalities and contributed to economic cultures during the birth of the two postwar German states. Therefore, the black market traders, the authorities who fought their activities, and even those who merely observed such goings-on are understood in this book not as mere objects being carried down a river of "external circumstances" but rather as historical actors.

Against a specific background of processes and events, Berliners not only traded goods for goods but also participated—while bartering—in political, economic, and cultural exchanges. Consequently, their bartering was accompanied by changes in social relationships; by support, disregard, or rejection of political interconnections; and by discursive shifts in the assignment of meaning.

Bartering transactions thus occurred in connection with a more general phenomenon that has recently become a focus of research: trust or mistrust vis-à-vis persons, institutions, and systems.[26] This scholarship regards trust as a strategy for overcoming insecurity or complexity.[27] This idea also holds at the level of individual and collective worldviews, for through a "concept of the world," complexity is transformed into "structured possibilities of one's own experiences and behavior."[28] The Berlin black markets of the 1940s can aptly be described as sites of constant insecurity that lacked mature and institutionalized mechanisms for building and securing trust—for example, state supervision, contractual security, and quality and measurement standards.

The relationship between "exchange" and "trust" turns out to be circular. A successful bartering transaction between people or the acceptance of (implicit) long-term bartering relationships between individuals and institutions both requires trust and simultaneously functions as a trust-building measure for future transactions. In contrast, mistrust can lead to the dissolution of trading relationships. This interplay fosters social cohesion that reaches beyond individuals acting on the basis of utility maximization.[29] By examining the nexus of trading and trust, the present study contributes to a cultural history of everyday household economic management.[30]

* * *

The concept of trading employed in this book encompasses two broad levels of analysis that require some explanation. The first perspective comprises the bartering practices of individual market participants aiming to achieve economic advantages. Central to the bartering culture investigated here, the micro-bartering level comprises Berliners' trading activities in the narrower sense of the word, namely, transactions in which goods, money, or services made an exchange possible. Following Max Weber, "exchange" in this context means "a formally voluntary agreement involving the offer of any sort of current, ongoing, or future utility in exchange for a utility . . . offered in return."[31] During World War II, against the background of a comprehensive state system of rationing and allocation, black market trading amounted to an illegal attempt to improve one's livelihood and signified an expansion of consumer sovereignty as well. Illegal trading undermined the logic of the allocation system, thus placing traders outside National Socialist conceptualizations of a "just" distribution of goods in wartime, which were beholden to the notion of the Volksgemeinschaft. Then after the war ended, illegal trading was tantamount to questioning the Allies' rationing systems and their establishment of functioning economic orders in the East and West. Behind this trading lay the experience of genuine shortages and scarcity, as well as a growing mistrust—reinforced by the experiences of World War I—in the ability of public authorities to ensure an adequate supply of goods. National Socialist leaders reacted to black marketeering with considerable concern. They expressed their anxiety in part via ad-hoc policies offering special rations in response to losses and shortages caused by heavy air raids. The formation of an informal economy, however, could no longer be stopped. Old-fashioned bartering, making special arrangements to pay for services with alternative forms of compensation, and illegally selling rationed goods existed side by side from the beginning. Market conditions—so much changed since the prewar period—affected above all the market participants' practices. Establishing contact with potential customers or bartering partners, evaluating products not subject to state-sanctioned standards, negotiating prices, and many more tasks presented participants with challenges, some completely new, that they met with varying levels of adeptness. In order to create the important foundation of trust, Berlin black marketeers adopted various strategies that enabled what Clifford Geertz has called a "personal confrontation between intimate antagonists." The forms of market organization and the participant strategies gradually established included compensating techniques such as the formation of networks primarily with people one knew, the establishment of spatial and temporal market routines, and the employment of certain marketplace conventions.[32]

At the same time, attitudes to individual goods changed, especially if these were not "anonymous" objects that one could buy today and sell again tomorrow but rather things one had possessed for a long time and become quite fond of, such as heirlooms or keepsakes.[33] Bartering frequently promoted its own "economy" for such objects, especially if the trading was motivated by hardship or an emergency. Going beyond the market value determined by supply and demand, this economy reflected the biographies of its participants. What should one, or could one, part with first or last?

This overlap of economic and personal values points to a complex process of reevaluating the familiar. The seemingly haphazard juxtaposition of objects and circumstances no longer where or how "they were supposed to be" was one of the most powerful experiences of the war and the early postwar period. It became necessary for Berliners to reassess—for themselves and others—what a necessity or a luxury was. The concept of luxury changed rapidly as a consequence. Corresponding to the supply situation, Berlin's bartering society formed its own hierarchy of goods, which reflected not only the general effects of supply and demand in the market but also individual privation and desire.[34] Further, in the same way that objects previously seen as "possessions" now became "goods," that is, a means of exchange, a new good appeared: information. For in contrast to the well-developed information infrastructure of legal markets, the Berlin black markets appeared to many of their participants as amorphous and confusing. The acquisition of information about the supply of goods, current prices, and reliable exchange partners could therefore become an important factor in determining success or failure.

These changes in Berlin's consumer goods landscape were related to the crisis of the official currency, which had two primary causes. First, the introduction of ration cards reduced the significance of the Reichsmark. Increasingly, ration cards for food and clothes took the Reichsmark's place, albeit without being able to render the same services as the currency because the cards were only valid for a certain period of time, for a certain location, and for a certain person. Furthermore, there was counterfeiting, embezzlement, and fraud. Second, in the interest of financing the coming war "silently," price and wage freezes had the desired effect of keeping inflationary tendencies in check, at least until the war began. Many contemporaries also measured economic developments against the crisis years of the early 1930s, which were still quite fresh in people's minds.[35] Nonetheless, these favorable circumstances could not prevent Berliners—especially toward the end of the war—from increasingly mistrusting the Reichsmark and its future value. Only after the currency reform would this lack of trust begin to ebb, and even then, the wartime and early postwar economic insecurity left a lasting impression. In response to this crisis of confidence, a whole series of substitute currencies existed alongside the official currency, among which the various cigarette currencies are only the best known. Additionally, because of the large number of international currencies in circulation during the occupation and the special situation of postwar Berlin as a divided city, foreign exchange trading developed into a continuous segment of the black market that outlived the currency reforms.

Up to now, works on the black market period seldom note that black markets could have many different segments. These varied according to the assortment of goods, the trading practices, and the sites where the trading took place.[36] Alongside everyday markets for food, clothing, and small goods offered by casual traders, semiprofessional and professional markets appeared for every imaginable kind of good. On top of this, transregional and even transnational distribution networks developed, for example, in jewelry and art, which allowed Berlin to become a center of international black markets that belonged to the world of organized crime.[37] Of course, the segments of the market were not distinct; there was a good deal of overlap between them.

The Berlin bartering culture led to changes in social relationships. Supervisors, bowling partners, teachers, and chance acquaintances—to name only a few examples—could become black market partners. New networks and network practices arose that could transform relationships between trading partners or lead to new relationships,[38] because bartering partnerships did not always build on familiar buyer-seller configurations, as happened, for example, when a business's regular customers and its owner traded with each other. Bartering could also profoundly change the character of existing relationships, creating dependencies or violent conflicts or transforming partnerships into friendships or love. Bartering culture led to the renegotiation of the relationship between the sexes during and after the war, especially. The gender of the bartering partners could play a decisive role in trading, whether men and women chose their bartering partners on the basis of gender, developed different strategies for establishing and maintaining contacts, or traded in romantic relationships and sex. Sexual services were indeed available for trade on the Berlin black markets. At the same time, sex became an important component of contemporary discourses, especially those on morality that thematized the behavior of the sexes in the markets. A widespread opinion held that bartering women not only traded in household goods but also offered themselves as prostitutes, forgetting their roles as loyal mothers and housewives.[39]

The appearance of "foreigners" in the markets also played an important role. In fact, the behavior of foreign laborers, forced laborers, and members of the Allied forces in the markets became a political issue for Berlin's black market society. In evaluating the roles of these "outsiders," we can see that people combined their general attitudes toward foreigners with anti-Semitic interpretations, xenophobia, and accusations against Germans who traded with them. This topic points beyond the level of contemporary Berliners' experiences and helps shed light on the role of the Allies, that is, on the distinctive relationships between the occupiers and the occupied. In times when things could simply be taken away, bartering—and gift-giving—yielded an additional gain for those who had lost the war: at least some limited, temporary freedom of action. This did not mean, however, that unequal entry requirements such as economic or physical power were completely eliminated from the bartering situation. Berliners responded quite differently to the various gestures of the victors, whether aggressive or reserved, when trading on the black market.

Trading as an everyday practice occurred between two poles. At one end, there was the act of "giving," which found paradigmatic expression, among the American occupiers, for example, in the candy given to children and in care packages. As a rule, these gifts aimed at getting something in return: sympathy and a friendly reception. At the other end, there was taking things, namely, the self-service practices of soldiers, the rapes, and the reparations. Most everyday trading oscillated between these two extremes. For example, because of the need to part with expensive jewelry for food "actually" worth a lot less, many Berliners saw bartering—even if only years later—as veiled theft. Moreover, the experience that threatening physical violence could cut short what up until then had been a "regular" bartering deal demonstrated that this situation could not be understood inherently as a "partnership." On the other hand, bartering also led to genuine partnerships between the vanquished and the victors. A number of Germans developed closer ties to their occupiers and sometimes used these bonds for social advancement.

Differences in dealing with the occupying powers and in perceptions of the occupiers' roles can be shown in an exemplary fashion by comparing German encounters with Americans and with members of the Red Army. Here one can see the effects of a clear difference in the degree of trust Germans held. The primary origin of this gap lay in ideologically charged stereotypes, some of which had developed relatively recently and others that were more deeply rooted, but all were very difficult for the Soviet "brothers" to correct, despite their efforts to appear to be partners.

Sexual relationships between Berlin women and members of the US and Soviet armies played a particularly important role in how the public evaluated relations between the victors and the vanquished, and these entanglements were debated in connection with the topic of bartering. Accusations of prostitution accompanied the individual predicaments of women who had sexual relationships with "the enemy." Moreover, such claims failed to acknowledge the whole range of different motivations these women had, ranging from genuine love to the need to earn a living. And although the power relationships that underlay these associations appeared quite clear on the surface, they could take on other forms in individual cases. Some Berlin women, for example, "kept" a series of partners or at least told themselves that they did. Nevertheless, various contemporary observers employed a variety of revealing phrases to describe relationships between German women and members of the occupying armies, revealing the dominance of stereotyping in their perceptions, including "Veronika Thank-You" (as a first and last name), "traitorous casual prostitutes," and "brutal members of the victorious powers who were taking advantage of their position." These stereotypes, which still have power today, did not do justice to the complexity of the bartering situations between Berlin women and the victors. Instead, they reproduced resentments and varying degrees of bitterness, insecurity, fear, and mistrust.[40]

Mistrust of "foreigners" was one of the characteristics of Berlin's bartering culture. Georg Simmel once described the modern urban lifeworld as a collection of encounters in which "strangers" depended on "certain outward appearances" in order to form an opinion of people unfamiliar to them.[41] For many in the Berlin black markets, this problem arose in a more acute form. The desire or need to barter led to an encounter between interested traders who could not "blindly" trust each other from the outset because they were not acquainted. Yet familiarity and the trust based on it formed a basic pillar of the Berlin bartering community as only those who trusted each other would trade with each other. This bartering culture required trust-building strategies that were essential to the practices of small-time and big-time black marketeers alike. These strategies were also important for the social fabric of this urban bartering society that comprised trading networks of varying size, complexity, and stability. One promising strategy for risky black market deals involved using existing networks among family members, friends, or acquaintances. What economic sociology has demonstrated with empirical analysis was certainly true in this context: an awareness of risk and insecurity encouraged traders to take advantage of "pre-existing noncommercial ties between buyers and sellers."[42]

Berliners who trusted their bartering partners—even if only after protracted scrutiny—opened up an extended sphere of action and prospects for the future. Admittedly, these prospects often failed to meet expectations in the prewar period, but they went beyond the lethargy that afflicted so many Berliners. This circumstance brings up another important aspect of Berlin's bartering culture: the reorganization of timeframes. Niklas Luhmann has pointed out that trust exhibits "a problematic relationship to time." "Whoever shows trust anticipates the future" and "acts as if he were confident about the future."[43] The way that casual black marketeers, in particular, handled their own relationship to time can be described as an ongoing but always dangerous attempt to attain a better, more secure future. In peacetime and in state-sanctioned markets, contracts provided long-term security. The permanence and stability of the state as a guarantor of the market meant that prospects were reliable for those who participated in it. In the Berlin black markets, however, the temporal constants of the prewar period had disintegrated. What remained were the remembered experiences of extreme inflation, currency decline, price gouging, and scarcity. These points of reference shaped the perceptions both of the black market traders and of the authorities who fought against their activities. Both expectations about certain levels of provisioning and assessments of future developments—of the war's course and of one's own economic and social situation—can only be understood against the background of previous patterns of experience.

As an economic and social phenomenon, trading on the black market functioned within its own temporal boundaries, which reflected local economic conditions and price expectations as well as the temporal confines of "everyday life in a state of emergency."[44] Time took on a new significance for many market participants inasmuch as they oriented their bartering practices toward changing price levels, thus attempting to integrate a different temporal aspect into their everyday lives. Initially, however, official allocation periods had provided the rhythm of everyday consumption. The rationing system that had been set up to limit consumption unintentionally ended up establishing its own economy for the thrifty or wasteful use of rationing cards within their specified periods of validity. Consequently, consumer sovereignty was subject not only to the dictates of limited supplies but also to the difficulties inherent in planning within limited periods of time.

The shortages required Berliners to reorganize their customary relationship to time in another regard. In this new context, one had to trade something "more valuable"—something that had only lost value in this exceptional situation of scarcity—for something ordinary that "normally" had no special value. Thus, one traded a piece of one's former and perhaps future prosperity for survival today.

In addition to these processes of temporal negotiation, spatial adaptations also played a decisive role. Trading in closed rooms followed different rules than trading on the streets; bartering between neighbors occurred within a more limited setting than did trading between commuters and city dwellers or the foraging of city dwellers in the countryside. Even with all the confusion and instability that accompanied these new extended market relationships, the markets as a form of public assembly had a remarkable level of organization similar to that of the legal (weekly) markets and the bazaars described by Clifford Geertz.[45] To be sure, it was almost impossible to create trust through what Anthony Giddens calls "facework commitments" because the impermanent character of the markets did not permit the ongoing establishment of stable and reliable relationships on the basis of routinized face-to-face interactions.[46] Nonetheless, the durability and dependability necessary for promoting trust and establishing positive conditions for conducting business could be established through compensating techniques such as building up networks and clients, operating at certain times and in certain places, and employing special market codes of behavior. Furthermore, these practices led to new, segmented market structures, which themselves helped to make the illegal business transactions more reliable and safe.

The chaos caused by the Nazi regime's "final battle" led to further changes in Berlin's economic geography. Near the end of the war and in the beginning of the postwar period, everyday life became increasingly local in its organization, reminding urban observers of a bunch of villages.[47] This patchwork corresponded to a tendency that had already developed during the war. Local bartering networks were formed and goods traded within limited spaces, turning upside down the modern transregional and transnational pattern of moving goods. On the other hand, black market trading in the large public squares of the city center, for example, around the Brandenburg Gate or Alexanderplatz, increased the catchment area for goods and—together with cultural events—gave rise to new forms of public sociability. The war had damaged or invalidated the old peacetime patterns of spatial orientation. Because of their very nature as places where people came together, the markets served as important reference points for a spatial as well as a moral redefinition of urban life in Berlin. The reconfiguration of Berliners' everyday spatial orientation vis-à-vis the controversial bartering sites promoted the reestablishment of a certain public order, however politically undesired, in the chaotic postwar years. At the same time, spatial adjustments moved the illicit markets to the center of public life and public discussions about these practices.

* * *

Besides exchanging goods, market participants exchanged meanings. Hence, the concept of exchange employed in this book comprises not only individuals' bartering practices per se but also the discursive elements of Berlin's bartering culture. Semantic changes indicated participants' attempts to reduce the complexity of Berlin's society as they observed and constructed phenomena like the black market and the other people who traded their wares in it.[48] The common German term used to describe the black market trader was *Schieber*. Literally "pusher" in English, the term not only meant "black marketeer" but also conveyed the more critical senses of "profiteer" (for the big fish) and "hustler" (for the smaller fry). The term "spiv," used frequently in wartime and postwar Britain, also comes to mind, although it referred only to men. Given the insecurity inherent in illegal trading, stereotypical labels and seemingly clear oppositional categories created perceptional and interpretive patterns that sought to delineate a morally and politically volatile phenomenon with stable assessment concepts, thus illustrating the crisis in trust. Labeling the market participants "stealthy traders," "black marketeers," "profiteers," "hustlers," or even "*Volksschädlinge*" (literally "pests" that attacked "the people" like insects devouring crops) drew a line between undesirable or antisocial behavior, on the one hand, and "small-time" trading or "private trading for one's own needs," on the other. Thus, it became possible to condemn a widespread illegal practice that could barely be controlled and simultaneously tolerate aspects of it—without ever having to establish a clear boundary. The flood of regulations and explanatory comments seemed to develop some relevant definitions, but they also led to confusion because they left room for interpretation. What exactly did "for one's own needs" mean? How were "war economy crimes" different from offenses against the Penal Code for Consumer Regulations?[49] Black marketeers and government authorities both made use of this room for interpretation. As attempts to reduce complexity, discourses on the black market and its workforce also represented negotiations over those precarious definitions that claimed to differentiate between the legal and illegal, moral and immoral, and loyal and disloyal. Within political-legal discourses and various discourses about everyday life, different black market concepts emerged that reflected participants' interests.

The black marketeer as a discursive figure embodied many levels of meaning that could be evaluated quite differently, depending on the context and the individuals or groups involved. If in the language of National Socialist propaganda, the black marketeer was asocial, Jewish, or foreign, if he or she was opposed to the Volksgemeinschaft in some way, and if he or she reminded people of the social misery of the inflation period, then this black marketeer could look like the "true" criminal in the eyes of the "small-time casual trader," whose own actions seemed like trifles in comparison. Instead of accepting the prosecuting authorities' terminology as the only valid definition of the black market, it is necessary to recognize the constructed nature of popular topoi in contemporary discourses and to try to reconstruct the complex exchanges in meaning that occurred. The politically explosive topic of illegal trading reproduced discursive conflicts over sovereignty in matters of interpretation, and these discourses expressed power relationships.[50] In talk about the black market and its traders, one could thus see who among the various participants, observers, and authorities had the power to define key terms of the relevant debates. On the other hand, each additional statement represented a new contribution that updated or rewrote the discursive fields in which these events transpired. Thus, planners in the Justice Ministry initially used the terms "war economy criminal" and "Volksschädling" to describe black marketeers, albeit without taking a public stance on the more common, well-known colloquialism "Schieber." This discursive strategy aimed to emphasize the transitional and temporary character of both the new regulations and the rationing system by linking individual criminal offenses to the war. Special circumstances called for special measures, according to this reading. As soon as the war was over, such expedients could be rescinded. In the final analysis, talk of "war economy crimes" was based on the regime's promise that the war and the rationing would remain a mere episode. Moreover, recourse to the terms "profiteer" and "spiv" brought the experiences of the inflation period immediately to mind. The National Socialist leadership wanted to avoid anything that depicted the coming war as a similarly chaotic period or new "Great Disorder."

This strategy did not pay off. On the contrary, the figure of the profiteer—to settle for the moment on just one translation of "Schieber"—came to dominate the discourse. Made popular in the 1920s in numerous cabarets, novels, and satirical how-to books, the profiteer had achieved the status of a colorful cult figure. By referencing it, one could articulate different meanings and connotations—from moral outrage and distance to admiration for this special kind of survival artist. Reference to this common figure, to vocabulary the masses understood, became ever more widespread when (politically controlled) newspaper articles on proceedings against "war economy criminals" popularized the topic. Authors tried to meet the widely shared and relevant expectations of their readers. Compelled to accept associations from the "upside-down world" of the inflation period, propagandistic usages of the profiteer figure emphasized its "subversive," "Jewish," or "foreign" connotations, contrasting the "harmful" behavior of the black marketeers with the ideal of the Volksgemeinschaft. To be sure, the concept had a basic meaning that captured certain actual practices of the traders and their outward appearance; however, its application to individual cases remained relatively open and dependent on context. Even statements from high-level party functionaries emphasizing the difference between occasional bartering of "little importance" in contrast to "commercial trading" supported an understanding of the black market that distinguished between the legal and the illegal, depending on the situation. Of course, this interpretation contradicted the rigid sentencing practices of the courts even in "smaller" cases, but it corresponded to the opinions of the many Berliners who engaged in bartering for "their own needs" and saw nothing wrong in that.

This unstable consensus functioned as long as ordinary Berliners had the feeling that the punishments for offenses against the regulations were just. In this context, any social imbalances or privileging of party functionaries and government officials became a political issue.[51] At the same time, such a consensus was only possible because law enforcement agencies uncovered no more than a small part of the offenses committed. The policy of fighting black markets was to a large degree symbolic policy that attempted to honor the National Socialist promise to ensure a just and sufficient distribution of goods. "Deviants," who through their behavior placed the system in question and who undermined trust in just distribution, were supposed to be publicly pilloried. Spectacular cases such as those involving embezzlement or large quantities of goods were particularly suitable, as were cases in which stigmatized classes of participants—including Jews, "foreigners," or prostitutes—traded among themselves or with other Berliners. Such cases, whose protagonists could easily be labeled "profiteers" from the outset, made it possible for both the state and the broad majority of consumers to believe in a boundary between acceptable trading "for one's own needs" and "large-scale profiteering," a boundary that ignored the gray areas.

This discursive constellation experienced a crisis with the appearance of regular public black markets toward the end of 1944.[52] The use of the capital's streets and public squares for illegal trading became an important component of a general discourse of crisis on the city's downfall. References to the previous war and its ensuing inflation as well as questions about who was responsible for the present breakdown all came together in voluminous talk about the black market and its protagonists. The leading characters in these discourses were foreigners, the Berlin women who traded with them and who were thus accused of prostitution, and the Berlin men who also participated in the illegal trade and who were consequently unable to live up to their normative masculine role as guardians of the public order. Accordingly, the image of the black market changed. Now trading was seen as a symptom of a comprehensive process of disintegration. One spoke of the markets primarily as phenomena in the cityscape that illustrated the decline of the moral order.

In the early postwar period, a new element supplemented the perception of chaos. It contradicted the observations of the newly established state offices. In place of the heaps of people in the streets being characterized as "contaminations of the streetscape" and disruptions in the "normalization of conditions," there emerged talk of "flourishing" markets. The operative metaphor was about being alive in this landscape of urban ruins. There was "new life," that is, sociability in an environment characterized by destruction. All the same, the image remained ambivalent. The gloomy moral and political discourse on the Berlin black markets continued to exist alongside these new, positive interpretations.

Two interpretive strands came to predominate. The first focused on the social distortions, the "high living" of the "big-time profiteers," and the misery of the destitute, mostly older city inhabitants. The second dealt with differing economic concepts in the East and West. Against the background of the founding of two postwar German states, economic concepts played an important role, and not only for specialists. Debates on the market economy, the planned economy, and their variations took up a lot of space in the newly established Berlin newspapers. According to the official Soviet and East Berlin view, the black market was the product of war and fascism. Moreover, it offered a propagandistically deterrent example of social imbalance because of the light it supposedly cast on unregulated market economies. Free market interpretations of Western provenance proved no less controversial. Especially the controversy following some remarks of the minister of justice Thomas Dehler brought to light the close relationship between policy ideas for a new economic order and the general black market discourse of this transition period. The *homo oeconomicus* behavior of the black marketeers, subsequently approved by Dehler, contradicted morally based defensive postures that contrasted the impoverishment of what was already called the "black market era" with the immoral lifestyle of the "big profiteers." Debates over the bartering culture's "moral economy" became especially heated in Berlin because of the competition between the capitalist and communist systems.[53]

Indeed, we need to examine the illegal bartering culture's significance for the new socioeconomic orders that emerged in East and West Germany after the war, and Berlin offers a suitable entrance point for such analysis because of its special situation as a divided city. A dominant, semi-official narrative of economic history served as an integrating myth in both German states. Each narrative told a success story that offered a sort of national legitimation. The thesis put forward here is that a good deal of this dialogue about economic facts was determined by the experiences of the chaotic bartering era, which served as a foil to these economic discourses.

* * *

Berlin's special nature makes it uniquely suited for a study of German bartering culture that reaches back to World War I and includes the history of everyday experiences relative to the developments in the East and West after the city's division. Here the illegal market as a predecessor of both the West German social market economy and the East German planned economy becomes the book's focus. These two aspects—the Berlin bartering culture's earlier history and its consequences—bookend the present study.

Chapter 1 deals with historic backdrops or "prologues." Specifically, it examines bartering experiences and semantics in Berlin related to World War I and subsequent inflation, and it looks at the sites and conditions in which bartering occurred. The experiences and the radicalized political language from this period formed the background against which Berlin's bartering culture developed during and after World War II. Chapter 2 then turns to the protagonists of the illegal trading networks. Using the history of Martha Rebbien's bartering network, this chapter investigates the social profiles of those who participated in the black market as well as the striking changes in social relationships that occurred under the conditions of the bartering culture. Individual black market practices are examined, as are the development of a degree of professionalization, changes in how people used space, and a specific kind of city making, as Berliners redefined their city in the course of their confrontations with the authorities. Already during the war, morally laden judgments of illegal trading revolved around the profiteer, a discursive element that contributed to discrediting above all the "usual suspects," that is, the fringe groups of National Socialist society.

Chapter 3 investigates the conditions that encouraged the Berlin black market scene to move outdoors into public spaces. The diverse crises of everyday life during the state of emergency that characterized the final months of the war and the initial months of peace promoted the development of a network of marketplaces throughout the city. Chapter 4 examines these sites, the logic of their locations, and their microstructures. Besides considering new practices and participant groups, including members of the occupying forces, this chapter focuses on the strategies of the German and occupying authorities to contain the black market. Finally, it looks at the goods that were traded and their significance for Berlin's bartering culture.

Chapter 5 integrates the development of the illegal trading into the "histories of a new beginning" under the auspices of the currency reforms in the East and West. It describes these reforms as the culmination of a process in which everyday life and high politics intertwined, and it asks what role the black market played in the birth of the new economic cultures on both sides of the German-German border.

The conclusion takes up these ideas and shows how they relate to the overall thesis that the black market was a radical market experience. If the Berlin bartering culture can be described as a space in which Berliners encountered confusing and often incomprehensible developments while also experiencing and articulating changes in their levels of trust or mistrust, then this space served as an important reference point for that yearning for stability and security that became so palpable in the 1950s.

CHAPTER 1

Prologues

The history of Berlin's wartime and postwar black marketeering formed a relatively distinct period with its own characteristics, but it did not represent a break with the prewar period. A line of tradition reached back to World War I and included the Roaring Twenties, the Great Depression, and Nazi Germany's rearmament economy. In the face of recurring chaotic economic conditions, a sustained discussion about correct moral behavior in the marketplace occurred that mattered to black marketeers and government officials alike. Likewise, the subsequent histories of traders such as Martha Rebbien did not merely repeat a well-known plot from World War I, when Berlin women used all available means to organize their everyday lives around obtaining enough food and fuel to keep their "home fires burning."[1] Rather, the histories of black marketeers like Rebbien presented sequels that referred back to such experiences and the political discussions accompanying them while at the same time manifesting new situations, new experiences, and discourses. One can understand these sequels only if one knows what came before.

The Semantics of Bartering and the Realms of Experience in Berlin after 1918

Black marketeering during World War II was dangerous. An indictment of March 31, 1945, charged Martha Rebbien, an unemployed waitress, with violating the War Economy Regulation, and the prosecutor Steinriede asked the court to convict her.[2] If the approaching end of the war had not intervened and her case had come to trial, Rebbien would most likely have received a jail term. To be sure, the judges of the Berlin Special Court who heard cases entailing war economy offenses did not always hand down the maximum sentences possible, but sometimes they imposed considerable prison terms, occasionally even the death penalty.[3] This rigorous approach toward those active in the illegal markets enjoyed broad public support for at least four reasons. First, in the eyes of many, such punishment merely put into practice the promise of equality and justice that the rationing program formulated, a promise that everyone in the Volksgemeinschaft would be treated equally and not according to class or milieu. To be sure, over time distrust and suspicion shifted to cases of real or alleged unequal treatment in criminal prosecutions. Initially, however, the sentences for convicted black marketeers could be understood as the judicial counterpart to the rationing system's distributive rationale. Second, broad support for tough punishments comported with a widespread perception that one's own bartering was about doing small "favors," not actual black marketeering. In this way, Germans established a clear boundary between themselves and real "profiteering," for which they could still indignantly demand harsher penalties without seeing any contradiction or hypocrisy in light of their own black market activities. Third, law enforcement agencies were soon swamped by a massive increase in the number of cases, and prosecutions could not be pursued in every direction.[4] In part, this circumstance resulted in indignation because illegal trading could apparently run rampant. On the other hand, the situation made it easier for one to classify one's own bartering as not worth prosecuting, even while still condemning the profiteering cases being publicly tried. Fourth, the practice of prosecuting black market activities had its own history going back to World War I. When National Socialist planners started to formulate regulations to prohibit the black market dealings they feared would come with the next war, the German public had already been discussing the black market in various social contexts for almost 20 years. The anti-black market policy between 1939 und 1945, in part symbolic but nevertheless enforced with a great deal of energy, could count on public support because of attitudes that had developed during and directly after World War I. Various groups rejected the "profiteers" and their practices. At the same time, the boundary between economics and politics blurred in discussions about illegal trading as inappropriate economic behavior became one of the most important discursive patterns of the interwar years.

On the surface of Nazi ideology, the black market does not appear to have been all that important. The basic elements of Hitler's worldview as propounded in *Mein Kampf*, in countless party publications, and by Nazi government officials called for revising the Treaty of Versailles, asserting Germany's leadership in the world, promoting the idea that Germans were a "people without space," rejecting the Weimar "system," and fostering hatred for Jews, communists, and other "alien elements" (*Volksfremde*). These interconnected elements formed an aggressive racist ideology that became the foundation for state action. Although pragmatic considerations often prevented, moderated, or sometimes radicalized the implementation of pure doctrine, the Nazi ideological edifice provided a general set of directions that could be interpreted and applied by various groups within the regime as party functionaries and civil servants worked toward what they believed the Führer wanted.[5]

Below the most visible level of the Nazi worldview, however, black marketeering was indeed important to National Socialists. The issue had already become controversial in the Weimar period. Moreover, it was well suited to exploitation by Nazi propaganda for establishing and reinforcing a whole series of stereotypes of enemies of the people. Referring to Weimar as a "republic of profiteers," National Socialist politicians characterized economic bartering transactions as a partnership of the few at the expense of the many, that is, as the "greedy transactions" of a "Jewish," "eastern-backward" or "western-capitalistic" minority at the expense of the German Volksgemeinschaft. Between 1939 and 1950, the Berlin bartering culture took shape not in a vacuum but against the background of individual and collective experiences—especially of the politicians themselves.

In the eyes of the National Socialist rulers, illegal black market trading had already undermined the morale of the home front during World War I because it had severely affected the system of rationing. It was also an emotionally charged and political topic. National Socialist propaganda sought to discredit the Weimar Republic by pointing to the supposedly corrupt cliques of the old "system." In caricatures, the republic was lambasted for "profiteering" and shady arrangements between business and politics. In fact, these symbols had formed an important element in Nazi rhetoric during the party's struggle for power. Already in 1920, taking action against "criminals who harm the public good" was in the party program of the National Socialist Workers' Association, which called "for the ruthless fight against those who through their actions harm the common good . . . extortionists, profiteers, etc., are to be punished with death, without consideration of their confession or race."[6] This disregard for "racial" gradations in the punishment of black marketeers might seem surprising in light of the unequal treatment meted out later.[7] In 1920, however, Nazi priorities were different. Expressing a genuine disgust with black marketeering, party propaganda also captured a sentiment shared far beyond their own circles.

The term Volksschädling (a human "pest" who feeds on the nation) was taken up in the title and text of a 1939 regulation, whose draft title was "Profiteers and Extortioners" (*Schieber und Wucherer*).[8] In 1920, the main Nazi press organ, the *Völkischer Beobachter*, had published a complaint about the "failure" of public agencies' efforts "against the nasty Volkschädlinge, the hustlers and extortioners."[9] At the same time, the term was used in political debates and discussions to defame and slander opponents. For example, the police headquarters in Munich included in its "political news" a remark about Hitler's speech in the Hofbräuhaus that denigrated Volksschädlinge: "[Hitler] [spoke] about 'Erzberger and his comrades.' This topic, relevant because . . . the case against Erzberger for tax evasion has once again been taken up, gave the speaker a welcome opportunity . . . to settle scores with these 'criminals and national pests.' "[10] Derogatory talk about illegal business practices in the Weimar Republic was supposed to make the political culture of National Socialism appear in a positive light—even though, from 1933 on, the upper levels of the hierarchy of the Nazi Party and the German public administration provided a refuge for black marketeering of all kinds.[11] Finally, the negative image of the "profiteer" developed between 1939 and 1945 had an inclusive function. Illegal trading was used to identify "aliens to the community" (*Gemeinschaftsfremde*) and thus strengthen the bonds of the Volksgemeinschaft.

Ultimately, the National Socialist "movement" succeeded because its adherents' ideological patterns of interpretation resembled those of the national-conservative mainstream and because National Socialists took up the reservations and fears of other socio-cultural milieus. Many decision makers and supporters of right-wing parties viewed the agony of the Weimar Republic through the lens of their revisionist, anti-communist, or anti-Semitic preconceptions about the importance of the "Fatherland" and the (re)establishment of a strong state; from their perspective, this promised to address the country's most pressing problems. These positions were popular above all in those circles for whom the very existence of the Weimar Republic was a scandal. The change of the political system in 1918 was overshadowed from the very beginning by many crises produced both by the war and by long-term processes of social change and ambivalent modernization in the nineteenth century.[12] As a result, the Weimar Republic comprised an amalgamation of social divisions that expressed themselves in particularly fierce political and social debates.[13]

In the public sphere, political discourse often seemed to be less a debate on issues and more an attack either directly or indirectly on parliamentary democracy itself, on its principal ideas and representatives.[14] The "battle against extortion and profiteering" was one major theme, employing "a central buzz phrase used in the revolutionary strategy of the communists," a synonym for capitalist exploitation. Criticism of the "profiteer," a discourse at once hostile to the republic, was more than just a platform for political agitation by the radical parties, however. It "permeated the language of all political groups regardless of stripe," as Martin Geyer noted.[15] The republic lacked a fundamental consensus. Not only did the parties opposed to the system question the legitimacy of the new state; the majority of the population and the elites began contributing to the erosion of the republic's stability soon after it was founded. Talking about the Weimar "republic of profiteers" accelerated this process.[16]

The rise of the National Socialist German Workers' Party (NSDAP), the Nazi Party, was possible, at least in part, because it seemed to promise an end to political disappointments by picking up on widespread worry and fear among different social and political milieus. The republic's crisis of representation reflected the frustrated expectations of many Germans who had transferred the modes of representation they had grown accustomed to in World War I, such as virtualization and dramatization, to everyday political life. The result was excessive demands made on everyday politics, which itself had become much more protracted, ambiguous, and complex. The typical Weimar-era rejection of efforts to reach complicated compromises that required patience was not compatible with the existing desire for clarity and community. Expectations of what politics could achieve thus generated an unresolvable paradox. On the one hand, there was the demand for a comprehensive national community, or Volksgemeinschaft, in which the "spirit of 1914" still resounded and in which improvements could be achieved ad hoc, and, on the other hand, discontent grew and political half measures came to be openly rejected. Indeed, Weimar politics quickly obtained the aura of not being able to uphold the moral standards of "good politics," while at the same time, this critique neglected the need for politics that would seek consensus in small steps and be able to transcend political partisanship for the sake of the public good.[17]

The scandals in which individual politicians and businessmen were accused of economic crimes, whether justly or unjustly, played an important role in public debates.[18] Beyond the discussion of concrete individual cases regarding corruption, venality, and illegal agreements, hateful polemic against the supposedly deplorable conditions of the Weimar Republic emerged in which some sought to discredit the entire state as a republic of hustlers. In the so-called Barmat Scandal, for example, right-wing politicians accused Social Democrats and entrepreneurs, especially Jewish ones, of fraud and bribery. This scandal became shorthand for opposition to the republic, enabling one to question the morality of the Weimar Republic and the politicians who loyally served it.[19] Already before National Socialists successfully jumped on this bandwagon and criticized the Weimar system under the mantle of a discourse about racketeering, talk of a "Weimar republic of profiteers" had established itself as a topos. Individual cases of economic crime were portrayed as typical of the entire war, as well as the revolutionary and inflation era, thereby turning the topos into a destabilizing discursive element.[20] In the resulting thought-world, the new state was no good. "All of Germany," wrote a journalist in 1925 in *Montag*, had become "a bar where profiteers meet, a clip joint, a crazy, ludicrous movie, a wild amusement park," all thanks to the revolution.[21] Such accusations, which came primarily from the Right, did not go unanswered. The *Berliner Tageblatt* and *Vorwärts* attempted to counterattack by taking up two scandals that were supposed to show that those on the Right were involved in inappropriate economic behavior as well. Some publications emphasized either the so-called Aryan or aristocratic background of those involved in speculative transactions to counteract the racist and social stereotypes of the right-wing discourse on profiteering.[22] On both the Right and the Left, therefore, the tension between general and particular interests was thematized, with both sides claiming to represent the general "public good."

These controversies held particular power because of people's experiences with rationing and black markets during and immediately after World War I. In the period of hyperinflation, what Martin Geyer calls the "disorganization of the market" had become clear for all to see. The collapse of the currency, reflected in the new banknotes and in the statistics published in the newspapers, had sweeping consequences for everyday life. Numbers and figures created an almost surreal atmosphere one new price record after another was broken, but this almost virtual omnipresence of crisis directly affected the real living standard of large sections of the population.[23]

Theretofore stable models of order were plainly breaking down. Such important guarantees of the bourgeois order as contracts and stable relationships among people, goods, and money no longer seemed self-evident.[24] That money "successively lost its function as an apparently neutral measure, a means to determine differences" was something many citizens found difficult to grasp. Ultimately, this development shook the foundations of society's moral categories and, as a consequence, strengthened anti-Semitic currents.[25]

In the debates concerning the illegal Berlin black market of the 1920s, the topic of shortages and the "perception [of] inequality brought about by state measures and subject to moral criteria" moved to the top of the political agenda.[26] Above all, unemployed persons and senior citizens living on either the dole or a small pension sank into poverty during Berlin's inflationary years. This necessitated a strategic reorganization of social and welfare services.[27] Initial measures such as public relief works could not stem the tide, however. The unemployment trend in the capital was worse than in the rest of the country. Long-term unemployed people had flocked there. At times as many as 40 percent of all those receiving unemployment assistance in Germany lived in Berlin. Two factors in particular lay behind this development. First, Greater Berlin, created just after the war, had suffered badly from the economic transition from war to peace because a large section of the armaments industry had settled in the area before and during the war. Second, the city became a place for refugees from the territories that Germany had lost as a result of the Treaty of Versailles. Both led to a worsening of the city's economic position.[28] The social dynamite exploded in the chaotic months of the hyperinflation. There were hunger and inflation riots in October 1923. These riots expressed anger, at least in part, against scapegoats, including Jews from Eastern Europe, many of whom lived in the Scheunenviertel. There were further riots in November in the Scheunenviertel, and businesses in the city center were plundered.[29]

Against this backdrop, the familiar wartime figure of the "profiteer" (Schieber) gained importance. Together with related concepts such as "speculator" and "war profiteer" (*Kriegsgewinnler*), it quickly entered people's ordinary vocabularies. As these concepts were closely tied up with experiences from both during and after the war and could be applied to a variety of different situations, the "profiteer" as a popular cipher came to characterize not only certain individuals but also the chaotic economic conditions themselves. Martin Geyer's observation about the speculator applies to the profiteer too. The "speculator [became] nothing more than shorthand with which the 'upside-down world' of the postwar period could be both explained and condemned."[30] At the same time, the image of the profiteer offered a suitable vehicle for stereotyping the enemy in ways important to National Socialism because it brought together anti-Semitism, anti-Marxism, anti-liberalism, and anti-capitalism.[31]

The figure of the profiteer was successfully instrumentalized because it represented the alternative to an imagined community that was "virtuous and German" but was facing the collapse of both its material and immaterial values because of runaway inflation. From this perspective, the black marketeer had seized the moment to make a profit in a period of general moral and economic decline, unscrupulously promoting his or her own interests at the cost of the community's. Especially scandalous was the profiteer's allegedly luxurious lifestyle characterized by conspicuous consumption.[32] This impression outraged many in all political camps, albeit with different accents. Whereas anti-republican commentators on the Right saw individual cases as typical of the whole Weimar system, Social Democratic voices charged that members of the mercantile middle class in Germany who had grown rich during the inflation were the ones behind the profiteering.[33] Newspapers on the Right, in particular, validated, created, and mobilized emotions and resentments vis-à-vis the republic and its representatives. The public's willingness to vilify perceived wrongdoers was correspondingly high. Focusing on the black marketeer—the wheeling and dealing profiteer—brought large sections of the fragmented Weimar society together in a community of outrage.

By venting their outrage, people processed their experiences, rehearsing a piece from the repertoire of the "culture of defeat."[34] Together with the experiences and interpretations of deprivation in the postwar years, talk of the "ignominious" or "shameful defeat" of Versailles pointed to the close psychological relationship between feelings of humiliation and a widespread desire to renounce political practices seen as dishonest bartering typical of the republic. Defeat, "loss of trust in the rules" during the inflation crisis, and discussions about reparations formed the focal points of a process of accommodation in which talk made with apodictic certainty was often only the other side of a widespread feeling of uncertainty.[35] A widely shared interpretation of Germany's defeat saw the republic's "compliance policy" as a symbolic reenactment of the military capitulation. "One not only wants to kill us economically, one also wants to take away our honor," explained the representative of the right-wing German National People's Party (DNVP), Count Posadowsky, in a meeting of the National Assembly on May 12, 1919, in the auditorium of the Friedrich-Wilhelms University in Berlin.[36] The linking of "war guilt" and reparations in Article 231 of the Treaty of Versailles opened the door for an interpretation that was only too plausible to many contemporaries. Ultimately, this interpretation resulted, as Gottfried Niedhardt put it, from "different forms and stages of reality denial" and from an "introverted defensiveness" that was unable to see anything positive in the treaty.[37] Contemporary critics saw the treaty conditions as a "defamation of honor" and wanted either to limit or even reject payments to the victors. What sociologist Adolf Weber has called the "tragedy of the reparations" was unfolding.[38]

The "compliance policy" of the government under Chancellor Gustav Wirth became a central topic, especially for those on the political Right, who responded to it with open hatred. In their view, whoever wished to negotiate the sum of reparations and therefore a debt pay-off with the victors conflated moral and financial debt; worse, such negotiations could not avoid acknowledging moral debt and so could only increase Germany's humiliation. Financial payments could not compensate for this loss of face. Rather, one could only eliminate the debt of honor by rendering it null and void. This perspective used a friend-or-foe topos based on a specific understanding of Germany in relation to England; it employed the dichotomy Werner Sombart had pointed to with the phrase "German heroes and English merchants." This polarity reveals the peculiar semantic mixture of economics, politics, and morality that typified these overheated Weimar debates. The supposedly clear distinction between the calculating Englishman and the morally impeccable German gave expression to a desire for clarity, for perceiving defamation. This desire comported with insistence on a clear division between different political styles. Negotiating (which also had a business connotation) was "not German" and suggested that gains here were achieved in back rooms instead of "in open battle." From this perspective, Germany's defeat was the result of a traitorous deal negotiated by a few people behind closed doors. These few became the "internal enemy" and were placed alongside the external enemy, the victorious powers because whoever partook in the "foreign" terrain of negotiations, consultations, and "backroom deals" committed "treason" in two ways. The "compliance politicians" not only accepted and acknowledged Germany's defeat and war guilt but, by engaging in negotiations, they also committed performative treason, so to speak: they participated in a mode of politics that corresponded to the political modus operandi of the enemy, and they sat down with this enemy at a table.[39] Such reservations were already apparent when the government stated in early 1919 that the Versailles demands were unacceptable. In the Prussian Assembly on May 13, DNVP Representative Hergt explained, "This unacceptability has to be without any reservations; there can be no partial successes; there can be no horse trading about the one or other point."[40] In other words, the assembly demanded maximum rigor, which doomed to failure any policy that took the actual political situation into account and accepted compromise.[41]

Strident opponents of the republic considered the Treaty of Versailles and the ongoing reparations negotiations—which perpetuated the experience of defeat—a great sin, even if they did not always explicitly say so. At the same time, talk of profiteers in public debates at the beginning of the 1920s evinced an interpretive framework closely enmeshed in the ongoing experience of defeat, thereby linking profiteering to the feeling of humiliation engendered by the reparations negotiations. The feelings of powerlessness among those who believed Germany had remained "undefeated in the field" converged on the profiteer. After all, this figure represented a group of people who had profited from the defeat. The ubiquitous black marketeer embodied a pattern of action. He or she was the "internal enemy" whose egotistical behavior—connoted as "commercial" and "Jewish"—corresponded to the "external enemy."[42]

Berlin was at the center of this discourse. Many elements of a comprehensive criticism of modernity—illiberal, anti-Western, anti-Semitic, and anti-Marxist—came together in an aggressive rejection of the metropolis as a symbol of the new age. Of course, the National Socialists' contributions were particularly vehement, but there were others too. In the nineteenth century already—for example, in Friedrich Nietzsche's writings—a persistent theme had been contrasting the "unnatural" life in the big city with an idealized provincial world as the site of real Germanness. The "pleasure, wrapped up in fear, of the man from the province" as he entered the world of urban spectacle, as Hanne Bergius has described it, was reflected in a whole series of contemporary representations of the city that centered around a concept of the masses, around what were assumed to be typical figures of the criminal milieu, and around the "unhealthy excesses" of a hectic city existence.[43] Berlin was considered the perfect example of such squalor.[44] For conservative cultural critics, avant-garde artists, and large sections of the population, the city represented the "whore Babylon," a remarkably vivid synthesis, both terrifying and fascinating, of everything in the new era that was wonderfully tempting and disgusting. The ostensibly omnipresent "Berlin cocottes" (prostitutes) formed a central motif of this male view of the city as they "embodied the eroticism of consumption." Hanne Bergius noted that contemporary written and visual representations of these Berlin prostitutes were strikingly analogous to other commodities for quick, anonymous mass consumption.[45] Various desires to satisfy one's own baser instincts were recast as urban consumer behavior and found expression in an almost obsessive fixation on a "new form of urban performance" that combined the archaic and the modern.[46] The temptations of the Berlin world of consumer goods encompassed both women's bodies and the products in the city's shop windows.

In this situation, the roles available to urban men faced threatening and fascinating challenges, and the alternatives were dubious, ranging from the violent and criminal to respectable in a "normal" way. These roles included outlaws of various stripes who appeared to have distanced themselves from bourgeois morality and adapted to the chaotic conditions of crisis-ridden postwar Berlin. And like the common descriptions of Berlin that combined the repulsive with the appealing and the adventurous, descriptions of contemporary criminals mixed moral reproach with admiration and the desire "to be a little bit like" them.[47] The profiteer or hustler was one of the most prominent criminal figures in postwar Berlin, appearing in the city's newspapers, motion pictures, and novels.[48] The two characteristics that made him so alluring clearly corresponded to those of that other metropolitan commodity, the "Berlin cocottes." After all, the profiteers had the money to afford these women and the chutzpah to deal with their challenging, even dominating, ways. The poem "Berlin Christmas 1918" by the German writer known as Klabund (Alfred Henschke) provides an example of this interpretive pattern:

> Nowadays the people sit together
> on the Kurfürstendamm with much hullabaloo.
> Diamonds and dames, a tailcoat with something in it,
> A mink coat, a heart of stone, a double chin.
> Pearls sparkle, the champagne sparkles.
> Cocottes mock: Whoever wants to can, of course,
> count out five fifty-mark notes for me on the tablecloth.
> Hey profiteer, my dear?—No, we can't be fooled.
> And while millions starve to death:
> We'll join another party instead.[49]

The only ones up to dealing, economically and attitudinally, with the sarcasm of the prostitutes were their masculine counterparts, namely, those "ruthless upstarts who used the anonymity of the big city to put on various high-powered masks for carrying on their hustling activities."[50] Only these two complementary figures knew how to make their way to their own advantage in this metropolis, which had become a dubious sort of "department store." The powerlessness experienced by many small-time and big-time losers of the war and the new postwar order were reflected in this conceptualization of the profiteer and the prostitute. The (male) gaze at these unwholesome men and commodified women was not simply passively powerless and jealous, however. It was active in that it aimed to transfer an unsettling experience of contingency into manageable moral categories. "How is the cocotte culture being paid for, this culture that has spread in this period of great hardship, when many small livelihoods in Germany are going bankrupt?," a reader of *Vorwärts* asked rhetorically, followed by the answer: "with the money that heavy industrialists and alongside them the profiteers have taken from the pockets of the savers, the creditors, the mortgage holders, and the underpaid working class."[51] National Socialists polemically took up this anti-profiteer and anti-metropolis sentiment, stating loudly that they would do everything they could to work against urbanization and that with them there would be a "turning away from (the) previous false paths of development: . . . urbanization, industrialization, Western ideas, [and] a global economy."[52]

On the political level, the mistrust in the arrangements of innumerable governing coalitions, which were perceived as seeking compromises rather than leading, reflected precisely this sense, formulated in the example of the profiteer, that one's weaknesses were constantly being exploited by the tricks of the powerful. Thus, war and defeat in tandem with power and powerlessness formed core motifs of the Weimar Republic's political culture, and these themes found practical, everyday support among the people, above all because of their experiences with ruinous inflation.

Accordingly, the topic of (political and economic) bargaining played a key role in the political debates of the 1920s. Talk of the "Weimar system," synonymous with "profiteering" and "corruption," brought together deep-seated feelings of hatred against "the politicians," "the Jews," and "the inflation profiteers." Rather heterogeneous groups shared this hatred. The various bogeymen they despised could all be associated with the reportedly dirty bartering transactions of black marketeers. The strong desire for leadership and a leader, for decisions, identification, and greatness, was a pipe dream that vehemently rejected the cumbersome, frequently incomprehensible political arrangements of the Weimar period as variations of shady bartering agreements.[53] Not by chance did those on the Right attempt to exploit the continuing negotiations on reparations for their own purposes. For example, they generated political agitation to oppose the Young Plan, in which Germany's reparation payments were to be renegotiated. By referring to these negotiations, right-wing opponents could easily demonstrate how they were different from the other parties by refusing not only specific reparation models but the process of negotiating on the whole. Regarding the new payment plan, a pamphlet from DNVP circles, for example, stated, "We are supposed to sell our children and grandchildren into slavery. Our fulfillment propaganda claims that the reduction of the annuities achieved by extending the length of time they are to be paid is progress, success, even a 'gift.' Whoever agrees with that deserves to be a slave."[54] The word "gift" expressed—in an ironic form—outrage over deal-making that right-wing circles considered unacceptable. The NSDAP took up this defensive posture when, in the *Völkischer Beobachter*, it accused the "establishment parties" of being responsible for the "enslavement of the German people" and added that the "Weimar Republic" was only "another expression for the tributary peace (*Tributfrieden*) of Versailles."[55] With this and other positions, the NSDAP generally put forward nothing but a "conglomeration of resentments and ideas that was widespread among the German Right and by no means original." What was new was the "passion," the "rigor," and the "dynamism" of the National Socialist movement.[56]

Disengagement from horizontal public negotiating, contracting, and trading relationships, which at the very least seemed to be based on partnerships, entailed more than just rhetoric. It was also reflected in the system of personality-based fealty that the National Socialists pushed through on the state level after 1933. National Socialism was founded on a "type of rule in which neo-feudal, personal loyalties had preference over bureaucratic structures of governing" and "formal status had been replaced by personal ranking within the Führer's entourage."[57] This process of replacing bureaucratic or elected relationships with personal ties corresponded to a massive semantic shift away from explicit bartering situations toward voluntary "gifts" and "sacrifices." Individual national comrades (*Volksgenossen*) made "presents" and "contributions" to the greater whole. If one understands exchange as an interrelation between at least two people whose aim is to cooperate in the form of some sort of compromise of goods, which is the result of negotiations, then the new political culture of National Socialism marked a radical shift away from exchange as mode of communication. The shift away from exchange relations, which were threatened by a loss of trust, toward demanding the greatest possible "unconditional loyalty" marked an important transformation in Germany's political culture during the transition to National Socialist rule.[58] This development did not mean that politicians and citizens no longer viewed their relationship, which was based on trust-building achievement, as an exchange.[59] The National Socialist leadership was especially keen to secure people's loyalty by making concessions, for example, in the question of securing adequate provisions. Even so, a massive propagandistic evocation of "victim," "loyalty," and "national unity" was required in order to offer large sections of the population truly attractive chimeras that promised to end the inner strife of the Weimar years.[60]

Thus, it was the renunciation of a political culture that had placed great value on complex rules and on the possession of knowledge about these rules that secured the willingness of a majority of Germans to participate in National Socialism. Of special importance in this regard was the "Führer myth."[61] The crisis of the Weimar Republic derived in part from its failure to develop a system of communication based on mutual trust that could have stabilized it. The Führer myth combined the hope and longing for "better times" with the possibility of attaching this hope to a single individual with a sort of raw, unadulterated trust. A personal tie to the Führer, orchestrated by propaganda and transmitted via mass media, took the place of a raw trust formed in face-to-face situations. This blurred border between unadulterated trust and the hope that someone would be able to bring about change converged in the hope for salvation with the Führer as "savior." Just how successfully this hope displaced democratic election and control procedures was revealed in Germans' willingness to criticize political abuses and individual state agencies while retaining a high level of trust in Hitler himself.[62]

At the same time, the "Führer principle" made it possible to eliminate some anonymous hierarchies in politics and the administration. This principle appeared to be the logical implementation of a personal and "organic" social structure in which people entrusted with tasks replaced checks and balances. In this way, National Socialist political culture represented something completely different, an alternative that ran counter to democracy with its procedures, patience, and compromises.

In this political culture, there was a semantic displacement of the concept of "loyalty," which took the place of democratic conceptions in which a citizen's trust in politicians was limited to a certain time.[63] This displacement could only succeed against the background of a political culture in which democratic procedure was perceived as deficient and under the conditions of a comprehensive crisis of modern "languages of trust" (including money), to borrow Harald Wenzel's phrase.[64] Against this backdrop, the new imagery was able under the mantle of "charismatic rule" to transcend disappointments with Weimar by offering hope for a better future. The crisis of the republic was in part caused by the inability of the political system's representatives to communicate credibility. Modern societies have to rely on abstract systems to provide mediation services at their "access points." Hitler's "charismatic rule" addressed precisely this gap; it was able to establish personal "raw" trust through "face-work" in the media. Alongside the National Socialist rejection of formulations taken explicitly from bartering, this charismatic rule proved to be attractive.[65]

The National Socialists set themselves apart from political competitors by means of consistent and sustained shifts in political semantics. Wherever possible, National Socialists described their policies with language that distanced them from the vocabulary of bartering and trading, which they discredited as an unacceptable mixing of business and politics. In place of negotiations and agreements, there were events. Not the political process but rather the result dominated the discourse. New organizations replaced those of the so-called Weimar system. "They have no system; they have an organization. They do not try to organize things rationally; they listen to what is organic in order to discover its secrets," noted Viktor Klemperer.[66] The concepts that best expressed this "organic" transformation were those like "Führer" and "trustee."[67] These terms suggested that a person had a definite role, that a person knew his or her place and was working for the good of the whole. Instead of political power, conveyed for a limited period, there was now personal power. "Loyalty" to the "Führer" was thus both the precondition for and a description of official and mandated functions.[68] Thus, at the level of public social relationships, National Socialism offered an integrating structure—"intense inclusivity in a society that had been scarred by deep divisions."[69]

As successful as this policy of disengaging from horizontal exchange relationships was, these propagandistic incantations could scarcely be reconciled with the new burdens of the war for large sections of the population. At the very latest in 1939, when a comprehensive system of rationing was instituted, the issue of trading was once again on the agenda, albeit under new circumstances.

Consumption Spaces between the Wars, Conditions of Interaction, and New Market Boundaries

Berlin's wartime black market was a new space for consumption that functioned according to its own rules. Illegal and lacking infrastructure, the black market forced participants to learn new bartering practices in place of what had been routine shopping rituals and procedures. Bartering took place in apartments, in cafés and pubs, in stores, or in the workplace. In many cases, these sites were where introductions were made and where potential traders could size one another up, as none of these sites was actually suitable for trading goods. Danger, security measures, and improvisation characterized the scene. Buying things illegally brought important changes to managing one's household resources compared to regular shopping. I look at consumer spaces in Berlin before the war and the trading methods as components of a consumption history that focuses on the interactions of the participants.[70]

The context of shopping and the scripts followed by buyers and sellers had changed in the legal market before 1939 since some small rationing measures had already been introduced in 1934 as an effect of Nazi consumption policies prioritizing at least to some extent rearmament over consumer goods supplies. Nonetheless, the wartime rationing measures marked a clear break. The regulations drafted to secure these measures set forth a relatively clearly defined space in which consumption could legally take place and thereby defined ex negativo the areas for black market trading. Three things will be looked at here: the sites where Berlin consumers conducted business in the prewar period, the new boundaries between the legal and illegal markets as drawn up in the relevant wartime regulations, and the goals National Socialist leaders pursued in formulating these boundaries.

When Karl Deutmann, who lived in Karlshorst, recorded his impressions of his "journey to the city" on June 24, 1945, the hustle and bustle of the marketplaces in the ruins figured prominently. Deutmann employed a telling formula. Although the activities in the Berlin streets seemed anachronistic—butter was sold out of kegs and there was a good deal of haggling over prices—Deutmann compared the illegal trading with a "street department store." There was a good deal of irony here because the difference between the "wild black market trading" and the "temples of consumption" that had once been so admired in the city was only too clear. Where a couple of years earlier elegant businesses had invited one to stroll and shop, now one could buy "outside, freely traded beets of some kind" on every street corner.[71] Descriptions of such contrast indirectly took up a discourse that had been popular since the nineteenth century, in which Berlin was described as a modern city of consumption. But how far had consumption really fallen? What did the Berlin consumption landscape look like before the war economy and the conditions of this "society in a state of disintegration" prepared the way for the illegal markets? What sort of consumption spaces and practices characterized the period just before the black markets?

In Berlin, largely because of the chaotic economic situation between the wars, there were heated, politically charged discussions about consumption. In quick succession, World War I, hyperinflation, and the Great Depression had determined living conditions. At the same time, the contexts for consumption practices were undergoing a long-term transformation that heralded the birth of a new consumer society. This development, which had begun in the nineteenth century, not only produced enduring changes in the everyday economic activity of Berliners, but it had also led to the creation of new consumer spaces and had even impacted the capital's appearance. Berlin had increasingly come to be described in terms of consumption. With the birth of the department stores at the end of the nineteenth and the beginning of the twentieth century, the city became a "consumption metropolis." Reports and fictional adaptations in literature and film established an image of urbanity defined by new shopping opportunities that were fascinating for some and suspect for others. The city had once held a spartan Prussian image, but that changed after the founding of the German Empire in 1871. In the boom phase of the 1870s, apartment houses on Unter den Linden gave way to fashion shops, restaurants, banks, and hotels. This was in keeping with imperial policy, which placed a high value on appearances. In the new Kaiser-Galerie, modeled on a gallery in Milan and completed in 1873, customers could enjoy the consumer experience in over 50 stores, cafés, and other establishments. Such sensational new buildings received a great deal of attention.[72] This trend continued after World War I. Consumption opportunities were now considered an essential part of the Zeitgeist and of contemporary lifestyles. Thus, observers in the 1920s often compared Berlin to Chicago, which they saw as a shining example in this respect. What people had in mind with such descriptions were above all the large department stores, such as the Kaufhaus des Westens, which opened in 1907. These businesses offered such an undreamed-of variety of attractively displayed products that shopping became a thrilling experience. At the same time, new entertainment facilities and even public advertising changed the cityscape, while posters and neon signs started to change how Berliners perceived their surroundings.[73]

For all that, descriptions attributing modernity and world power to specific sites of consumption did not have much to do with the everyday lives of Berliners. Such accounts, whether positive or negative, overlooked the diversity of consumption spaces that typified the city. Alongside new forms of the retail trade, there were still traditional forms of shopping at markets or with peddlers, street vendors, and "flying exchanges (*fliegende Börsen*)." These distribution points continued to exist for a long time. They continued to shape many quarters of the city into which the new consumer world of department stores, retail shops, fast-food stands, and entertainment facilities was only slowly making inroads, if at all.[74]

The topos of modernity was probably also the expression of a rhetorical break because Berlin in the 1920s looked like anything but the modern consumer city: the images of chaos—recall Deutmann's description—stood in stark contrast to the new forms of presenting goods and of shopping.

As far as bartering went, Berlin saw plenty of it already during World War I. This kind of trade continued into the early 1920s, largely unabated by the "extortion courts (*Wuchergerichte*)."[75] There was a whole series of terms for the new black market practices: *Schleichhandel*, which meant "illicit trade" and conveyed a sense of sneaking or creeping about (*schleichen*); "chain trade," which pictured goods passing through the hands of many middlemen; "wild [unauthorized] street trading"; and "profiteering (*Wuchergeschäft*)" in the sense of charging extortionate prices. The distinction between "real" and "wild" street trading, in particular, preoccupied many outraged observers and reflected the fact that at the beginning of the 1920s, legal street trading was more widespread than in the 1930s. But illegal trading also proliferated. According to contemporary estimates, the number of participants increased by the thousands between 1920 and 1921.[76] As such, illegal trading became a problem for rather different groups.

The topic was mentioned in numerous petitions and letters between the Berlin police headquarters and the city government. In June 1919, the police division responsible for enforcing trading laws reported to the Berlin municipal authorities that the "wild street traders and their following" have attempted "to establish themselves on Küstriner Platz after [having been] driven out of the Schönhauser district and the Andreasplatz." The policeman in charge assured that he was "doing all he could . . . with all the means at his disposal" to stop the "wild street trading, which is spreading in a most annoying manner." That this was not an empty threat soon became clear. The authorities advanced with military squads against the unwanted trading.[77]

Markets were in fact strongly regulated. The various "market police regulations for municipal market halls and weekly public markets" in the individual Berlin districts determined, for example, the "market area" and "freedom of access." The planners had also thought of "business conducted while walking" and immediately prohibited it. Market stands had to display both their proprietors' names and the goods' prices. "Loitering" was forbidden, "as well as violating basic decency or disturbing the peace, hawking wares or auctioning them off, and preventing or disrupting purchases and transactions with physical force or by outbidding or indeed by any other means."[78] These regulations made the contrast to unregulated "wild trading" in the streets all the more apparent. Complaints about unregulated trading began to pile up at municipal offices from shop owners afraid of the competition who objected, for example, to the poor hygiene where illegal street trading took place. They also bemoaned disturbances caused by hawking and pushing, or they simply protested the underhanded competition.[79]

Food producers and the Berlin Market Hall Association also criticized street trading. A complaint from 1919 stated that although many people suffering from disabilities, war injuries, and unemployment sought "to create a source of income for themselves through street trading," these efforts could not be allowed "to degenerate to the degree that whole streets" were no longer available to "public traffic." This problem was particularly serious "in the area around the two central market halls on Neue Friedrichstrasse and Alexanderplatz." Under pressure from these complaints, municipal authorities called for "a stronger police presence to keep the area around the market halls, in particular, as well as the most important traffic routes, free from street traders."[80] Residents and shop owners alike complained about congested streets and access roads.

The Berlin police seem to have been most receptive to this last point. They had been trained to see the streets as the site of "street politics" and understood street trading as a disturbance of the peace, which they subsumed under the concept of "traffic problem."[81] They kept meticulous records of the preferred black market trading sites and at the same time used raids to gain the upper hand, albeit with only partial success. Yet as a letter from the Stettin Food Office made clear, there was no legal foundation for such police actions. The police justified their approach with reference to street regulations because other applicable regulations did not exist. Stettin authorities therefore intended to amend the regulations to enhance their control.[82]

Street trading had become a political issue, and it remained on the agenda in Berlin throughout the entire Weimar period. Political parties represented in the capital city's government had rather different opinions about the practice. The Social Democrats (SPD) and Independent Social Democrats (USPD) often supported street traders. In their opinion, poor Berliners—and thus the war's real losers—depended on street trading, and the right-wing coalition against the practice was primarily interested in protecting and representing the interests of "the propertied classes," "wholesalers," and "capitalists." In the meeting of the Berlin city council on March 4, 1920, SPD representative Zimmermann responded to someone who had interrupted him and associated street trading with profiteering and hustling:

> When one speaks here of profiteers and hustlers, then I could say with the same justification that the merchant class, too, is riddled with [them]. . . . I need only refer to the large department stores Wertheim and Tietz, who put their retail outlets on the best corners. The merchants, too, systematically move their businesses to the busiest parts of the city.[83]

His party viewed street trading as a "necessary branch" of Berlin's economic life. Street trading not only created jobs for those not so well-off but also ensured that there was a quick and cost-effective distribution of goods. Of course, "real businesses" had to be strengthened, and one had to cooperate with merchants toward the "elimination of all abuses."[84] USPD representative Nawrocki explained only a few weeks later, on May 26, that the measures against street trading demanded by the Liberals and the DNVP were an expression of political patronage: "As a matter of fact, they see a certain danger in the possibility that the street traders could have a moderating effect on prices, so that the businessmen cannot increase prices as much as they would like. During the war, businessmen played fast and loose with the proletarian population."[85]

By contrast, liberal and conservative representatives emphasized that street trading harmed retailers and that the bulk of participants were not the poor but criminals. Furthermore, in their opinion, the "wild hustle and bustle" led to "disfigurements" in the "cityscape" and massive traffic problems. The city council member from the Economic Party of the German Middle Classes (aka Wirtschaftspartei or WP) made some remarkable statements that read like a prologue to the sort of scenes that became characteristic of the Berlin black market in the 1940s:

> You all know it—you only need to go into the streets where there are lots of people; it doesn't have to be in the west, it can also be in the center of the city—when you walk home you often hear: cigarettes, chocolate! But the man never has anything in his hands. Rather, he takes everything out of his overcoat. Is that legitimate street trading?

The answer to Roeder's rhetorical question was clear. He agreed with city councilman Frank that unregulated trading should be prohibited. To be sure, the latter took the position "that it would be very difficult today to draw a clear line between honest and dishonest street trading." At the same time, however, Frank also took a "strong stand . . . against the havoc—which is spreading more and more—of smuggling, price gouging by middlemen, and black marketeering." The "men of action in this business" are "people who are well off, who live in the western part of Berlin, and who earn millions in this profitable business." These same people also controlled the trade in currencies, securing for themselves "huge profits by trading in foreign currencies." Furthermore, Frank pointed out "that in the western part of the city, street traders were conducting a flourishing trade in cocaine." In spite of the fact that it was very difficult to distinguish between "honest" and "dishonest" trading, he called for "the government to take appropriate measures to protect fully the interests of legitimate street traders [and] to suppress the illicit trade on the streets."[86]

Frank gave voice to a moral division in the city that would persist for a long time to come. Remarks by city councilman Warthemann continued in a similar vein. Warthemann asked whether traders in the Weinmeister and Grenadier Streets were "Berlin citizens." He surmised that they were not but were "Jews who had come to Berlin from the East." "We cannot and must not," he continued, "allow such trading in the streets of Berlin to continue." The Liberal Democratic (FDP) representative Hausberg supported such appeals. He spoke of the "vermin of economic activity" that had to be "removed from our street life."

In his reply, SPD representative Zimmermann stated that he wanted to make people aware of the disproportionately harsh measures against street traders. He saw grave differences between the small-time street traders and the circles described by Councilman Frank: "the contraband trade works with wagonloads and whole trains, whereas the street trade cannot push whole wagons and trains of groceries, etc." In response, someone cried out, "We denounce both." Clearly, the streets had become a contested consumption space, yet Berlin street traders would remain familiar figures in the city into the 1930s.

The moral economy expressed in such statements did not only reflect views on decent behavior in the marketplace but also showed an awareness for the outward appearance of the city's public spaces that had changed a lot since the prewar years. Did street trading really fit into the picture of a modern metropolis? Yet street trading was not necessarily backward per se. As late as the second half of the nineteenth century, it was considered typical of big city life.[87] During the 1920s, a significant portion of these traders were news vendors; in 1929, there were 3,700 officially registered news vendors in Berlin alone. The sale of newspapers in the city streets came to symbolize the need for information, imparting an image of speed and rapid change that seemed essential to modern urbanity.[88] On the other hand, just as this branch of the mobile business seemed to fit well with the image of a modern metropolis, hawking small items and foodstuffs on the street could be considered backward because it stood in contrast to the new, opulent business premises. With its direct confrontation between buyer and seller, the seemingly provisional presentation of goods under unhygienic open-air conditions had something old-fashioned (if endearing) about it. The authorities were not indifferent to such appearances. On the other hand, the state made money on the itinerant traders. Only in 1937 did the revenue generated for the state by the itinerant trade tax decrease significantly, by around 80 percent compared with 1929.[89] Furthermore, street trading created jobs for the lower classes, above all, for women, senior citizens, children, and people with handicaps. Thus, allowing such trading was a matter of socio-political significance.[90]

Alongside street trading, market halls shaped the Berlin consumer landscape between the wars.[91] With the slaughterhouses and the indoor market halls, the city provided "the most important facilities . . . to organize the distribution of food" in Berlin.[92] Whereas the market hall in the Neue Friedrichstrasse was exclusively for wholesalers, the other ten halls, spread over the whole city, were open to wholesalers and retailers alike. The market halls flourished so that by the late 1920s, their total floor space once again expanded. Within three years, the floor space increased from under 27,000 square meters in 1926 to 28,000 square meters in 1929. Some 500,000 tons of fruits and vegetables were sold here in this period.[93]

To understand the transformation of the urban consumer landscape in the first third of the twentieth century, we must keep in mind that in 1927 there were still regular hay and straw markets in Wedding and Friedrichshain, and horse markets in Charlottenburg and Spandau.[94] Whereas, the new had arrived in the form of modern consumption temples, elegant cafés, and music halls, for example, on Potsdamer Platz, Unter den Linden, and Kurfürstendamm, consumption spaces in other parts of the city that seemed anachronistic remained. Most important for the everyday Berlin consumer were the regular weekly markets, at which, above all, foodstuffs were sold. In 1927, there were 114 weekly markets in Berlin, both public and private, with more than 250 market days per week. The 58 public markets were spread out relatively equally throughout those districts that were not part of the central city; the most important were Charlottenburg, Schöneberg, Steglitz, and Treptow. The markets in the city center were exclusively in the hands of private businessmen.[95]

Street trading, market halls, and weekly markets remind us that not everywhere was Berlin becoming a new, modern consumer city. All the same, things were changing. In Berlin, too, retail trade came to be what Uwe Spiekermann calls the "foundation" of the new "consumer society."[96] One important objection to street trading as a whole thematized the insecurity of the illegal or at least ephemeral business in the street. "I must emphasize," explained the city councilman Dr. Falckenberg, from the national liberal German People's Party (DVP),

> that the shopkeepers are stable, that they live there, so that the customer who buys something that does not fit or is poorly made can go back to the shopkeeper and return it. The street traders, however, disappear in a minute, and whoever has been deceived by them has simply lost out.[97]

This was a decisive point against street trading. On the other hand, Falckenberg's remarks reflected a contemporary perception that the customer had grown accustomed to the secure spaces of retail stores. The modern retail business met this need for security. And that it did so was, alongside its decentralized and efficient distribution function, one more reason for its success.

To an ever greater degree, retail stores and large department stores crowded out more traditional consumer spaces. Between 1924 and 1932, the number of large department stores, cooperatives, and other stores with a wide variety of goods increased significantly throughout Germany, although smaller and medium-sized stores still formed the backbone of retail in Germany.[98] In the business census on May 17, 1939, a total of 31 department stores were registered. Just under 23,000 people worked in them. For standard price, variety, and bulk goods stores, there were 30 entries and a comparable number of employees, 19,000.[99] According to the same census, there were even more retail businesses for food and beverages. By May 1939, their number had increased quickly to 31,395. There were also about 7,000 clothing shops.[100]

The expansion of the retail and department store trade laid the foundations for a new culture of shopping that profoundly affected the everyday lives of consumers, especially in terms of how people interacted with one another. A new set of roles developed for buyer and seller that were subject to rather fixed rules. "Shopping," observes Spiekermann, "was transformed into a ritual, where the process, aim, and subject of commercial communication between retailer and consumer were increasingly regulated."[101] Yet these new rules were ambivalent. On the one hand, there was greater anonymity, something generally attributed to life in the big city. In place of personal relationships with a shopkeeper and their accompanying forms of interaction, there was now a relatively uniform pattern of paying without a longer sales talk. Prerequisite for this change was the standardization of both goods and prices. At the same time, the situation was characterized by a limitation on competition left over from the war and inflation years. Until the late 1920s, the prices for bread and other baked goods were set by law throughout Germany. Milk prices were specified by local officials. At the same time, name-brand items with standardized prices made up over half of all food sales. Only a couple of goods such as salt, sugar, and lard were sold as "competitive articles."[102] Together with price levels established for policy reasons, the introduction of price standards ensured that there would be a different sort of shopping. These standards enabled people to orient themselves quickly; a lengthy, protracted inspection and examination of the goods was no longer necessary. Thus, how one shopped changed. Shopping became more anonymous, could be completed much more quickly, and promoted new expectations for the behavior of buyers and sellers.

On the other hand, the shop as a "basic innovation," to use Spiekermann's phrase, strengthened relationships between vendors and their regular customers; indeed, it made such relationships possible. As a new consumer experience in the nineteenth century, especially in regard to communication, the new store created space for a new, recurring, and therefore secure shopping experience. It became much easier for the customer to enforce his or her demands—for example, in regard to the quality of goods. Furthermore, shopping took place in a social context that went far beyond a simple exchange of goods. The small corner shop in particular was the ideal trading site for not only goods but also gossip. The decentralized distribution network of small retail shops was not only modern, but it also provided the starting point for social integration in the supposedly so anonymous big city. Small retail stores broke down the complexity of the modern metropolis into comprehensible units.[103]

When the National Socialists came to power, the conditions for street trading in Berlin changed considerably. The National Socialist measures that affected the consumption landscape were not solely motivated by ideology but by a bundle of motives that mixed ideological guidelines with questions of city planning and public health, in addition to strictly economic policy calculations.

Perhaps most important were those conceptions of the National Socialist leadership—specifically of Hitler and Goebbels—that aimed at a complete "cleansing" of Berlin's appearance. After what Goebbels called the "battle for Berlin," the "red Moloch" (the communist-infested metropolis) became the object of National Socialist transformation gigantomania.[104] Berlin was not only the center of Germany; it was also the center of the National Socialist theater of power. From 1933 on, the National Socialist claim to power found expression in torch and military parades, spectacles at the Olympic Games, and urban development. Berlin was not only the metropolis of government and administration; it was also the most important site where the well-ordered, powerful masses marched. In these ostentatious displays, the National Socialist leadership found an expression of support.[105] "Berlin is Germany and Germany is Berlin" were the words in a 1937 booklet commemorating the 700th anniversary of the city's founding. Scarcely had the National Socialists "established the city as *their* capital when they claimed to have turned it into a bastion of order, decency, and correct thinking," whereas before it had been little more than an accumulation of male brothels, amusement temples, and drug markets in their eyes.[106]

The Nazi takeover of the city involved the city's administration and public spaces. Dr. Julius Lippert, chairman of the NSDAP faction in the city council and Reichskommissar for Berlin, was responsible for the "cleanup." After years of bitter street battles between communists and the SA, paramilitary National Socialist troops ruled the streets of Berlin, whereas the Berlin police preferred to act against fringe groups. In December 1933, newspaper articles celebrated "the cleansing of Berlin," stating that "the measures of the Berlin police and their results find the support of everyone. The capital city is freed within a few months from an evil whose scale represented an unacceptable annoyance to Berliners and to visitors in the city."[107] In fact, this violent "pacification" of the streets appears to have enjoyed the approval of the populace. It hardly mattered that the city's transformation and the resulting new National Socialist cityscape were the products of terror.

The anti-Jewish policies of the new rulers formed a central aspect of violent Nazi control of urban space. The prohibition of street trading for foreigners, which affected especially eastern European Jews, so-called *Ostjuden*, and which was supposed to keep the city streets "pure," brought together anti-Semitism, "cleanup" policy, and local commercial policy. From the perspective of the new rulers, unauthorized or "wild" street trading was incompatible with "clean" German streets and therefore had to be prohibited. This policy comported with existing anti-Semitic attitudes, but there was something new about it. It was not limited to spontaneous or individually planned attacks. On the contrary, actions against street trading were radicalized and systematized. This National Socialist ideal of "German cleanliness" bore fruit in public spaces during preparations for the Olympic Games. To improve the image of the city abroad, "measures to impress foreign visitors with Berlin's civility included a roundup of beggars and known con-men, as well as a prohibition on price-gouging."[108]

Other aspects of Nazi ideology also played a role in reshaping the city's consumption spaces. This was particularly evident in the idea of a collaborative relationship between buyers and sellers as an organic constituent of the Volksgemeinschaft. In the 1930s, state regulations increasingly specified certain roles for merchants as well as for consumers. In theory, both sides were understood to be partners with equal rights who were supposed to act in the economy for the good of the whole. As a result, medium-sized retail stores were increasingly supported, whereas large businesses, small stores, and itinerant traders were suppressed.[109] Between 1933 and 1941, authorities drastically reduced the number of business licenses. If in 1933 there were still 6,620 street merchants, by 1941 this number had declined to under 2,000. In particular, the municipal administration limited street trading in connection with preparations for the 1936 Olympics, because in its eyes street trading did not conform to the ideal of a clean and modern metropolis. The beginning of the war was also a pivotal moment, although it was much less dramatic because it was part of a general trend to restrict consumption for the duration of the war.[110]

On top of these anti-Semitic and ideological motives, there was economic policy. Here National Socialist Germany pursued two contradictory goals. On the one hand, the regime worked to increase armaments production. On the other hand, it worried that its armaments policy could hurt consumption and therefore cost the government popular support. These dual concerns required careful balancing, which Hitler himself underlined in 1935 in the face of a strained supply situation.[111] The issue of "adequate provisions" was explosive because of the experiences of World War I. The National Socialist leadership believed that hunger since 1916 had played a decisive role in the home front's collapse in 1918. A starving home front was not to endanger the state ever again.

To be sure, the capital received particularly favorable treatment when it came to provisions for the populace. But even in Berlin, food supplies were limited by raw material shortages.[112] Well before 1939, the precursors of wartime rationing affected everyday life in Berlin, as the government quietly began to ration certain goods. Already by the mid-1930s, attentive observers noticed the state taking the first steps toward a war economy with a regulated supply of foodstuffs. The necessary measures for agricultural products had already been "planned in detail," according to a 1934 report from SOPADE, the Social Democratic Party in exile, which had sources in Germany. Indeed, the "sales and market regulations" for foods such as milk, butter, and eggs "certainly also [reflected] important pricing policy goals." At the same time, they constituted "the completed framework of a command economy in the event of war."[113] Only a year later, SOPADE correspondents noted that the deputy to the Führer "at the beginning of October [1935] . . . still repudiated the introduction of compulsory rationing or a ration card system." By the end of November, however, "an indirect card system was introduced for all fats in the form of customer lists at retail shops and butchers." This procedure, the authors supposed, was chosen "because one wanted to avoid reintroducing the ration cards that had been so hated during wartime."[114] Already in June 1938, as a result of the restrictions and limitations, a black market for rationed foodstuffs started up in Berlin. For example, the authors of the SOPADE report suspected that the eggs being offered for sale in the city were part of a slowly expanding illegal black market.[115]

These new market conditions resulted from an economic policy that was primarily interested in rearmament and that viewed consumers as a potential risk.[116] The introduction of the Four-Year Plan in 1936 constituted a milestone in economic policy as the regime's economic preparations for war aggravated declining conditions in the consumer goods market. The consequences reached all the way down to the relationship between merchants and consumers, for now it was important to cultivate one's contacts in order to receive preferential treatment. At the same time, every purchase could provide information about one's—perhaps improper—consumption habits. Merchants thus became potential agents of a steadily spreading surveillance culture that sought "deviants" outside the Volksgemeinschaft. As a result, power relationships shifted against consumers in favor of sellers; the retail trade became a seller's market. Together with the regulations that enforced the rationing, these new market conditions defined the legal consumer spaces that Berliners increasingly attempted to get around during the war.

The emerging Berlin black market constituted an evasive action, as often happens in markets with a regulated consumer supply. It was the exception that occurred in the supply-demand relationship in the context of prohibitions.[117] Economic theories explain the formation of black markets as a response to regulatory measures. Such restrictions lead to a decline in supply, which in turn increases demand and affects black market prices. When officials undertake no further measures, the relatively small amount of goods in demand initially flows to those who first set up their shops, who have privileged access to the goods in question, or who know the right people. Finally, black markets can arise "if adherence to a maximum price at distribution points cannot be guaranteed or if goods are traded *after* their distribution at other sites."[118]

On August 27, 1939, five days before the Wehrmacht invaded Poland, the National Socialist government required Germany's inhabitants to use food ration coupons, although initially the authorities exempted bread, flour, and eggs. The longer the war lasted, the worse the supply situation grew. Consequently, more and more goods became subject to rationing, and officials had to regularly readjust the size of a permissible ration in light of worsening shortages. In 1940, the percentage of freely available foodstuffs sank to 20 percent of total revenues.[119] Rationed goods were dispensed at distribution points set up in existing stores. Although the first shortages could be compensated for, in the summer of 1941 weekly meat and meat product rations had to be reduced by 25 percent to 400 grams for ordinary consumers. The most far-reaching changes up to then in the basic living conditions of the German people came on in February 1942: bread, meat, and fat rations were reduced drastically.[120] This was a turning point. A subsequent increase in rations was temporary and only served propagandistic purposes. A stabilization in 1943 also did not last long, and rations remained meager. Military developments were decisive as the destruction of streets and trails by Allied air raids hampered the distribution of goods throughout the country.[121] Production declined further, and massive problems with distribution made things worse. The winter of 1943–44 saw a new low. Finally, in the last year of the war, "the food situation worsened to a frightening degree." According to Gustavo Corni and Horst Gies, the average nutritional value of rations for ordinary consumers sank by about 40 percent over the course of the war, and the situation in the cities was especially dramatic.[122]

Government-issued ration cards complicated things further by linking goods and time in an unfamiliar way. In contrast to money as a means of exchange, which ideally could be converted for an indefinite period into the future, ration cards had only limited security for equivalent values, which furthermore depended on the course of the war. The operationally effective fiction, according to which a collective trust in currencies is both a precondition of their stability and simultaneously something that perpetuates this stability, could never be achieved to the same degree by the substitute currencies of the allocation system. Just the opposite: the responsible state agencies repeatedly had to assert that the supply situation and thus the system of providing food and goods were not at risk, in the process conveying their own concern. At a meeting in early 1944, the magistrate was informed by City Councillor Dr. Petzke about the general situation and upcoming reductions.[123] Petzke explained decreases in rations, periods of frost, and problems in the provisioning of coal. At the same time, however, he mentioned that he had been successful "at the Ministry for Public Food Administration in pushing through an allotment of 250 grams of herring per head in Berlin for the near future." Not without pride he added that "the herrings are already underway." According to the meeting transcript, "laughter" followed. Nonetheless, Petzke's next remark showed just how precarious the situation was and the extent to which not only consumers but also planners calculated only for the near future as this adjustment was only to last for four weeks.[124] The tense situation clearly caused problems for more than just the ministerial elites as is evident in the concern Petzke retrospectively expressed vis-à-vis coal supplies:

> The situation back then [in 1940/41] was, if you remember, extraordinarily precarious, for we had to declare effective March 31 that although the entitlements had not all been handed out, the ration cards for coal were no longer valid.... This was a step that we did not want to take because, of course, such measures shake the trust of the population.[125]

The phrase "trust of the population" can be considered a key concept. Often the authorities did not particularly trust those receiving the rations. Long before black marketeers such as Martha Rebbien were arrested, planners in the Justice Ministry had anticipated such cases, and by shifting the boundary between what was legal and illegal, they defined a new market space; by describing the practices allowed, they set forth ex negativo the framework for the emerging black market. What, authorities asked, would happen if the war were to continue for a long time and a large number of Germans on the "home front" attempted to get around the rationing restrictions and improve their standard of living?

The people who asked this question were able with a certain justification to refer back to the experiences of World War I, when increasing numbers on the "home front" integrated illegal bartering practices into their everyday lives.[126] Naturally, this was also a special worry of the National Socialist leadership—even an idée fixe of a group of men, the logical consequence of their interpretation of the defeat in World War I, which saw a weak "home front" as a decisive factor in the German setback. Both the experiences and the interpretation of these experiences formed a benchmark that people used to assess their situation at the beginning of World War II. Thus, the legacy of World War I formed the backdrop to the formation of bartering networks in Berlin that Martha Rebbien and many other Berliners engaged in.

The regulations were supposed to help prevent social disintegration, but they generated confusion. When in March 1948 Hamburg Oberregierungsrat

Herbert Klüber published the third edition of his overview of the "Gesetzliche Grundlagen zur Schwarzmarkt-Bekämpfung" ("Legal Basis for Combatting the Black Market") ten years after its initial publication, the legal situation had become even more confusing.[127] To Klüber's great disappointment, a decade after the first regulation had gone into effect, it was still not possible to fight illegal trading "on the basis of a uniform law." Rather, "an extraordinarily large number of regulations" was required.[128] Alongside regulations on how to proceed against black marketeers, there were regulations on the war economy, on consumption, and on price law as well as, at least in Klüber's list, 12 more regulations.[129]

The most important regulation, which set forth the framework for all further interpretations of "black market trading," was the so-called War Economy Regulations (Kriegswirtschaftsverordnung, or KWVO).[130] This regulation called for jail time or—in especially serious cases—for the death penalty for those who destroyed, set aside, or held back "raw materials or goods that are a part of the vital needs of the population, and who through this maliciously endangered the covering of this need" (§1 paragraph 1). The same was true—according to the following paragraph—for certificates concerning the right to obtain certain benefits as well as the manufacturing and use of such documents. Those who committed fraudulent acts to enrich themselves would also be fined (§1 paragraph 3).

Concepts such as "setting aside" or "vital needs" were a matter of interpretation, and judges viewed them in different ways in their rulings. Was one to perceive "in the relocation of a storage location for a certain good a diversion of such" within the context of the KWVO, as was stated in a court judgment from 1940? Did "luxury articles and beauty products" fall under the category of "vital needs?"[131] In an article for *Deutsche Justiz*, Berlin public prosecutor Karl-Heinz Nuse explained early in 1940 what the War Economy Regulations meant in his view. They were primarily supposed to "catch a certain sort of criminal, namely, the 'war profiteer, the hustler'," in order to ensure that a situation such as had occurred in World War I could not happen again. "Whereas in the First World War, at least in the first few years, war profiteers and hustlers were able to act undisturbed—their behavior harmed their own people and contributed significantly to the collapse of the home front—with this regulation we have eliminated such a possibility," wrote Nuse. The regulation gave judges and prosecutors a "strong weapon to use against the parasites." The judges, Nuse continued, should not "shy away from the death penalty if one of the criminals" had "shown himself or herself to be an especially asocial personality." On the question of the meaning of the passage "vital needs," Nuse added,

> the provisions of §1 aim to ensure the well-ordered functioning of the economy, especially to ensure the provisioning of the population with all those goods to be included under the concept of vital needs. The definition of the "vital needs of the population" is broad. Not only are articles one needs to stay alive included, so, too, are coffee, tobacco, and alcoholic drinks. Indeed, there are few items which do not fall under §1.

The National Socialist justice system described all black market trading as offenses against the regulations listed above and subsumed them generally—even those which, according to the files, belonged to other groups of crimes—under "Offenses against War Economy Regulations." Only in individual interrogation records as well as in the written judgments do terms such as "black market trading," "smuggling," or "hustling" appear. Of course, in his speeches, Hitler captured quite well the public's attitudes toward "hustling." He stated many times that "one should use barbaric punishments against the professional hustler." On the other hand, he also stated that one should not "stop trains and buses . . . in order to search for what might be just three eggs bought or stolen from a farmer."[132] How this "program" could be put into practice was a problem that occupied a whole legion of employees in the various ministries and local state agencies. The formulation of the regulations and the further debates to flesh out the details as well as determine how to ensure adequate enforcement took up a great deal of National Socialist planners' time and energy. These discussions circled around how to sustain and uphold public order and a stable "home front." The German Justice Ministry remained the most important supplier of keywords for the elaboration of this policy both on the national and the local level. The strict centralization of the National Socialist justice system above all in the realm of the so-called jurisdiction of a special court of law meant that decisions made in Berlin decisively shaped National Socialist black market policy. The special courts were responsible for enforcing the most important sections of the regulations. Even if one can recognize local differences in sentencing policy, one must assume that the general lines of the policy were decided on the national level and that furthermore—given its importance—it was constantly monitored.[133]

At a meeting in the German Justice Ministry, Freisler emphasized that it was necessary in wartime "to eliminate every symptom of decay, to start when these symptoms are barely recognizable" and "to eradicate every sign of discord."[134] Moreover, questions of adequate punishment had to be reevaluated. This was especially true for the "holding back of vital and essential foodstuffs," which was the equivalent of "stabbing the German people in the back."[135] With an eye to the situation on the "home front," Justice Minister Gürtner stated on the same occasion, "in war . . . even at home one's personal fate has to be subsumed, without consideration, to the defense of one's people."[136] The Berlin municipal authority, Brombach, added that

> in the present war, which has been forced upon us, securing the vital needs of the German people is one of the government's most important tasks. On 27 August 1939, in order to guarantee a just and equal distribution of consumer goods, the government issued the "Regulation for the Temporary Safeguarding of the Vital Needs of the German people (RGBl. I, p. 1498)." This regulation introduced rationing coupons . . . for a large number of consumer goods.[137]

The judges of the special courts could mark a person who had committed offenses against War Economy Regulations as "harmful to the nation" and, in so doing, as a rule, assign a harsher punishment. As a commentary in the *Deutsche Justiz* from 1940 made clear, under the rubric "Decisions by German Courts," "it is simply not true that offenses against War Economy Regulations do not correspond to the conditions in Paragraph 4 of the Regulations against Crimes Harmful to the Nation." However, in these cases, there had to be "substantiated reasons to be found especially in the state of war, which had not yet been taken into consideration in the elements constituting the war crime."[138]

In the following years, such strict and relatively concrete guidelines described the space within which legal consumption practices were possible. The opposite side of this coin was that whoever disobeyed these regulations had to reckon with the possibility of severe penalties or sentences. That was the result of a policy of securing political authority and power that took into account and, to a degree, accepted illegal trading during the war—with good reason, but which at the same time also defined this as an illegal activity. Taking a look at it from the state's perspective, there was no getting out of this dilemma. Intelligent solutions were not even discussed, such as attempting a limited legalization of bartering in carefully controlled spaces. This would turn out to be a burden. For it very quickly became clear that regulations and punishment would not be able to curb massive illegal trading.

CHAPTER 2

The Wartime Networks: The Martha Rebbien Case

Early in the war, trading in the Berlin black market took place primarily in networks. Unlike late in the war or immediately afterward, people could not just visit an existing market and choose their partners from among those there at that time. Instead, they had to establish contacts and make arrangements to meet. This clandestine part of the Berlin barter culture, between 1939 and 1950, has long been overlooked by historians.[1] And yet this phase was more than just a prologue. Rather, in this phase, manifold displacements both at the practical as well as at the discursive level occurred that make it an important part of urban bartering culture between the beginning of the war and the development of the economic societies of East and West Germany.

At the center of the story here are the activities of one woman, Martha Rebbien, and of the participants in her black market trading network around the Gesundbrunnen city train station in northern Berlin. Using this example, we can follow the important changes that characterized everyday life in the huge metropolis under the conditions of a barter culture, including new everyday consumer habits and practices. The first part of the chapter investigates how bartering networks came about, the degree of professionalization of bartering practice, the social profiles of the participants, and the changes in social relationships engendered by bartering in the city. The second part investigates the changes in the use and perception of urban space. These changes constituted a specific form of collaborative city making, a practical and moral renegotiation of urban spaces and their residents. The third part concentrates on black marketeers' unique way of dealing with goods and currencies. It looks into the steps toward professionalization and into the "tagging" of money and the meaning assigned to various bartering equivalents. That bartering culture did not remain limited to the practical dimension of exchanging goods can be seen most clearly in the evaluation of the protagonists. The fourth section examines the discourse on the hustlers during the war and thus the core of the aforementioned ongoing debate concerning moral rectitude in managing one's household. In principle everyone was guilty of some bartering. Which groups were most often accused of being hustlers by the outraged Volksgemeinschaft? One would perhaps imagine that fringe groups, especially, would be at the center of practices considered so harmful to the people. Yet Martha Rebbien and her bartering partners do not clearly fit this profile.

The Participants and Their Practices

The history of Martha Rebbien and her bartering partners is a case study with which one can describe and analyze the characteristics typical of the Berlin black market during the war. Of course, we can only discover the degree to which Rebbien's history is representative if we compare her case with others. This investigation is based on an analysis of 183 individual cases, a sample created from the lists of the cases of the public prosecutors at the Berlin Special Court in the Landesarchiv Berlin. In order to avoid distortions that can arise if one starts with one case and then merely follows the cross references, I systematically examined every tenth dossier from the list. In individual cases, I was able to elaborate on or verify previous findings by means of cross references. Martha Rebbien's case makes a good example because the police and investigator reports make it possible to reconstruct, relatively clearly, the history of a bartering network over a four-year period. Furthermore, the records are complete, having remained undamaged by the war.

The unemployed waitress, 55-year-old Martha Rebbien, had operated for at least four years as a black marketeer in the German capital at the time of her arrest on November 9, 1944.[2] In her indictment, the prosecutors concentrated on the last two years, 1943 and 1944. The investigators' reports compiled from painstaking research paint a picture of a brisk business. Although the reports convey things through a certain lens, the records of interrogations and notes render characteristic details of Berlin's black market. The police and public prosecutors' records comprise over 200 pages and include materials on the black marketeers who participated in Martha Rebbien's bartering network. The investigators were interested above all in identifying the participants and determining the quantity of goods traded. Who became acquainted with whom, when, and in what way? How was business initiated and conducted, and what prices or what equivalents in terms of goods were paid? What were the living conditions and motives of the trading partners? In the end, Berlin police received information on more than 60 people, carried out dozens of interrogations, and confiscated goods worth hundreds of Reichsmarks.

In order to obtain the information relevant for a court case, the policemen were forced to reconstruct the everyday bartering practices of Martha Rebbien. Using the snowball principle, they followed leads from the center outward. More than once investigators came to a dead end (above all because of high population turnover in the city). On the other hand, the police also discovered links to other networks. In principle, every member of the Rebbien network could also have been a member of another network. Under the surface of everyday legal life in Berlin during the war, there were a large number of bartering networks of different sizes, which generally intertwined with other networks in some way, forming an overarching network. The people who were interrogated not only mentioned names, but they also told, even if only in passing, how they had established, cultivated, maintained, and terminated contacts. From this, we can analyze the strategies participants used to establish contact with possible partners, establish trust, or find suitable trading places. And, of course, we can analyze the individual bartering transactions themselves.

At the same time, the police reports give an impression of the significance bartering had as an everyday activity for a large number of Berliners. All the methods and strategies of the illegal business were mentioned, such as keeping an eye on possible suppliers and customers, the turnover of goods, et cetera. Martha Rebbien, who was the center of her bartering network, had direct contact to at least 20 people and indirect contact to at least another 20 (see Figure 2.1). The actual number is likely even higher as the police were presumably only able to expose a portion of her business relationships, as the prosecutors asserted in their indictment.[3]

A considerable portion of the work of the Trade and Safety Supervision Service (Gewerbeaußendienst), the police, and the Gestapo consisted of conducting surveillance of local "hot spots," following tips from the population, and engaging in the grunt work of exposing complex exchange relations.[4] The Berlin police, prosecutors, and special courts enforced the mistrustful National Socialist policy, which aimed to confront any possible destabilization of the "home front" with a comprehensive juridical catalogue of regulations and punishments. On November 9, 1944, they caught up with Martha Rebbien and some of her bartering partners.

Police records make it possible to trace the bartering deals between Martha Rebbien and her partners back to November 1940. The picture becomes more diffuse the further back one goes, either as a result of the witnesses' inability to remember or their unwillingness to give out information or because the Berlin police and prosecuting authorities were most interested in information they could use in prosecutions. All told, one finds references to over 30 meetings in which bartering transactions were initiated, prepared, or concluded. Of these, 11 took place in the last week before Rebbien was arrested, that is, between November 2 and 9, 1944.

Martha Rebbien's business activity went through a number of phases, each reflecting external circumstances and events. Rebbien had to move three times during the war, twice because she had been bombed out. The war on the home front, during which the capital was attacked by British and American bombers, had a direct impact on Rebbien's everyday life—and thus on her illegal business. As can be shown in the well-documented last phase of her business career, she built up her bartering network in the confined spaces of her district or *Kiez*. Moving for her, therefore, meant that she had to build up a new network of

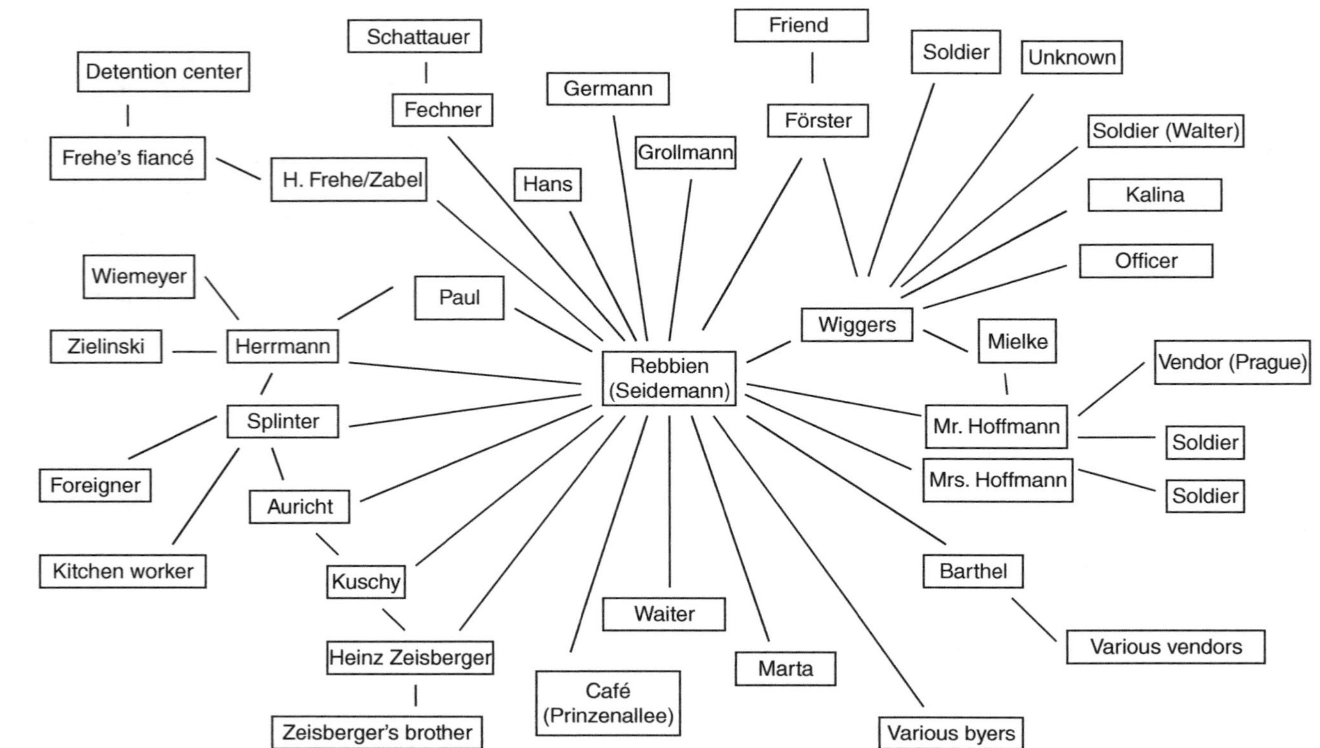

Figure 2.1 The black market network of Martha Rebbien

bartering relationships. In the last phase, the sites where contacts could be initiated and where traders met and conducted business were almost exclusively near the Gesundbrunnen train station and Rebbien's apartment on Swinemünder Street, where most of the participants also worked and lived.

In the course of a protracted investigation—the interrogations produced new suspects and witnesses, and lineups were used to try to clarify facts when there were contradictory versions of events—slowly but surely the picture emerged. Although Martha Rebbien confessed immediately in her first interrogation on November 18,[5] she insisted that she had been "merely the go-between for other, larger suppliers" and "that she had not earned much money doing it."[6] The goal of the investigation that followed was to discover who the other individuals were as well as the extent of the business—in short, to discover the full extent of the Kiez bartering network around the Gesundbrunnen.

On November 24 the investigators got an indication of the earliest ascertainable date of Martha Rebbien's career as a black market trader from Hanna Zabel. From November 4, 1941 to April 1, 1942, Zabel had sublet her apartment to Rebbien (and lived with her), and she told the police of her difficulties with the accused.[7] Approximately 4 percent of all citizens in Berlin lived in such often conflict-laden arrangements, where one's behavior could easily be monitored by others.[8] Rebbien's quarrel with her landlady apparently had to do with her illegal business. Zabel named Rebbien's "behavior and . . . social interaction" as the reason for her hostile stance and for her ultimately successful attempt to get Rebbien out of her apartment. "She had a lot of visits from people I don't know," Zabel explained in her interrogation and continued, "I often had the feeling that the people visiting made a less than reassuring impression. I can't say what the people wanted there, as I wasn't much concerned about that and wasn't home very much." She also denied "quite strongly" that she had ever been a "supplier of coffee, canned meat and chocolate," goods she claimed to have received from her husband, a prison warden. Rebbien, however, incriminated her former landlady, stating that Zabel had indeed given her diverse foodstuffs.[9] Zabel also confirmed Rebbien's own testimony that she had already become a black marketeer in 1940. Even before the wartime black markets in Berlin were established, Rebbien had taken an initial step into illegality. In 1937 she had been convicted of embezzlement and sentenced to a year in prison.[10]

A Network Arises: Trust and Contacts

Being able to trust one's trading partner in Rebbien's network, as in all black market networks, was a fundamental component. Using the example of the Rebbien network, we can examine some of the important strategies black marketeers used to build up, stabilize, and sustain trust. A central problem for all Berlin black marketeers was initiating contact with potential bartering partners. It was crucial for Rebbien and her partners to find the right mixture of prudence, on the one hand, and trust or confidence, on the other, as demonstrated not least by the demise of the Gesundbrunnen network. Because Rebbien had conducted business with Erna Kuschy, allowing her to see behind the curtain of her bartering practice, Kuschy was able to pass on information about her to the police, resulting in the dissolution of these bartering relationships by means of the police and public prosecutors.

Trust and mistrust are thus the critical elements of any bartering practice in several respects. Partners have to be able to trust that the others will uphold the imperatives of conspiracy. Martha Rebbien, for example, tried to build up trust by telling potential bartering partners that if she were arrested she would not betray them.[11] Investigating authorities, in their efforts to fight the black market, made use of this problem in that they attempted to win over "persons in a position of trust" who for their part had tried to win the trust of their bartering partners in order then to "misuse" it by "entrusting" the authorities with their knowledge. There was no absolute security for the participants of the Gesundbrunnen network. But one could attempt in a number of ways to minimize the danger.

One of the strategies was to trust only those with whom one was already acquainted.[12] There were a number of advantages in starting up a conversation with someone one knew and involving them in business transactions. First of all, one did not have to engage in tedious searches, which saved valuable time. Second, depending on the degree of familiarity and the credibility of the first person, one could assume that the other candidates for bartering were more credible than just any complete stranger. Friends of friends had already been tested in regard to their trustworthiness. There was thus less risk: further tests could be less extensive or could fall away completely. Third, obtaining "personal data" was often already combined with a preliminary discussion, in which persons interested in trading could ask their intermediaries whether or not they were at all interested in certain goods or if these were to be obtained from them. Information about a person's credibility could also be combined with an exchange of information concerning the assortment of goods, which, in turn, also saved time.

Martha Rebbien chose a whole series of bartering partners in this manner (see Figure 2.2). Such multiplex relationships in which bartering relationships were built up on the basis of other relationships (colleagues at work, neighbors, or friends) formed in all likelihood the vast majority of all bartering relationships in Berlin between 1939 and 1945.

The trading cluster depicted in Figure 2.2 is based on the multiplexity relationships of the network participants. The participants in the network were acquainted with each other mostly as colleagues at work. With the exception of two participants, they all worked as waiters and waitresses in one of the bars or restaurants in the Gesundbrunnen Kiez. The relatively high network density (0.24)[13]—which led to greater social control, that is, monitoring by other people—had both positive and negative effects. On the negative side, it increased the likelihood of conflicts (and of betrayal), but on the positive side, it enabled the black market participants to exchange information and goods quickly in a narrow and limited "network space."

Yet Martha Rebbien went one step further. Instead of restricting her trading to acquaintances, she "expanded," by contacting Friedrich Wiggers, another illegal trading broker. Of course, Wiggers had been introduced to Rebbien and

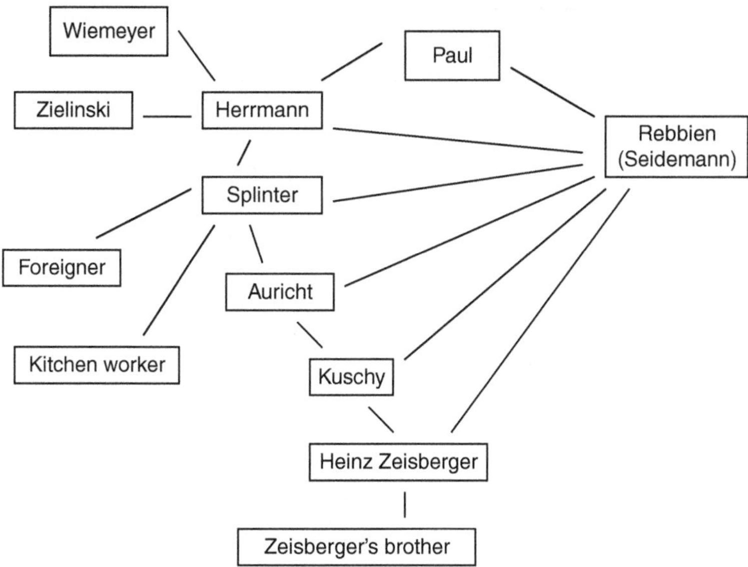

Figure 2.2 Cluster 1 of Martha Rebbien's black market network

was thus not a complete stranger. Indeed, they had a common acquaintance. Wiggers and Rebbien had become acquainted through Ursula Förster, whom Wiggers had met at Rebbien's former and Förster's current workplace, the restaurant in the Gesundbrunnen train station. Förster had often met Wiggers here and had become "better acquainted" with him.[14] According to Wiggers, he established contact with Förster in September 1944. Ursula Förster confirmed this and described their first meeting: "I became acquainted with Wiggers about a month ago in the restaurant in the train station in Gesundbrunnen. He told me that he was a traveling salesman, and that he sold Maggi [a well-known packaged spice blend name]." All in all she met him five times, usually in a café on Danziger Street. Already at their first meeting she had noticed "that he spent a great deal of time in the restaurant in the train station in Gesundbrunnen." When she asked him "why he did this, he did not really... give a sufficient answer."[15] Finally, she took him with her to Rebbien's apartment, where he was introduced to a "Martha." After this Wiggers visited Rebbien once again under the pretense of asking about Förster. On this occasion a "bartering transaction" took place. Förster and Rebbien had already discussed the topic of a "bartering transaction" in the presence of Wiggers: "We talked about all sorts of general topics. But we also talked about goods now being sold on the black market. The conversation turned to city handbags. Wiggers said he had some that he could sell. He said that he could give Rebbien about 10 of them."[16]

Martha Rebbien disagreed with Förster's version of the story and stated that when she had first met Wiggers on November 2, there had been no talk of business.[17] Still, Wiggers came back to her "on the same day... a couple of

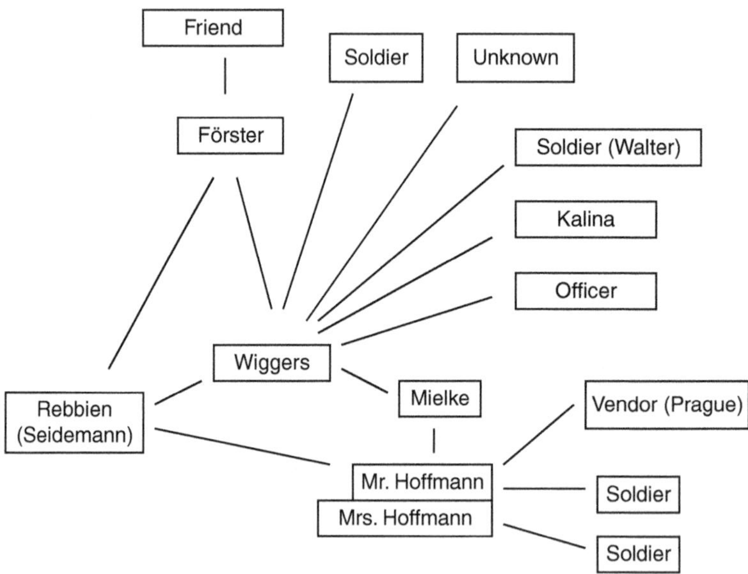

Figure 2.3 Cluster 2 of Martha Rebbien's black market network

hours later" and asked if she "had a use for shopping baskets." The business relationship then became steady. This relationship considerably expanded Rebbien's network. Through Wiggers she had access to a new network cluster (Figure 2.3).

This expansion brought together two business models of illegal trading because Rebbien and Wiggers followed different strategies in building up their illegal business relationships. Wiggers acted in his black marketeering primarily as a representative. In order to do business, he spoke to people he was not acquainted with in bars and cafés. In contrast to Rebbien (in Cluster 1), he thus avoided the dangers of a high degree of social control. This is evidence of the relatively low density of his network cluster. Wiggers accepted the high price of initiating contacts with all that entailed—for example, testing their reliability—in order to be able to avoid the monitoring of multiplex relationships. This strategy can be characterized as targeted action. Wiggers ensured that his relationships were non-binding by maintaining anonymity and keeping them secret. On top of this, he had skills he had acquired as a "representative in the food industry." He was already well acquainted with how to address people and to engage them in sales talk. Now he adapted his actions to the needs of illegal trading—being careful and keeping secrets—and thus developed a successful black market strategy.[18]

As a result of Wiggers's involvement in Rebbien's network, her network provides an example of two different methods of network formation. On the one hand, there were those (like Rebbien) who chose to bet on a higher degree of multiplexity in their black market business relationships. This method had a number of advantages. Being acquainted with some of her partners from other contexts, Rebbien could preselect them and reduce the danger of being discovered. She not only saved time by doing this, but she was also acquainted with the economic circumstances of her partners, their credit rating, their preferences and their characteristics, and their ability to get at goods in demand. On the other hand, as her relationship to Erna Kuschy shows, there was no guarantee that the bartering partners she selected would follow the rules of the illegal business—most importantly, the rule of secrecy.

Wiggers for his part relied on non-binding bartering relationships. He became acquainted with his partners in places that were semi-public, said little about himself, and thus lessened the risk that other social factors could harm his business. Yet this entailed a lot more work. He had to invest a great deal of time and energy in initiating and cultivating his contacts. Whereas Rebbien conducted the largest part of her business in her own four walls, Wiggers's black marketeering involved going from door to door as an "anonymous" representative, addressing strangers.

Such encounters with strangers were problematic, especially if one had little practice in them. The case of the Croatian worker Stevo Calic offers an example of how black marketeers had to overcome mistrust little by little before they could do business with each other. Calic had come to Berlin in February 1942 for a "work assignment" at AEG. Soon he "stayed away from work without permission" and traveled to Swinemünde and Vienna before returning to Berlin in February 1943.[19] In the restaurant "Aschinger" on Alexanderplatz, he became acquainted with a fellow Croatian, Vladimir Savo, who offered to provide him with a certificate of need for food ration cards, for 100 marks. However, Calic was careful vis-à-vis his new acquaintance because he did not yet know or trust him. He wanted to hand over the money only after the cards had been delivered.[20] Trusting a person, trusting in a regular bartering transaction, and trusting in the goods themselves went hand in hand here, as in all black market business transactions. Hildegard Mielke, who belonged to Cluster 2 of the Rebbien network, described once how a bartering relationship between strangers became consolidated when she recounted how her bartering partnership with Wiggers had started.[21] In her interrogation on November 28, she said that she did not know the person police described as Wiggers by name. Wiggers had introduced himself to her as "John" and had answered her "many questions as to his name" by saying merely that "names do not matter here." He also did not give his exact address but rather only spoke of an apartment near Danziger Street.

Mielke and Wiggers had become acquainted in the restaurant "Dachgarten" on Badstrasse: "I wanted to get something hot to drink and I sat down at a table where three men were already sitting. Wiggers and I started talking. Because I wanted to get married, I wanted to buy wedding rings. I told Wiggers this." Mielke did not say whether or not she had made the remarks in regard to the wedding rings with the intention of finding out whether Wiggers might be a potential supplier or if the conversation coincidentally turned to the rings.

Wiggers replied that he could supply the rings, whereupon Mielke gave him her address. Eight days later the rings were exchanged; the two bartering partners had already agreed the night they first met that two postage stamp albums and detector equipment with two headphones constituted his payment in return. The two sat together in her apartment and ate a piece of salmon together that Wiggers had brought. Eight days later, when Wiggers brought the wedding rings, the "case was closed" and the bartering transaction was over. However, "after another eight days, Wiggers stood once again in front of her door. He had brought with him a roast duck" and asked if Mielke wanted to have it. In the interrogation, she explained, "I had no reservations about taking the duck. He didn't want me to pay for the duck. I didn't want to take it as a present, and I gave him a hair dryer." A couple of days later, they exchanged goods for money for the first time. Wiggers brought flour after Mielke had a need for some. She bought the flour for ten marks per pound, as well as some tobacco. "On the same day he brought along a blouse, dark blue, which he wanted 150 marks for." The bartering relationship became steady. "Over time," Mielke told the police during her interrogation, Wiggers obtained from her "another birdcage, a small piece of silver for technological uses, and a broken fountain pen." However, these things were presents; no further reckoning with other goods took place.

The bartering transaction between Wiggers and Mielke is a good example of how a bartering relationship was successively built up through repetition beyond what originally had been viewed, at least by one party, as a single transaction. From someone looking for and someone offering a ring, a firm configuration for exchange was developed. Wiggers, as a "representative" of black market goods, regularly approached Mielke; he used the fact that she had been looking for a wedding ring as an opportunity. Whether or not he actually had two wedding rings when they had become acquainted in the "Dachgarten" restaurant or whether he was simply trying to procure them in order to be able to win a further customer for his goods, cannot be established with certainty. The fact that it took him eight days to deliver speaks for the second option. The history of the bartering partnership between Friedrich Wiggers and Hildegard Mielke is thus, from the traders' perspective, a success story. Seller finds buyer and wins his or her trust, leading to further business transactions. At the same time, it also testifies to the effort and energy required to participate in this illegal business. Instead of simply going into a business, one had to bring along a good deal of time and be able to keep calm in the face of risk to acquire the product desired—if it was available at all. Having to deal with these adversities was the everyday practical challenge that all black marketeers faced, whether they were "little" or "big," "clever hustlers" or fearful "occasional, private traders." But is this popular breakdown of the group of participants even true? A closer look at the bartering networks not only helps to identify different roles people played in the illegal markets but also serves to deconstruct some of the apologetic rhetoric about the black market and the people involved in it.

Network Positions, Professionalization, and Methods of Bartering

Our analysis of bartering practices can build upon much excellent theoretical and empirical work on the nature of networks. Integrating such work into our analysis helps us to better understand the network character of the phenomenon and to determine more exactly the structures and the relevant details at the level of practice. Thus, one can investigate the different roles played by various actors as well as processes of group formation and adaptation. Black market trading practices can be differentiated according to the centrality of the actors, the degree to which they were integrated into the network, their cut-point positions, bridges, network paths, and last but not least, the density of networks and their parts. These characteristics illustrate the logic of illegal trading.

The police investigations form the basis for reconstructing the individual networks. Of course, these records have a certain perspective. Although Berlin police attempted to develop a comprehensive picture of the activities and the contacts of traders who had caught their attention, they had to rely on the willingness of witnesses to cooperate and were unable to follow up on every tip and every individual contact.[22] This means that the records evaluated here are only part of the picture and indeed distort the perspective. Police investigations followed the logic of the snowball system; they were, however, not free of pragmatic considerations. Policemen set priorities in their investigations, and thus the picture of complex bartering networks was centered on individuals or groups of individuals rather than the whole picture. I assume that the networks reconstructed here are incomplete. However, individual positions within the network and different degrees of professionalization or different types of black marketeers can be clearly identified.

In the case of the Gesundbrunnen bartering network, with the inherent restrictions on entering networks in the illegal Berlin markets, various power positions evolved that solidified into so-called broker positions.[23] People who were privileged because of their access to goods that were in demand or because of their greater efforts to get goods could use their position to profit as brokers of the network. Brokers are defined as those who "no longer [exclusively exchange goods] for their own interests, but rather do so in the interests of a third party, who themselves have no access to the bartering partners." These professionals "[act] in an entrepreneurial spirit" by calculating the supply and demand situation and by "allowing themselves to be paid with extra profits for their mediating services in trading paths blocked by social structures."[24] They used the advantages they had or had acquired concerning contacts for obtaining goods that they themselves were not necessarily interested in consuming. They could resell these goods to other traders in the network who were either less privileged or interested in the goods for an additional charge (commission). Brokers were thus not only occasional, private traders; they also took on the role of vendor in the illegal markets.

However, the transition from non-broker to broker, from occasional, private trader to professional trader, was not abrupt; one did not advance from being an amateur to a professional "hustler" from one day to the next. Rather, there were successive levels of professionalization, and semi-professional participants can be distinguished from others. Often after one had taken the step into black market trading as a business, a whole series of options opened up in regard to optimizing one's business by means of, for example, bookkeeping methods or high credit standards. Professionals of the illegal Berlin business systematized their business processes as much as possible under the adverse conditions of illegality. At first glance, one discerns two types of black market traders: occasional, private traders and brokers. The group of brokers, though, encompasses traders who employed such different trading practices and had such different business sizes that it appears useful to differentiate between small and large ones.

The criteria that distinguish the three types (occasional traders and small and large brokers) are the amount of time invested, the quantity of goods traded (or the sales), the degree of network connectedness, the covered area of their "markets," and the extent to which they had developed professional accounting and organizational methods. In the networks that have been reconstructed, the broker as a rule had a central position with a higher degree of connectedness than the occasional, private traders who were usually located at the fringes. Exceptions to this rule are found above all among brokers who specialized in goods that were especially difficult to obtain (goods that were traded across borders).

Time was a decisive factor. For Martha Rebbien and her bartering partner Wiggers, the black market was a full-time job; they were, therefore, among the brokers. The most important preconditions for being able to conduct black market trading professionally were relatively unlimited availability and the possibility of combining legal and illegal business activities. Martha Rebbien was able to maintain a network of considerable size successfully only because she did not have any other regular job.[25] Brokers whose occupation overlapped with their black marketeering activities had a special position. Those who owned bars or who were salesmen, independent retailers, or waiters came up most frequently in the case reports.[26]

Others conducted their black market trading only in their free time. Occasional, private traders such as Hildegard Mielke traded only every now and then, usually because they needed something, many only for special occasions such as organizing festivities (birthday celebrations, Christmas, or leave from the front) that required "something special."

The second criterion, sales, presents something of a problem as it does not clearly distinguish occasional, private traders from brokers, at least not when considered in isolation. In the language of National Socialist justice, it was effectively defined as the line between trading "for one's own need" and "commercial smuggling"—where to draw this line, though, was one of the most controversial debates of these years.[27] Ultimately, this boundary was implied by the quantity of goods and was not definitively resolved but was left to the discretion of the special courts. Looking back, it is quite easy, as a rule, to correlate the quantity of goods with the type of merchant—especially if this is only one criterion among many under consideration. The source of goods also helps to clearly distinguish one type from another. Hildegard Mielke, for example, traded goods she had personally owned but could dispense with and not the goods that she first had to obtain. This distinction also relates to a trader's area of operation. Brokers had far larger areas in which to trade their goods that could be transregional or even transnational.[28] In addition, the number of bartering partners recruited helps us to measure the full size of a black marketeering business—a number that can be defined as a degree within a network. Of course, specializations could lead to even large brokers not necessarily needing to achieve a high degree if they conducted their business primarily as middlemen for goods especially difficult to obtain.

This brings us to the final criterion for analyzing the type of merchant: systematizing techniques. These techniques could consist of such specializations but also of certain accounting practices or security measures.

Overall, it can be said that the three different types of merchants in the Berlin black market can be differentiated by their different practices and activities and by the size of their black market businesses. These factors in turn correlate in most cases with the position of the actors in the network. Martha Rebbien and Wiggers were small brokers. The time they invested and the degree to which they had already started to specialize in certain goods or to systematically organize their trading business were quite different from those who only participated sporadically in the black market. On the other hand, their practices never reached the level of professionalization of the large brokers.

The example of a broker Hermann Weese from Neukölln makes these differences quite clear. Weese was the principle actor of a bartering network in Neukölln that traded primarily in jewelry provided by a Dutch supplier. Weese systematized his trade for example by exchanging samples. Weese, who had a billiard room on Hermannplatz, arranged for the sale of this jewelry that had crossed national borders by showing potential bartering partners sketches of the rings he possessed before he concluded the transaction. As one of Weese's bartering partners explained in his interrogation,

> in order to be able to strengthen what he had told me, especially in regard to the rings he was selling, he pulled out of his wallet two to three charts or tables on which he had drawn in pencil the individual rings available. He said that he could not always carry the rings, even if he wanted to sell them, so he had made sketches to show potential buyers. It seemed to me that he had about 50 to 60 rings sketched in this form.[29]

Instead of carrying around the valuable goods, the Neukölln jewelry merchant lowered his risk by using small cards to advertise his rings. Weese's business practices thus resembled those of a registered retail business—putting him somewhere on the scale between the necessities of the illegal business and modern forms of advertising.[30] Weese's bartering practice was not only highly specialized, but it also met the other criteria of regarding him as a large broker. These included using transnational "weak ties" in the Netherlands, mixing—and thus hiding—his illegal activities with the business in his billiard room, building up a local distribution network, which covered at least the market in Neukölln, and developing a working relationship with the police in order to safeguard his business.[31]

Social Profiles

According to the image of the hustler popularized by the media, black marketeers were mostly young men, classical social climbers. Hustlers were young, independent, and without scruples. They lived in style, having become well-to-do by means of their illegal wheeling and dealing and by using their existing (business) contacts for "dirty" deals. Yet did this correspond to reality? Perhaps a more realistic picture of the social reality for black marketeers can be found by examining the members of Martha Rebbien's bartering network. How representative was the Gesundbrunnen black marketing network? Was it a special case in its social composition, or was it a representative cross section of Berlin black market society during the war? Valuable clues can be found by comparing the social profiles of Martha Rebbien and her partners with the analysis of the personal data of a sample of 500 people indicted for offenses against War Economy Regulations.

The data consist largely of information suspects themselves provided in their police interrogations. Analyzing the statistical data of the Berlin public prosecutor is quite easy. The police interrogation form asked for information both on the suspect's occupation and income. However, this information proved to be problematic in many regards. First of all, occupations were often expressed in ambiguous and vague ways.[32] For example, it is not always clear whether someone described as a baker owned his own business or was simply employed by someone else. Further, "worker" covers a broad range of activities requiring various training and correlating with quite different levels of income.

Nor is it always possible to reconstruct how reliable income statistics are. Some delinquents may have believed that stating a low income illustrated a certain poverty that they hoped would reduce their sentences. The incomes of the self-employed are even less clear. As a rule, police officers accepted the information provided by the person being interrogated without undertaking further investigations or asking them to provide supporting documents. Usually the estimates of those being interrogated were simply noted with the phrase "their own estimate" written on the side. In July 1943 these inadequacies induced the director of the trade inspection service to address the problem in an "Order of the Day," in which he criticized the fact that "many cases only indicate sales but not profits and then only for 1942." Further, there was no information at all concerning the extra profits. In order to provide Division IV, which was in charge of these investigations, "with a clear picture of the income and surplus profits obtained exceeding the price . . . especially the sales and the profits achieved during 1939–1942" were to be highlighted "and the increase or decrease in profits should be described in the form of percent," at least in those cases "where an especially harsh punishment [wa]s called for." Furthermore, the police were to note whether the income had been "determined" or if it was "only an estimate."[33]

There are also uncertainties concerning suspects' occupations at the time of their interrogations. Often people being interrogated listed vocational qualifications and occupations from the prewar period. It was by no means certain that they were still able to practice these occupations. As the war economy had brought about displacements and shifts in the structure of the occupations, it was possible that they had become soldiers and were receiving soldiers' pay or that they were working in another field in the meantime. In part, the analysis can compensate for this imprecise information considering the text part of the interrogation, where individuals sometimes gave more information concerning their careers. At any rate, we have to keep these limitations in mind when we look at the statistics.

Nonetheless, the data do provide evidence of the social nature of the participants in the black markets, as they do allow us to make plausible interpretations, even if we need to treat them with caution. The black market was largely a market of opportunities and was thus different from markets that had specific entry requirements. Martha Rebbien, for example, belonged at first to a minority in Berlin's black market society, simply because she was a woman. Around 70 percent of the accused were men. In her network as a whole, the ratio was about 50–50. Furthermore, Rebbien, who was in her mid-50s, was older than the average female black market trader. The average was around 40 (see Figure 2.4).

What especially stands out is the high percentage of 40–50-year-old female black market traders. For one thing, this reflects the high percentage of this age group in the population of Berlin as a whole. In the census of May 17, 1939, there were 418,000 women in this age cohort, making it the second largest, only exceeded by the group of 30–40-year-old women.[34] Another factor explaining the high number for Rebbien's age cohort is the occupational groups (see Figure 2.5).

What is striking here is that the vast majority of the indicted women were employed. Only 7 percent were unemployed, including Martha Rebbien, or were "housewives" subsumed under the category "none." The most important occupational groups were the self-employed and employees with low incomes, as in the larger society. The percentage of female employees in 1939 was especially high in the civil service and in providing services in the private sector.[35] But the high number of female black marketeers who had some form of employment

Age of female defendants (in years)	*In%*
<20	2
20–30	17
30–40	20
40–50	42
50–60	13
60+	4

Figure 2.4 Age of female defendants in cases of war economy crimes

Occupation group	*In%*
White-collar employees/civil servants	43
Self-employed	26
Workers	22
Non-identifiable	7
Small trade	2

Figure 2.5 Occupation groups of female defendants in cases of war economy crimes

Age of male defendants (in years)	*In%*
<20	1
20–30	15
30–40	25
40–50	28
50–60	20
60+	11

Figure 2.6 Age of male defendants in cases of war economy crimes

can be explained by two factors. First, of those who had jobs, many worked in restaurants and bars. Martha Rebbien, too, before she lost her job, had worked as a waitress, which meant she had dealt with and had access to foods that were in demand. Second, having an occupation gave these women opportunities to establish contacts in semi-public spaces such as shops, restaurants, bars, or even government offices. Women who worked had greater mobility and thus a broader set of acquaintances.

The picture of indicted men looks much different (see Figure 2.6). What is striking is the underrepresentation of 20–30 and 30–40-year-olds compared to the older generations.[36] There is an obvious explanation for this: members of the older generations (40–60) were often exempted from military service because they were already at a point in their career where they were considered "indispensable" whereas a large percentage of young men served in the army.

The distribution of occupations among male black marketeers has two standout groups: the self-employed and the lower-ranking civil servants and employees. If one looks more closely at the composition of the self-employed group, which included master craftsmen, then a connection quickly becomes clear. This group included a large number of grocers, bakers, tobacco merchants and tailors, owners of garages and repair shops, innkeepers, and restaurant owners. All of these people had access to goods in demand. The illegal trade in food, textiles, tobacco, and various services was above all a second-hand market: one had to have access to goods that were scarce to enter the market; that one could reach circles of customers easily through legal business contacts also made this easier. At the same time, people who worked in these fields were continually observed by the police. Among the routine tasks of the trade inspection service was to monitor

Occupation group	*In%*
Self-employed	20
White-collar employees/civil servants	20
Workers	18
Small trade	11
Merchants	11
Unemployed	5
Others/non-identifiable	13

Figure 2.7 Occupation groups of male defendants in cases of war economy crimes

businesses and restaurants. The probability that one would be discovered was correspondingly high, which also contributed to the percentage of the accused in these occupations being overly high (see Figure 2.7).

The group of the lower-ranking civil servants and employees was composed above all of employees in the hotel and restaurant business and food agencies. On top of this there were truck drivers, railway employees, as well as factory safety and postal service workers. What was true for the members of the first group was also true for this one. Employees in hotels, canteen kitchens, restaurants, and bars also had easy access to food. They had opportunities as well to make contacts in their workplace. It was easy for a waiter to recruit his customer base from among the restaurant patrons. Where other people would have to undertake complex and elaborate searches to find people, these black marketeers were able to dip into a large reservoir of potential bartering partners.

When comparing the groups of indicted men vs. women, an inequality becomes clear. Whereas the indicted men reflect a relatively representative cross section of the social classes, the women's group was dominated by members of the lower classes. There appears to have been an inhibition threshold that middle-class women had to overcome that made it more difficult for them to find access to the illegal markets. A large part of the market activity uncovered by the police took place in bars and restaurants, which, given contemporary moral attitudes, were hardly open to middle-class women.

Even if one was successful at entering the black market, participating in it was stressful. Alongside the pressure of illegality and the danger of being discovered, trading often had an impact on the social relationships of the partners.

Bartering Culture and the Transformation of Social Relationships

The illegal bartering transactions of the participants in the Berlin black markets were social and cultural facts. These facts had an impact upon society as a whole and on the web of social relationships, just as they also reflected the breakup of existing structures. An analysis that only considered the economic aspects of the illegal trading would fail to see one of the most striking characteristics of the "black market era": the markets became a catalyst of a comprehensive process of re-evaluation which brought forth a different urban social reality at the level of interpersonal relationships. Illegal trading, one of the most important institutions of everyday interaction for Berliners during and after the war, was built up around personal contacts and at the same time confirmed and intensified these contacts.[37] Black marketeers renegotiated friendships and love relationships and relationships to their neighbors, supervisors, and subordinates under the conditions of the Berlin bartering culture. Symmetrical and asymmetrical relationships between formerly acquainted participants were either revised or confirmed. New partnerships into which one had entered solely for the purpose of the bartering transaction could take on new directions. Thus, participants were able to transcend accepted borders between social milieus and social roles and effect new distributions of power that had not previously been customary.

In this way, Berlin's bartering culture turned one of the trends of modernity on its head. Modernity's trend toward "disembedding" interpersonal communication and replacing it with an impersonal system of social rules[38] was turned upside down by the complex trading practice of Berlin's black marketeers, which undermined money as a generalized, symbolic sign. Illegal trading also challenged the "reembedding services" that had cropped up in reaction to the processes of increasing anonymity. This was because the polite act of not paying attention and the specific beat of life in the big city, which had begun to characterize life in the modern metropolis, made it difficult to establish bartering partnerships. Those who participated in the black market were required to modify their patterns of communication, at least in part. This was easier for them to do when other social relationships could provide the foundation for future trading.[39]

The majority of bartering partnerships built on existing social relationships. The participants were already acquainted with each other as neighbors, friends, or colleagues before they became "intimate antagonists" in the illegal markets.[40] It made sense to fall back on existing contacts, especially if these had proven reliable in the past, as this precluded the need to spend a great deal of time searching for contacts. Black marketeering was based on existing links yet also changed the character of these contracts.

There was a basic change to all types of social relationships under the conditions of the barter culture. As participating in black market trading was equivalent to taking a step into illegality, it meant that any relationship of trust that had already been created between bartering partners was once again tested and—if found trustworthy—deepened. Especially when bartering partners traded with each other for a longer period, they shared the experience of taking part in something that was not allowed and was even prosecuted. The conspiracy in turn had two effects: an increased dependency on one's partner, for the partner could betray one at any moment, and, as a result of this, a strengthening of the relationship's cohesion, as the social relationships between the participants became more intense. All bartering relationships were subject to this process, independent of the distribution of power. On the macrolevel of Berlin war society, this development promoted the formation of an everyday life that carefully compartmentalized its components. This everyday life was characterized by a "shadow world" formed alongside legal procedures and spaces and occupied by an increasing number of citizens. Moreover, this shadow world demanded that participants—at least for a while—lived some distance from the "normal," everyday life, which was closely monitored by the authorities and by large sections of the Volksgemeinschaft. Thus, in a sense the black market represented a process of privatization. The black market had removed itself from the urban public space controlled by the National Socialists and created a sort of counter public space that was largely apolitical. National Socialist black market policy, which aimed to reduce the amount of black marketeering to a minimum, merely moved the activity "into the underground." That this "underground" existed was the result of the regulations prohibiting it. It was the activities of the black marketeers and the changing conditions filling this space with life that ensured its establishment as an independent and persistent social reality in the everyday life of Berliners. The far-reaching consequences can be shown in detail in four examples.

1. The "normal" type of social relationships between people who exchange goods or services with one another is that between buyers and seller. Black market traders often fit this pattern by extending previous legal relationships under quite different conditions: the baker who "sold" bread that was not part of the official allotment alongside the goods he had been officially allotted and who in return allowed himself to be "provided" with other goods, or the seamstress who traded custom tailoring for meat. There was a typical script for interaction underlying these relationships between customers and sellers. Researchers into socialization and the psychology of relationships make a distinction between "role relationships" and "personal relationships."[41] Between the seller and the customer, there were "stable patterns of interaction," mutual expectations in regard to one's roles: " 'Role' describes here the expectations, culturally determined, in regard to interactional behavior."[42] Both sides are acquainted with one's own and others' expectations and practices concerning the interaction. Furthermore, they were in possession of a script for the situation in which they found themselves.[43]

At the same time, there was never a pure, clear (theoretical) distinction between role relationships and personal relationships even in the trading in legal markets. Buyers and sellers did not just rely on abstract, given understandings of roles. Indeed, this was all the more true the longer there was a relationship between a customer and a merchant on the corner, for example. Instead, a common history formed the context of the relationships: merchants and customers were, as participants in the events in a particular quarter "in the picture," aware not only of what was going on, but also of each other (their preferences or customs). All the same, the relationships that were defined by the roles that they had to take differed from other social relationships such as love relationships, in which the pattern of interaction depended primarily upon the personalities of those involved: the personalities of the other person are of less significance in role relationships. In principle both the role of the customer as well as that of the vendor could have been acted out just as well by another person without changing anything important about the pattern of interaction, a situation that pertained all the more the more impersonal the relationship was.[44]

Shopping is certainly one of the most important everyday situations in a consumer society. However, especially in grocery stores, there was a decisive difference in the buyer-seller relationship between the legal and the illegal sectors. In the legal sector, shopping followed well-established rules and rituals. One could expect a certain assortment of goods to be available; these goods could be examined on the spot and acquired for a set price. In the black market these rules did not apply. A set of goods was the exception.[45] Even when trading with those who specialized in a certain assortment of goods—for example, with bakers, tailors, or tobacco merchants—one had to take advantage of opportunities. Not all goods were available at all times, nor could one make demands in regard to certain brands or other special wishes. In place of the superficial inspection or examination of goods that was possible in modern retail trading, where the quality of standardized goods was certified by the state, it was now necessary for customers to monitor the quality and quantity of the goods being sold themselves, even of the most fundamental product characteristics. Finally, the price often had to be negotiated.

To be sure, many customers did not make use (at least at first) of the possibility of haggling and paid the price the vendors demanded. For one thing, this was a sign of the huge demand and of the increased power of the vendors. For another, dispensing with haggling over prices corresponded to the old pattern of interaction between the buyer and seller.

However, one could observe learning processes on both sides: vendors who found that the prices they asked for were paid without any haggling attempted in the next transaction to raise their prices—often with the terse observation that "prices have gone up."[46] They could count on newcomers not being informed about prices, and therefore as a rule they had an information advantage vis-à-vis occasional, private traders. Customers for their part learned (partly as a result of the behavior of the vendors) that prices in illegal trading, unlike prices in stores, were flexible and could be negotiated. The free play in the setting of prices confronted the customer with new challenges. Merchants who were well trained in their regular occupations in methods of appraising value, and in calculating and negotiating prices, had decisive advantages. In contrast, participants who were not professionally trained had to learn these things if they wanted to compensate for this disadvantage—provided that they were willing and able to engage intensely with the framework of the illegal trading. Occasional, private traders who were able to afford it tended to pay more than they had to in order to have as little "contact" with "shady business." The negotiating position of those who were living in hiding was especially limited because they were politically persecuted and therefore had no legal rations.[47]

In this way power relationships in the illegal markets shifted. Previous customer protections from abuse did not exist in the black market. Accordingly, those offering goods had an advantage. The difficulties in obtaining goods in short supply during the war and the postwar period privileged those who worked in occupations that gave them access to such goods (e.g., retailers, manufacturers, and the food or textile trade) and who were thus able to enjoy the advantages of a supply oligopoly.[48] The numerous shortages, organized by rationing, opened up for retail business owners a number of potential consumer channels, so that the purchaser was limited in his ability to determine how the transaction would be concluded. Dissatisfied customers had almost no possibility of redress, except, of course, to break off the bartering relationship, engage in negative advertising, or—and this was very risky—inform on the other.

If customers wished to avoid being swindled, they had to immediately recognize counterfeits or imitations or even the diluting of goods (thinning down, mixing in inferior product components, etc.) and mention these observations to negotiate a lower price. In black market transactions, the consumer bore the full risk of testing the quality and the full cost of conducting such controls. The consumer in the illegal Berlin markets did not have any enforceable rights like those guaranteed by the state in legal markets.

This asymmetry in the buyer-seller relationship in the black market was only partially compensated for by the social integration of the business. From the perspective of the customer, there were numerous advantages in bartering relationships with brokers with whom one was personally acquainted as a business partner. Retail business owners, in particular, who knew the value of regular customers, proved to be more reliable bartering partners.

2. During the 1920s the "new woman" appeared as the protagonist of a modern feminine way of living and working. This development was accompanied by a motif that thematized the logic of give-and-take as an expression of gender-specific power positions. Engaging in sexual bartering transactions with male supervisors in order to advance socially was both part of the everyday realm of experience of a growing number of female employees as well as a hot topic being debated during that era. In Erich Kästner's novel *Fabian. Die Geschichte eines Moralisten*, a contemporary commented on one actress's doubts about these practices: "Does that surprise you? Isn't that why you came to Berlin? Here goods are swapped and exchanged. Whoever wants something has to give whatever he or she has."[49] The black market merely rendered such amalgamations of sexual and socioeconomic trades more visible. One does not, however, have to assume that the existence of such a market necessarily had a negative impact on intimate relationships.[50] In the public discussions concerning the illegal markets, the association of (material) trades and sexual favors played an important role. The behavior of German women who traded with "foreigners," especially—that is, during the war with foreign laborers or forced laborers and after the war with Allied soldiers or displaced persons—provoked the displeasure of many observers. In the eyes of many, women who engaged in such trading were committing treason. The myth of the rapid capitulation of German women in May 1945 describes nothing other than the alleged "major sin" of the women and girls who "sold" themselves to the victors for—according to the obsessive, primarily masculine view—a couple of cigarettes or pairs of nylons.[51] Marlene Dietrich's "Black Market Song" from Billy Wilder's film *A Foreign Affair*, which takes place in Berlin, treats bartering as something prostitutes engaged in. The female lead, played by Dietrich, offers "kisses for chewing gum," hinting at the relationship

between illegal trading and prostitution. The topic of trading for sex was ever present.

However, apart from the question of the role that bartering and (occasional) prostitution played in the precarious definition of a moral economy in the postwar period, it is clear that already during the war the illegal trading of goods and sex of the Berlin black marketeers, both male and female, were closely intertwined. And this is true as well for other types of personal social relationships in the black market—economic practices and multiplex relationships had a reciprocal influence on each other.

Love partners engaged in a constant give-and-take in any case: signs of affection sometimes took the form of objects, of presents. These signs not only sustained the friendship but also served as evidence of one's feelings. As a rule, they formed an important part of that complex social reality that can be characterized as love—long before marriage as a special contractual relationship came into play. Inasmuch as a love affair aimed to become a (long-term) partnership, factors that have little to do with romantic love influenced the choice of a partner, such as similar backgrounds, status, and income.[52] Presents, and other exchange processes that dispensed with the veil of one-sidedness caused by the time delay of gift-giving, thus played a central role in the game of love. They not only served as evidence of one's feeling but also informed the partner being wooed about one's social and economic power.[53] Under the conditions of the limited supply of goods, partners of both sexes who were able to "supply" products in demand could increase their market value. To be sure, there were many factors to choosing a partner, and the partner's ability to ensure a certain standard of living was only one of them. However, in the context of an unclear family situation, insecurity in regard to food and supplies, and insecurity in regard to one's own future, this factor could indeed prove decisive. Of course, the overall context during the war changed considerably. Because so many men had been drafted, there was a large surplus of women in Berlin. Thus, the contemporary shortage phenomenon existed in the marriage market as well or, more generally, in the partnership market. Meat, fats, and textiles were in short supply; so, too, were men. This was a source of worry not only to women but also to the state agencies responsible for National Socialist family policy. The absence of men made it more difficult for women to find a partner and led inevitably to a declining birth rate.[54] This, however, ran counter to the plans of National Socialist leaders, who had made having a lot of children the foundation of their expansive and racist reshaping of Germany and of all of Europe. Official efforts to promote racially desirable heterosexual relationships and thus to work against "sexual segregation" during the war found expression in state sponsorship of letter exchanges and of events where people could get acquainted.[55] These efforts, however, were largely unsuccessful. By far the vast majority of contacts initiated for the purpose of finding a sex partner did not take place under the auspices of the state.[56]

This finding is substantiated by analysis of the black market as a contact exchange. If one understands Nazi family policy as an intervention in the market and as efforts to create an official market for founding partnerships, then the black market can be understood as an "alternative" infrastructure—a much more successful alternative. Considerable parts of Berlin's black market functioned as a partnership market. In approximately 20 percent of all the black market trading cases I examined, I found evidence that sexual and bartering relationships were closely interwoven with each other. The barter of goods as well as various forms of providing love and care for others were closely related to one another.[57] This overlapping took place at two levels. On one level, black market trading as a gregarious social practice provided the ideal environment for people to become acquainted with potential lovers. Whether one was alone, married, or widowed, the black market, a market with a great deal of personal closeness, brought men and women together under the mantle, sometimes as well as under the pretext, of trading goods, functioning as an important site of everyday (sexual) interaction.[58] In this, it was unimportant whether partners were already acquainted with one another. In every case the trading sequence followed a logic of social exchange that corresponded closely to how lovers became acquainted with one another: from addressing a person to testing a person to completing a transaction. The example of Wiggers from the Rebbien network, who as a broker engaged in bartering transactions with a whole series of women whom he regularly met in cafés or in their apartments, makes it clear—independent of whether the designation "friendly relations" (*freundschaftlicher Verkehr*) used in the language of the bureaucracy implied sexual relationships—that black market trading increased opportunities to meet people.[59]

Furthermore, the two markets were quite close to one another or even shared the same space. Restaurants and bars, among the most important sites for clandestine industries, also served as contact sites for black marketeering groups. Often people exchanged both goods and intimacy. Just as the two markets cannot be kept distinct from one another in terms of space, so, too, the dividing line between material and social or physical bartering equivalents often remained vague. Where, for example, was the dividing line between giving a gift as a friendly gesture or as part of a seduction, and where did "paying for" a partner begin or end?

In extreme cases, black market goods could be seen either as a payment by a client to a prostitute or as a present, as is shown by the example of a fish merchant who stated in his interrogation:

> in the Central Market Hall I heard that in a house on Alexanderstrasse 42, at the apartment of a certain Miss Bienert, there was a sleazy hotel with pretty women. I, too, went there a number of times in order to have sex with a woman called Pia. After the first meeting . . . she received 10 marks from me. In about five other cases I gave Pia some fish as a gift . . . . It could have been overall 6 kilograms of fish, which Bienert and Pia shared.[60]

Obviously it was easier for the person visiting the brothel to declare that the exchange of goods for sex was a present, whereas paying for sex with money was socially unacceptable. With this, the bartering culture blurred unequivocal classifications. To describe the black market as a market of love relationships amounts to differentiating among a wide swath of different transactions as well as differentiating among the interpretations of these transactions and the relationships themselves.

Of course, the complexes of "providing for" and "partnership" have always traditionally been quite close. An example that makes clear the changes accompanying the shifts caused by the war, the allocations, and the shortages is the case of Elisabeth Hanke and Edgar von Vahl. The two became acquainted in January 1940 in a restaurant. Hanke came there after work to spend a couple of hours with her colleagues. Von Vahl was a regular patron.[61] Leaving aside the emotional aspects, which can only be hinted at and which therefore will not be taken into consideration, the bartering transactions between Hanke and von Vahl are a classic case of trading in scarce goods. Hanke had access as an employee in the Rationing Card Office 12 in Charlottenburg to food ration cards. As she told the police—with a certain amount of pride—she herself played a role in deciding whether or not those who for whatever reasons had not picked up their ration cards in the allotted time would still receive their contingent of ration cards:

> Whether or not things were in order was more or less a question of instinct and tact. If I wanted to reject a request by a Volksgenossen to hand over the cards, then I had to go to the supervisor and he would decide. I could, however, approve the request on my own.[62]

On numerous occasions she embezzled cards that had not been picked up and thus became an interesting acquaintance for all black marketeers:

> One evening in November I sat down after work in the Löwenbräu in the Tauentzienstrasse. A man sat down next to me . . . . We started to talk, and he asked me where I worked. I told him that I worked in a Rationing Card Office. In the course of further conversation the man informed me that he had some coffee that he had received from France that he wanted to get rid of, and that he would be able to supply me with fabric. I badly needed cloth for a coat. He made it very clear that we could do business with each other.[63]

However, in the case of her bartering relationship with von Vahl, the situation was obviously much more complicated. If previously she had merely bartered with the men in the "Löwenbräu," when she became acquainted with von Vahl emotions played a role. For Elisabeth Hanke, von Vahl represented a scarce good: men. In her interrogation she stated that her first marriage had ended in divorce in 1931 and that she had been identified as the party at fault. Since 1933 she had lived with her mother and her sister in their apartment in Zehlendorf.[64] Under these circumstances, there were obviously good reasons she wanted to catch von Vahl. He had attended the Cadet School, had worked as a farmer and as a bank accountant, was divorced, and had worked since 1939 as a civil servant in the German Aviation Ministry. According to his own statement, he earned 500

RM per month.[65] Thus, he fulfilled two important measurable criteria, alongside those that cannot be analyzed such as his emotional qualities or his appearance: he had a certain status, and he was present.[66] And other women appeared to find him attractive. In her interrogation Hanke repeatedly stated that her bartering partner and lover was idolized by other women, which only increased his value in her eyes.[67] As, furthermore, he seemed to know this, the price increased. Not only did Hanke repeatedly pay for him, invite him to dinner, and pay for a trip that they took together by taking "rationed goods out of public distribution."[68] Sex was also among the goods Hanke was willing to trade. She stated in her interrogation that although she found it unpleasant, she allowed herself to be seduced by von Vahl to engage in "indecent" sexual practices. On top of this she was willing to make false statements both to him as well as, later, to the police. She suggested to him that she was reasonably well-off (in spite of his income von Vahl clearly still had debts to pay); vis-à-vis the police she covered him in regard to his participation in the illegal transactions as long as she could and was only convinced to make a much more complete statement about her black market transactions after a conversation with her lawyer. She later admitted, after von Vahl had been taken from the interrogation room, that she had lied to him about what she possessed because she could imagine, "that (he) would rather have a woman with him who had money than a woman without money."[69]

Von Vahl's services were non-binding. The time they spent together and the alleged prospect of a common future and of getting married were the goods that he could trade:

> During the trip von Vahl had held out to me the prospect of marrying me, or of moving in with me into a four-room apartment. I was to take care of the house, but I was also supposed to continue working. To be honest, I didn't take the offer seriously.[70]

However, although she supposedly did not take the offer seriously, Hanke appeared to continue at the very least to have hopes in regard to a common future. Her attempts, however, to tie von Vahl down were unsuccessful. He claimed that when he had looked at an apartment with her this had been non-binding. According to Hanke, he told her they were "in the same boat" after he found out that the police were investigating them, in order to make her understand that he was standing by her. Only when Hanke observed in the police interrogation that her bartering partner and lover did not appear to be holding up his part of the bargain did she change her tactics and incriminate him by revealing his part in the illegal bartering transactions.

Not always did the pressure applied by the investigating authorities lead bartering pairs to mutually accuse each other, causing the partnership to end. In some cases, the relationship became especially intense because of the police investigations. The sexual desire, the consumption wishes of the participants, and the conspiratorial community of the bartering partners created a peculiar mixture. The role constellation of a pair of lovers running away from the authorities rehashed in numerous works of fiction took on concrete form in such cases. Like Bonnie and Clyde, many lovers experienced their relationships as a special oneness. The secrecy, one of the basic preconditions of illegal trading, stimulated the erotic relationship. As "partners in crime" the black marketeers experienced an extraordinarily close oneness. This intensified the drawing of boundaries vis-à-vis the environment (in this case perceived to be dangerous) that helped to constitute the pair. As they further developed their conspiratorial methods, forged common escape plans, and went into hiding together, this strengthened that feeling of singularity characteristic of love relationships: "we, and we alone, belong together."[71]

An especially striking case of such "partners in crime" was the relationship between Erich Bruselat and Margot Engel.[72] It was a bartering relationship and a love affair, and they shared the excitement of being on the run. Although (or perhaps because) Bruselat had suspicions in regard to Engel when she had become acquainted with him and had hired a private detective to conduct inquiries into his—as it turned out—quite glamorous way of life, she entered into a relationship with him.[73] In her police interrogation she later stated that because of the "sexual contact," she had "become a slave" to Bruselat, the former managing director of the nightclub "Lichtburg."[74] Whether that was true or whether that was merely an effort to protect herself can no longer be ascertained. It is certain, however, that Margot Engel used Bruselat's black marketeering competence. To be sure, she stated in her interrogation on November 4, 1944, "I reject the claim that because of my relationship to B., I or my relatives enjoyed any economic advantages."[75] However, Bruselat was able to demonstrate that his "expensive lifestyle" was ultimately connected with the exquisite presents he had purchased for his lover in the black market.[76]

When the busy black marketeer, who, among other things, had repeatedly transported goods from East Prussia to Berlin via airplane, had to go into hiding, the story of a pair on the run began.[77] Engel shielded her lover, deceived the police officer conducting the investigation, and met secretly with Bruselat and with someone who claimed he could forge passports in order to give him the photos necessary for the forgeries. Switzerland was their common destination.[78] Although the course of events in this case was quite dramatic, it should not deceive one about the fact that the described effect of a "partners in crime" situation played a role in less spectacular relationship dramas, too.

3. Bartering touched on at least two taboos. According to prevailing beliefs, love was something that, at least in its true, romantic form, was not to be based on material performance, as long as social conventions (partnership and marriage) were upheld. There was a complex set of rules that distinguished between acceptable and unacceptable forms of behavior. This points to the great importance of these conventions, at least in bourgeois circles. The second taboo was that for business within the family, the rules of the free market were not supposed to apply. "A household," in the words of Max Weber, was "economic and personal . . . : solidarity toward the outside and communistic use and consumption of everyday items . . . on the inside on the basis of unity and strict filial

piety."[79] To be sure, this initially applied, Weber continued, only to "pure" and "primitive" forms; however, "the household communist principle that 'one does not calculate' " continued to exist "as the essential characteristic of the 'family' household."[80] And in the context of "helping one's neighbors," along the lines of "doing each other favors," Weber recalled the still valid principle that "brothers do not haggle over prices."[81]

Therefore, bartering did not merely supplement the relationships between family members by adding another variation of social interaction. Rather, it fundamentally called into question the concept of "family." Was a family not characterized by the fact that one could not raise the topic of economic services, or if one did, then only in conventional forms such as parental care? Could one exchange goods with family members, could one barter with a brother, a sister, or an uncle, that is, calculate prices or even insist on one's advantage? "Hustlers" as popularized in the media were individuals who pursued their shady business alone. One could not even think of them as family persons. From the perspective of the "normal" and "decent" Berliner, hustlers were "asocial." In contrast to this ideal fiction, black marketeers were often not only family oriented, but they also used their families to assist them in their illegal business and even bartered and traded with them. The popular talk about "hustlers" thus did not do justice to the family context of many black market trading networks. The verdicts of the courts, published in the state-controlled press, against those who had committed offenses against War Economy Regulations and the descriptions of black market business transactions they contained, denounced especially the "transgressions" of black marketeers who had worked with their family and made references in such cases to the apparent "asocial" character of the families. This use of language accorded with National Socialist discourse policy, which bet on the use of stereotypes of perpetrators that aimed to stigmatize those alleged to be foreign to the community to increase the cohesion of the Volksgemeinschaft.[82]

This did not stop a whole series of participants from choosing their bartering partners from among their family members. In part, these family members were merely intermediaries. For this purpose black marketeers remembered that they had an extended family, even distant relatives, that perhaps they had not seen or thought of for years. The chance to obtain goods in demand or to carry out lucrative business transactions could reawaken family ties that had been dormant for a long time.[83] All the same, the convention remained that wherever family members bartered with each other, these business transactions were generally not perceived as bartering or at the very least were not labeled as such. "It's true that I once received 100 cigarettes from my sister," said the 40-year-old Martha Tomczak in her interrogation at the police station in Schöneberg. However, she did not pay for these cigarettes; rather, she "did a favor" for her sister "in a different way."[84] Her sister confirmed this later when she was interrogated. She said that she had "not received and also not demanded" any payment for the cigarettes.[85] That which black marketeers quite openly labeled a bartering transaction when the business was conducted with strangers was, as a rule, considered a "favor" when family members were involved. Among sisters, in a variation of the rule cited by Weber, one did not barter and one demanded nothing in return.

However, this was not true for all market participants. Diverse black marketeers moved beyond such conventions. For example, the engine mechanic Arthur Wissel, who was employed by the Awia aircraft factory in Prague, described his transactions in the following manner:

> In September 1944, as I was visiting Berlin, I brought back with me from Prague some bottles of alcohol. . . . In the beginning of October 1944 all of a sudden [a supplier] brought me 45 bottles of alcohol of various brands. I paid him 110 marks per bottle. In December 1944 I brought these 45 bottles . . . to Berlin to my wife. . . . My wife paid me 130 to 140 marks per bottle.

Even if Wissel did not speak of "bartering" or of "selling," it was clear that he expected a higher price from his wife than he had paid when he bought the bottles. Business transactions involving married people were a conflict-laden practice, testing the strength of the relationships. The same was true of relationships in which only one of the two partners engaged in bartering, while the other rejected this "hustling." The illegal business separated the partners and produced massive tension. Such conflicts escalated regularly when the police made the consequences clear to those involved.[86]

4. Among the most regular, everyday contacts were those between colleagues at work. Therefore, it is not surprising that bartering in the workplace was widespread in Berlin. One was acquainted with one's colleagues; one had friends among one's colleagues and thus the necessary steps had already been taken toward creating a level of trust. A remarkable transformation of social relationships in the workplace took place because of the bartering culture—less among colleagues of equal rank and more in the relationships between subordinates and supervisors. The asymmetrical distribution of power in these well-defined roles could be profoundly changed by the bartering practices, even to the degree that in some cases the roles were reversed and supervisors became powerless and dependent on others at work.

The metalworker Emil Gierschner, for example, undertook on behalf of his supervisor a business trip to Ostrowo to trade old clothes for food for himself and his colleagues.

> In Berlin I packed an old suit of mine and four other suits from colleagues at work or from acquaintances (!), two pairs of boots and men's underwear. . . . I talked earlier about colleagues at work; I am now willing to name names: 1) my factory manager Schumann—who gave me one pair of boots to take along. . . . The goods which were received in exchange for clothing were supposed to be distributed among those named above.[87]

Furthermore, his supervisor Schumann provided the necessary travel permit and gave his employee vacation so that he could carry out these transactions. Participating in such transactions meant that a much more complicated relationship replaced the clear distribution of power between subordinates and supervisors that increased the status of the weaker party. Such displacements had long-term consequences on the structures of authority. In extreme cases it could lead to the complete dissolution of existing structures of power and order, as in the case of the warehouse management at the "Generalbauinspekteur der Reichsstadt Berlin." As became clear in the rather comprehensive investigations—there was even talk of the intervention of the "Reichsführer-SS"—the complete management of the warehouse had participated in and approved of embezzlement and "hustling." As a consequence, the structures of authority almost completely dissolved. Subordinates told their supervisors "to their face" that they were "hustlers" and were able to get away with it because the supervisors feared being reported to the police.[88]

Such developments affected not only interpersonal relationships but also large social networks and urban spaces. The changes in everyday life in Berlin during the war were accompanied by innovations or improvements or striking continuities in the use and perception of urban spaces. The black market trading functioned as a lens shaping contemporaries' perceptions of their city. Both the participants in the black market and criminal prosecutors, as well as mere observers, were participants in that process of city making, in which the city of hustlers practically and rhetorically came to life.

Bartering Spaces and Movement Patterns

Over the course of 1944, already before illegal trading moved into the streets and squares of Berlin, black marketeers began to use some public places for trading. They integrated well-known meeting places, in particular, into their bartering practices. For example, Elisabeth Hanke and her bartering partner Strassburger from the Gesundbrunnen network used a flower stand at Wittenbergplatz as a place to meet as well as a place to trade.[89] One no longer had to make an appointment in order to barter. The elevator operator Otto Stock stated on February 13, 1943, in his police interrogation that he had known that "on Linienstrasse, on Rosentaler Platz, there was a lively black market." So he went there shortly before Christmas "to see" for himself "what was going on" in the Spandau district. And as a matter of fact, "there was a dense gathering of people at the corner of Linienstrasse and Kleine Rosentaler Strasse."[90] As the statement of another witness made clear, it was still a good idea, even in September 1944, not to undertake such bartering transactions outside during the day. In this case, the transfer of 1,200 cigarettes took place on the Hohenstauffenplatz. The witness received the goods, "in the public square," but only "in the evening."[91]

Another public site for bartering was the weekly markets, for example, on Winsstrasse in Prenzlauer Berg. Here, in the hustle and bustle of the marketplace, one could exchange goods without standing out. People who barely knew each other, such as Frau Kehler and Frau Menge, who before had only greeted each other but had not had been "friendly" with one another, met here in January

1945 and started up a conversation, and finally one of them offered the other some meat as part of a trade.[92]

As is made clear by the history of the origins of Martha Rebbien's trading network, the transactions during the war occurred "in public" to varying degrees.[93] Trading outside was the exception; enclosed spaces were preferred. In part, these spaces were commercially defined. Illegal trading took place in sites generally reserved for legal business such as bars or restaurants. Because these sites were coded as sites of urban socializing, it was easier to use them for illegal trading. Encounters and consumption were their very basic functions and were still possible here, as they had been before. Of course, new practices changed well-established concepts of space. Trading changed the character of existing urban spaces, and even those who did not participate in black market trading faced the consequences of illegal trading.[94] Furthermore, in the black market, the relationship between what was near and distant changed, and existing concepts of privacy and publicness were called into question. It was necessary to go to quarters of the city or to places that were further away, and these trips built only in part on existing patterns. Why did female Berlin black marketeers prefer certain spaces? What impact did illegal trading have on the urban, regional, and transnational patterns of movement of those who participated in the markets? Which routes for trade and flows of goods linked individual market areas to one another? How did such shifts and displacements in how space was used modify the perception of certain sites? And, finally, what did the mobility requirement for participating in the market mean for different groups of people being to participate successfully in the trading and to be able to profit from their allocated rations?

As we have observed that a large part of black market trading took place in rather limited spaces, we now turn our attention to the structures of the city districts and to individual bartering sites such as apartments and restaurants. Of course, beyond this, patterns of movement extended over the complete urban space, the surrounding countryside, and all of Europe. The shifts in the use of everyday space were above all products of the techniques developed to ensure secrecy. Trading was likewise one of the sites where a confrontation between black marketeers and prosecuting authorities concerning the use of urban spaces at different levels of the public sphere took place.

The Structures of the Districts and the Sites of Encounters

Martha Rebbien's bartering network offers some clues regarding the spatial organization of the black market during the war. What is most striking is the space in which it was conducted, the local district or Kiez. Rebbien hardly ever left her Kiez to conduct her business—not to procure goods to replenish her supply, to arrange to meet customers, nor to hand off the goods.

The central area consisted of a couple of streets around the Gesundbrunnen train station. The bartering activity thus occurred right next to one of the most important "bottlenecks" of the Berlin public transportation system. As Erich Giese's study on the "future suburban train network for Greater Berlin" from

1919 has already shown, the train station that lay to the north of the city had the greatest amount of traffic among the train stations on the line that circled Berlin. Already in 1912/13 over 9.5 million people passed through this train station. Almost half of them were either coming or going from the northern suburbs. Even in 1936 the number of tickets sold in Gesundbrunnen was significantly higher than in one of the best known and centrally located train stations in Berlin, Alexanderplatz.[95] This volume derived from the station's use largely by the working class; large segments of Berlin industrial factory workers came through it on their way to work.[96] The trading between Martha Rebbien and her bartering partners took place mostly within one square kilometer of this transportation hub. The apartments, bars, and cafés on Badstrasse, Bellermannstrasse, Swinemünderstrasse, and Brunnenstrasse as well as those on Prinzenallee were part of this central area. The trading of the network participants thus took place within the spheres of everyday life; everything was within walking distance. Repeatedly, Rebbien described her walks through the streets of the district to the police.[97]

There were a number of reasons to trade in the Kiez. For one, it was necessary for people to live near each other for them to develop trading relationships and to exchange information over goods, prices, possible offers, and interested parties. Most black marketeers did not have a telephone. Only Erna Kuschy had one. Anna Auricht at least could be reached at her landlord's.[98] Sending things via mail was difficult, took time, and increased costs. A large percentage of traders, therefore, had to be able to visit their bartering partners to deliver or pick up goods.[99] On top of this, to take advantage of the trust-building "pre-existing non-commercial ties between buyers and sellers" with neighbors or with other district acquaintances required physical proximity.[100] It was thus logical for traders to build up a trading space that they could manage and keep an eye on. Ultimately, the Gesundbrunnen Kiez, teeming with bars and cafés, supplied a good infrastructure; some participants were already well integrated into the Kiez because they worked there as waitstaff. Consequently, trading in Rebbien's network fit very well into the already existing everyday relationships among people and spaces. This was one of the conditions for the black market's relatively long record of success here. This local neighborhood formed the basis of the illegal everyday trading in the Berlin black market. In almost every one of the cases investigated here, one's district in Berlin was also where one did business.[101] This is not really all that surprising. For already in the nineteenth century, relationships among neighbors had often developed into patronage networks; "the owner of a shop in the quarter who gave [his customers] credit . . . was integrated into such a neighborhood system."[102] "Occasions for informal mutual assistance among equals," too, functioned as a catalyst, which helped define the neighborhood as a space encompassing "sociability."[103] In this space the black marketeers could conduct their business in relative security.

By moving frequently from one apartment to another and by visiting the same restaurants, bars, and train stations, traders wove their illegal activity into their everyday routines; the different sites of the district were joined together into a network of black market trading centers. Indeed, only by means of such repetition could individual districts become black market trading centers. The area in and around the Gesundbrunnen train station was one such center because black marketeers like Martha Rebbien conducted their business there; the black marketeers helped the restaurants and bars become central meeting points for illegal trading. This points to a spatial concept that extended beyond one's own neighborhood. Rebbien's Kiez had become attractive to commuters who had previously used the transportation hub to get to the inner city and now, with the black marketeering, could use it for its new, alternative infrastructure. Trading in the Kiez expanded the market's catchment area, opening up opportunities for local merchants to improve their sales. Even black marketeers who up until now had not been to the quarter could go to northern Berlin in search of bartering partners, as one witness said in her interrogation, "to buy cigarettes in restaurants or bars around the Stettin train station or the Gesundbrunnen train station."[104] The location of this trading space had advantages for both sides. The local Kiez market was able to expand and thus profit from the central location. This enabled commuters to appear quickly and without any problems on the spot or to conduct their business while on their way to work or on their way home from work.

The illegal trading expanded the district not only by adding a new infrastructure; it also changed the character of individual meeting spaces in the district, including, of course, the participants' apartments. As "central sites of private life," apartments were profoundly important to urban life.[105] Activities that took place in apartments were largely private. To a certain degree, other people and the law did not have a right to enter this space. Of course, privacy was limited, de facto, by legal regulations, norms, and also the social control of the neighbors. On the other hand, privacy was the ideal of the bourgeois family.

One was safe in one's living space, and such a space was to be protected from too much outside interest.[106] Bourgeois ideals of privacy had slowly influenced how bourgeois families lived as well as how their apartments were designed. The interior was considered women's space; the organization of the space within the living quarters reflected gender differences in that, for example, the kitchen was separated from the "living room."[107] This trend was part of bourgeois culture, but its impact extended to the working class, where a trend toward the "privatization of family life" could likewise be observed.[108] The apartment as the "box of the private man" corresponded to a "need for closure" that transcended class.[109] Having an apartment meant "upholding the feeling of being protected, both symbolically and in reality";[110] this need became especially apparent when one had lost it. The southern Westphalian Gauleiter Albert Hoffmann, who was considered an expert on the air war, was particularly sensitive to this. In meetings in August 1943, for psychological reasons, he argued against housing those who had lost their homes in temporary settlements as the director of the Deutsches Wohnungshilfswerks, Ley, had advocated. Hoffmann felt that it was better to find housing for them near where they had lived—even if this was only provisional, because it would perhaps avoid irritating those who had lost their dwelling.[111]

Losing one's apartment was a major event for many Berliners. The "loss of the familiar living space" often led to a "desperate search for a new interior space," to attempts to try to at least simulate "provisional, unconnected living quarters." The familiar interior of one's own apartment offered security and the possibility of "well-defined areas of different levels of privacy." The hallway, for example, could mark the area where one would decide who was a client or a guest. The loss of such stable sites for doing business was one of many "deep cuts into the customary everyday order." The absence of an apartment, "of space for intimacy, of space at all" would characterize "the lives of millions of people" from the moment of the loss "until well into the 1950s."[112]

If one takes the number of apartments built in Berlin as an indicator, apartments became even more important in the first half of the twentieth century. Between 1929 and 1932 and between 1937 and 1940, there were significant increases in the number of apartments; all in all, 272,361 new apartments were built between 1925 and 1944.[113] The number of apartments increased from 1,210,602 in 1927 to 1,551,356 in 1939. This number was highest at the beginning of 1943, when there were 1,562,641 apartments. The bombing lowered this figure; in 1943 alone, over 200,000 apartments and houses in Berlin became uninhabitable. At the end of 1944, there were only 1,222,085 units.[114] Most of the apartments hit by bombs—around half—were in the densely populated "central city" (Mitte, Tiergarten, Wedding, Prenzlauer Berg, Friedrichshain, Kreuzberg).[115] The newly built housing was evidence of a continuing housing shortage. At least in propaganda, National Socialist city planners emphasized that they wanted to preserve and renovate the working-class housing in Berlin. From 1934 on, especially, these efforts were intensified as it was useful, from the viewpoint of the new rulers, not only to use this policy "as a means to produce consensus" in those districts suspected of being "red" but also to use these labor-intensive but not capital-intensive measures to create jobs.[116] All the same, at no time did the government succeed in making enough apartments available. Apartments remained a scarce commodity. The housing shortage persisted throughout the war, exacerbated by the concentration of the government administration in the capital and the influx of arms industry workers.[117]

Of course, this does not change the fact that "one's own four walls" became a preferred site for Berlin black market trading during the war. Apartments remained a relatively private space and were thus difficult to control. In them, black marketeers were able to meet with their bartering partners undisturbed, to examine goods, to haggle over prices or other terms of exchange, and to conclude their transactions.

This did not have to have been the intention of those involved. Often, in conversations concerning the general supply situation, people revealed that they knew a supplier. Sometimes, one encountered this information accidentally, as, for example, in this statement about a female black market trader under interrogation: "One Sunday, Drosdowska, the woman who has been indicted, overheard in her bed how Anita Schwarz and Dubtschak were talking . . . business. Sometimes one came to know of crimes by chance—even though one had not wanted to. Drosdowska therefore also received a ration coupon from Schwarz."[118] One's living space, thus, likewise became a site of unintentional proximity that could endanger black market trading. Allowing those only coincidentally in the know to participate in the business was one way to buy their silence. However, apartments as a rule served as sites for initiating mutually desired bartering transactions.

National Socialist efforts to control the private sphere of the Volksgenossen made it more difficult for black market trading to develop undisturbed. A whole series of state measures and new forms of everyday interaction undermined the private character of encounters both in the neighborhood and in apartments. These state measures aimed to establish the "National Socialist claim to absolute power in living quarters."[119] The introduction of the Hitler salute subjected even the simplest interpersonal communication between neighbors to the everyday culture of surveillance that integrated the majority and exposed the minority.[120] Social control among neighbors increased continuously as reflected by punishments meted out for offenses against the "Regulations on Radio Use"; in addition, the naming of block wardens and fire protection officers further permeated the private sphere.[121] Informers divulged the crimes of family members and neighbors to the authorities.

As Robert Gellately has noted, "Germans . . . not only paid attention to criminals and deviants, to social outsiders and ethnic minorities; they also mutually stalked each other."[122] This integration of the Berlin population into the structure and functioning of the National Socialist regime took place partly by means of people's willingness to adapt to a system of mutual surveillance that found expression even in harmless-seeming institutions such as emergency services or courses on how to run a household. Thus, urban living space was penetrated, or squeezed, simultaneously from "above" and "below." State surveillance and people's willingness to inform on one another are two ends of a broad scale of practices that could make one's living space dangerous for illegal trading.[123]

The large number of denunciations demonstrates the importance of black market trading in the relationships between neighbors, especially as the number of unknown cases remained high.[124] Attempts to bring the living quarters of the Volksgenossen under state control were never fully successful. Illegal trading, for which at least a minimum of privacy was needed, remained widespread. Thus, black market trading promoted movement away from public control in an era filled with community (such as the "housing community" and the "bunker community").[125] Those who bartered in their own homes insisted on their right to privacy and retained or indeed won back part of their sovereignty over their living space.

Yet this sovereignty was always threatened: Neighbors paid close attention to comings and goings, as an unusual number of strangers or people with unusual luggage suggested illegal business. Social control in the neighborhood was directed against any possible "hustling," as evidenced by the statement Rebbien's landlady, Hanna Zabel, made.[126] The "housing community" registered the goods "brought up" at birthdays in the neighborhood that suggested special "connections" with great suspicion. A police report from district 107 shortly before Christmas 1944 provides an example of such observation:

> [T]he local police were informed confidentially that . . . Paul-Heinz Brinkmann . . . has not had a job for months and that he is earning his living through black marketeering. As a rule, according to the informer, he brings his black market trading goods into his apartment during the night from Friday to Saturday. He then sells these same goods over the next few days to buyers who call upon him in his apartment.[127]

The use of apartments for bartering had a lasting effect on well-established living concepts. Rooms for relaxing, for familiarity, for privacy, became—at least temporarily—rooms for doing business. Some rooms were set up as business rooms and others as storage space. Sometimes there were hiding places set up to keep bartering transactions secret from other people living in the apartment. Anna Auricht, an employee of the German National Railway, stated in her interrogation that Martha Rebbien generally went "into another room" when Anna was present because she herself "did not want to have anything to do with the whole thing."[128] Black market traders who regularly used their apartments as sites for bartering had to adapt their private space to the requirements of the illegal business. For example, a customer remembered: "I can say nothing definite about the people who went in and out of G.'s apartment. When I visited him, he showed me a separate room and we conducted our business there. I seldom saw his visitors face to face."[129] Apartments served both as places where vendors handed over goods as well as for deliveries. Interested parties were asked to come to the vendor's apartment for either negotiations or merely the transfer of the goods.[130]

When Berlin black marketeers used their apartments to barter, they negated the distinction between public and private space, one of the most important in everyday urban life. The door to the apartment and the hallway as the threshold to one's everyday living space became more permeable. This endangered the security of this space and created tensions among family members or roommates, presupposing as it did a considerable willingness to take risks.[131] By no means were all roommates willing to take on this risk, nor were all traders able to use their own living spaces. For those afraid to expose their homes in this way, conducting business in a restaurant or a bar was an alternative. However, trading in these rooms was also risky because there were people one might run into and other potential witnesses among the public.

Why did so many Berlin black marketeers prefer to conduct their business in such semi-public spaces such as bars, cafés, or restaurants? There were many reasons. Because there was a limited public here, these sites provided a useful platform for many of the integral black market practices. First of all, these were normal spaces for people to meet; encounters between bartering partners thus looked in no way suspicious. Where else could one—disguised within institutionalized socializing—dare to begin a business transaction and dare to meet a new business partner? If the bartering partners came regularly, if they were among the regular customers, then they had the advantage that they were well acquainted with the local customs, with the employees, and with the guests.

For the civil servants of the Berlin trade inspection service, surveillance was a routine part of the job. At first, though, they did not have to combat black marketeering. Rather, their tasks were to monitor prices as well as enforce health and liquor regulations and such things. When they had to start fighting illegal trading, though, it made their lives considerably more difficult. Unlike monitoring prices or observing business transactions between customers and employees in a bar or a restaurant, this new sort of surveillance required different investigative techniques, such as planting police informers in suspicious circles and eavesdropping on conversations.[132] On December 30, 1944, for example, following a tip from a "confidential" source, two policemen went to a restaurant in Schöneberg and conducted an "inconspicuous surveillance" of the personnel. In their report afterward, they noted that one of the waiters in the restaurant not only "conversed quite actively" with a guest but also received "numerous cigarettes" from this guest. They searched and arrested him immediately.[133]

The police felt that such methods had become necessary because restaurants and bars offered a mixture of clandestine activity and openness, of privacy and public realm, which was favorable to illegal trading. For one thing, restaurants and bars, as public spaces, enabled traders to meet a potentially infinite number of bartering partners. For another, the size of the rooms and privacy they offered groups of various sizes secured traders a certain control over their networking or bartering partners. Entering a restaurant and engaging people in conversation was a harmless act, in no way suspicious in and of itself. Such encounters could, however, at any moment turn into trading situations without this being monitored.

But even the relatively manageable public nature of restaurants, bars, and cafés was not sufficient for some black market traders. Instead of transacting their business at a table or at the bar, they used such spaces only for negotiations and retired to other sites for handing over the goods. A police informer, for example, noted the following events:

> On 12 October 1944, around 20:00, I observed a person with a briefcase in the restaurant Schirmer in the Linienstr. . . . I could see that the man went to the bathroom with his briefcase and a number of other people and that this occurred a number of times. This is how, as is generally known, the bartering transactions were conducted.[134]

And a participant reported on the bartering trade by waiters and guests in the "Hotel Bristol," which was next to the Schöneberger City Hall, that on the day of his arrest he had handed his bartering partner "around 16,500 marks," which came from the sale of goods. This money transfer, he remembered, "took place at the door to the restaurant's toilets."[135] Less careful local traders did not have to retreat to the toilets but could offer their goods directly in the restaurant. Typically, they kept their goods in an inconspicuous bag or briefcase. For example, one witness remembered: "in the last four weeks before S.'s arrest, I saw him enter Frau Lipp's bar with a briefcase . . . he was always selling stockings. He always came at around 21:00." Every day he sold as many stockings as he could fit in his briefcase. [136] When asked about this in his interrogation, S. admitted that "it had gotten around" that he sold stockings. He merely disputed the alleged extent of his business.[137]

It was especially easy for waiters to deliver their goods. News of their prices and delivery methods spread quickly among their customers—especially among their regulars—so waiters merely had to wait until guests addressed them with the "right" question. They did not even have to know them. As the waiter of a restaurant in Schöneberg said in his interrogation, "I do not know the names of the guests in question, nor can I say where they live. The sale of these cigarettes took place like this: the people in question asked me for cigarettes and I laid a pack on the table, without naming a price." Such transactions took place without lengthy and protracted negotiations. As the customers paid a fixed amount without asking the price, this information was obviously generally known.[138]

In the districts where there were a lot of restaurants and bars, a bartering network often developed among them. Traders in these networks visited a number of bars and restaurants and traded goods they had acquired in one bar or restaurant in the next. One trader, for example, who was obviously quite successful trading in this fashion was incriminated when a bartering partner told an investigating officer about the trading network in the restaurants of Spandau. Her partner had used the "Münze" in the Münzstraße to procure his goods, as here he could "buy everything from the Dutch and the French" and then resell these goods in neighboring bars and restaurants.[139]

Such areas profited from a market-movement pattern used both by small brokers as well as occasional, private traders. Often, people conducted their black market business in the same way that city dwellers legally bought supplies. Inevitably this led them to centrally located bars, restaurants, and stores that had a reputation for black market trading. Sometimes they had already visited such sites for "legal" reasons, thus bringing new (illegal trading) and old (familiar environment) together. They found it easier to visit the site since they had already been there, and they could feel more secure if complications arose.

These market spaces for district-crossing traders were contiguous with the well-known centers of social activity, including the bars and the stores in Spandau around the Oranienburger Strasse, on Alexanderplatz, on Friedrichstrasse, around the Cottbus Gate, or the restaurants and cafés at Kurfürstendamm.[140] For occasional, private traders from other parts of the city, the distance from their own apartments made these areas attractive sites; it was less likely that these black market traders would run into their neighbors. Unpracticed occasional traders appreciated the anonymity. This was a clever strategy, considering the large number of investigations prompted by information supplied by neighbors. Yet these traders also had to accept that these locations were closely monitored by the trade inspection service.

This sort of information about trading opportunities reinforced such black market trading centers becoming more established in the city up to the point when the sites of illegal trading turned into a well-known urban infrastructure that coexisted and sometimes was enmeshed in its legal counterpart. One investigation indicates that traders did not need to know each other at all. One accused

City district	*In%*
Mitte	16.7
Charlottenburg	11.5
Prenzlauer Berg	9.8
Schoeneberg	7.5
Kreuzberg	7.5
Wilmersdorf	6.9
Wedding	6.9
Neukoelln	5.2
Lichterfelde	4.6
Other	23.4

Figure 2.8 Defendants' places of residence in cases of war economy crimes

trader told interrogators that he had decided to go to a particular place because he "had heard that foodstuffs were being sold in these places." The policemen found it implausible that he claimed not to be acquainted with his unnamed partner, but he insisted it was true: "I had no connection to these places, and I can only say that I went there purely by chance."[141] Black marketeering thus pulled in new interested parties, expanding the catchment area of a bar where black market trading took place and further concentrating trading in certain sites.

Centers of Black Market Trading

In order to draw a picture of the spatial distribution of the black market in Berlin during the war, it helps to take a look at where the accused lived (Figure 2.8).

Analysis of the residential areas of the arrested black marketeers shows that most trading during the war took place within local networks. This analysis also points to where the trading centers were and where illegal business was concentrated. Mitte was clearly the most important black marketeering area in Berlin, followed at some distance by Charlottenburg and Prenzlauer Berg. Schöneberg and Kreuzberg were in the middle of the pack—about equal to Wilmersdorf, Wedding, Neukölln, and Friedrichshain. Lichterfelde, Lichtenberg, and Friedenau followed closely behind and what was left, about 15 percent of the whole, was distributed across the rest of the city.

Overall, black marketeering was concentrated in the center of the city; more than two-thirds of all defendants lived in or near the city center. Mitte and Charlottenburg, in particular, already established as sites for consumption and amusement, provided attractive spaces for trading. Indeed, these two large central areas of black marketeering, only separated by the Tiergarten, were both centrally located and boasted numerous stores, providing an ideal starting point, with a limited public, for clandestine trading. Some numbers indicate the concentration of this legal infrastructure, which was so important for the black market. Almost half of the 10,128 bars and restaurants with "full licenses" to sell alcoholic beverages in 1938 were located in the center of the city. This number declined up through March 1941, but only minimally to 9,809, and the distribution remained the same.[142] The distribution of hotels and guesthouses was similar. Of the 18,685 beds for hire in all of Berlin in 1937, 9,612 were in Mitte and 2,188 in Charlottenburg. Almost two-thirds of these were in the districts where most people lived. Between 1932 and 1942 the number of overnight stays more than doubled. In the third year of the war, there was a new record, with 1,990,333 "overnight stays by non-Berliners."[143] Retail stores, too, were similarly dispersed. The business census from May 17, 1939, revealed that approximately 48 percent of all Berlin retail businesses were located in the city center. The distribution of employment was even more pronounced: 55 percent of employees worked in one of the central city districts.[144] The decline of the smaller and middle-sized firms in the Berlin consumer goods and textile industries contributed further to the previously somewhat industrial central district becoming "more and more a residential and business district."[145]

All in all, this concentration of consumer spaces in the city center, increasingly also the western part of the city, was a development that professional observers had already noticed in the 1920s. In 1929, Berlin Mayor Gustav Böß had realized that

> the trend of the development in the center of the city is [moving] . . . from east to west. The main business areas, which originally were in the old city to the right of the Spree, have extended beyond Unter den Linden, Friedrichstrasse, Leipzigerstrasse and Wilhelmstrasse to the Potsdamer Platz and the area around it.

This had resulted partly from the development of the public transportation system ring, the center of which was the train station at Potsdamer Platz.[146] Consequently, Böß had correctly predicted how this would develop further: "the area around the Zoologischer Garten will become a part of the inner city, even if of a different sort."[147]

However, to attribute this concentration of black market trading centers emerging from analysis of the defendants' residential districts solely to the centrality of the Berlin consumer spaces and the opportunities they provided would be to neglect police bias in their practice of combating the trade. Indeed, one has to assume that the investigative activity of the trade inspection service was largely selective and contributed, along with other paradigms for interpreting the cityscape, to generating this distribution of "black market centers." To be sure, the trade inspection service had at its disposal a comprehensive network of "support points," and these points had to report weekly to the supervisors of their division on the events in their relevant segments. However, when an "initiative Sonderkommando" was established in July 1942, which was responsible directly to the director of the division and which could be deployed for "special controls" throughout the whole city, the detection and work on the crimes was no longer organized around a particular location.[148] From that point on, investigations were concentrated in areas prioritized by the police.

Even when investigative work remained centered around a certain location, subjective decisions played a role. All of these factors need to be kept in mind because they relativize the picture provided by the police records. In extreme cases, criminal prosecution depended on the involvement of individual policemen. For example, some especially committed policemen spent their free time pursuing perpetrators of offenses against the War Economy Regulations.[149] On top of this, individuals working on cases could impact the classification of crimes, for example, by setting the income level "as a percentage . . . the turnover and profit realized from 1939–1942" because they wished to encourage "an especially strong punishment."[150] The work of the trade and health inspection service was certainly not purely rational and objective; rather, it took place within the context of guidelines of interpretation, which formulated a political evaluation of the black marketeering.

The phrase "it is widely known that in this area black market trading transactions are taking place" regularly appeared in police notes and in written verdicts. It formed a part of a collective process whereby official agencies and "simple" urban dwellers divided up the urban space of Berlin into moral zones. By prioritizing individual sections of the city, in a practice known in ethnomethodology as "crime producing," the police anticipated, confirmed, and even strengthened the moralistic subdivision of the city. This pattern built on a long tradition. Already during the Kaiserreich, certain sections of the city had been defined "from above" as "political fields of conflict."[151] Delineating such "problem districts" helped to shape perceptions, influencing the practical measures criminal prosecutors took against "hustlers" in the bars and against the "underworld" in the middle of the city and in the "decadent west." Such patterns of perception, developed over a long period, included the practices of persecution against "Jewish," "asocial," and "underworld elements," for example, in the Scheunenviertel or in the Friedrichstrasse. The Scheunenviertel, in particular, had already had a bad reputation shaped by anti-Semitic resentments during the Weimar Republic.[152] Berlin's city planners considered the area a "disgrace" and tried to remove the old Scheunenviertel from the city. Toward the end of the 1920s, following the plans developed by Hans Poelzig, city planners attempted to improve the region by constructing apartment for the "new middle class" in it.

These efforts were only partially successful. National Socialist plans to reshape this city district seemed to pick up where the Weimar Republic had left off. However, the National Socialists also interpreted the redevelopment of the Scheunenviertel as the structural implementation of a racial-ideological policy of modifying urban space or—as Harald Bodenschatz put it—as "political and social cleansing, as a new interpretation of the old, historic section of the town."[153] For example, a "local history" publication of 1938 stated that

> in a few years . . . we will barely recognize the streets in this part of the city, which was once ruled by the Jew and where the Reds committed their worst murders, where Horst Wessel fought, suffered and died . . . , a new city will rise up, with sunny apartments and with Germans as occupants.[154]

In the police work of the 1930s and 1940s, therefore, two strands of interpretation converged in which the district was construed as a "problem district." These two tracks are not identical, but they do overlap.

Of course, the Berlin police also built on their anti-drug experiences of the 1920s.[155] A book written in 1924 by retired detective Ernst Engelbrecht, in which Engelbrecht describes his experiences in raids against the Berlin "underworld," gives an indication of this. Written to be sensational and appeal to a popular audience,[156] the book, and especially the chapter "Cocaine Epidemic in Berlin," not only acquainted readers with the common practices of drug dealers (middlemen, selling in the street and in certain restaurants and bars, etc.), but also pointed out trading and consumption centers, "primarily in the west and in the south of Berlin." Engelbrecht named "a large number (of) cocaine cellars" where those in the know got their cocaine, located primarily in and around Charlottenburg and the Wittenbergplatz, the "central meeting point of homosexuals." He named the Zoologischer Garten train station as a further trading point; indeed, the "most important trading site" of the "wild cocaine trading" was in the "Zoo-Diele," the waiting room for first- and second-class passengers.

Engelbrecht's description corresponds, both in terms of the sites he named as well as his labels for the drug scene and for black marketeering, to the patterns of perception of those fighting the Berlin black market during World War II. Engelbrecht demanded, for example, "strong action against cocaine dealers." He spoke of "wholesale dealers" with middle-class professions, for example, pharmacists or doctors, which enabled them "to deal part time in cocaine."[157] Engelbrecht's book gave some insights into the police work that divided the city up into criminal areas and, at the same time, underscored the semantic proximity between the black market and the drug market and subsumed the protagonists of both under the stereotype of the hustler. The continuity of these descriptions of criminality could be maintained without any difficulty because they built on a discourse on hustlers that, in its anti-decadent approach, condemned certain districts of the city—such as those of the "well-to-do west." It is therefore not very surprising that the better "bourgeois" districts, such as Dahlem, Zehlendorf, and Lichterfelde, hardly appear in the official records documenting black marketeering. To be sure, in these districts, too, there was black marketeering—as is shown by individual cases; however, the police paid little attention to these activities, which likely significantly distorted the distribution.

If one reads the statistics as evidence of a view of black market trading centers shaped by the perceptions of the state actors, what stands out is that these centers clustered into two groups: first, primarily "working-class" and "Jewish" districts—Spandau, the Scheunenviertel, and northern Berlin; and second, sites of "decadence" or "luxury" in western Berlin. Charlottenburg, Schöneberg, and Wilmersdorf, in particular, were associated with the black market, suggesting lavish and wasteful "luxury" (rejected by both the working class and the middle class).[158] Such calumnies, which denounced the alleged Bohemian lifestyle of a "decadent west," harked back to a tradition of labeling the boomtown that continued to be applied after World War II. For example, a commentary in the *Tagesspiegel* referred in 1947 to the alleged, historically developed difference between Schöneberg and Charlottenburg: around 1870 in Schöneberg

> one believed that one was open-minded, well-to-do and ambitious; one was solidly middle class, with a promising future . . . . This self-understanding was by no means so utopian if one considers that at that time Charlottenburg was not much closer to Berlin than Potsdam is today from the city borders, and the Kurfürstendamm was still the stuff of speculators' dreams.[159]

Even if what was meant here with unreliable, shoddy, and thus disreputable practices were the real estate speculators at the end of the nineteenth century, the association was with the "nouveau riche," with parvenus, an accusation that hardened into a cliché. There is a hint of this in Alfred Kerr's harmless description of western Berlin as "an elegant small town . . . in which people live who can do something, who are someone, who have something, and who think that they can do, be, and have three times as much as they really do."[160] At the same time, the attention paid to this reflected the fact that internal migration was possible and that since the 1880s ever more Berlin Jews had moved into the western districts of the city. Already by 1910, 40 percent of all Berlin Jews lived here. The synagogue in the Fasanenstrasse, finished in 1912, visually marked the process of the Jews "having arrived" in western Berlin. In 1925, Wilmersdorf, with 13 percent, had the highest percentage of Jewish citizens. Certain areas, such as the Hansaviertel in the Tiergarten and the area around the Bayerischen Platz in Schöneberg, had developed into concentrated areas of Jewish life.[161]

People viewed the city morally along two axes in accordance with these preconceptions. On the one hand, one assessment, which informed the work of the Berlin police, saw asocial "swarms of small hustlers" in Spandau, Prenzlauer Berg, Wedding, and sections of Kreuzberg and Neukölln. On the other hand, there was the condemnation of the "elegant café visitors" of the "well-to-do west," who were considered "thoughtless spendthrifts" who seemed to fit the category of the smart, hustling parvenus. This image built at least in part on older patterns of interpretation from the 1920s. This division adapted anti-Semitic stereotypes and, at the same time, spatially implemented the scapegoat mechanism that helped to create social unity at times of crisis. Such attributions made it possible for people to distance themselves morally from behavior they did not like and were therefore useful in labeling behavior that was "harmful to the nation" as the practice of specific minorities, whom one could assign to certain spaces. Accordingly, the concept of the Volksgemeinschaft itself provided an ideal template for the black market crisis discourses that began in 1944; construed in a broad consensus with official agencies already during the war, it structured a vague, flexible interpretation of black marketeering that loaded certain city districts with various negative connotations concerning trading that could be deployed as needed.

Goods from All of Europe

Among the peculiarities contemporaries ascribed to the black market was the assortment of luxury goods it had available. And typically, luxury was associated with choice foreign products transported by streetwise hustlers across the whole continent. But the reality was more profane. Even small brokers in the Berlin black market brought together both local and transregional dimensions—as did their professional "colleagues." The black market adjusted the geography of markets. For one thing, the black market provoked a contraction in the city. Instead of being able to choose consumer spaces freely, everyday traders now often turned to their own district and organized their transactions around neighborly relations. This was very similar to the organization of rationing, which required customers to shop at a local neighborhood store; one had to be registered at a store to pick up one's rations there.[162] Yet the black market opened up new possibilities, especially as its sphere of influence for goods expanded as the army advanced. Some Berlin merchants knew how to exploit these new markets and became the driving force behind the movement of goods out of Berlin, which established illegal networks with France, Poland, the Netherlands, and the Soviet Union. Alongside the old, common ways of shopping in the neighborhood and commuter business in the city, these distant markets opened up new possibilities for black marketeers. These did not, however, achieve the same degree of organization as legal, transnational wholesale trade.

The extensive postal traffic with German soldiers in the occupied territories formed a special variation of a transregional market link, integrating Berliners into a trading network that spread over the whole continent. The vastly expanded radius of private, long-distance relationships provided an ideal basis for shipments of goods. In the luggage soldiers on leave brought home from the front, there were goods from all of Europe. The significance of this was soon quite clear to the responsible agencies, who formulated new regulations to curb such practices. For example, the Supreme Command of the Wehrmacht issued a whole series of "regulations" on the "sending and taking of goods" from the occupied territories, establishing maximum amounts.[163] "Along with one's official equipment," it stated, everyone is allowed "only to take along as much luggage as he can carry in both hands without the assistance of straps or of carrying devices." What constituted "official equipment" obviously had to be more clearly defined. According to the Supreme Command, this included "for those providing their own uniform (*Selbsteinkleidern*) the officer's field case, for officers or civil servants suitcases with a tight, hinged lid."[164] Apparently, there was a reason for such counter measures—the military leadership had not failed to recognize that officers were bringing home vast quantities of "gift souvenirs" from foreign countries.

The quantity of goods one could send by mail was limited. Furthermore, the "responsible commanding officer" could prohibit the sending of certain goods, at least de jure. De facto, however, it was almost impossible to stop soldiers and other members of the army from sending goods, and the practice flourished.

This was not changed by penal provisions that expressly and "strictly" forbade "the divestment for profit of imported goods to strangers either through sale or through bartering."[165] It was not just in Berlin that illegal trading was a part of everyday life; it was also conducted by German soldiers and by many departments in the occupied territories themselves. Although, for example, "Reichsführer SS" Heinrich Himmler repeatedly pointed out the relevant prohibitions, the SS, too, bought goods in local markets.[166]

However, the market traffic that extended beyond the boundaries of the city was by no means limited to members of the army. Berlin's black marketeers, regardless of their level of professionalization, participated not only in the local markets in individual districts or between different parts of the city, but also in bartering transactions with a much wider range. In part, they brought in goods from the area surrounding Berlin or from sites with which they were previously acquainted. Large brokers employed supply services for this. They merely had to supply the contacts and the commissions to transact their business outside of the boundaries of the city; they left the transport to liaisons, who also assumed the risk associated with such transport. The example of Hermann Weese from the network around the Hermannplatz in Neukölln illustrates the connection between a locally organized trading network in the city and the transnational networks of the Berlin black market. Weese occupied the decisive intersection: through a middleman he received gold from Holland, which he was then able to sell in the local markets in Berlin. But even small brokers organized their trade in part beyond the boundaries of the city. Regular deliveries from Krakow, Warsaw, Bulgaria, or Holland were not all that rare.[167] The goods that flowed through Martha Rebbien's network came both from nearby as well as from Hamburg or Prague.[168] Of course, foreigners living in Berlin who could have goods sent from home had an advantage. Because of the scarcity of particular goods, they could often demand very high prices for goods still relatively easy to obtain in France, for example.

Facilities that brought together soldiers on leave from the occupied territories or from the front with local Berlin traders proved to be especially successful. One example of this was a brothel in the Alexanderstrasse, not far from the Alexanderplatz. Indeed, the brothels in Berlin quickly moved up to the very top of the list of suspicious sites that needed to be monitored to control the black market. On November 6, 1943, the police in Mitte reported that "brothels, in particular, and these sorts of undertakings . . . are often visited by people" who want "to sell rationed goods at vastly inflated prices." It was "a matter of experience that prostitutes, especially, given their relatively high incomes, did not have any inhibitions in this regard" and bought anything they were offered "indiscriminately."[169] This description was simply false in that not all Berlin prostitutes had high incomes. It also distorts the picture by neglecting the trading by men that took place in the brothels.

Prostitution, that is, exchanging sex for money or goods, was an integral part of Berlin's illegal bartering culture. As Annette Timm showed using the example of Berlin, the prostitution policy of the NS regime changed during the 1930s and at the beginning of the war. On the one hand, Berlin authorities considered prostitutes asocial, strictly monitored them, and kept them from publicly practicing their trade.[170] On the other hand, their services were very welcome for strengthening soldiers' and workers' morale. National Socialist policy toward prostitution evolved over time from rhetorical and legal marginalization to increasing acceptance until the practice finally became an instrument for providing the most effective and thorough social mobilization of German wartime society.[171] The state considered setting up, organizing, and maintaining brothels necessary both for the soldiers as well as for workers on the home front. Alongside brothels for local civilians, state agencies also established some for "foreign workers," which sometimes presented organizational problems. In February 1942, a report by the relevant agencies stated that "establishing brothels" for foreign workers "in Staaken and Königsheide is acceptable." However, the report immediately pointed out that negotiations to establish similar facilities in Wilhelmsruh and Friedrichsfelde "are not moving forward," as the main planning office had still not issued any "site maps of the available property." This was all the more remarkable as the construction had to move forward and both the "Herr Minister"—this was Göring—as well as the "Main Security Office" had already pressed to have this issue "taken care of."[172] Clearly, the Interior Ministry and the subordinate authorities thought that it was very important to have both an adequate supply of brothels as well as a clear separation in the different facilities for different groups of customers. To justify setting up this special brothel system, it was repeatedly pointed out that it protected Germans. When Germans visited the brothels, the government supervision enabled measures to prevent the spread of sexual diseases to be taken, and when foreigners visited brothels, German women could be protected from sexual assaults.[173] Whether or not this breakdown of groups was effective, it soon became apparent that brothels contributed to undesirable black market trading, which would generate considerable problems for the prosecuting authorities.

The illegal trading in the Berlin brothels and among street prostitutes formed part of the black market built on customer-client relationships. Traders were able to build on established relationships of trust and familiarity. The bartering relationships between clients and prostitutes also benefited from the fact that one could count on anonymity in this "shady" business, which created an excellent environment for illegal trading. In the Berlin brothels and hotels, customers and prostitutes met one another in a carefully controlled clandestine atmosphere, which provided ideal conditions for black market transactions. In many cases one gave only one's first name (not always the real one.) If further information was volunteered, it was in good hands with the owner of the brothel, whose very livelihood depended on her respecting the wishes of her customers.

The mutual anonymity extended to suppliers and customers limited social control of brothel trading. The customers could depend on their bartering partners remaining quiet. The madame of one brothel, Clara Biniek, explained to the civil servants of the trade inspection service, "Strangers with whom I am not acquainted are not allowed in the rooms."[174] As it turned out, she made exceptions to this rule if customers or potential suppliers were either introduced by regular customers or if the business promised to be profitable. The problem was that male visitors not only desired sex but also wanted alcoholic drinks and tobacco, for which she did not have a license. Accordingly, Biniek began to look for these goods in the black market, and ultimately she discovered the black market as a business. The demands of her customers, their desire to consume food and liquor, gave rise to her career as a black marketeer. From the very beginning, this branch of her business overlapped with her regular brothel business; over time it developed into a profitable second line, and ultimately it earned her more than her regular business. According to her own statements, she received 10–15 marks for a glass (2 cl) of schnapps. Customers wishing to "be served" by one of her two "monitored girls" had to pay on average about 20 marks, and Biniek received half of this.[175]

As a rule, customers paid cash for sex. However, as a police report from March 13, 1945, noted, it was also common to pay in kind. As "primarily businessmen" went in and out of Biniek's business, "the illegal acquisition of food was especially easy." Retailers and shop owners, who found it relatively easy "to take away" something from their contingent, particularly relied on this form of trading, as evidenced by the fish merchant Heinrich Kierspel. As the official of the trade inspection service noted with outrage, Kierspel had been "deferred from military service" for his business, but, instead of dutifully organizing the distribution of fish for 3,500 customers as he was supposed to, he had "gone so far" as to withdraw his goods from his intended customers. Accordingly, the policeman wrote, "his behavior . . . in the sixth year of the war" was to be considered "especially reprehensible."[176]

Whereas Kierspel and others like him may have failed their duties "as trustees of just distribution," as "Volksgenossen who were supposed to prop up the National Socialist supply system, and as comrades in arms on the 'home front'," the second group of traders in Biniek's brothel got off relatively easily. These were the soldiers who stopped off at Biniek's "accommodation," as the investigation showed, with their goods from occupied Europe, making it function as a site linking local and more distant distribution networks. Only some of the soldiers made use of the services of the "girls." Others were primarily active as suppliers of foreign goods brought in their luggage. For example, a delivery of cognac from France found its way to Berlin in an army rucksack. How the soldiers came to be in possession of the goods in question cannot be reconstructed in most cases, although the civil servants of Berlin's trade inspection service did confiscate cans of meat from the stocks of the army near Biniek. The sources were thus bought or commandeered not only foreign goods but also army stocks and stolen goods.[177]

There was thus a special trading relationship between the capital and the occupied territories. Through interfaces such as the brothel in the Alexanderstrasse, soldiers could introduce small presents into the local distribution system of the Berlin black market economy. In return, the soldiers received goods withdrawn from the legal supply chain, above all food, but also the "services" of prostitutes. Consequently, one can speak of the home country as a place to relieve the strain, a place to recuperate, and a place where "girls" offered their bodies for goods that had been brought from abroad. On top of this, the brothel brought together two groups of male participants: the soldiers and local Berlin traders. Thus, state-sanctioned prostitution ultimately functioned as a catalyst for illegal black market trading. That this compensation for physical and psychological stress removed itself from state monitoring and led to disastrous misallocations of supplies was clearly not what was desired. From the perspective of the authorities, it was good that prostitutes supplied a service important to the war effort; yet these same authorities considered it scandalous that at the same time, they withdrew goods from local Berlin food markets.

The overlapping of the front and the home and the changes in the structure in local districts and in black market centers resulted from a spatial reorganization of everyday life in Berlin under the conditions of the barter culture. These processes ultimately reflected individual and group mobilities. Women, men, and youths who had mobility also had ample opportunity to use what the black market offered to their advantage.

The different black marketeers' conceptualizations of the use of space displayed gender- and milieu-specific discrepancies. The practice of visiting restaurants in certain districts remained reserved primarily for men, or women from the lower classes. Women of the middle class would almost never visit one of the black market centers in the Scheunenviertel, in the area around the Silesian Gate, or in Mitte. If they did, they had to reckon with the potential for earning a reputation as "fallen women" or as social people.[178] Middle- and upper-class women found it best to develop bartering partnerships in cafés or restaurants through acquaintances. Women caught trading in bars—as random samples show—were employed almost exclusively in "menial tasks" and had a lower income. Of course, all women could use their own private rooms and the local distribution networks in their respective city districts. Thus, the black market maintained the gender-specific discrepancy in the use of space that pertained to most spaces; men had access to almost all public spaces, whereas women were restricted to a rather limited domestic sphere.[179] Those not blocked or bothered by such obstacles had, in the black market, a whole series of possibilities for creatively shaping their own bartering practices or adapting them to the particular circumstances. This applied to both the goods and the currencies in which business was conducted in the illegal markets.

"Illegal" Currencies, Bookkeeping, and Goods

> Since money, as the existing and active concept of value, confounds and confuses all things, it is the general confounding and confusing of all things—the world upside-down—the confounding and confusing of all natural and human qualities.
>
> Karl Marx, *The Power of Money*[180]

> The feeling of personal security that the possession of money gives is perhaps the most concentrated and pointed form and manifestation of confidence in the socio-political organization and order.
>
> Georg Simmel, *The Philosophy of Money*[181]

Contemporary descriptions of the chaotic activity in the black markets appear at first sight to be accurate in at least one regard: a barely manageable "currency disorder" prevailed. Goods had replaced currencies. Ration cards and ration coupons had taken the place of money. The Reichsmark, as a currency, no longer had a stable value nor the normal functions of a valid currency such as exchange and settling accounts. What one could buy for money today one could buy tomorrow only with cigarettes. The dissolution of the boundary between goods and currencies seemed inexorable so that the use of "normal" means of exchange likewise seemed impossible. Yet can we assume that people who traded with one another sometimes over weeks, months, and years, who negotiated, calculated, and made agreements about prices, and who were engaged in understanding the rules of the business or, indeed, in rewriting these rules failed to develop a system for dealing normally with "their" goods and currencies? This seems unlikely. It is much more probable that, in the face of the dissolution of stable areas of practice, such attributions of chaos simply reversed the widespread negative interpretation of the modern money economy, which cast money as a demon and a medium of selfishness and social indifference. Many contemporaries were painfully aware of the loss of the function of money for reducing complexity and expediting action. Confronted with the consequences of the "money disorder," they would have preferred the unambiguous relationships between people, money, and goods. By rejecting the "currency chaos," these interpretations overlooked the fact that the "chaos" had its own rules.

One can only talk about money and its social effects in the plural—this is the quintessence of analyses in economic sociology—which examines the very different everyday practices of distinguishing between and "marking" various sorts of money. Money for managing the household, savings for education, donations, and gifts are only some of the categories used to distinguish various expenditures and give them a social meaning, which varied starkly by gender and class.[182] These distinctions took the bite out of the idea that money capitalism obliterated social contexts and interpersonal relationships. Simmel's judgment that money belongs "to those standardizing ideas . . . which themselves submit to the very norm that they themselves are" needs therefore to be put into perspective.[183] Even if the expansion of the "modern" money economy had a "standardizing" effect, these relationships remained caught up in a network of social meanings wherein family relationships, friendships, and other group relationships were not abandoned; rather, people attempted to bring their money practices into harmony with social facts. This was certainly true for Berlin black marketeers' handling of their currencies. Not only did the Reichsmark retain its validity as the legal currency for a long time, but it was also accepted in the black markets as a common means of payment. The prices on the black market were both calculated and paid for in Reichsmarks. This officially recognized currency continued to function both as an accounting unit and a means of exchange. A black market trader who had wanted to go into the city to barter said in the fall of 1944 in a survey that he had explicitly asked one of his acquaintances the price "in the black market in Berlin for a kilo of butter." He remembered that she was able to give him precise information: "Frau K. told me that a kilo of butter cost about 120–130 RM."[184] For small brokers, especially, who worked on commission, the paper currency proved to be an important exchange medium.

As the goods being traded often could not be divided up, it was easier for the profit to be paid out in Reichsmarks.[185] The population's lasting trust in the value of this currency resulted from two contradictory feelings. On the one hand, this trust limited the fear of inflation, which prevented mass flight into material assets.[186] On the other hand, the existing juxtaposition provided fertile ground for diverse trading practices that utilized the official currency in growing black markets as a perfect accounting measure and opened up greater flexibility. Furthermore, the RM still had the advantage that—at least temporarily—it did not lose its value as quickly as ration cards, which were distributed for a set time period. The RM therefore remained the preferred currency for black market trading. Nonetheless, during the war some black marketeers avoided the RM and explicitly demanded payment in kind.[187]

Black marketeers sometimes treated their illegal profits like "normal" household income. For example, the cloth merchant Capaldo admitted that he had no records concerning the fabric that he had sold on the black market and that he had also not given out any receipts. And indeed, he had his son deposit the RM just like any other income into his account at the Dresdner Bank, where it was mixed in with the money that he had earned legally.[188] As a rule, however, traders kept the various monies separate from one another; they kept money and other means of exchange from the black market at home or made sure that these were quickly turned around and converted, for example, into food.[189] This approach coincides with behavior patterns researchers have often analyzed in regard to groups participating in at least partly illegal activity. The reasons for the quick turnover of illegally obtained goods varied; it could be simply to acquire something new, something one actually desired, or to get rid of evidence quickly. Possessing such goods weighed heavily on one's conscience, and a rapid turnover could provide relief.[190]

The division between "legal" and "illegal" monies meant that profits made in black market trading seldom found their way into the legal retail trade and instead were used primarily for further black market transactions. It is obvious why this would be the case when goods were used as the means of exchange, as there was scarcely any possibility of reintroducing them into the legal retail trade. However, even if a merchant sold, for example, a suit or a clock on the black market for money, it was quite probable that he would reinvest the profits in black market goods or buy food on the black market.[191] Although the circulation of money and goods in legal and illegal consumer spaces continuously overlapped, merchants attached importance to being able to distinguish between the two. "Clean" and "dirty" monies had a different (moral) significance and were kept separate from one another. Special purchases, such as gifts for children, Christmas, birthdays, or weddings justified crossing such borders. Many traders used such arguments to part with money or things they had actually not intended to use for consumption and especially not for illegal transactions.[192]

Other traders attached less importance to keeping their monies distinct. It was a common practice to use one's "savings" to buy black market goods if one had already found a buyer. As a rule, most traders used the profit from these transactions to buy consumer goods, but they might also use it to expand their black market business. The commercial clerical worker Heinz Binder, for example, who drove to the outskirts of Berlin to buy some pork from a farmer in March 1945, stated in his interrogation that the 1,450 RM that he had paid for 27 kg of pork was his "own money," which had "(come out) of his savings."[193]

In weighing punishments, the courts did not distinguish between the use of rationed goods or ration cards for transactions. In the judgment in the case against Elisabeth Hanke and those indicted with her, the judges of the Berlin Special Court wrote "that ration cards for essential products are to be considered equivalent to the products themselves" as had been "repeatedly emphasized in numerous decisions by the respective Special Court."[194] Ultimately, the proper handling of food ration cards by the employees of the Rationing Card Office was an especially sensitive realm within the war economy. The accused, who had been convicted of embezzling ration cards, had, through "her wicked example called forth the danger of imitation by a third party and of rebellion by other people against the state's distribution system." In the court's view, however, the "people" had to "be able to rely upon the fact that the Ration Card Office" worked "honestly and reliably . . . and that every infringement w[ould] be strictly punished."[195] Even though the courts aimed to punish trading in ration cards and bartering with goods equally, this helped to blur the boundary between officially approved means of exchange and what were, in a strict sense, goods for trading.

The blending together of goods and currencies as means of exchange resulted not only from certain practices among black marketeers but also from a complicated substitute system of cards, ration coupons, and real goods. The confusion this created found its expression in official designations taken from the money economy. For example, the ration coupons for tradesmen bore relatively unspecific names that had nothing to do with the good for which they were valid, such as "*Punktschein* (point certificate)," "coupon," or even "*Punktescheck* (point check)."[196] For individual traders, in particular, who regularly managed large amounts of rather varied "ration coupons," viewing such substitutes for money as currency was even advisable, especially as these corresponded to contingents that gave them a certain flexibility in regard to time or quantity, which normal consumers were not aware of. The ration cards thus had a flexible exchange value, which meant they could function like a currency such as the Reichsmark, storing value and providing compensation.

The system of allocation, as rigid and normative as it was compared to unrestricted shopping, could also be flexible. The best example of this was a distribution introduced to calm the "population" after air raids, so-called special allocations. As special allocations were not part of the normal ration scheme, in which contingents were restricted to a particular time period, black marketeers could quickly integrate them into their trading practices. And because these special allocations were not included in the individual allocation plans and could be more freely exchanged, they were very popular means of exchange. Black marketeers reported again and again that the goods they were trading had come from such allocations. There was, of course, a reason for this. Because these special allocations were handed out irregularly, after air raids, many allotments went unclaimed, so they became available to shop owners for trading. Moreover, the paths these allocations took were difficult to control, which made stating these special allocations as the source of one's goods both a way to protect accomplices and to deny that one was trading in stolen goods.[197] The situation for contingents from the period before the war was similar.[198]

The currency practices of Berlin traders thus helped to reorganize goods and currencies. In short, they helped to organize and constitute the black market as an alternative infrastructure. The official distribution system organized an infrastructure "from above"; the black market alternative was a means of correcting this, albeit one that competed with the public order. This competition contributed, on the one hand, to establishing and perpetuating the boundaries between legality and illegality, without, however, containing the phenomenon on a sustained basis. As confiscated black market money from police searches and arrests was clearly marked as such, the state at first glance seemed to undo the blending of legal and illegal goods and currencies generated by the bartering transactions. The confiscated black market goods were eventually moved from the evidence rooms of the police departments to appropriate distribution points, which then transferred the goods once again into legal retail spaces. For example, the police carefully listed and then passed on the black market goods seized from Martha Rebbien in exactly this way. They were especially enthusiastic when seizing goods from such "unscrupulous war vultures."[199] One final report, after harshly describing the suspect, concluded with concern about rapidly redistributing the seized goods into the regular distribution pathways:

> in order to ensure that the goods will not be destroyed by the terrorizing air raids, we ask that you inform us quickly what is to be done with them. As it is not possible to ascertain who the owners of these goods are, we suggest that we turn the fabrics over to the Economic Division and the boots over to the NSV.[200]

This concern was well justified because, especially toward the end of the war, goods sometimes were destroyed before they could be redistributed. For example, the trade inspection service reported on March 13, 1945, that the goods confiscated from black market transactions in a brothel had been given to the "disabled persons division of the urban hospital" because they were "perishable"; the report neatly listed a total of 17 items, including several liters of alcoholic drinks, goose liver, and canned goods. Moreover, the report stated that many of the goods stored in the police headquarters on Magazinstrasse had been destroyed in the March 10, 1945, air raid.[201]

Money that was confiscated was sent down different paths, establishing once again the division between goods and currency. For example, whereas the confiscated goods in the example cited immediately above were sent to the disabled persons division, the confiscated money that had been paid for those goods, 250 RM found on the accused, was deposited in the "cash office of the police for safekeeping" together with the 14,807 RM found on the brothel's madame.[202] A large portion of black market money was processed in this way and thus brought under the supervision of government institutions (by means of receipts and documents) and once again made legal.

Bookkeeping methods give an indication of how professional an individual black marketeer in Berlin had become. Once business activity had achieved a certain size, it became necessary to write down information to keep track of pending deliveries, provisions and debts to be paid, contacts, and even prices. Traders' notes and records are still in the archives and—the police often used them as evidence—are therefore carefully preserved. These documents reveal that bookkeeping styles ranged from amateurish to professional.[203] They include telephone numbers, price calculations, and systematic lists on other documents or in the margins. In their note-taking techniques, the vast majority of black marketeers never achieved the degree of accuracy one finds in the very carefully maintained lists of the Berlin police. When the bartering partners were already acquainted with each other from relatively close multiplex relationships, they were merely building upon already established relationships and did not need to note much beyond the items and exchange values.

Black marketeers bartering with unknown persons, however, needed to record more information. As a rule, they needed to exchange (and thus, often, record—depending on the number of trading contacts and their individual memory capacity) information concerning meeting places, telephone numbers, and goods in demand. Individual or chance trades could be noted on any sort of paper one had brought along. If the number of contacts and transactions increased, black marketeers often carried lists of telephone numbers or calendars. Some pages contain calculations or lists of names with telephone numbers associated with goods and prices. In his interrogation, Martha Rebbien's bartering partner Friedrich Wiggers, for example, explained that his notes of names and goods represented completed transactions but that some were also memory aids to remind him of certain requests people had made.[204]

Such improvised bookkeeping served, first and foremost, as a memory aid. If one had a large business, like Martha Rebbien's, one could not possibly remember all the prices, amounts, times, and names one needed. Furthermore, notes could serve as evidence if trading partners disagreed about terms. A written note did not necessarily have to convince the other person but did tend to make an impression, especially if the other person had failed to write anything down. Reference to a bookkeeping method conveyed an impression of professionalism that improved one's negotiating position.[205]

Bookkeeping was necessary for growing one's business. Only those with some form of record-keeping could compare long-term prices, identify demands, and thus improve their business. Traders who thus systematized their work documented that they had at least a partially professional attitude to their black market business. They organized their time, contacts, and business commitments around

Goods and services	*In%*
Food and ration cards	23
Clothes and fabric	23
Tobacco	19
Services	13
Jewelry	3
Drugs and weapons	3
Foreign currencies	3
Other	13

Figure 2.9 Goods and services in black market transactions

their illegal business. The degree of organization reflected in one's bookkeeping style revealed the importance black market trading had for participants. Further tools included notes concerning supply and demand. For example, an "acquaintance" of Erna Kuschy, Heinz Zeisberger, passed a note to Martha Rebbien with the shoe sizes of Kuschy, himself, and his brother so that she could find the right shoes. According to Rebbien's statement, Kuschy and Zeisberger had done this to "produce evidence to prove that Rebbien was engaged in black market trading."[206] Regardless of their intentions, the police valued such documents as evidence, and thus the example documents a common, widespread practice, not only used by informers.

What goods did black marketeers trade most often? Figure 2.9 gives an overview based not on the amount of goods but on the percentage of transactions in which the individual groups of goods appear.

At first glance, this information does not seem surprising. Rather, it shows that the most important goods were rationed ones, which were in short supply: food and textiles. Tobacco products are third because they were used not merely as consumer goods but also as currency. The most important services were those of tradesmen, such as, for example, those of a tailor, with services paid in kind. It is interesting that jewelry—that is, valuables that were personal possessions—did not play an important role during the war. At the same time, the low figure for weapons and drugs shows that the black market offenses being analyzed here did not conform to the traditional business transactions of the underworld; this was truly an "everyday" black market.

The goods included here under "other" reinforce this idea: these were primarily household goods and furniture that cannot easily be categorized and, as keepsakes, often had a special significance well beyond their actual value. Personal "valuables" only played a very important role after the end of the war—at the very least in the public perception and in Berlin black marketeers' self-understanding—pointing to a fundamental change. Bartering deals during wartime were also an attempt to improve one's own income. It was only when the supply situation worsened in the postwar years, when there were no more deliveries from the occupied territories and harvests were poor, that a section of the Berlin black market became the "poor man's market," where people traded their valuables for necessities. This new market then became the focus of outrage in the insecure and suspicious postwar society.[207]

The Usual Suspects: Stereotypes of Hustlers in the Postwar Era

The Nazi regime had faced a dilemma concerning its black market policy. On the one hand, the hustler, or Schieber, provided a useful negative symbol. Highlighting and denouncing individual cases made visible the border between the Volksgenossen who submitted themselves to the rationing war society in which one did without any "selfish" black marketeers. In this, the hustler helped to integrate that society. On the other hand, the hustler concept had its problems. At first, the jurists in the Justice Ministry did not use the concept, even though it would have been very easy to draft an explicit anti-hustler regulation, because they wanted to avoid any association with the "turnip winter" (1916/17) that would remind people of shortages, hunger, black market activities in wartime, and the chaotic inflation era.

Whoever spoke of "hustlers" reminded Germans of their experiences in that "upside-down world." Concepts prefixed by the word "war," by contrast, held the implicit promise that rationing and the consequences of the war economy, such as punishing offenses against these regulations, would remain temporary. The expression "Offenses against War Economy Regulations" was designed precisely along these lines. It designated a special, war-related condition, which called for special measures that would in no way be comparable to conditions after the defeat of "1918." However, this avoidance strategy was never consistently applied as it was too self-contradictory. The image of the hustler formed in the early 1920s turned out to be very popular during World War II.

Innumerable publications in the 1920s and 1930s, ranging from pamphlets full of politically charged defamations to cabaret-like performances, had portrayed the "hustler" for the first time as a formative figure associated with a series of allegedly typical behavioral patterns. Alfred Müller-Förster's reader, whose title translates to *Reheated Potatoes: A Booklet for Politicians, Hustlers and Chimney Sweeps, for Reich Presidents, Shoemakers, Ministers, Virgins and Those Who Wish to Become Such*, attempted to parody the relationship between politics and "hustling."[208] Max Brinkmann's *Kleiner Knigge für Schieber* [Little Etiquette Manual for Hustlers] described the embarrassing situations Berlin "hustlers" and their wives could get into as *nouveau riche*—for example, at formal dinners or in the theater—if they did not put aside their *petit bourgeois* attitudes and failed to take on the manners of "high society."[209] Above all, "hustling" and "hustlers" had become the negative symbols of an "upside-down world."

This discourse thus put black marketeers in a negative light long before National Socialist propaganda, and most Berliners held this view of them as well. The stereotype of the public discourse simplified and exaggerated the "hustler," especially concerning the complex issues of the illegal economic activity. Yet the individual characteristics of the hustler in this discourse could be associated with real people and real events. The pattern of perceptions of the "hustler" and the actions of real hustlers mutually influenced each other. Looking at the figure of the hustler from the perspective of discourse analysis, what is especially interesting is the ways it structured perceptions, which could be called up as a set of attributes, assigned, and thus confirmed. Language functions as a series of preconceptions, sorting and organizing "possible experiences according to guidelines of the figures of speech, the metaphors, the topoi, the concepts, the textualization, indeed, the ability to articulate, which at the same time shapes and limits our consciousness."[210]

To a large degree, the wartime hustler discourse picked up on well-known motifs. Even the lawmakers and judges who were bound to utilize the concepts associated offenses against War Economy Regulations started expressions from it. The term Schieber appeared regularly both in indictments and in written verdicts. For example, a Berlin Special Court verdict stated that the accused had become "a 'hustler' " by his behavior and that "such phenomena, which played such a sad role in the last war and which contributed significantly . . . to undermining the will of the people" had to be prevented by applying the laws strictly in such cases.[211] The use of the popular concept points to a semantic shift that ultimately acknowledged the power of the existing stereotype. The term "those convicted of offenses against War Economy Regulations" was too unwieldy for everyday colloquial language to refer to black marketeers. Even more unwieldy was the phrase "Offenses against the Verbrauchsregelungsstrafverordnung (Penal Code for Consumption Regulations)." This did not even make clear who the actors were. Such terms could not displace the simple and convenient term "hustler."[212]

The persistence of the older figure had definite advantages for the Nazi leadership. Although it might have reminded people of World War I, it made it much easier to stigmatize black marketeers as "social outsiders" or Gemeinschaftsfremde.[213] These two interpretations remained the predominant interpretations during the war as can be seen in the two very different groups to which the term was most typically applied. The first consisted of fringe groups on the edge of society, even though their most important offense was quite often not illegal black marketeering but was, rather, their foreignness and purported asocial nature, which Nazis wished to eradicate from the "body of the people." This policy picked up and modified resentments that had been cultivated in Germany for generations and was directed above all against Jews, foreigners, prostitutes, and alleged criminals. As in the anti-foreigner and anti-Semitic discourse of the 1920s, this Nazi discourse mixed racist and economic discourse elements together. The second group consisted primarily of young men who seemingly made their money without any great effort and flaunted their wealth. There was often little evidence against them, even though it was derived from the culture of surveillance of everyday life in Berlin. These young men fit the image of the "hustler" as a war profiteer, as someone who profited from crises and who had become the object of envy and fear of many Germans during the inflation period. Yet there was also a third and final group comprised of individual traders who traded goods in demand. Many Berliners assumed from the start—and as we have seen this was not completely without foundation—that shop owners or hospitality employees in hotels, restaurants, or bars like Martha Rebbien were involved in illegal trading. This, too, was not a new phenomenon; the trading among middlemen "which drove prices up" at the beginning of the Weimar Republic had been the focus of numerous consumer protests.[214] The relationship of broad sections of the population to this last group is important, especially in regard to the consequences of the "black market era."

But let us look first at the first two groups, the "classical" fringe groups and young war profiteers. The phrase "those convicted of offenses against War Economy Regulations" appears only sporadically in the vast majority of informer letters to police, complaints, and witness statements. Instead, the terms "hustlers," "smugglers," and "black marketeers" are used repeatedly. Even Hitler, the final authority in Germany, avoided using the vocabulary coined by the judges of the justice system when he spoke of black marketeering.[215] Almost everyone spoke rather of "hustling food" than of "being convicted of offenses against the War Economy Regulations." Authorities in the police and justice systems who combated black marketeering were no exception. For example, the "counter-intelligence representative" of the Daimler-Benz factory in Berlin-Marienfelde turned over a number of foreign personnel to the police for "hustling food."[216]

In numerous letters to the police informing on people—letters which often led to police investigations—the recourse to the terms "hustling" and "hustlers" was especially striking. For example, an anonymous informer from Kreuzberg in the winter of 1943 wanted "to bring the police's attention to a number of large hustlers." The author continued, "The previous leaseholder Frohlschläger, a street girl from Alexanderplatz, understood how to draw a large number of shady dealers and hustlers to herself in the bar" to earn money to pay her rent to W. Moreover, "Jews were given shelter and the goods were sold preferably to such at huge prices" in the restaurant, and W. had begun "running the hustler business with even more verve by himself and O. in their apartment." After advising the police on how and when to conduct surveillance, the author referred to a second case in nearby Schöneberg, where a fish merchant had allegedly stored all sorts of possible goods that he sold at "enormous prices." Clearly, the anonymous writer believed he was carrying out a mission as he closed with a warning: "after these cases are taken care of, more will follow. Heil Hitler."[217]

This letter informing on neighbors brings together with the "street girl," the barkeeper, the Jews, and the fish merchant representatives of nearly all the groups typically accused of being involved in illegal trading. Another anonymous letter mentioned the only group not addressed in the first example: foreigners. The letter writer highlighted the contrast between his Nazi perspective and credentials and the shameful acts of foreign hustlers. "As a National Socialist and a fighter for the National Socialist worldview, as a veteran of 1914–1918, who received the Iron Cross I and the Iron Cross II as well as the medal for bravery and the purple heart," he felt compelled to inform on a Belgian waiter who had offered him cigarettes with a total value of 1,000 RM. "We Germans," continued the outraged letter writer, "are with all of our thoughts and souls for our Führer and

Fatherland. It is our faith that gives us the strength to endure all the hardships. And then these annoying foreigners come and are so shameless as to quite openly carry out extortion with our common property." In any case, he had tried to get to the bottom of the "dark intrigues" and had come across "a center of black market trading" with "a large number of French, men and women," who had set up an apartment as a "smuggler band" and whose irregular comings and goings suggested they were not involved in any sort of "honest work." The letter writer wanted to know that the authorities would make "short work" of them.[218]

Although prosecuting authorities did not make "short work" of foreign black marketeers, whenever they did arrest and prosecute "foreign workers" or other foreigners living in Berlin who participated in the black market, harsh sentences would be handed down. For example, the judge of a local court wrote in his written explanation of the verdict against Belgian traders that it is "especially irresponsible . . . when foreign workers who have found work here use their stay in Germany to conduct their hustling business and in such a careless and reckless manner make money on the side."[219] The trade with food rationing cards among "foreigners," another report stated, had "taken on epidemic proportions."[220]

Foreigners could sometimes profit considerably by selling goods sent from their home countries that were hard to get in Germany except on the black market. In a letter intercepted by the Foreign Letter Inspection Service of the Gestapo in Cologne-Riehl, Belgian worker Robert Parmentier described this activity to his parents in these words:

> In regard to food, one does whatever one can to help oneself. I can tell you that I am not suffering from hunger, but you would be amazed at what I am doing to get food. . . . Only one example: here in Germany you can hardly find any film, and I sell at least 50 rolls of film every week. You can imagine what sort of profit I am making.

As he did not want to mail all the money home, Parmentier had gone on a shopping spree and bought, among other things, a suit, a gramophone, and numerous books.[221]

In spite of these advantages, foreigners ("forced laborers," "foreign workers," and other foreigners who were at least temporarily in Berlin) were not nearly as well represented and numerous in the black markets as contemporary descriptions and some historians would suggest.[222] Foreign women accounted for 5 percent of market participants, foreign men around 15 percent. If one considers that the number of foreign workers in the city increased during the war, the percentage was comparatively small—at least from the evidence of the Berlin courts. Up through 1944, across Germany the number of foreign workers rose to about 7.7 million. This represented about 20 percent of the labor force and about 10 percent of the population.[223] The number was further distorted by more intensive surveillance of foreigners in camps and in the city than of their non-foreign counterparts.[224]

Surveillance was at least as intensive when Jews participated in black marketeering. In the summer of 1943, the local Berlin court heard a case in which one of those accused was listed as a "Jewish half-breed." The case involved the wholesale perfume firm Walter & Liebe.[225] The two owners, Ulrich Walter and Karl-Heinz Liebe, sold different sorts of cosmetics and had business relationships with perfumeries in Vienna, Prague, and Milan. Their shop was in the Uhlandstrasse in Charlottenburg. The prosecutors indicted them on July 5, 1943, charging them with having secretly "sold goods for around 20,000 RM" between April 1941 and the summer of 1943. A letter to the police had got the ball rolling.[226] G. Müller, a soldier, had filed a complaint leading to the indictment, in which he made all sorts of anti-Semitic comments. Müller wrote that as "a soldier who since the first day of the war" had been fighting "for a better future for our Fatherland," he had been passing by the Hotel Imperial "on a short business trip through Vienna," when he saw, to his "great surprise, the merchant Walter . . . with (his) girl" coming out of the hotel. Müller suspected that Walter had presented the woman accompanying him as "his wife." Scrupulously, the soldier noted in brackets: "Thus, a false report, I will look into it the next time I am in Vienna." Müller's description developed another aspect of the popular cliché of the hustler in describing him as someone who wasted money on women:

> Walter is half-Jewish and ran away from the military after the decree of the Führer regarding the half-Jews. Now he is once again conducting his business, and has been for more than two years, in the Uhlandstraße. There he earns loads of money, as he is engaged in all sorts of crooked transactions.

Recently, Müller continued, Walter had been in Prague quite often, where he had had "a Jew make many shoes" for a long time, and on top of this brought back "suits, furs, and the like." The owner of the perfume shop, Müller suspected, had to have "a battalion of shoes and clothes at home." The letter writer was even outraged by Walter's alleged consumption of food. Walter had bought food at "high black-market prices," had traded "goods for food," and furthermore had only exchanged goods from his own assortment when he received something he needed in return. Müller also cast suspicion on one of Walter's employees, who was "also half-Jewish and probably working (with Walter)." He called the owner of the business a "person harmful to the nation," who insulted and abused "everyone and everything in the Third Reich," and engaged in "extensive whisper propaganda." It was "extraordinarily bitter" for the fighting men that they had to fight "under unimaginable suffering and affliction for Greater Germany," while the "half-Jews as business owners" made loads of money and, moreover, behaved like "political swine." How could it be "that a half-Jew could be the owner of this business?" The soldiers, Müller charged, hoped "to see a change as soon as possible." He concluded with a summary:

> to conduct fraudulent transactions, to buy food for the highest prices on the black market, in short, to lead a life such as we decent businessmen cannot afford even in

> peacetime, while valuable men are dying for Germany's greatness out on the front once again [is a travesty]. Many of my comrades are already buried in foreign soil and I myself may die today or tomorrow. At least take a close look at this man and see that this half-Jewish vermin, who is an active enemy of the state, cannot have himself a business. Walter has a decent Aryan partner, whom he has probably cheated badly, but who can't do anything about it right now as he has been drafted into the army.[227]

The final police report carried forth the anti-Semitic tone of the denunciation: "Although (Walter) as a Jewish half-breed must have had an excellent business given his partner's absence, he was only interested in earning his money through dirty business transactions."[228]

Such remarks, which took up the National Socialist state doctrine of anti-Semitism, were by no means rare. At the same time, they contained references to another motif commonly applied to hustling: the suspects' conspicuous consumption. Conspicuous consumption was a prominent theme in the case of Erwin Frank and his cohorts. He was interrogated two days before his thirty-third birthday by policemen from Schöneberg. Frank, who had been born in 1911 in Berlin-Lichterfelde, claimed that he was a self-employed businessman and lived in an apartment on Babelsberger Street.[229] This was a good district; Babelsberger Street was not far from the Bavarian Quarter, which had been developed around 1900 by the Berlinische Bodengesellschaft and had become a good residential area. Representatives of the liberal bourgeoisie, above all, doctors, lawyers, intellectuals, and artists, lived in the large apartments—some of them with up to 12 rooms.[230] It seemed that the young man enjoyed it here. He always had some cigarettes for friends and acquaintances who visited him. Frank was, as became clear during the investigation against him, a broker in the Berlin black market. Not only did he have at his disposal as a grocer a widespread network of individual colleagues with whom he could trade, but he also had contact with an office manager of the German Allocation Offices for tobacco products.[231] The exact number of cigarettes he had traded remained unclear—the numbers fluctuated between 15,000 and 50,000. A policeman estimated that the total value of the goods that Frank and the other members of the "wartime black marketeering band" had traded was around three million RM.[232] Lance Corporal Wagner, who was one of Frank's bartering partners, was court-martialed and sentenced to death "because of black marketeering and for bribing a civil servant."[233]

A case such as Erwin Frank's had all of the characteristics of scandalous hustling. As a matter of fact, both the public prosecutors and the police spoke in this case of a "Major Crime against War Economy Regulations" and described the participants as "war profiteers." However, a large portion of those who participated in the Berlin black markets did not correspond to this image of the "splurging hustler, with a hedonistic lifestyle of luxury." Exchanging a few food rationing cards or attempting to barter for some candles for a relative's birthday did not fit these categories. All the same, traders who only traded "for their own needs" could not be sure that they would not be labeled "hustlers." The boundary between reprehensible hustling and lesser offenses was not clear, which made it possible for those in power to determine the patterns of interpretation to describe various wide-ranging cases as examples of "unconscionable hustling."

At the same time, it was easy for the Berlin police, as well as witnesses who informed on their neighbors, to incorporate their impressions about black marketeers into the stereotype of the hustler. In the case of 32-year-old Max Scheffler, who between 1940 and 1942 embezzled numerous barrels of industrial oils and traded them on the black market, what witnesses as well as investigators immediately took notice of were the characteristics that made Scheffler a prototypical hustler. These included his worldliness (Scheffler spoke a number of languages), his red Mercedes convertible, which he regularly drove through Berlin, his love affairs (to make things worse, one of his girlfriends was French), and his extravagant lifestyle (according to a witness, he "lived in style").[234] The car and his love affairs, above all, took up a great deal of space in police records. Meticulously, the investigator noted the dealings of this hustler with his German girlfriend, Lieselotte Stange, who allegedly had become a "victim of Scheffler, who sought pleasure without inhibition" and had become his slave because of his sexual practices. Even though it became necessary to interrogate Stange in the course of a manhunt for Scheffler, who had succeeded in making a getaway in his automobile, the interrogation certainly did not have to extend to the defloration of a young woman.[235] In this, as in the careful investigations into his possession of the automobile, one observes a focus on Scheffler's "typical" hustler characteristics. The police added the key to Scheffler's Mercedes convertible to the police records like a trophy after they had succeeded in arresting Scheffler and confiscating this automobile, with which he had humiliated the police during his escape.

This fixation on the automobile as a key characteristic of hustlers repeated the view of conspicuous automobile consumption that ranged between horror, envy, and fascination. In the "Roaring Twenties," the automobile had become a characteristic of the modern dandy lifestyle.[236] In the minds of many contemporaries, as is evident in the actions of the investigator, young and apparently successful men of Max Scheffler's caliber had role models such as the "gentleman author" Arnolt Bronnen. In the 1920s, Bronnen had invested the unprecedented sum of 12,000 marks in a "fast car" in order to roar like "a tiger in the asphalt jungle" to speed "through the streets of Berlin."[237] Owning and driving an automobile expressed both urban modernity and a Bohemian lifestyle, as well as forming a means of social differentiation.[238] In Thomas Mann's short story "Disorder and Early Sorrow," the only person who owned an automobile was a stockbroker described as follows:

> A pale, tall youth with pearls in his shirt, the son of a dentist; he is nothing less than a stock market speculator and lives . . . like Aladdin with his magic lamp. He has a car, serves champagne to his friends at expensive dinners, and enjoys handing out

presents immensely whenever he can, expensive little presents of gold and mother-of-pearl.[239]

Many observers simply did not understand the modern, "speculative" money economy and especially how it created wealth. For many contemporaries, both the money economy and driving cars—signs of "modern times"—were not just positive but were envied and hated. Alongside a reassessment of existing social and economic patterns of order (such as those between creditor and debtor), the experience of acceleration—such as in the devaluation of the currency in the hyperinflation—generated uncertainty among contemporaries. "The [people doing the] devaluing are driving automobiles and the law is running after them, out of breath," is how in 1923 an observer described the attempts of the legal system to adapt to new formulas of what was just and equitable.[240] All three of them, Mann's stockbroker, the author Bronnen, and the hustler Scheffler, counted among those who had been able to keep up with the signs of disintegration and who had therefore been able to "enrich" themselves. At the same time, they exemplified an individualism that appeared to set itself apart—demonstratively—from the idea of the Volksgemeinschaft. From the perspective of many Volksgenossen, many of these men had come undeservedly to their wealth (and thus to luxury and women) because they did not do any productive work. As a "money man," the speculator embodied "the highest possible degree of individualism and—because his actions were not bound by tradition—of freedom."[241]

Concerning Scheffler's case, those who incriminated him made him out to be a hustler above all because of his conspicuous consumption of luxury goods, travel, and women. Often the second-hand information provided about Scheffler and his activities formed a conglomeration of "traits" that made him appear to be a hustler.[242] For example, the washerwoman Emilie Paul, who got her information from her son-in-law, who himself had worked with the accused, mentioned Scheffler's "hoarding trips" in which he allegedly used secret storage places in his car; she also mentioned a trip with his French girlfriend to France—people talked of 50 liters of cognac, of trades in foreign currencies, and of stashed radios.[243] The son-in-law, in turn, had heard stories of secret smuggling automobile trips from a coworker, of "signals" using a flashlight at night, and of a trip to Paris.[244] Thus, he was not at all surprised to hear that Scheffler was wanted as a "smuggler."

A specific sexualization of the hustler was a core motif of the stereotype, with negative connotations similar to those in the canon of anti-Semitic attributes. Integral parts of this topos that were often repeated were promiscuity, an ability to seduce women, a preference for young and pretty girls, and "perverse" sexual practices. With this, the hustler took his place in a gallery of ancestors of intra-community stereotypes of the enemy constructed through attributions of sexual deviance, which, in part, were projections of desires.[245] The conspicuous consumption practices of the hustler were closely associated with his sexual conquests; in this interpretation, it was easy for him to seduce young and inexperienced women with all sorts of presents he could afford because of his illegal practices, rendering them prostitutes.

A respected source, oft-cited and well-known journalist Ursula von Kardorff, shows that even observers who did not usually adopt the stereotypes of the hustler all too frivolously were not immune to using them. She wrote in her diary on April 12, 1944:

> Recently, in a bar it became clear to me what is to come. Next to us sat a couple, she in a dirty pullover, he in suspenders. They had Advocaat in a large water bottle and offered some to the waiter. As we finished our miserable meal with a pudding with a poisonous color, they were served roast duck, and with this red champagne. These are the types to whom the future belongs. With us, everything is at a tipping point; every day our downfall can come, but these types will be on top in any regime.[246]

It was easy for the concept to be used in this way because, for one thing, it was relatively ambiguous and open. When asked to define the characteristics of a hustler, most observers would have been able to name only some of them. This openness made it possible to attribute certain characteristics on a case-by-case basis: for example, one could describe trades in one's own circle of acquaintances as courtesies while condemning another case unequivocally. Of course, such outraged accusations and suspicions relied upon a set of core hustler features, including typical practices such as conspicuous consumption (of goods that were scarce), smart ("streetwise") appearance, and a certain lack of scruples. Other characteristics referred to outer appearance, such as dressing elegantly. It was no coincidence that the suit was a defining hustler characteristic both for Thomas Mann and the soldier Müller.

The characteristics assigned to the hustler centered above all on the automobile. This was in part because the automobile was a symbol of wealth, but also because it implied mobility. The hustler was always on the move; he was here today and there tomorrow; he traveled abroad or drove with his car through the city. As a result, he appeared to be uncatchable—and at an advantage. Moreover, unlike other Volksgenossen who were tied down to a place or a job, he was in charge of his own time and decided where he was going for himself. The hustler—this comes through repeatedly in contemporary statements—was his own boss and was not responsible to anyone. From the perspective of the observer who was not "free," this was immoral but also attractive.

Interestingly in this context, people who were involved in black marketeering were often accused of being "indolent." Hustlers did not have to work because they could earn their living completely by means of their illegal business. Usually, it was not clear if the hustler first became a hustler and then realized that he was indolent, or if it was the other way around and that particularly indolent persons became hustlers because it fit their temperament.

All of these attributions functioned to make at least the Volksgemeinschaft, if not the hustler, unambiguous by meaningfully including the majority and excluding minorities both discursively and practically. Because people in the wartime society saw themselves exposed to a whole series of massive social shifts and rearranged hierarchies, their need to bring order and clear meanings into increasingly contingent conditions and to find scapegoats for developments increased. This is precisely what made it possible to reassess complex situations and questions according to moral standards that did not allow any gradations but simplified the understanding of wrong behavior by attributing it from the outset to certain groups of people.

CHAPTER 3

Destruction, Disorientation, and New Patterns of Order: Changes in the Black Market Landscape during the Transition from War to Postwar

> The notion of extermination is exemplary in Berlin. In the unerasable city, the impression one gets when looking at the photographs . . . is that the one thing that was not erased in all the bombings—and almost everything was—were the streets: the makings of the streets, the curb, only a few centimeters high.
>
> (Daniel Libeskind, *Radix—Matrix*)[1]

In the last months of the war, the landscape of the Berlin black market changed. Alongside the trading in closed spaces, markets now became visible in the city. They became a new sort of public space. Of course, individual trading partners had already used streets and street corners as trading sites. However, no later than in October 1944, groups of black marketeers became a permanent presence in "focused gatherings."[2] There were a number of reasons for this. Alongside the difficult supply situation, this development was part of a comprehensive crisis of urban life under the mantle of "everyday life in the state of emergency."[3] Agencies whose job it was to uphold public order were increasingly reduced to mere observation. The brutality the government used against "quibblers," plunderers, and deserters was one side of the state exerting its power when it was no longer able to disguise all the signs of disintegration.[4] Among these, increasingly, were the appearance of black marketeers in public spaces and a specific form of consumption. These signs were both contributed to and reflected in the crisis of everyday life in the city.[5]

In the confusion of the last weeks of the war, absurd situations arose. On April 23, 1945, for example, members of the Japanese embassy threw an encoding machine with the name "Hinoki" (life tree) into the Krumme Lanke, a lake not far from Grunewald.[6] They did this as a security measure because enemy forces were advancing, but they need not have wasted their time. The British had already broken the code and had read intercepted telegrams with great interest, hoping to find relevant information on conditions in the city. It was not only German security authorities, such as the SD, but also enemy intelligence services that were interested in the living conditions in Berlin, which fostered the development of alternative infrastructures. London wanted to be well informed about the military strength of the German troops and was also interested in the city's "morale," in everyday life there. On March 15, 1945, decoders distributed the summary of an intercepted message classified as "Top Secret U[urgent]" to the Foreign Office, the military staffs, and MI5. The decoded text was from the ambassador, General Oshima, to his supervisor, the Japanese foreign minister in Tokyo, and informed the Axis Power allied with Germany about the "living conditions in Berlin." This telegram was one of Hinoki's last acts.[7]

The British officials analyzing the long telegram filtered out the information that was important to them about the state of the infrastructure and the nature of everyday life in the capital of the Reich. The report was primarily concerned with the breakdown of public transportation, including subway trains and trams, and with the scarcity of everyday provisions. The almost constant alarms were, as the ambassador expressed it, "certainly annoying." On the whole, the telegram conveyed an image of a city in a crisis, a city with almost no contact to the outside world. Still, analysts reported that the Japanese diplomat still felt

> that in spite of the continued presence in Berlin of large numbers of foreign labourers and Soviet prisoners-of-war labourers there is no evidence of anxiety as to the maintenance of order. Petty thefts of food, liquor, tobacco, etc., continue, but he has not heard of any particular increase in robberies or violent crimes.

Furthermore, the ambassador had noted that "although food 'points' are being limited in various ways, one's rations can still be obtained so that at least a minimum livelihood is assured." The state agencies, the analysts conveyed from the report, still largely had the situation under control.

It is not known what the various British agencies did with this information. They would have been well advised to view the report critically because the ambassador was interested primarily in supplying his officials with gasoline and also had to combat the disloyalty of his subordinates.[8] Oshima no longer really knew what was going on in his embassy. Because he was fixated on the gasoline problem, he reported to Tokyo that "the allowance of 200 litres [of fuel] hitherto assigned to the Embassy has been stopped as from March. Supplies are accordingly being bought on the black market in exchange for coffee, though even such purchases are becoming more and more difficult." What he did not take notice of, however, was that alongside these officially acknowledged efforts to ensure that his vehicles would be able to operate, Berlin's black market had planted itself in the embassy. The building, erected in the 1930s in the embassy district of Tiergarten as a National Socialist prestige object, had become a site for illegal trading.[9] The Berlin police were much better informed about this than the ambassador. As the astonished policemen at the police station in Schöneberg found out on September 5, 1944, the automobile upholsterer Eduard Sternhagen, whom they had interrogated on a different matter, had received both eggs and radios from members of the embassy.[10] It was extremely likely that the 360 eggs Sternhagen had acquired for 700 RM from a chauffeur at the embassy with the name of "Lio or something like that" came from the embassy as well. Such a large number suggested official sources. At best, one could pardon the Japanese ambassador's ignorance as a consequence of not needing to be interested in such "small" offenses. This, however, would be further proof that the criteria used to measure whether public order still existed had shifted enormously.

This shift in standards emerged from the gradual disintegration of normal living conditions, which took a sharp turn for the worse with the heavy air raids on the city. "All signposts of the LTI [Lingua Tertii Imperii, that is, the language of the Third Reich]," Victor Klemperer noted in *The Language of the Third Reich: A Philologist's Notebook*, "either point to or from Stalingrad."[11] With this statement, Klemperer, in his analysis of the Third Reich's language, got to the heart of an experience many contemporaries shared and that historians would later note. After the strategic military defeat in the winter of 1942/43, which was also disastrous from a psychological standpoint, there was a swing in public opinion and signs proliferated, indicating that a growing number of Volksgenossen were losing their confidence and that people were more willing to be critical.[12]

The events of 1943, which began with the defeat at Stalingrad and which marked the turning point of public opinion, when confidence was replaced by skepticism or even by defeatism, also marked a turning point in the lives of many of Berlin's citizens. For various reasons, everyday life was directly affected. Many of the life stories captured in the records on the black markets took a new direction in the course of 1943. Above all, people were forced to become more mobile.[13] Many of those indicted and suspected of participating in the illegal markets were confronted with the same problem: they had been bombed out and had had to move. Such turning points in an individual's life did not always correspond to "historic" dates reflecting developments at the front. It was not 1939 but the air war, which had intensified since November 1943, that confronted many Berliners with the reality of war. There was no space in the war society for a public discussion of the terrible experiences of being bombed. The "collective injury" caused by the bombing could scarcely be articulated if normal life was to go on merely a short time after the raids.[14]

Before the war and, though less so, even in its first year, urban life had been characterized by continuity and routine. Individual actors and the city as a whole used "normal" rhythms in order to survive. Individual "patterns of action," being automated, provided a great deal of relief as they made life easier. The inextricable interrelationship of subconscious body control and everyday activities provided most citizens with a feeling of security under largely unaffected conditions of everyday urban life. Routines made a sort of normalcy possible and could themselves "reproduce continuously both the personality structures of the actors in their everyday activities as well as the social institutions."[15] They provided for body practices that contributed to an individual's experience of security. The body and the "experience of the movement of the body" formed "the center of forms of action and forms of consciousness," and it was the "activities of the body in the flow of action" that were "immediately involved in the ontological security or attitude of 'trust' towards the continuity of the world and of self implicated in the *durée* of day-to-day life."[16] Such experiences were not dangerous until well into the war, as shown by pictures from the first years of the war. Many routines remained "normal," such as trips to the swimming pool, trips through the city, normal working days, et cetera, so that individuals could experience a minimum of security every day.[17] As they did so, city dwellers repeatedly experienced as new the self-evident validity of the everyday world as a guarantee of social order; the practice of everyday routines suggested "normality."[18]

Although the first air raids generated a great deal of fear, most people living in the city, at least those who did not live or work in the districts hit by the bombs, were not directly affected.[19] Still, some observers noticed first signs of the coming disintegration in the course of 1943. Ursula von Kardorff, for example, who worked as a reporter for the *Deutsche Allgemeine Zeitung*, made the following notes on September 25 in her diary:

> In our house there was only a small fire on the roof. . . . In many places there were small phosphorus flakes . . . , which fortunately we could cover with sand. . . . Finally we were overcome with a sort of fatalistic merriment. We looked for something to drink. . . . Then off we went. We came to the Kurfürstendamm. . . . "Around the Memorial Church" other powers than those of the times of pleasure had turned on the lights. . . . The zoo has been hit hard; many animals are assumed to have died and others escaped. It is an eerie feeling that on any street corner a tiger might suddenly appear.[20]

At this point, although this was a terrifying experience, it was also exceptional and somehow exotic and ended well (a tiger at the Memorial Church!). Two days later she reported, "in the newspaper office everything goes on as if nothing happened. Berlin is so large that many colleagues did not even notice the air raids. The Promi [Propaganda Minister Joseph Goebbels] admits that the attacks were by far the worst that any city has ever experienced."[21]

Only half a year later, the perception was completely different. On March 1, 1944, Kardorff wrote, "Today once again everywhere an alarm psychosis, because exactly one year ago, on the 'Air Force Day,' the first heavy air raid against Berlin took place. How harmless that all was back then. One almost looks back with a certain longing."[22] Karl Deutmann, by contrast, had had a dark foreboding during the air raids in the summer of 1943 when he wrote in his diary, "The houses shook and trembled . . . will you continue to live, you sea of houses of Berlin, or will the wings of death spread over you, over a dying city? The people are quiet and the streets are emptier than usual. A large city holds its breath—and waits."[23]

Not all citizens were equally affected by the changes in urban life wrought by the air raids. Although it mattered a great deal whether one lived in the middle of the city or close to large parts of the infrastructure, the dominant feeling was that fate determined whether one was bombed out, so, in principle, it could happen to anyone. A good number suffered this fate more than once. Martha Rebbien had to move three times between 1940 und 1944, twice because of damages caused by air raids. Such forced moves led to major changes; as a rule, it was necessary to set up a new apartment and to determine new supply chains. "My wife and I have just moved again—for the third time," Karl Deutmann noted in his diary in February 1944 and continued,

> Once again I have pounded nails into the wall of the new apartment and sealed off the windows with cardboard. Once again my wife has found a place for our stuff, cleaned everything, made it pretty and cozy, wound up the cuckoo clock, placed flowers on the window sill, and did it all with great care and a positive attitude.... The day before yesterday the owner of the apartment returned.... Therefore, we will be moving again in the next few days—for the fourth time.... I wonder if it will be the last?[24]

Moving not only meant that apartments had to be repaired in a makeshift manner but also brought bureaucratic problems. One had to be allocated a new place to live; new furniture had to be applied for; the government agency responsible for the ration cards had to be visited; new allocations for new address had to be entered on the ration cards. Often, these bureaucratic problems were not so easily solved, as the above example of the returning apartment owner shows. There was thus plenty of incentive to try to get around these difficulties, with "wild" (unofficial) rehousing and relocation quite often the consequence.[25] Moving was a very painful experience for many because they had lost their belongings. It was a precarious experience of mobility, as it meant the disintegration of the space where one felt at home. Furthermore, moving to a new part of the city brought unfamiliarity with the new surroundings. Even if the loss "of the feeling of being at home in one's apartment" did not have to "lead to the breakdown of one's feeling of personal identity," for many it remained a traumatic affair.[26]

On February 1, 1944, Ursula von Kardorff wrote in her diary, after she had gone to Neuhardenberg for a few days to get away from the air raids:

> To be able to sleep undisturbed for four nights; this is a gift today.... Better not to think about all that could still happen.... Our house was hit in the last air raid by a bomb. Nothing is left of it at all. The other seven apartments where we lived in Berlin are no longer standing either. I feel in myself the growth of a wild vitality, mixed with defiance, just the opposite of resignation. Is that what the English hope to achieve with their attacks on the civilian population? One certainly does not get worn down. Everyone is caught up with himself. Is my apartment still standing? Where can I get tiles for the roof, where cardboard for the windows? Where is the best bunker? The catastrophe, which affects Nazis and anti-Nazis equally, welds the people together. Furthermore, after every attack there are cigarettes, real coffee,

> and meat. "Give them bread and they are attached to you," the Grand Inquisitor in Dostoevsky says.[27]

At the beginning of the war, it was primarily the NSDAP that "looked after" the population after air raids. After the first major air raids, coping with the damages was reorganized and became the responsibility of the Commissioners for the Defense of Germany (*Reichsverteidigungskommissare*), which established "Regional Operations Staff" (*Gaueinsatzstäbe*) to "combat heavy damages after air raids." They were increasingly unable to find available substitute apartments, food, and articles of daily use. As the war continued, providing for the population became an ever more urgent problem.[28]

Being bombed out, as well as city-country transfers, even if temporary, undertaken directly because of the war or for a better supply situation, meant that the city experienced more new patterns of movement and dissolution than usual. There were also shifts in everyday practices, in the allocation of the roles between the sexes, and between older and younger citizens. Once the tension of the air raids ended, according to Kardorff,

> among people who had lost nothing, a merriment broke out that could not be held back by anything, and the numerous men who were separated from their wives spent their evenings with less restraint than their wives, who are bored living out in the countryside, would ever suspect. All bonds and attachments have ended; nothing is taken seriously in light of the possibility that one could die today or tomorrow. What indeed will be left standing after this disintegration?[29]

And on one of the evenings at the grand Hotel Adlon, during which she occasionally sought relaxation and recreation, she found her assessment to be correct:

> There it was, the fast life. Lots of men. Only a few elegantly dressed women. Husbands whose families have been evacuated are only all too happy to be comforted in their loneliness. Bad luck for these young women when once again a certain order is reestablished and they are forced to recognize they were only temporary.[30]

The phenomenon of disintegration not only affected fixed spatial and temporal criteria used for orientation but also had an effect on role behavior and social relationships. Previously firm commitments became less important or were at least questioned.

Berlin became a city of chaotic events, only partly adhering to the trade-off and substitute patterns established by the state agencies. One's daily routine adapted to the conditions of the war. Indeed, urban life itself in some sense adapted and found new patterns. This included well-practiced behaviors such as fighting fires and finding cellars and bunkers, as well as the orderly distribution of food at the distribution points. Such state-organized substitute infrastructures remained intact for a surprisingly long time, although they had deficits and were increasingly supplemented and replaced by other non-state infrastructures. The most striking evidence that the authorities were losing their ability to maintain a well-ordered urban life emerged in the program to evacuate some of the city's population.[31] Between the summer of 1943 and the end of the war, around 1.2 million people left the city, leaving behind about 2.8 million. As those remaining were largely oriented toward defense, Berlin took on more the character of a fortress than a city.[32]

The Berlin youth welfare offices saw one cause of the massive disintegration especially during the evacuations. Their reports concentrated particularly on the effects these measures had on children and youths and determined that the evacuations, necessary "as a consequence of the air war," had broken up families, so that many youths—especially young women—lacked a "well-ordered home."[33] Young people were often "left to themselves," "not responsible to anyone for their time or their actions," and so they sought "opportunities that made the world of being grown-up appear to be desirable." There were reports of attempts to misappropriate someone else's property and of the "temptation to take things" many were not able to resist. There was an increase in the number of cases "where after air raids youths described themselves as people who had allegedly suffered damage from the raids, allowed the corresponding certificates and money to be handed out to them, and received all of the benefits of a person who had suffered material damage from the air raid (*Fliegergeschädigter*)." In general, the number of "criminal offenses directly related to the air terror against the civilian population" increased parallel to the "damages caused by the air war." The increase occurred "in all sorts of different cases of children of both sexes (although there were very few cases of little girls) and of young women." Commentators sought to explain these facts with reference to a "playful urge for activity, a certain love of adventure, such as is called forth by the war experiences in young people," and a "desire to explore and investigate the unknown" that enabled youths to do things that would border "on being criminal acts if they were adults and were held responsible for their actions."

Children, reports continued, were ultimately "not aware of how serious what they had done was, as it was part of the events of the war." Although they could distinguish between right and wrong, they were tempted in many cases, as in the saying: "an open door may tempt a saint." In the end, the "possessions of other people . . . simply lying around, unsupervised" were "more tempting than ever"; indeed, they almost "invited" people "to pick them up."[34] The "young people" had grown up quickly "through the war experiences," which exposed them to things "far beyond the realm of normal everyday experiences." "[I]nterventions in family life caused by the war, the adjustments in professional life, the progress of everyday events at work and leisure," especially, made "youths feel again and again the war as an objective fact."[35] Repeatedly, the breakup of the family was seen as the cause. Discussions centered on "insufficient supervision of the children," of the "absence of the father," of the "heavier demands on the mother as a result of her work and the difficulties in running the household," and of the "absence of supervision at school." In their uncontrolled freedom, many youths therefore went on "extended travels of discovery through the bombed out areas of the city" and committed thefts. Often the thefts had a clear motive. "The black market among the children" played "an important role."[36]

The criminality among children and youths slid into the spotlight especially when the public practices of foreign "offenders" were involved. For example, a report from the last days of the war stated that "in the streets and in the train stations . . . in the course of the winter one could repeatedly observe children trying to sell pedestrians colorfully painted toys for bread coupons." These were "children from eastern worker camps" selling "goods . . . made by adults in a form of disguised begging."[37] Overall, it was noted that the "youths who were roaming around" lacked a "strong hand" because of war-generated circumstances. The comprehensive process of existing patterns of disintegrating order extended both to everyday routines and moral standards. The references to the increasing coarseness of children and youths most drastically portrayed this process.[38]

However, such tendencies were by no means limited to youths. Criminality was an "escalating" phenomenon among many groups.[39] In the postwar period, lawyers and sociologists spoke of a "criminality of total ruin."[40] Freiburg public prosecutor Karl Bader, for example, maintained that criminality had "become a lifestyle" and attempted to get to the heart of the issue concerning observed changes in his book on German postwar criminality.[41] In 1927, he stated, a murder in the countryside would have had the population's attention "from near and far . . . for months." In contrast, during wartime, when one heard about such a crime, "one shrugged one's shoulders, and even hideous and repulsive murders, which were still brought to prosecution during the complete breakdown in the last days of the war, almost disappeared in the confusion of everyday life."[42] The number of serious crimes committed in Berlin was not much higher. Of the 11,724 people convicted by the Berlin courts between June 1945 and June 1946, approximately 10,000 were guilty, either directly or indirectly, of economic crimes. These included, above all, theft and offenses against the Verbrauchsregelungsstrafverordnung (Penal Code for Consumer Regulations), of which illegal bartering transactions were examples.[43]

Contemporary descriptions regularly associated such moral upheavals with the visible destruction of the city. The change in the city's outer appearance corresponded to a mental breakdown among many of its citizens. Just as Berlin's buildings lay in ashes and rubble, every individual's state of mind was also affected. The disintegration of well-established systems of order caused a crisis with a moral dimension. In light of these issues, finding a new orientation was, in one sense, a strictly practical problem, such as, for example, orienting oneself spatially in the increasingly destroyed city. Previously simple movement patterns, such as the everyday trip to work, now became much more difficult. Ursula von Kardorff noted that it "sometimes took her four hours to get to the office" and, once there, there was not much hope of actually working. "It is more for appearances, so that one makes an appearance there."[44] But there was also a new orientation of consciousness. In view of the daily danger, the disorder, and the loss of life, "small offenses" did not seem to matter very much. "Transgressions" such as serious law violations were a common topic of contemporary discourse.

What was one allowed to do in the present conditions, and what not? In the chaos between the war and the postwar period, this question took on profound significance. To what could "marginal ethics," perceived by contemporaries as one of the characteristics of the time, be applied?[45]

Treating the crises of the city and of individuals as parallel events first became possible in the context of the now disjointed spatial relationships.[46] The air raids established the vertical dimension as the most important spatial reference, changing the direction people looked every day to up into the air. They looked because they feared the danger of the bombers in the sky, the area above the rooftops of the city marked off by searchlights, fire, and smoke, the burning roofs themselves, the apartments with their endangered furnishings, and the largely empty and "out-of-order" streets. At the same time, another new direction was looking down into the cellar, the counterpart to looking up because of the attacking airplanes. With the beginning of the heavy air attacks, bunkers and cellars became part of the standard repertoire of everyday spaces in Berlin, turning into a "major feature of everyday life during the war."[47] On January 25, 1944, Kardorff described a typical bunker situation in her diary:

> recently I was . . . in the bunker at the zoo. Spooky. When the flak begins to start, a herd of human animals runs in the dark to the entrances, which are small and much too narrow. Flashlights go on and everyone screams "Lights out!" The people push and prod into the building, and once one is in, one is surprised that it more or less went ok. The walls of the bunker, massive, coarsely hewn stone blocks, have the same impact as the stage setting for the prison scene in *Fidelio*.[48]

Beginning in the winter of 1943/44, everyday life in Berlin increasingly moved underground to the cellars and other protected spaces. Underground life was not primarily in the bunkers because these were not yet completed; the building projects initiated under General Building Inspector Albert Speer were far behind the original planning schedule.[49] Instead, beneath the Berlin apartment houses, a "system of paths and tunnels" had come into being. In them, as in the bunkers, some order was supposed to be maintained, with a clear hierarchy—air-raid shelter wardens and bunker wardens, as well as marshals, in control. But hunkering down in these emergency shelters became ever more torturous. Alongside acute danger, hygiene was insufficient. Accordingly, the mood swung between panic and apathy. Reports from doctors in the bunkers registered "that people who were usually quite proper and neat have become brutish and crude; suddenly, after the loss or the destruction of their possessions they have become cave dwellers." Irritability and violence were often the result.[50]

The crisis of the city manifested itself in its loss of sovereignty over the section between the street and the roof's edge—that is, the part that, in peacetime, was most characteristic. To the degree to which people, when they left the protective spaces, lost the protective roof as a point of orientation, the street as the space in front of the body gained in importance. The air war transformed the closed spaces of the city as well as the public spaces and thus the mode of existence and the mode of movements of survivors. In the "city of ruins," everyday life shrank more than ever to the height of people's bodies and thus to the precarious space of personal encounters.[51] An example that illustrates this reduction of available urban space is that of changes in leisurely strolling through the city. "Strolling" constituted one of the most prominent forms of movement in the city in peacetime.[52] That aimless movement, turned toward the street, the people, and the architecture of a city, which could also always turn effortlessly toward the shop windows and make the transition to urban consumption, expressed an individual pace and conveyed relaxed sovereignty. Those who strolled slowly through the city set themselves apart from the hectic, purposeful streams of movement and allowed themselves simply to enjoy the spectacle of the city. Strolling meant taking one's time, appearing to be uninvolved but really perceiving the whole city as an urban living space. It was a luxury but a democratic one that allowed people to demonstrate their command of this typical urban appropriation. Such movement patterns were only possible because they could take place in a familiar and unthreatened urban environment. Strolling was thus also an act that reaffirmed one's familiarity with one's surroundings, establishing once again secure environments and arrangements, which at best led to only small corrections of what one already knew. The city landscape that one registered as one walked through it was an agglomeration of institutionalized, durable arrangements that were not only reliable but also able to convey certainty.[53]

All this was no longer possible in the landscape of ruins. Strolling along the city streets now only existed in people's memories of the city before the war. Ursula von Kardorff likened the movements of the people she had observed hurrying into the bunkers to a "nervous multitude of ants" and spoke of life in the endangered city as being equivalent to "the lives of termites."[54]

After the war, when the situation was more secure, it once again became possible to stroll through the markets. This was greeted with relief as being able to do so was an essential part of the discourse wherein the markets and their fields of activity registered as signs of peaceful times and of normalization.[55] Kardorff noted on September 20, 1945, "In the evening, I was on the Kurfürstendamm. Pretty girls with ribbons in their hair and purses on their arms stroll between English, American, and French soldiers."[56] However, negative connotations could also resonate in such descriptions. Those who continued to miss their customary urban practices and security-signifying routines terribly saw in this strolling a disproportionally nonchalant behavior that only occupiers and hustlers could—quite literally—afford. To these people, such behavior seemed inappropriate when the city appeared to be a "pile of rubble" and many citizens were worrying about their very survival. The contrast between one's sequence of motions and the "setting," the destroyed city, was particularly stressed in such interpretations. Individuals acting in an old-fashioned manner in a destroyed city drew attention.

In his diary, Karl Deutmann recorded his impressions from numerous walks through the city in the spring and summer of 1945:

> Ride into the city. Berlin has become a pile of dirt and rubble. . . . On all of the streets and squares there are piles of ruins, out of which barricades are built.

> Wherever a better café is still open on the Kurfürstendamm, well-fed women in men's suits flail about on the padded seats; these women have most certainly never moved a finger for the German people. . . . What has become of you, my beautiful, clean, shining Berlin? A violent, invisible wrecking ball has torn down the palaces and churches, universities, theaters, museums, department stores, villas, elegant streets, embassies, travel agencies, sports centers, ministries, train stations, factories, market halls, restaurants, working-class districts and districts of villas—all torn down and all that is left is dust. Ashes and—nothing. That's life. . . . We who have survived will have to be hungry a great deal in the near future and we are going to have to fight bitterly every day of our life. This is spring in Berlin.[57]

What bothered Deutmann, above all, was the "well-fed women flail[ing] about," actions which stood in sharp contrast to the destroyed city. A couple of weeks after the end of the war, on another tour through the city center (via Adalbertstrasse in Kreuzberg, the Michael's Church Bridge and the Alexanderplatz up to Brunnenstrasse), Deutmann focused on his tentative movements through the city, which had replaced a normal walk:

> The streets are, as much as is possible, cleared of rubble, so that the traffic once again can move along, albeit with difficulty. . . . At times one walks on a carpet of dust. Or one walks like a tightrope walker on wobbling, flat slabs of stone that lie on the steel girders of a leaning, destroyed bridge. . . . The city is a pile of rubble with an eerie effect, with haunting shapes of former houses, streets, squares and districts. Russian soldiers move through the city of rubble; car horns beep.[58]

In this chaos, black market meeting places became central reference points in people's perception of the city. "On a street corner," Deutmann added to his above notes,

> there was a wild black market going on. Here one could buy or exchange anything. Depending on the quality, Russian soldiers and officers gave some pounds of butter, meat, tobacco, or money to the Germans for a wristwatch. Suits, shoes, underwear, stockings, shirts, rings, pocket watches, and much more were available.

Deutman had gotten a headache from all the "hustle and bustle" and was relieved when he and his wife once again left Berlin.[59] Only slowly would these negative assessments of the black market be joined by more positive ones. Many observers never changed their attitude vis-à-vis the "hustlers" and their "behavior harmful to the nation." On the contrary, toward the end of the war, with defeat imminent, they responded even more sensitively to the black market as a symptom of disintegration. In the "Reports on the Mood of the Population by the Army Propaganda Division" (Stimmungsberichte der Wehrmachtpropaganda-Aktion), which attempted, in the style of the SD reports, to trace the mood and the attitudes of Berlin's population, illegal trading played a central role.[60] Public trading engendered indignation. To many observers, public trading appeared to herald the coming defeat because it reminded many of the end of the war in

1918. In recorded statements, the disintegration of the existing order, the black market as the symptom of this disintegration, the imminent defeat, and the fear of inflation formed a symbiosis. From this perspective, black market trading was the visible symbol of this process in the image of the city. If illegal trades could take place "in broad daylight" in public squares, unchecked or even in front of the police, then the end was not that far away.

The negative attitude of "everyday Berliners" and of the Nazi leadership came together in this condemnation of hustling. Again, one can see that a significant number of city dwellers agreed, at least in their basic evaluation of the situation, with the National Socialist propaganda slogans.[61] However, the political leadership and the population had rather different reasons for coming to the same conclusion. To be sure, both sides had reason enough to fear the defeat and thus to reject the black market as an (alleged) harbinger of imminent personal misfortune. However, from the perspective of "common men," who did not see themselves as having political responsibility, the looming "doom and destruction" was more significant. To them, the black market symbolized, above all, the disintegration of an existing order, no matter how "abnormal" and "out of joint" this order might have been, as well as increasing uncertainty. The experiences of the inflation era were thus associated not only with military defeat but also with a chaotic period in one's personal life. The full effect of such associations found expression in the popularization of the hustler figure who always profited from this disorder. For these observers, the emergence of hustlers and hustling thus signaled the onset of disorder and at the same time reminded them of their own experiences of deprivation.[62]

The discourse on the black market and the discourse on the looming doom and destruction thus followed and modified familiar patterns of interpretation of the experiences of the end of the war in 1918 and the inflation period.[63] This included the subtext in which in a whole series of expressions linked the illegal hustling activities to treason. The accusation that traders undermined public order was made quite explicitly about foreigners, in particular. Although foreign workers had been stigmatized as special elements who had advanced the black market in the earlier war years as well, now, in the face of imminent defeat and with the "wild vagabonding" of camp residents who had lost their homes to bombing, the reactions became more virulent. There were repeated complaints that this group of people was especially responsible for the flourishing trade in the public squares and restaurants.[64]

Germans who traded were judged differently according to their gender. Observers interpreted illegal trading by German women and girls as especially reprehensible if it had been "conducted with foreigners." In this case, as well, trading with foreign workers had previously been branded as an "evil," yet it now moved into the center of public interest. The members of the Army Propaganda Division noted numerous expressions of outrage thematizing the behavior of German women trading publicly with foreigners in cafés:

> In the bars and cafés in the center of the city . . . but also in the bars and cafés of the so-called better west . . . on Kurfürstendamm—one can see over and over again

> that German women are behaving in a way that is more than offensive. Apparently they think nothing of allowing themselves to be kept by foreigners.... It is especially regrettable that these so-called German women even sell their honor for cigarettes.... The German women and girls who are present are not at all interested in the other Germans there, but rather sit exclusively with the generally well dressed foreigners and then later take these foreigners home with them. At the same time there is also a good deal of bartering going on between the girls and the foreigners, for example, silver rings for meat ration cards.[65]

The talk about "traitorous" German women was a precursor to the discourse on "the speedy capitulation of the German women in May 1945," women who stabbed the Volksgemeinschaft in the back in a particularly shameful way by trading with foreigners. The sexual connotation could not be missed. When "being kept" was spoken of in connection with trading, the accusation of prostitution was in the air. This included the description of what was being bartered, as well, with cigarettes and jewelry regularly being mentioned. The image of "easy" or "fallen" women who gave themselves to foreign men to indulge in excessive patterns of consumption of luxury goods determined these patterns of perception in the Berlin black market discourse. This image picked up on stereotypes from an earlier black market discourse when newspapers, for example, had reported that the cafés of the "well-to-do west" were preferred sites for this business. The city's division into certain types of people in certain spaces that these stereotypes established was adapted and enriched with the new paradigm of foreign and potent men.

What was most scandalous about the bartering of German men, by contrast, was the failure of the masculine forces of law and order. When it was German members of the army or the police doing the bartering, comments were particularly indignant.[66] In this perspective, the participation of German men in uniform illustrated most poignantly that law and order was collapsing and that defeat was that much closer. An SD report from November 1944, for example, stated that the police "in most cases simply looked on without doing anything or even participated in the buying."[67] The discursive construct of the failure of the masculine forces of law and order was the passive corollary to the masculine hustler figure. Whereas hustlers knew how to take advantage of the situation and thus harmed the general public, policemen and members of the military police failed by doing nothing to stop the illegal activity. Consequently, collective failure and individual cleverness were two sides of the same coin. In the same way, talk of "bands of hustlers," that is, coordinated criminal behavior, could still be clearly differentiated from the interests of the community. This questioned the relationship between the individual and the community, between pure egotism and a minimum of collective solidarity. In this way, black market trading became a symbol of defeat and a medium of attributing guilt that incriminated certain segments of the population and made them responsible for the downfall and its expected consequences.

Such conflicts displayed rather different ideas about the morally correct use of city space. Just as new spaces and their uses began to shape and characterize everyday life in the city, old spaces and uses had to be abandoned or repurposed. The streets, as the most important public areas in the city, changed especially rapidly. In 1937 streets and squares had made up about 10 percent of the developed city area.[68] At the end of the war, about 40 percent of the buildings had been destroyed. A large part of this immense pile of rubble blocked the streets.[69] It had already become increasingly difficult to utilize the street system for its main function as an urban network of thoroughfares during the war. Pedestrians had to climb over piles of rubble ever more often; in some places it was impossible to get through. On top of this, the Berlin streets became the background to scenes of vast destruction. One noticed dead bodies in the streets. Deutmann described the effects of an air raid in February 1945:

> In the area around the Spittelmarkt and on Moritzplatz whole streets have disappeared, along with the people; all that is left is the ruins of the houses. On Neuenburgerstrasse, which was near the Halle Gate, a vocational school for girls was hit; hundreds of girls had sought shelter in the cellar. Later the parents stood before the torn up, denuded corpses and did not recognize their daughters anymore.[70]

Looking at Berlin's streets after another air raid, Deutmann remarked, "Anything one can imagine, anything this life requires, is in the streets, strewn with the shells of fire bombs of all different calibers. Pictures, letters, pianos, and mattresses. It was a sad picture on a beautiful summer Sunday."[71]

"You will no longer recognize Berlin," Goebbels had promised Berliners, alluding to the grand reconstruction plans the National Socialists had for the capital. However, the citizens would soon have difficulty finding their way around for another reason. The expanses of rubble made it difficult even for experienced pedestrians to find their way. Street corners, street signs, businesses, stores, metro entrances, and many signposts were gone or no longer visible. "This Berlin!" complained Ursula von Kardorff, "The streets previously so clean have become squalid."[72]

The spatial references of everyday life in the city had quite literally come apart, and the temporal organization had lost its rhythm. The war dramatically disrupted the daily routine of night and day in peacetime, with its relatively stable periods of work and leisure. Ursula von Kardorff wrote on February 11, 1944, "Yesterday the daily alarm. A nervous mass of ants heads quickly to the terrible cellar of the publishing house; between volumes of books in the archives and underneath the water pipes one sits and waits to find out what will happen . . . haggard women and girls, hunched, hobbling men."[73] Indeed, some of the most common motifs in contemporary descriptions of the time were the periods in the bunkers and the end to daily rhythms. "Early this morning there was a huge dark gray cloud of smoke," Deutmann wrote of one such experience,

> then the sun disappeared like a red ball in the dark and was not able to force its way through until midday. Up through the afternoon burned paper and ashes rained

> down on us. After a hard day of duty, which had seen so many tired and weary people, men, women, and children, afraid of another air raid, rushed in droves to the public trains to leave the city.[74]

A couple of months later he wrote, "As we left the bunker the sun had disappeared; the skies were cloudy. Over the whole of the city center there was a huge ocean of thick smoke, fed by innumerable, small and large fires. . . . On this day, in the streets of the city it was night at noon."[75] This time disorder had a particularly negative impact on many Berliners. The irregular phases of being awake and asleep, and living in a state of constant vigilance, perpetually fearing the next attack and thus not sleeping well, affected Berliners' health, leading to exhaustion and sometimes complete breakdowns: "At night one started up out of one's sleep, suspecting that bombs were falling."[76]

The slow but steady disintegration of fixed frameworks of time and space as well as the erosion of norms of behavior had the effect not only of promoting alternative infrastructures, such as public black markets. This disintegration also affected legal everyday trading sites in Berlin, such as municipal market halls. In a heavy air raid during the night of November 22–23, 1943, Martha Rebbien lost her apartment on Swinemünder Strasse.[77] About 200 meters away, Reich Defense Commissioner Joseph Goebbels in his command post "felt that the whole government district was burning." The Wilhelmplatz was almost as "light as day." While Goebbels was describing—with a curious distance, given the destruction around him—this "modern war" as "nothing but a great horror," Central Market Halls I and Ia, likewise not far away, were badly hit.[78] "The shops in the halls burned to the ground," noted the report of the city's finance department, "the roofs, were destroyed most of all, down to the iron frame. The galleries in both market halls were destroyed; the flooring was very badly damaged and as a result is no longer waterproof." Yet interestingly, people adapted immediately to the new situation:

> In spite of this heavy damage the market still functions regularly under the galleries and in the passages. The daily stay in the vending stalls makes especially heavy demands on the proprietors of the stands because at present there is very little difference between this market place and a market out in the open.[79]

Because of the difficulties, the proprietor of one stand asked for a "reduction in rent," which was granted "only until the provisional roofing of the Central Market Halls is installed." The booth rents sank for the short term by a third. Yet the conditions in the market halls remained precarious. A good half year after the end of the war, the fee question remained open. A memorandum from October 23, 1945, of the division of the Berlin municipal authorities responsible for the markets noted that a final "modification of the scale of fees" for the market halls had not been made because one had to see how business would develop.[80]

A familiar site for legal shopping had been partially shut down over night; its outer appearance had come to resemble the street trading. Although no records show that the partially destroyed market halls were turned into black market trading sites, other examples indicate that damaged legal consumer spaces often quickly mutated into sites of illegal trading. The damages seem to have reduced people's inhibitions, transforming what legal infrastructure still existed into illegal trading spaces.[81]

Among the conditions that opened public spaces up to black market trading was the crisis of temporal and spatial everyday routines, of well-established role models and social relationships. The transition from familiar routines to improvising made a "virtue," as was so often described in contemporary sources of adapting to new conditions and transcending the boundaries of previously acceptable behavior.[82] In addition, the worsening supply situation prompted ever more people to participate in the market, which also drove the activity out into the streets. These conditions altered the cost structure of an individual's participation. The expansion of the market activity made it much more difficult for the prosecuting authorities to enforce their sanctions in the phase of disintegration between the looming end of the war and the development of new administrative structures under the Soviet occupation power. The Berlin black markets that gathered in public spaces emerged in this vacuum of state order.

The critical moment came at some point in the last half year of the war. For the moment, there was no going back, especially not only because, after war's end, successfully established meeting points offered some protection from prosecution but also because the new rulers had reduced the punishments for such crimes.[83] According to a public opinion poll conducted by the Institute for Public Opinion Research in Allensbach in 1948, 52 percent of responders in West Germany stated that they had participated in the black market before the currency reform.[84] Given the disreputable illegality of the market, the true number was probably even higher. Even if a good number of these were only occasional, private traders, the numbers alone meant effective criminal prosecution that would deter criminals and win back public space was no longer possible. A system of public trading places was coming into being that quickly spread through the whole city. This new public form of the Berlin black market resulted in part from the chaos, from the disintegration of the legal routines of everyday life. However, similar to the black market trading in networks during the war (which also continued to take place alongside the public markets), the trading in public spaces followed rules. Some of these were adapted from existing conventions; some had to be developed in the new trading practices. The transition from accidentally meeting or from making individual arrangements to meeting to trade in marketplaces with relatively stable hours and alternative market regulations began with the transitional phenomena described here: destruction, disorientation, and new patterns of order. At the end of this process, by the summer of 1945, there were public black markets with their own market regulations that became a permanent part of the city.

CHAPTER 4

Black Markets from the End of the War to the Currency Reform

New Spaces: Public Black Markets

The appearance of Berlin's black markets changed toward the end of the war. The public black markets emerged as the state's control over the city began to erode and a new form of political control had not yet been established. Although illegal bartering transactions continued to take place in apartments, restaurants, and in other open public locations, marketplaces also sprang up at this time, open to the public, where bartering no longer had to be pre-arranged. Henceforth, those who wanted to exchange goods could assume with relative security that they merely had to visit one of the well-known places to meet others interested in exchanging goods. Expanding the areas involved in market activity made business considerably easier. The costs for the participants likewise decreased. Traders who had not previously dared to engage in bartering in the open street and violate city ordinances now found a new situation. The larger the crowd of people meeting publicly to exchange goods became, the lower was the threshold to join in. A self-fulfilling, self-generating process set in that new countermeasures were no longer able to stop, let alone reverse.[1]

Central Locations: The Logic of Distribution

It is not clear what happened to Martha Rebbien after April 10, 1945. Perhaps she built on her old contacts and continued to trade without getting caught by the authorities. Perhaps she stopped her illegal trading. It is more likely, however, that she became a participant in one of the open public meeting locations in Berlin. Her story cannot, in any case, be followed past this point because whatever she did, she did it anonymously. Compared to the network of structures in wartime, anonymity was one of the main characteristics of the new black marketeering. The disappearance of Martha Rebbien is indicative of this shift to relatively anonymous public trading. The more visible the marketplaces became in the city, the easier it was for individual traders to hide in the crowd. Instead of detailed investigations of individual cases, the everyday work of Berlin police concentrated on large-scale raids in which over 1,000 people could easily be arrested at once. These raids did not just occur at the few places captured in the pictures in the historical chronicles of the period. From the summer of 1945, a network of black marketplaces extended over the entire city.

If one looks at the network of bartering sites, two things stand out: above all, the number of marketplaces. Even if one excludes unclear cases—for instance, when the proximity of the markets in question is too close to distinguish between regular and black markets—60 black marketplaces remain. If one counts the swap markets officially set up by the authorities, where it can be assumed that illegal black marketeering regularly occurred, then the grand total of known or registered sites (either in police reports, newspapers, and personal accounts) increases to 75. This surprising number is all the more remarkable in that the unclear cases could make it considerably higher. The second conspicuous characteristic is the discernible regularities. For example, there is a clear distribution of markets along the S-Bahn ring (city-wide, above-ground tram network) that functioned as an outer boundary for broad swaths of Berlin; there are also clusters of markets in Charlottenburg, in the western and eastern inner-city areas, in the area around the swap market on Brunnenstrasse between Wedding and Prenzlauer Berg, as well as at the Silesian Gate.

With these areas of concentration, the system of public black markets adopted patterns established in the early phases of the war, as the majority of black marketeers who had been arrested also lived in these neighborhoods. The most important open public black markets in Berlin were in the center of the city and in Charlottenburg and Wilmersdorf, west of the city center. The Tiergarten, with its large park an impediment to effective raids, functioned as a revolving door between the two core areas,[2] resulting in an east-west axis offering the residents of other Berlin districts a variety of starting points for black market activity. To the north of the center, the black markets of the old Scheuenviertel and Spandau were linked. The Brunnenstrasse (an officially founded swap market positioned further to the north) also developed into an additional important institution of the black market cityscape, both in the swap market itself and in areas adjacent to it. The swap markets on Frankfurter Allee and at the Lichtenberg railway station in the eastern part of the city, likewise, also functioned as sites of black market trading. The area around the Silesian Gate formed the core of the Kreuzberg-Friedrichshain black market scene, which built upon the black market trade in restaurants and bars already established there during the war. As this area (Friedrichshain) was near the eastern harbor and the Upper Tree Bridge, it provided opportunities to exchange greater quantities of goods on ships.

Of course, the distribution of public black markets is also heavily shaped by official sources, so, as we repeatedly saw before, we can expect the surviving records from the prosecuting forces to distort it. Yet the question remains of whether this picture strictly reflects police report patterns or if there were not other reasons for this pattern. The open public black markets in Berlin arose spontaneously. However, their positioning within the city was anything but random or spontaneous. Rather, it followed a developmental logic that factored in several conditions. The large trading centers fulfilled exactly the function described in the theory of "central spaces" as distribution points for specific trade segments at these locations. Karl Deutmann described the traders and their assortments of goods with the following words:

> [We] visited the "black market" at the Brandenburg Gate. Here American and Russian soldiers buy and sell everything from watches, clocks, items of clothing, rings, jewels, boots, binoculars, cameras, razor blades, and fur coats to stockings and women's silk underwear. Many Americans and Englishmen buy only watches, clocks, and jewelry. The Russians, however, buy clothing for their women and give, in return, beyond what they pay for the product, food such as butter, sausage, bacon, sugar, or bread.[3]

Other sources confirm Deutmann's assessment of the assortment of goods and traders in the central markets. One female contemporary, for example, described the route to the black market at the Reichstag as follows:

> [I went] on this day straight through the Tiergarten and came out near the Reichstag. I had to go through thousands and thousands of people; the black market was in full swing. Many Russian soldiers had butter, bacon, sugar, and other delicious things we hardly recognized anymore. Starving, desperate people brought their last precious jewelry and exchanged it for something to eat.[4]

As central places, the trading sites now formed the allocation nodes of a new, alternative infrastructure where goods that had some value were traded for goods that met daily needs. They were spaces where the mostly German suppliers could sell their valuables to Allied soldiers while these same valuables had been on offer for the German buyers in the city's shopping venues before and for some time even during the war. The concept stayed the same; only the direction of the transfer of goods had changed.

This points to distribution being a fundamental criterion for economic agglomeration. Economic geography and urban studies have developed nuanced but different models for describing this phenomenon. In urban studies, for example, Michael Porter applied the concept of evolutionary processes to investigating the competitive advantages of cities and regions.[5] The aim of his analysis was to recognize and formulate the guiding mechanisms whereby cities and regions—similar to neoclassical agents—attain competitive economic advantages. Economic geographers, on the other hand, point to the geographic and economic historical differences of competing regional and urban locations. Cities, in particular, function as spaces with historically developed features that define them as economic entities and guarantee them a niche in national and regional reference systems. When studying economic entities such as marketplaces and their spatial distribution, one simply cannot ignore specific local rules and regulations, mores, and traditions.[6]

A good example that illustrates the mutual influence of various factors in the development of a black market in Berlin is the history of a smaller exchange area not far from the Silesian Gate in Kreuzberg. A report by a Kreuzberg citizen describes its beginnings:

> My company's first big building project, an apartment complex on the corner of Cuvrystrasse and Schlesische Strasse, was owned by the gastronome F., who owned a big establishment on the corner, formerly known as the "Hackepeter." He had shrewdly recognized the times and set up a huge lunch table and buffet.... A black marketplace had developed in front of this restaurant, where food and grocery items along with ration cards were exchanged and traded; the cigarette trade played a big role as well. All around the Silesian Gate, similar to the situation on Bernauer Strasse, the black marketplace grew and grew... Many businessmen used this opportunity and settled on Schlesische Strasse, as [they did] on Bernauer Straße, building huge stores. The black market was especially attractive to the citizens from East Berlin, who came via the Upper Tree Bridge and thus significantly expanded the circle of customers.[7]

These observations indicate the complex interaction of factors in the development and establishment of black marketplaces. In addition to the macro-conditions, infrastructure played a decisive role. Indeed, the establishment of black markets often entailed transforming meeting places already well known as legal consumer spaces. Not by chance did the distribution of illegal trade locations throughout the city follow the pattern of development of pre- and postwar legal consumer spaces.

In the Kreuzberg example, the hotel and restaurant businesses were an attractive starting point as they allowed for a critical mass of agents to easily interact in and around the building. Whereas other cases might have led to illegal trading in the store, the social hustle and bustle of this city street corner presented an opportunity for public meeting and trading. Furthermore, the restaurant was favorably situated vis-à-vis the public transportation system. It could be easily reached by commuters from Friedrichshain and Treptow and also benefited from the long-term bottleneck at the Upper Tree Bridge arising from the lack of passable bridges nearby.[8] A final factor was the area's reputation as a center for black marketeering developed during the war. Those interested in bartering knew this area as "Kreuzberg 36" and already recognized the restaurants as consumer space. Therefore, they did not have to change their daily routes through the city to visit the area. The neighborhood was already established as a center of black market activity, and it merely changed its outer form by adding a trading site. Thus, along with the infrastructure conditions, local traditions of consumption such as black marketeering centers already developed during the war played a decisive role in the development of public black markets.

Site history affected the development of the trading centers in the city center as well. In addition to benefiting from their central location, the marketplaces at the Reichstag, Tiergarten, the Brandenburg Gate, Alexanderplatz, Potsdamer Platz, as well as the Zoo train station distinguished themselves from their district marketplaces by their "fame." All these marketplaces had a touristic tradition. Already in the 1920s and 1930s, visitors to the city had taken sightseeing tours of these spots or were more or less forced to deal with them if they formed part of the transportation infrastructure. By around the turn of the century, cities were coming to be identified by their most striking squares and buildings. This sort of identification would continue to influence visitors' images of Berlin. Black markets in the city center conveyed images of exotic and mysterious undertakings. The *Times* of London, for example, regularly reported on the black market activities at Potsdamer Platz, on the shopping boulevard Ku'damm, or in the area between the Brandenburg Gate, the Reichstag, and the Tiergarten.[9] American magazines printed anachronistic-seeming pictures of hustling with German traders and occupying soldiers communicating via hand signals. These images transmitted a picture of postwar Berlin in which the anachronistic conditions stood in stark contrast to the consumer metropolis of yesteryear.[10]

Naturally, it was not only these famous squares that profited from their location in the public transportation system or even from being on the borders between Allied sectors—such as the area between the Reichstag and the Brandenburg Gate. Smaller meeting sites for illegal trading also used existing transportation hubs as a starting point—whether or not the hub was a functioning means of public transportation or simply a footpath. Train stations, regional train stations, and underground stations developed into important centers of black market trading.[11] There were at least two reasons for this. First of all, the stations formed one of the most important points of spatial orientation for Berliners' daily routines. The extension of the railway system and the immense increase in the numbers of commuters made the train and public transportation system major factors in the lives of Berliners. The new infrastructure supplied a useful and effective system of reference Berliners could use to generate "mental maps" of the city.[12] Paths in and through the city could be memorized along the "routes" of the metro lines and the interconnections and could be integrated into a repetitive daily routine. Schematic outlines and maps reorganized and shaped the image that both Berliners and visitors had of the city. As black marketeering was not much different from "business trips," the stations of the public transportation system formed semi-natural passageways and waiting rooms, as well as economically relevant meeting places.

Secondly, metro and train stations functioned as important meeting places so that whoever wanted to could stay awhile and start up a conversation with other people, even though these encounters had a timeframe fixed by arrival and departure. The transitory character of the black market business, created from the dangers of illegality, thus found its complement in the timeframes traditionally ascribed to train stations. Furthermore, train stations and metro stations had served as meeting points before the black market period. Meeting someone at the train station was an integral part of the urban lifestyle, so it was not suspicious. Moreover, some train stations opened certain rooms to the public during the cold winter months of the postwar era, so-called warm rooms where the (provisionally) homeless could find heated shelter. Like almost all infrastructure facilities used by human social groups, these warm rooms were also transformed into trading sites.[13]

Beyond being transportation facilities, many metro stations were also consumer spaces, with small restaurants and shops. Cigarette and newspaper stands and even retail stores had already begun to influence the image of the "train station" in the 1920s into a consumer space. Even where such sites of consumption were not present, the ticket counter still remained as a consumer space that combined the daily experience of shopping with the public transportation system.

Figure 4.1 shows a small black market at the ticket counter of the Schnönhauser Allee train station in Prenzlauer Berg in 1945. As locations tied to the individual movement patterns of the city, facilities such as these public transportation stations brought groups of people together. At the station, the ticket counter formed a meeting point for focused gatherings of everyday life within the station's larger space. Consequently, public transportation facilities were ideal meeting places for exchanging goods.

Next to the black market centers and the traditional weekly marketplaces it was above all the established exchange sites—some of which covered the same ground as those after World War I—that formed the starting points for illegal

Figure 4.1 Black market at the ticket counter of the Schönhauser Allee train station (Prenzlauer Berg)

Source: LAB 1 NK, Nr. 373689, date of photograph: July 12, 1945.

trading. "The black market blossomed after this war just as after the First World War," remembered Heinz Frank, who was 35 when the war ended, "in some cases in the same places."[14] In August 1946 Frank walked to get some tomatoes for himself and his wife. With a map of the city in his head and with the knowledge of the black marketplaces after 1918, he took the shortest route, going to all the major black marketplaces in the center of the city. Apparently, the interaction between "direct experiences and practical necessities" allowed Frank to complete a mental map of the illegal Berlin consumer landscape during these critical times that considerably assisted his orientation in the black market era. His mental map functioned as a "subjective, inner spatial image of a part of his surrounding environs," with which he could mark the illegal markets as important sites that he could visit later.[15]

"I didn't know . . . which black market I would honor with a visit," Frank said, describing his tour through the Berlin black market scene. "In part," he remembered, "public transportation was already up and running, but I decided to walk."[16] Shortly after he left his apartment in Schöneberg and "visited" Potsdamer Platz, he decided "to go to the black market on Münzstrasse."[17] On his way there, he went to Potsdamer Platz and other attractions and also visited the black market squares in the Tiergarten, in front of the Reichstag, at the Brandenburg Gate, and at Alexanderplatz. Arriving on Münzstrasse, he got caught in a police raid after he had bought the tomatoes he wanted for 70 RM. He came home that night without the goods. "However, the next day," he reported, "I went out and visited the black market at the Bülow Arch." His motivation was clear. He "did not want to look for very long."[18] He did not wish to risk another fruitless odyssey across Berlin's inner city, so he decided to take the shorter route (again based on his knowledge of the black market scene from World War I).

Apparently, Heinz Frank had a clear idea of the assortment of goods offered at the various marketplaces as well as where they were. His route enabled him to visit all of the larger marketplaces in the city center, and he seemed to know that the object he was seeking—tomatoes—could be found at the market on Münzstrasse. In other words, he had knowledge of the structure of the distribution of goods in Berlin. The markets around the warehouse district (Scheunenviertel) and in Spandau traded typical end-user products, above all grocery and food items.[19] This exemplifies the overlapping of the assortment of goods between legal and illegal distribution centers because even though illegal trading had disrupted existing structures, certain elements like central locations or products typical of certain spaces remained. They stood in a sometimes longer, sometimes shorter, line of consumer tradition, and they made it easier for people to find their way in the seemingly chaotic system of public black marketplaces (out of which an orderly pattern emerged soon enough).

Insecurity and New Routines: Practices and Techniques in the Black Marketplaces

The consumption practices of Berlin's black markets were spatial practices. Goods and suppliers were sought; goods were offered, tested, and exchanged. In the process, a complex system of spatial rules and regulations arose that allowed the black marketplaces to appear highly organized despite their fragile nature. What appeared to be a chaotic hustle and bustle, in truth, followed rules that ordered diverse patterns of role playing and interaction and body language and rendered conflict-laden, illegal trading a successful, constant, social, and spatial institution in everyday life in postwar Berlin. It is important not to conceive of the marketplace as an amorphous, accumulated heap born out of the necessity of the day. Such a description merely perpetuates the simplistic *Trümmerzeit* discourse that pushed the "black market era" into a diffuse, historical "no man's land." To gain more insight into this time, one should consider how the complex order of the black markets emerged and perhaps improved everyday life.

To better understand the nature and importance of these marketplaces as "focused gatherings," it helps to look at Berlin's legal weekly markets, market halls, and official swap markets. The decisions Berlin's municipal authorities and Allied commanders made concerning consumption formed part of a history of modernizing the municipal markets and their rules and point to postwar normalization, hygienic considerations, and contractual security. Out of the innumerable drafts, variations, and existing market regulations, competing interests managed to carve out a canon of decisions about the marketplaces.

Ideally, according to this canon, the markets were to be spatially and temporally fixed. "Marketplaces and market times" were some of the most important specifications contained in the market regulations.[20] They regulated the exact location and opening and closing times for each market square, as well as the exact quantity of legal goods that could be traded. In addition to prohibitions on certain items, there was a prohibition on "mobile trading activities." Moreover, the canon regulated the arrival and departure routes to the market square, the setting up and taking down of the stands, as well as the fees to be paid. What differed most from the black marketplaces was the limits on trading activities and the official, printed code of market behavior. The former placed the distribution rights of the market stands in the hands of local district administrators in the Berlin municipality, according to which "no one has the right to any certain stand. Nor does any merchant at the market have the right to pass on his market site to another party."[21] The rules for "Maintenance and Appropriate Behavior at the Market," in turn, required market traders to publicize their identity (using a sign with a name and address) and regulated hygienic standards and lighting. Importantly, traders had to comply or pay a penalty.

The organizational forms of the illegal trading activities appear to have developed spontaneously and, therefore, at least implicitly, at times remain unclear. Nonetheless, they generated a space of relative transparency and security. The temporal framework provided an important element of consistency for the public black markets. The large squares at the Brandenburg Gate, the Reichstag, and the other important meeting places were "open" daily, only interrupted by the inevitable police raids. These relatively fixed market times guaranteed traders a stable infrastructure and certain minimum expectations. Unlike trading in networks, it was not necessary to make exhaustive arrangements and appointments. Those interested in trading merely had to visit one of the well-known squares to meet with other traders and acquire new information. The opening and closing times were, of course, determined by extenuating circumstances such as light and climatic conditions. If it was raining, the market at the Alexanderplatz, for example, moved partly to the underground subway station. Generally, the market was outside only during daylight hours.[22]

A different temporal specification of market parameters resulted from seasonal trading activity. Before holidays, especially, market participation increased with many who otherwise abstained frequenting the black market. Occasional, private traders sought Christmas decorations or flowers, for example, so that some illegal trading was a seasonal business. Accordingly, illegal trading for these seasonal items overlapped significantly with the legal Berlin Christmas market.[23] At the same time, illegal trading fluctuated by the day of the week, with Sundays being particularly well attended, as one police report noted.[24]

Potential market participants could be just as certain that they would find bartering partners at one of the larger trading centers as the black market was flexible in reacting to police disturbances. Over time, patterns of movement became routine, enhancing market flexibility. This allowed for a market that had suddenly disappeared to reappear at a different location, or traders would wait until a raid ended and return to trading at the same location after the police had departed.[25]

The temporal framework eased the burden of participating; so, too, did the spatial stability of market activity. The illegal individual trading spaces constituted a spatial inside-outside relationship that structured the markets on the microlevel, much as the stands and spaces were formally defined in the legal markets. Black markets, consisting of at least two participants of traders, formed a mobile, indeterminate, yet identifiable entity. The margins—the most important sign of the market's amorphous character along with the movements within the crowd—spread out and were themselves always moving, thus embodying the "indeterminable," "overflowing," and "steadily growing" nature of illegal trading practices. At the same time, these characteristic pushed the identification of participants and the point of market entry into a gray zone where the precarious crossover from being a moral observer to an immoral participant took place. In contrast to the official swap markets, which one entered at stipulated points after purchasing a ticket, black market trading places were in principle open on all sides.

The outer border of the market was only absolutely clear when the police marked it with a raid ring. For many Berliners, the illegal markets were the first place they came into direct contact with the police when they were encircled by a chain of policemen, loaded onto trucks, and taken to the police station on Dircksenstrasse. Although these actions quickly became peaceful and routine, numerous memoirs give over a good deal of space to describing the raids.

The disturbing experience of being involved in a police raid left a deep impression. The state, present in these raids, expressed itself physically in the formation of these police raid rings, enacting its power to "draw boundaries." Whatever happened to be within the police ring belonged for the moment to that entity. Only in the second step of the investigation did police begin to distinguish between those one could and could not prove guilty of a crime. At this point, the police ring's definition of the market as an anonymous, mass phenomenon was broken down into individual, moral categories of illegal black market traders. Eyewitness reports did not initially address the question of whether their authors actively participated in trading and concentrated instead on the raid as an overpowering experience.

The markets were the product of a communicative action that reconstituted itself from scratch every day. The participants formed a social entity—the market—by physically coming together, perceiving one another, negotiating, gesturing, speaking, and exchanging goods. This market entity functioned, on the one hand, as a phenomenon that participants could anticipate, and, on the other hand, as something that they could constantly form anew, reproduce, and modify by their practices. The public trading sites of the Berlin black market era thus had both a material and procedural component; they were comprised of a specific material infrastructure and interactive processes, and the urban sites made of stone, surrounded by buildings and heaps of rubble or ruins, provided the space for participants' practices. Both together gave birth to the Berlin black market as a social phenomenon and institution of this critical transitional period.

To analyze the history of Berlin's black market from the perspective of the logic of interaction at the microlevel, it is necessary to contextualize this history by looking at the physical condition of the city's inhabitants and their daily experiences. Generally speaking, during the war and the postwar trauma, daily life took on a new quality of physicality. The closeness of death, injury, disease, and hunger pushed the body as a medium of historical experience into focus.[26] Although the danger of being killed by the military slowly subsided as tensions eased in Berlin after the end of the war (although, nevertheless, it never completely went away because of the uncertain situation), the question of procuring one's daily sustenance remained crucial. Not to be forgotten were also the climatic conditions within a city that suffered from an acute housing shortage and lacked sufficient combustibles for winter heating.[27] While black market trading helped some participants overcome the precarious supply situation and thus improve their standard of living, it was, nonetheless, hard work and an imposition to the extent that they had to learn new and unusual rules of interaction and overcome a general situation of uncertainty.

To speak of the black market as a market of closeness is to take the physical experiences that inevitably accompanied illegal trading into consideration. In Berlin's marketplaces, bartering partners met each other in an unusual manner and under exceptional circumstances. Whether participating out of necessity or acting voluntarily, traders nonetheless encountered many strangers, which brought with it difficult processes of differentiation in the establishment of "territories of the self."[28] The illegal marketplace was a site for injuries, feelings of insecurity, discomfort, social uneasiness, and inferiority. The precarious character of Berlin's illegal consumption spaces becomes clearer as one views the varying situations more closely. To begin with, one had to approach a market.

Figure 4.2 Black market in Wedding district (Müllerstrasse)
Source: LAB 1 NK, Schwarzer Markt, Nr. 7862.

The traders approached the site from a certain distance, waited a certain amount of time, gained an overview of the situation, assessed the danger (the presence of soldiers or police), and only after this brief retarding moment did they act. "Small groups of people were standing around everywhere and haggling," was how one person described her first encounter with public trading. "First I looked around to see what was being offered and finally wound up with a group selling clothes to the Russians."[29] Nonetheless, Figure 4.2 shows clearly that experienced black marketeers, for whom trading had become an everyday job, or who felt certain that there was no danger, simply approached various groups without hesitation.

Before participants could assess the market situation and look for goods or for well-known faces, they had to successfully enter the market. This process functioned in what Lynette Lofland, describing the behavior of individuals in public settings, termed an "entry cycle." To navigate one's entrance into the market, one could not simply use customary practices from other well-known public situations like restaurants (such as hanging up one's jacket or making contact with the host), utilizing a code that prescribes each phase of entering a public space.[30] Perhaps the moment of a last body check (such as checking one's hair or one's clothes) also played a role in the entry cycle. Often people got rather dressed up before going to the market square, much as they would dress up before going shopping. Anna Fetting remembered that before she visited the black market at Potsdamer Platz, she put on her "pretty, burgundy red dress . . . My missing husband," she explained, "had always liked this dress on me so much, and that is why I brought it along with me when we fled."[31]

Contemporary summer photographs show most of the participants in fashionable clothing. The men are generally pictured in a shirt and a blazer, and sometimes also a tie, as a rule a hat and—even in summer—an overcoat. The ostentatious display of all sorts of jewelry is also conspicuous. While this

Figure 4.3 Women with jewelry in a black market in Zehlendorf, July 10, 1948
Source: LAB 1NK, Schwarzer Markt, Nr. 998.

seemingly tacky display of jewelry was a part of dressing up, it also represented a way to present goods to be bartered. This type of advertising on the body had already become predominant during the war. Black marketeers announced themselves as trading partners by displaying their rings, watches, and other jewelry, utilizing their bodies as display cases (see Figure 4.3).[32]

Although entering the market space remained difficult for many participants despite such preparations, the fluctuating borders and lack of clarity about internal and external spaces made it a little bit easier. The existing delineations within the market made it easier to look for goods or trading partners yet remained fluid to enhance flexibility. The nature of the situation—be it one of supply, demand, or supply and demand—was decisive for the movement patterns of the participants. Suppliers positioned themselves either by taking a fixed position or by covering a small area by strolling about in it. For example, one participant at the market at Brunnenstrasse described putting her "open suitcase on the ground" and concluding her first transaction before being interrupted by a raid after which she simply "returned to [her] spot" to make some more money.[33]

Such spatial distribution with fixed "spots" functioned at the illegal marketplaces just like they did in their legal counterparts, where one's own body and objects "centrally marked... personal spaces [and] owned territories." Magda Thieß, for example, who found herself set up at the black market despite initial reservations, spoke of her black marketeering " 'colleague' right beside," alluding to a temporary yet stable spatial distribution.[34]

Goffman describes these situations in theoretical terms. They involve "situational territories" distributed on a first-come, first-served basis. This division required the presence of the participant and could be disputed. The "personal space" surrounding the potential seller became a sort of shop space open to potential buyers. At the same time, this space was exposed to "territorial attacks" from potential vendors (especially those selling similar goods). This complex bodily social form of black market organization, which was highly prone to conflict (and had to do without certain regulations like market stand rights), affected the "smallest possible personal space," the body. "Injuries" to the established "territory of the self" (important for one's sense of self) occurred when others got too close, too aggressive with their voices or gesticulations, or violated (via unallowed contact) a person's "shell" (i.e., clothing or body).[35]

In interaction theory, the individual groups of merchants in the marketplaces could be described as so-called F-formation systems.[36] Such interaction clusters come about "whenever two or more people sustain a spatial and orientational relationship in which the space between them is one to which they have equal, direct, and exclusive access."[37] As individuals have control over their own individual "transactional segment" defined by their bodies that they attempt to maintain and defend, the space between two or more persons encountering one another can be described as an "o-space." This describes the spatiality in which the individual transactional segments overlap to form a "joint transactional space." The most important act, trading, takes place in this space. Most interesting for the investigation of these small group clusters or F-formation systems is the observation that they are able to retain their structures when a single participant leaves the formation and is replaced by a new participant or when the remaining group members renegotiate a new "o-space." A behavioral code stands ready to enhance member participation and stabilize the sites of interaction.[38]

As the groups of black marketeers met for the purpose of trading, the groupings formed vis- à-vis or L-forms of organization. This is a sign of "competing pairs" (to be differentiated from "cooperating pairs" or "separately acting pairs"),

Figure 4.4 Groups of merchants in a black market in Berlin (around 1946)
Source: LAB 1NK, Notstände nach 1945, Nr. 252899.

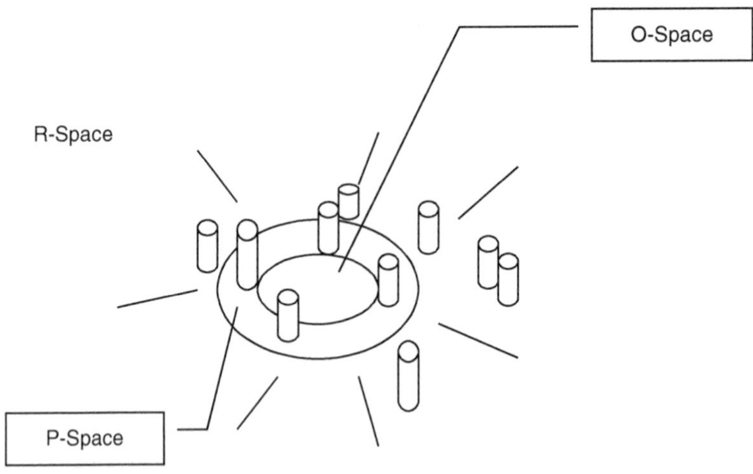

Figure 4.5 Schematic representation of the F-formation system

to whom Geertz's concept of "intimate antagonists" aptly applies. Figure 4.4 exemplifies such F-formation systems. Figure 4.5 is a schematic representation of this organization.

The pictures of the bartering situations show that evaluating partners' goods formed a closed gathering, so that the "o-space" grew smaller.[39] While customers investigated the goods, sellers appeared to be participating in this process in

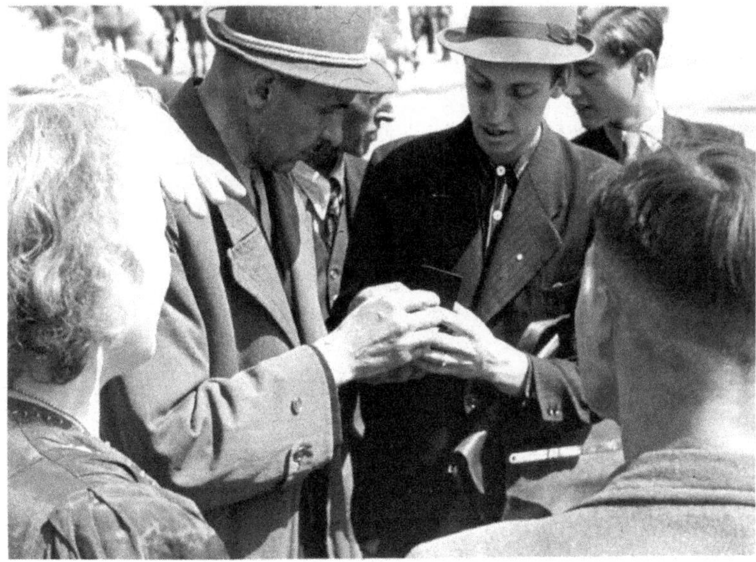

Figure 4.6 Evaluating goods and negotiating in Berlin's black market (around 1946)
Source: LAB 1NK, Versorgung/Schwarzer Markt, Nr. 252901.

reevaluating their own goods. This situation marked the point in time when bodily contact was the closest between black market traders. Potential buyers touched the goods handed to them for examination, turned the goods over and over, perhaps even attempting to smell them, and then eventually handed them back to the sellers before beginning or concluding price negotiations (see Figure 4.6).

In such situations, traders could not avoid touching one another. With bodies screening the investigative moment, small groups formed around the marketplaces; often a participant would join an initial group of two, looking over the shoulder of the bartering partners, pressing them slightly from behind. Naturally, this led to conflicts as the original small "buffer zone" (the "r-space") became smaller and was occasionally "violated." If black marketeers had their goods on their bodies—for example, in the pockets of their overcoats—then the inspection of the goods resulted in relatively intimate contact between buyer and seller.[40]

For many participants, meandering among thousands and thousands of people and withstanding the physical encounters involved in the exchange situation were very problematic. Many black marketeers described these feelings of insecurity, which correspond to a phenomenon that behavioral psychologists refer to as "crowding stress."[41]

This often manifested itself when one approached a small group on the margins of a market. Interested parties wandered about and then approached a single person or a small group around a supplier, as Anna Fetting did. She "had no experience in such things" and was "somewhat queasy and nervous" when she reached the market at Potsdamer Platz. Yet finally, she calmed her nerves. Her description of her experience conveys the general atmosphere:

> I walked towards a young Russian roughly my age and offered him my coat. He didn't want to have the coat, but he was very enthusiastic about my dress and said repeatedly to me, "you take off, I buy, 1000 mark".... Through sign language I made it clear to the Russian that I wanted to give him the dress and that he should wait a bit. I hurried to a set of ruins, always looking behind me to see if the Russian was following me. Wearing only the overcoat, I brought him the dress and received 1000 marks for it.[42]

Traders had to withstand physical contact in the black markets. Feelings of shame and shyness could be a real problem. If intimate contact made traders feel uneasy or distracted, they either had to avoid the market, work to overcome their discomfort, or find someone unbothered by this to act as their proxy. Irmgard Chambula, for example, who found the black market "a lot of fun," traded on behalf of a friend:

> my longtime colleague Ille, too old-fashioned to consider visiting the market, still had some old blouses from her adolescence.... I said to her, bring the things along, perhaps I can get rid of them.... I barely had the blouses displayed on my arm before they were all gone. Ille was very pleased when I... told her everything was sold.[43]

The friend's "old-fashioned" nature suggests an array of possible motives that might have kept people from visiting the black market, from lack of knowledge about the unusual practices and general shyness to fear of a violent attack. Violence could arise from close physical contact or from sexual aggression as the boundary between trading goods and forms of situational prostitution was not always clearly defined; some male participants (as well as many of the public observers) sometimes simply assumed that female participants were prostitutes. To give "a kiss every now and then" for food was common when trading goods.[44] Of course, there were certain areas of concentration for prostitution. Nevertheless, women who were interested only in trading goods usually had to contend with sexual solicitations and harassment as well.

It helped if one could assume a demonstratively laissez-faire attitude. One of the terms most often employed for the movements in the marketplaces was *schlendern* (to "loiter" or "meander"). On the one hand, this term carried positive connotations that helped move the black market experience out of the context of the bunker era into the normalcy of shopping. On the other hand, the term aptly described the gait and attitude of the black market participants, who balanced outward nonchalance with business acumen. Their aim was to engage in trading as well as to signal non-involvement in case of a police raid. Additionally, this "loitering" made it easier for black marketeers to make the rounds and establish contacts, because both sides (seller and buyer) could go slower. This slow approach was necessary to compensate for the lack of clear spatial parameters, such as doors and counters, that one finds in normal stores. The slowness was also necessary because there were no spatial definitions to expedite the search for a particular good. Finally, this type of gait reflected the movement patterns of inner-city shoppers that had been established before the war in large metropolises. In this way, the black market became a sort of "department store on the street."[45]

Over time, participants were able to master these approaches and contact situations and tended to do better the more often they engaged in them. Novices visiting the black market were often lost and scared; they didn't know how to approach a potential bartering partner. As a rule, approaching traders and making contacts followed certain patterns. In some cases, for instance, the seller called out his goods—louder or softer, depending on the level of danger—by listing his available goods. In other cases, a silent presentation of the goods sufficed, although it was important for them to be able to disappear quickly into pockets, bags, or suitcases if necessary. The transience of illegal trading was thus also reflected in the presentation of the goods, as captured in many photographs.

Without a doubt, squalid living conditions essentially forced many participants into trading, so that they could not afford the luxury of exaggerated modesty. Nonetheless, the physical demands of the black market presented them with great challenges. Out of necessity, one paid most attention to outward appearances when inspecting a bartering partner—in contrast to the networking process during the war. These included the partner's clothing, which said something about the trading partner's class, status, fashion sense, and the hygienic condition of the goods. One also looked at the trader's physical features. Old, injured, and weak persons presented less danger in case of conflict. This was important because the only authority participants could fall back on was their physical strength. An overt display of self-confidence (based on the black marketeer's physique) could signal trust, but it could also indicate black market experience, which, when coupled with an ostentatious show of jewelry, could mark him as a "hustler" or "sly fox" and thus as potentially dangerous. The inspection of the partner's appearance was decisive for each black marketeer. This inspection, unlike the situation in most retail shops or in the department stores, applied above all to the potential partner in illegal trading and only secondarily to the goods themselves.

In recent years there has been increased interest in sociological studies on the role of trust in the "performative construction of markets."[46] For illegal Berlin trading, "trust as a sedative in bartering relationships" was of fundamental importance. In order to break down or at least to minimize the high "hurdles for bartering relationships" in the marketplaces, trading partners had to be able to trust one another at least minimally, as trust was the foundation of all interpersonal communicative action.[47] For the most part, it was a performative, self-promoting act on the part of one of the trading partners that signaled credibility to the other. In response, the other trading partner was then motivated to perform the same act.[48] Because the black market had little institutional authority, the success of the market largely depended upon the performative actions of the bartering participants. In contrast to what economic models anticipate, "softer" factors played more of a role than "rational" calculations in traders' decisions. Participants' economic practices were determined by spontaneous judgments, fleeting impressions, and incidental evidence.[49] What the research literature considers special features of "market relationships in modern societies" applies equally to the so-called anachronistic conditions of Berlin's black markets. Precisely these conditions demand "risky performance without always the aid of exact knowledge of the trading partners, without long-standing trade relationships, and are based on only the incomplete observation of trading activity with others in an insecure and lawless situation."[50]

Using play-acting, suppliers were able to signal their trust to buyers and thus put themselves in the position of being able to conjure up the prerequisites for a successful business deal. In a sense, these performances fabricated the successful exchange of trust before the bartering transaction began. The barriers for trading activity were lowered on the one side as the gestures led to a "calming of the trust-giver" and gave the trading situation a definitive frame. These also represented the first move in the trading game, "into which the participants took turns drawing themselves further step by step."[51] Some possible strategies of performative presentation fall under the following categories: binding, congruent expectations, competence, and integration. In the case of the binding strategy, a lengthier trading discussion made it increasingly difficult for the buyer to terminate the discussion, since the principle of reciprocity demanded a response after the seller had invested so much time in trade negotiations. Congruent expectations could be raised by presenting a shared similarity with the potential buyer. Terminating negotiations with trading partners with whom a situational familiarity or trust had been established based on similar lifestyle symbols was much more difficult when one dealt with members of a different social class. In Berlin's illegal black markets, the supplier's investment in signals of competence was an ambivalent issue. Signaling too much familiarity with the peculiarities of the black market could be understood as hustler competence, which raised the partner's fear of deceit. Consequently, signals that testified to the trader's integrity were more important. Sometimes this could be achieved more effectively when one did not show too much familiarity with the etiquette of the black market and, rather, conveyed a certain naivety or insecurity.[52]

In order to be able to apply such methods, one had to participate regularly in the market. Experienced participants used the strategies described, learned from their disappointments, and slowly but surely professionalized *bonafide* black marketeering routines. When one repeatedly traded with the same partners, one fulfilled an economic goal; partners who repeatedly engaged in business transactions with one another also created an opportunity to balance out the advantages or disadvantages of one transaction with the next one.

Furthermore, repetitive trading—with or without the same partner—gave participants the chance to gain experience and thus to gain an edge and improve their position in a volatile market fraught with deceitful practices. Repetition meant learning. Only when one had become a regular trader did one acquire the chance to correct past mistakes and become a serious business partner who knew the ins and outs of illegal trading. Once initiated, participants quickly structured their trading activity. The basic methods of illegal trading (like information gathering) became a part of their everyday routines quite quickly.[53]

However, this space of a relatively stable and thus secure trading routine did not remain undisturbed. Above all, the unrelenting efforts of prosecuting authorities to combat these practices made life difficult for illegal traders.

Power Vacuums and New Black Market Policies

The courts would continue dealing with black market cases long after the currency reform. One example should make this clear: Leo Weissenberg was convicted in March 1943 by the Berlin Special Court as a "person who had committed an offense against the War Economy Regulations," and more than 16 years later, the first criminal division of the Berlin Court of Appeals reopened the case.[54] Early in 1959 the man's daughter submitted an appeal to the Berlin court; she wanted justice. What had he been convicted of? During the war Weissenberg had sold some women's and children's coats as well as several meters of fabric to someone who was indicted with him. Instead of charging textile points for the goods, as required by the "point obligation" regulation introduced in 1942, he had sold them for money. The judges of the Special Court sentenced him to two years and three months. As the ruling of the Berlin Appeals Court tersely recorded, he was "handed over on 16 July 1943 after partially serving his jail sentence . . . to the Gestapo" and then was taken "to a concentration camp" where he "passed away." The daughter, living in London, referred in her appeal to the Law for the Restitution of National Socialist Injustice. Yet she was only slightly and partially successful. The Appeals Court reduced the sentence from two years and three months to one year.

In their decision, the judges argued that the War Economy Regulations on which the Special Court had based its verdict had not been a National Socialist regulation. In their words, the War Economy Regulations served "neither to strengthen National Socialism nor did they aim to establish and implement National Socialist ideas." Rather, they had been issued "in order to protect the vital needs of the population, to ensure the supply of goods, which were no longer available in sufficient quantity as a result of the war." The law therefore had served "the interests of a population in distress." Further, there was no evidence, they maintained, that Weissenberg's status as a Jew had had any discernible impact on the Special Court's verdict, as could be seen from the fact that the person indicted with him, who was not Jewish and who was even a Nazi Party member, had received just as harsh a sentence. Although the Appeals Court was supposed to overturn convictions if the perpetrators had committed crimes to avoid the consequences of racial or other persecution, it ruled that this was not the case in this instance. Although the judges assumed that Weissenberg "had already suffered considerably from the existing persecution at the time of the offense," they refused to acknowledge any evidence that the situation had been extraordinary. Nonetheless, the opinion of the court was entirely self-contradictory. Elsewhere in the decision the Appeals Court stated that "the Special Court [had] taken [Weissenberg's race] into consideration as something to increase . . . the sentence" so that "subjective considerations" had come into it and admitted that the defendant "had been obliged to take special precautions because of his race."

The key argument in the Appeals Court decision was that the War Economy Regulations had not been a Nazi regulation: the "regulations to secure the supply of the population with essential products in times of hardship" had also been "applied in their full severity" after the "removal of the National Socialist regime" and were not repealed in Berlin until July 26, 1949, with the passage of the Economic Offenses Act. Indeed, the court continued, Council Control Law No. 50 of March 20, 1947, had amended and extended the War Economy Regulations, even prescribing "a life sentence" for severe violations. If one looks not only at the legal texts but also at the historical context and the legal practice at the time, it becomes clear that this reasoning was a farce. From a legal perspective, however, it was correct; the continuity of the sentencing framework illustrates the problem of trying to control the black market, which was not specific to any individual system.

On August 22, 1946, in a lecture entitled "Fighting Hustlers and Black Marketeers," broadcast by Sender Berlin, Strucksberg, the president of the Appeals Court, in explaining contemporary "attitudes toward the administration of justice" regarding illegal trading, called this "battle" an "important task" for the justice system.[55] Referring to black market trading as "the present very serious and very difficult situation," he maintained that the system had to take up "the battle against the hustlers relentlessly and ruthlessly and continue until these have been destroyed root and branch." Penalties, he felt, were not high enough to act as a deterrent, so that "from the outset the large hustlers and their associates in the black market merely [incorporate] the costs of potential penalties into their price calculations." The Allied headquarters had explicitly asked for a better deterrent in their order of May 21. The sentences against those who "hustle food and other black market traders," Strucksberg argued, thus had to be "so high that they worked as a deterrent." The "intended atonement" could only be achieved with fines so high "that the criminal not only does not profit, but rather, just the opposite, has to suffer very severe losses . . . which under certain conditions . . . should be expanded to confiscating his property." In order to protect the general public from criminal hustlers, "extenuating circumstances [should] take a backseat to the consideration that absolutely every citizen of Berlin" should receive the "food and other vital articles" he is entitled to by law. Strucksberg's reasoning, in this case, utilized the National Socialist category of harming the community (*Gemeinschaftsschädlichkeit*) under different parameters.

As Strucksberg saw it, continuity was the key to the judiciary's efforts to combat and control the black market. Although he emphasized the independence of the courts, it in no way contradicted their independence to remind "the judges of their duty while administering justice, given the public's extremely difficult fight for food and sustenance . . . to help and always to keep in mind that in all criminal cases . . . utmost severity in punishment and maximum speed in criminal procedure is an imperative." As he explained to the criminal judges at one meeting, the poverty of the Berlin population required punishments of "utmost severity." Working together with the occupying powers, he had done everything necessary to make it possible to speed up the court cases and "to check to see that the sentences were not too mild." Strucksberg concluded that "all those unprincipled elements who especially by stealing, misappropriating, or embezzling farm goods" had unlawfully removed "essential and necessary food and basic goods from a population seriously struggling to survive" should experience "severe punishment." This was the only way that the justice system could noticeably contribute "something essential to the immediate and complete extermination of black market trading."

"Utmost severity" and "complete extermination"—these phrases constituted the logical semantic development of the rigid policy against illegal trading that National Socialists had publicized and practiced. However, since the Allies had occupied the city, the policy, guidelines, and initiatives in the "battle against hustlers" were no longer determined by Germans alone. Rather, the occupying powers now had control. Berlin's situation was especially peculiar, with the representatives of five nations—each with rather different experiences with illegal trading—participating in formulating an anti-black market policy. Prohibition in the USA, shortages in the Soviet planned economy, and rationing in wartime France and Great Britain were their respective points of reference, no doubt making the black market seem familiar.[56] These different experiences were likely the reason that the Allies developed rather different ideas about how one could and should fight the black market. Indeed, the black market policy ultimately became an integral part of the increasing competition between the systems that reflected a bipolar world order in the streets of Berlin and was also fought out there.[57] On the one hand, this resulted from differing understandings of politics, society, and views of mankind. Whereas the Soviet occupiers, shortly after they took the city, began to send the black marketeers they caught directly to work assignments, the Western Allies at first looked on, somewhat baffled, and then decided to follow a criminal justice procedure regulated by prosecuting authorities.[58] The meager results of long negotiations to reach a common position found expression in the so-called Control Council Law No. 50, which took until March 20 to be signature-ready and contained little that was new. Its three articles dealt solely with infringements by government officials who oversaw the administration and implementation of the rationing process, which were to be punished by fines or prison sentences.[59]

The drastic way of dealing with "hustlers" and "black market traders" of the Soviets (and thus the Soviet-controlled Berlin police) soon became routine in the Eastern parts of the city and in the Soviet Occupied Zone. In East Berlin, the court trials against individuals were used to "morally discredit capitalism," with repeated references to the way that black market trading displayed "inconsiderate advantage-taking" of the market reality.[60]

Yet it took a while for this image of the hustler to be consolidated and employed in East-West confrontations. Initially, the Allies simply responded to everyday problems in their measures to combat the black market. At first, and especially because of the chaos of Allied policies, the Allies largely built on National Socialist policies in both the legal foundations, which in some parts changed and in some parts kept Nazi regulations, and in police measures to pursue and prosecute black marketeers.[61] The power vacuum, the legal uncertainty, and the staffing issues associated with establishing a police force free of National Socialists created broad insecurities in how to proceed. Especially in the beginning, this made the job of the Berlin police extremely arduous. A note from September 18, 1945, comparing police surveillance to fighting windmills makes this clear.

A young man who, although only a candidate for the police force, had been appointed head of a price monitoring agency, had shared his lament with the leading department. He "explained that under the given circumstances, especially given the current personnel conditions in his department, proper police work was impossible." For one thing, the price monitoring agency and the Trade and Safety Supervision Service did not have sufficient personnel. He also mentioned a lack of expertise in the area of price laws and material police law. On top of this, what he called the "social classes working against the law in these matters" often proved to be first-class professionals and rather smart characters. All in all, the young police officer described the status quo as a conflict between "an understaffed police force unburdened with specialized knowledge . . . against an extensive, professional, rather knowledgeable circle of lawbreakers in its efforts to create order in what is currently an especially important area for the general public." Under the given circumstances he saw no chance of carrying out his job even somewhat successfully. These well-trained professionals had existed "in sufficient quantities" in the police headquarters before May 1, 1945. To replace these would be very difficult, especially because "for reasons pertaining to staffing policy one should refrain from reemploying former policemen." The note included comments on over 20 individual cases that dramatically exposed the shortcomings of previous police efforts. In concluding, the head of the monitoring agency, clearly overwhelmed, asked that his note not be passed on to trade supervision or to the head of the department "so as not to worsen their morale for further work."[62]

In their helplessness, the authorities also attempted to reign in the black market using the classical tools of the press and information office. In a broadcast address, the head of the Press Office of the Berlin Police Headquarters, Alfred Fritzsche, told Berliners that they should not rely on the police but should themselves become active in the battle against black market trading and protect themselves against illegal business activity.[63] Fritzsche noted that it was "striking how easy some people make it for the bandits" and that newspapers carried stories of "fake policemen" who weaseled their way into searches and confiscations by showing false identification cards every day. In a dramatic warning about the dangers accompanying black market trading, he noted the "dark end" of many "[d]ark dealings with acquaintances active in the black market" and referred to a case from Neukölln where "just recently two men had been robbed and murdered . . . who had engaged in black market trading in their apartment with two people with whom they were not acquainted." Further, he exhorted listeners to ask "people who repeatedly show up in a house . . . without a certain purpose being apparent . . . calmly and respectfully why they are there." Also, he advised that "in light of the days becoming shorter," lamps be put up because "light is the enemy of all dark characters!"

This warning about the dangers of black market trading, however, could be regarded as a topos of futility. "Vigorous steps should be taken to rouse public opinion against the growing black market through propaganda in the press, in films, and on the radio," demanded a report of the British Building Industries Branch in the summer of 1946. "Trade Union Organizations should be used to the full. The United States Authorities should be invited to take similar steps."[64] These repeated appeals largely served to illustrate the authorities' failure to effectively combat the trading.

Of course, such appeals were obviously insufficient in a city filled with public sites for black market trading and hustlers. Accordingly, the authorities pursued a two-track strategy, which carried on National Socialist practices in its repressive elements, even though penalties were less severe than those imposed by the Nazi justice system.[65] In some respects, however, the procedures did break with the practices from before 1945.

First, the authorities insisted, similar to the authorities before 1945, on prosecuting all black market crimes strictly. In their opinion, these crimes were incompatible with the existential interests of society, leaving few mitigating circumstances. Although a zero-tolerance policy might not have been enforceable, the authorities considered it desirable. A second track was new: authorities attempted to control the existing desire to barter and trade by legalizing some of the bartering. One was not allowed to trade objects of value or food in officially recognized and supervised swap markets; one could, however, swap basic commodities. At the same time, criminal prosecution measures were realigned and expanded.

Criminal Prosecution and Symbolic Politics

From August 1945, the Berlin police believed they were once again in a position to fight the black market in a somewhat orderly fashion, principally by means of regular, sometimes daily, police raids in which up to 1,500 people would be arrested. They were taken to the police headquarters on Dircksenstrasse, where a large courtyard, made available by destruction from bombing, provided sufficient space for the large numbers. The goods were taken from the black marketeers, who were registered and in serious cases sometimes brought before a summary court. Most only received a fine. Serious or repeat offenders sometimes received jail terms.[66]

Everyday market activity was only slightly impaired by this. During raids market activity moved elsewhere for a short time, to the next marketplace or to side streets. As soon as the people were taken away, the traders returned, soon joined by those who had been taken away in the raid but who had not been arrested.

The Berlin police's talk of vigorous criminal prosecution referred therefore not so much to their success but rather to their efforts. Accordingly, both the raids and public statements need to be understood above all as symbolic and verbal appeals.[67]

This was true, for example, of what the Deputy Head of the Police and the Head of the Department of Commerce Noack said when in May 1946 he spoke publicly about black market trading. The theme of the event was "Down with the prices—fight price gouging and hustlers." Noack referred to some keywords from headquarters in trying to convince his listeners that the police were successful in their struggle against the street hustlers of Berlin. Immediately after the new German police had been reorganized, he began, they "had started to fight price gouging and hustlers, with all the means at their disposal" and would "continue, with great determination, to root out what is left of the hustling." Wanting to make an impression, he went so far as to claim that the police had succeeded "within the course of a few months" in "eliminating . . . up to 80%" of black market trading.[68] Without explaining how he arrived at this number, Noack praised the smooth cooperation between the Price Monitoring Agency, the Trade and Safety Supervision Service, and the police. Indeed, the newly organized Price Monitoring Agency, which had begun its activities "all of a sudden at the beginning of the month," had registered 1,322 offenses in the preceding 14 days. Over half of these had occurred in the Soviet sector, and the fewest, namely 112, had occurred in the French sector. Those who committed offenses against price laws were handed over to the local or district Trade and Safety Supervision Service. Some were fined or had their trading certificate revoked. A significant number, Noack claimed, were also arraigned before the appropriate courts and, when convicted, sent to jail. Noack described "price profiteering, price gouging, and the black market" as the "worst curse on the economic health of the Berlin population." In his closing remarks he appealed to his listeners: "help in the struggle against hustlers and price gouging, support the police and the Trade and Safety Supervision Service, and insure amongst yourselves that every Berliner acknowledges this cancer and helps the police fight it."[69]

The vice commander of the municipal police, Wagner, said something similar in an interview with the radio station Sender Berlin on August 6, 1946, a large part of which was devoted to police measures against the black market.[70] Emphasizing the success of the measures, which he attributed to the thorough and resolute efforts of the police, he almost appeared to believe that the black market would soon be a thing of the past. After they had discussed the organizational problems of police work, radio reporter Peter-Sven Schlettow asked Wagner to summarize what had been accomplished by "the numerous large raids which have been carried out in the last few days." Wagner replied that black market trading and hustlers had "almost completely disappeared from the streets," and the new "battle" was now to "remove this criminal activity from the bars and restaurants and dark alleys."

The optimistic picture Wagner drew here did not, of course, correspond to the reality that the black market continued to flourish in the city's streets and squares. Furthermore, the police had difficulties because many people did not trust them. This problem went back in part to the discourse on bartering after 1918, which had questioned the legitimacy of the police. And policemen were themselves active as black marketeers. Accordingly, an already suspicious public fell back on well-known discursive strategies, modernizing the old motif of general mistrust in state agencies and their questionable trading practices. This mistrust was directed above all against the police and the Allies, bringing together defensiveness against higher-ups and the experience of humiliation in dealing with the victors. The mode of articulating this mistrust, too, was quite familiar.

When the machinations of official agencies became known, talk quickly turned to scandal. Under the title "Shady Business Transactions of a Police Department Head. Confiscated on the Black Market and—Passed On," *Der Morgen* reported in January 1946 on policemen participating in black market transactions. Two leading officers had been caught attempting give an acquaintance the black market rugs and radios they had confiscated.[71] Alarmed by this report, the police headquarters inquired in the police division mentioned in the article who "had floated" the article and who the department head might be who was also mentioned.[72] Although the journalist portrayed the incident as "sensational," he also claimed that considering "the energy with which our courts are proceeding against these cases of corruption," one could assume that such cases would be "completely cleared up and . . . eliminated once and for all."

This public image that the police and courts presented of themselves was certainly well received by the media. Interestingly, the journalist used this case as a starting point for a few general reflections on the role of the police in the black market. He applied a variation of that well-known distinction between the "big" and the "little man" to the ranks of the police and the prosecutors. Although he had no sympathy for corruption among senior officials, he defended the "lower officials" who might not understand all the details of such matters. To illustrate this difference, he narrated the story of a police candidate: "sadly the boots were far too large for the person who had received them. He therefore decided to swap them and went to the black market—an unusual move for a police candidate! And there he stumbled into a police raid." The story suggests more a lovable fool than someone who had broken the law. And the reporter praised the decision of the summary court, which found the candidate not guilty.[73]

But was this popular differentiation between "ordinary folk" and "great scoundrels," because it matched the self-perception of most of market participants, not responsible for diminishing the success of the criminal prosecution? Did legalization not offer better chances for removing the fertile ground for illegal trade?

Legalization and Initial Confrontations

Criminal prosecution was the first element in the authorities' two-pronged strategy in their battle against "hustlers" and the black market; the second was to legalize trading by setting up legal swap markets. These had a clear set of rules and were tightly regulated and controlled by the police.

The first "Market Regulations for Swap Markets," published by order of the Allied Forces Headquarters, came into effect already in October 1945. It stated that "only the direct exchanges of used goods from private ownership" was permitted at swap markets, "during which one item was exchanged for another." Money was only "permitted in this regard" as was necessary to "make up for the difference in value between the traded items." The value of the items bartered was to "be within 75% of the price for similar new articles in 1939 (cut-off date August 30, 1939)." Furthermore, "food, drinks, and tobacco of all sorts as well as precious metals (were) banned." "Commercial trading" and "trading new goods" were strictly prohibited. The remaining conditions were intended to keep markets operating smoothly; they set forth the well-known parameters of a market with governmental oversight such as market hours and rules of behavior. Ultimately, access to the market was supposed to be regulated through entry tickets costing one Reichsmark.[74] However, the very first experiences with this legalization tool would prove sobering.

On August 30, 1945, in one of the first broadcasts of the new radio station, Sender Berlin, in which "hustlers" had been accused of being "parasitic" elements, the announcer referred to new, "effective measures" the municipal authorities had taken "to meet the very human need to trade goods."[75] "[A]n official, public swap market" was to be held on the grounds of the "private weekly market" on Brunnenstrasse from September 4. Every Tuesday and Friday between 9 A.M. and 5 P.M., every "civilian [would be able to] either sell or exchange used goods, with the exception of food and alcohol, gold and silver, and other precious metals." This arrangement was to prevent "goods being withdrawn from effective public control."

Many Berliners were well acquainted with the deficiencies of these measures. A report by the Berlin station, which described in detail the swap market on Brunnenstraße, spelled out the problems with these efforts to legalize the trading of used goods as indicated in "numerous letters" by listeners complaining about market "conditions." One of the letters was from Ludwig Oberreuter from Neukölln, who expressed his disappointment that the legal swap market seemed to be more of a black market: "When one demands 800 to 1000 marks for second-hand shoes, or 4000 marks for second-hand suits, or 200 marks for stockings, these are not healthy and sound conditions. We are not helped by this."[76]

The complaints did little to change things. Attempts to exclude certain categories of goods and to establish a framework for prices linked to prewar levels did not reflect the realities of the relationship between supply and demand like the black markets did. That the swap markets did not bring what the Allied agencies and the Berlin police had hoped for was one thing; it was quite a different matter that they even bolstered the black markets because they provided ideal opportunities for illegal traders to make contacts. It was impossible for market supervisors to determine whether bartering transactions adhered to market regulations, so this instrument to fight the black markets actually engendered a new black market infrastructure.

In the middle of 1947, although the Allied Command had closed six of the swap markets because they were so chaotic, Friedrichshain and Mitte remained black market trading centers. As the police inspectorate of Lichtenberg recorded in June 1948, the black market moved into the gaps these closings generated—"if only to a smaller extent." This was not at all surprising as the markets usually were close to main transport hubs or were centrally located. According to the police, large crowds made it easier for black marketeers "to disappear quickly into the broad mass of people."[77]

In the part of the city that would become East Berlin, HO shops (Handelsorganisationsläden, shops regulated by the state trade authority) constituted the second attempt to legalize trading and also ultimately failed. The shops were soon considered "little islands of the West in the East," where rationed goods were freely available although vastly overpriced, at least in the beginning. In truth, the HO shops simply set up a second system for shopping alongside the rationed economy. By means of expensive products, this system was supposed to prevent illegal trading and to absorb purchasing power. In the end, the HO shops were used to close the gap between financially strong market participants, who could afford to buy goods at black market prices, and all others, who simply did not have the money or the means to buy such goods. This system was thus diametrically opposed to the ideals of equality and justice of the East German ruling party, the Socialist Unity Party (Sozialistische Einheitspartei, SED). In the long run, this distribution system especially hurt those with a lower income who could not afford to go to the HO shops, not least because it removed high-quality products from "normal" distribution paths. Consequently, the HO system came to symbolize the regime's failure to develop a successful policy for supplying the population; it demarcated a new social division.[78]

Over time, the different economic and political concepts in the West and East to combat and control the black market came to the fore, rendering single cases less important than questions of principle, in part because the different authorities pursued the cases with different degrees of intensity.[79] For example, the Department for the Municipal Economy and the Soviet-dominated Division IV of the Berlin police agreed to keep official channels short, supposedly to counter black market trading with effective retail businesses. They established the "Commission for Prohibiting Commerce," in which officials of the Criminal Investigation Department and the Trade Inspection Service as well as trade union representatives participated. The commission was "to review . . . all the processes of the Trade Inspection Service and Division K, which (investigated) the criminal offenses of businessmen" to see "if in the interest of the realization of the two-year plan it was necessary to terminate (sic!) immediately the trader who is a self-employed businessman." The district offices were responsible for revoking business licenses. The anti-black market policy was thus adjusted to be in line with the SED campaigns against the private sector. The efforts to combat and control the black market became a welcome excuse and starting point to harass the private sector out of ideological motivation.[80]

The efforts to combat and control the black market became more than merely measures to establish a public order that people trusted so that everyday life could resume. After 1946, they also pertained to negotiating sociopolitical concepts and stable spaces within the context of the Cold War.[81] Against this backdrop, the cases of black marketeering in which the Allies could accuse each other of participating in and promoting black market trading became a political issue unto themselves. Some of these accusations involved individual cases—for example, when individual Allied soldiers were caught trading in the black market. Yet accusations the Allies made against each other that the other side was systematically intervening in the market to hamper their efforts to bring about order were much more explosive.

Conflicts

The public Berlin black markets were sites of conflict and at times violence, even at the level of everyday encounters. In order to avoid violent fights between members of the Allied forces and German participants, the Berlin police generally carried out raids. The military police and the Allied soldiers usually stayed in the background to "cover" their German "colleagues."

All the same, scuffles and brawls often broke out. The situation was especially precarious when German policemen who were supposed to combat illegal trading encountered occupying soldiers. This happened, for example, in April 1946. In a letter to the British headquarters in Charlottenburg, Soviet-appointed Berlin Police Chief Markgraf complained about the "mistreatment of a policeman" by "members of the British Occupying Army." Obviously drunk, the British soldiers had thrown the police officer "to the ground, punching him and kicking him" because he had apparently gotten in their way while carrying out his routine checks.[82] Although such incidents always had to be settled through official channels, the police chief's intervention nonetheless signals that the whole matter had a political dimension. This history of the Berlin police and their role in the division of the city suggests that Markgraf readily built conflicts such as this one into his confrontational strategy.[83] There is no record of any British response.

There is a record, however, of a much more significant story that took place on the next higher level documenting the systematic involvement of Soviet institutions in the Berlin black market. Starting in 1946, a number of Soviet companies in the Soviet Occupation Zone—in part local branches of firms headquartered in Moscow—were involved in domestic and foreign trading. These firms distributed goods and exported to the countries of the Soviet bloc and the West. "Rasno Export," the best known of these, was soon notorious among Berliners for supposedly taking advantage of the needy by buying up valuables and paying with cigarettes at black market prices. British Agencies described "Rasno" correctly when they wrote:

> The Rasno agency is directly responsible to the Ministry of Foreign Trade of the USSR in Moscow. . . . Rasno maintains headquarters in Berlin [and] has the apparent purpose of earning dollars and other effective international means of payment. It is responsible for exports of German merchandise and valuables to foreign countries; and many of its transactions affect the German black market in a direct or indirect manner.[84]

In November 1947, the British Economics Division of the Trade and Commerce Branch in Berlin compiled the results of a comprehensive investigation into Rasno's system of trade.[85] The investigators drew up the distribution system in graphic form so that their superiors could get a better overview (Figure 4.7).

The complex distribution system consisted of various groups that sold tobacco goods at black market prices, thereby injecting the goods into the Berlin market, paid with valuables or in foreign currencies. The British authorities classified the effect of this large business venture overseen by the Soviets as rather explosive: "There can be no doubt that Rasno has been channeling a sizeable volume of

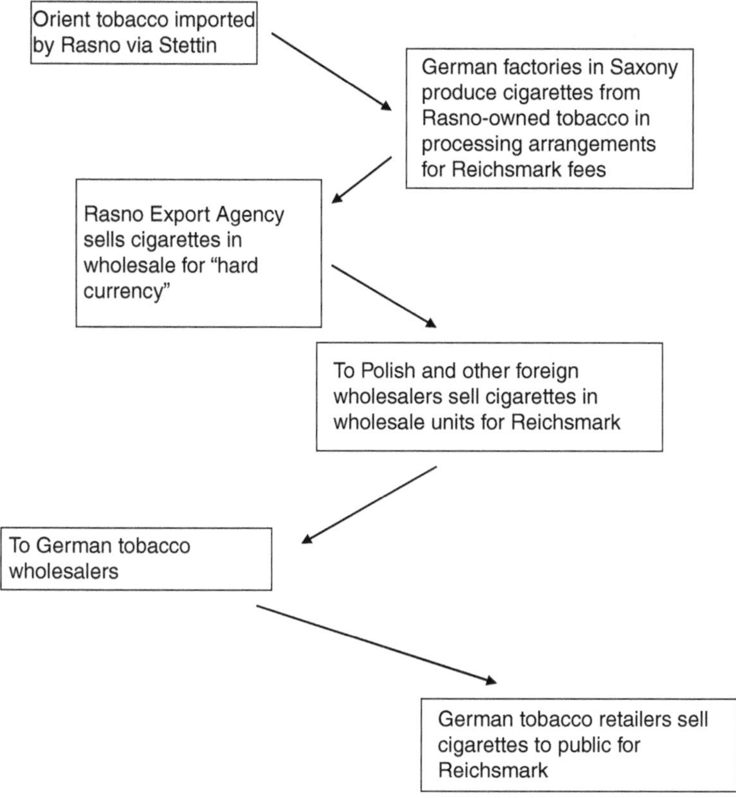

Figure 4.7 Distribution system for Rasno cigarettes

goods into the black market, although the agency does not seem to appear to be a direct seller of Marks." What especially upset the Trade and Commerce Branch was the fact that "the size of the Rasno supply of cigarettes and other goods and the official protection granted to their distribution have given the black market a status that makes prosecuting black market trading difficult." The British observers pointed to the acquittal of some black marketeers in the Soviet sector. The judge had written of his grounds:

> In almost all public squares of the city . . . food, drink, and clothing are being sold openly at black market prices. This occurs with the knowledge . . . of the competent German and Allied authorities, who clearly tolerate it. It would be a parody if the market ordinance of the Berlin Magistrate were invoked to punish persons who are compelled by the conditions of the time to sell necessities of life, at a time when black market trading is flourishing in the city, and tolerated by the authorities.[86]

The example of the Rasno company made it clear to the British agencies that it would not be easy to combat and control the black market. The illegal market was not an enclosed entity in a clearly defined space. In this respect, the findings of the British investigators, who had concentrated above all on exposing "large-scale black marketeering," contradicted in certain ways their understanding of the black market as "organized crime" or rather confirmed it, if one was willing to see the Soviet state as a part of it. Black marketeering in Berlin had not only been embedded for a long time in a network of international trade; it had also become a tool in the political confrontation between the two sides of the Iron Curtain, which would pull postwar Berlin into the center of international attention.

Consequently, efforts to combat and control the black market had not only to address administrative deficiencies and economic policy decisions that, given the chaotic postwar conditions, favored rationing and economic management over liberalizing the market. Rather, these efforts also had to take into account the black market's suitability for political agitation across sector borders.

One Allied measure that differed from the policies of the National Socialists was the selective legalization of trading. Otherwise, elements of continuity prevailed both in the measures themselves and in their impact. In terms of the big picture, neither the Allies nor the National Socialists were ultimately able to control the black market. The structure of black market was flexible and adapted easily to changing conditions and the shifting threat of prosecution; participants assumed the risk of arrest and fines. Even if this may have deterred some who only occasionally traded at Gesundbrunnen or Alexanderplatz, the professional traders regarded this as one of their occupational hazards and incorporated it into their pricing and manner of conducting business.

Thus, on the one hand, there were obvious structural reasons for the Allies' difficulty in developing a coherent and effective anti-black market policy. Foremost among these was the inherited problem of the shortages and their management. But there were other factors as well, including the occupiers' own involvement in the trading. The marshal himself was a black marketeer—this configuration undermined the credibility of those who claimed to be fighting the black market and, along with the mass nature of the hustle and bustle of the marketplace, fostered a certain nonchalance among Berliners in dealing with illegal trading. This nonchalance was, however, always endangered, not only because the trading remained illegal but also because of new arrivals to the scene that black market participants would now encounter directly.

New and Old Participants

Russian and American Occupation Soldiers: The Victors as Trading Partners

When American President John F. Kennedy visited West Berlin on June 26, 1963, the people's enthusiasm hardly knew any bounds. The reporter of the *Süddeutsche Zeitung* described the trip to Germany as a "four-day mass rapture." In his study of the Kennedy visit, Andreas Daum has written that the trip was a "pop-cultural, interactive performance, difficult to control." The performance found the right balance between exuberance and compliance, thus illustrating the "degree of political Westernization of West Germany" and the maturation of Federal Republic's democracy.[87] In Daum's view, the Berlin Airlift was another event that positively influenced the relationship between Berliners and the Western superpower. Having begun in the summer of 1948, it marked a "psycho-strategical turning point" and strengthened the "special relationship" between America and Berlin.[88]

Merely 18 years after the war had ended, Berliners in the western part of the city celebrated the visit of the highest-ranking representative of the former enemy, the young American president. Two days after Kennedy's visit, on June 28, the Soviet head of state, Nikita Khrushchev, visited East Berlin. This was, so to speak, the answer to Kennedy's trip, employing a logic of symbolic acts characteristic of Berlin. For the entire Cold War, the city was a site for the struggle between East and West, both real and symbolic. Khrushchev was likewise received with enthusiasm. However, the mobilization of the masses in the East was largely controlled from above.[89] Although the relationship of the population in both German states to their respective Allied power(s) was never without tension, it was especially problematic in the East. This had a history. Berliners welcomed Khrushchev as the representative not only of the former enemy but also of a "race" that had been denounced as "subhuman" not long before. National Socialist propaganda had stirred up and promoted latent antipathies and stereotypes during the war. The National Socialist atrocity propaganda, for example, had described the Soviet Union and the approaching Red Army as barbaric butchers.[90] The accounts of the popular morale from the Wehrmacht propaganda office had regularly registered the population's fear of acts of revenge and noted the "desire . . . that Anglo-Americans reach Berlin before the Soviets."[91] Indeed, the occupying soldiers of the Western armies were somewhat surprised when Berliners greeted them with cheers. Under these circumstances, the official non-fraternization policy could not be enforced.[92] Of course, the positive reception of the Americans also resulted from the experiences Berliners had had with the Russian occupiers immediately after the end of the war. Mass rapes, especially, were etched deeply into the collective memory, and it was often impossible to deal publicly—or even privately in an adequate way—with this past.[93]

The situation had reversed for the defeated Berliners when the Red Army captured the city and the Allies moved in to occupy it. "The only carefree people," noted a reporter of the Berlin *Telegraf* in March 1947, "are the soldiers of the occupying powers." For them, a trip in the Metro was a fun diversion whereas "the former privates . . . are probably thinking back to the time when they were the occupying power," when they were the "carefree and lighthearted" ones.[94] The reporter, thus, pointed out the peculiar situation that the occupiers had become the occupied, that the conquerors had become the conquered. What exactly the *Telegraf* reporter meant by the "carefree and lighthearted" nature of the occupation in Europe remained his secret. At any rate, he regarded the occupiers' life as quite comfortable. Maybe he had some concrete notion of the comforts available to a large part of the occupying regime because the occupation by the German Army had opened a multitude of economic possibilities for soldiers and bureaucrats behind the line.[95] An entire pack of "Eastern hyenas," as business employees and the families of civil servants had been called, had enriched themselves at the expense of the population of the occupied areas. A secret report from 1943 noted that "bartering" had been "the only thing which [had even interested] a large percentage of the clerks working in the Ukraine."[96] Another observer compared the steady spread of "smuggling enterprises" in the Ukraine with "Negro tribes 'trading' glass beads for ivory."[97] In the occupied territories, members of the occupying administration as well as the Wehrmacht, police, and private firms had participated intensely in the illegal trade.[98] The polycratic coexistence of different agencies, the disparity of supply and demand between the rich and the poor in the occupied areas, and the authority of the German occupiers had provided ideal conditions for extensive illegal bartering of food and luxury goods.

But maybe the *Telegraf* reporter was also projecting his observations of the Allied occupation back into war times. Most Berliners experienced the "new masters" and the occupation as humiliating. "Then, to my horror, it became clear to me," wrote one woman, "that we were no longer Germans, that Germany no longer existed, that we had become the underlings of the respective victorious powers, and that every German had become a nothing."[99] That the Allies required trained nurses to report for compulsory labor service was "proof" in her eyes that Germans were no longer regarded as "independent human beings." What had happened to make such a substantial part of the Berlin population respond so positively to the visits of the American president and the Soviet head of state 18 years after the end of the war—even if one takes the politically engineered mobilization in the east into account?

The airlift in the Western section was perhaps the most important symbol of external assistance, one that helped Germans dismantle their mistrust of their former enemy. This spectacular action was, however, only one especially charged symbolic event in a broad contemporary discourse, in which different practices of giving and taking were negotiated. These reflected Germans' understanding of their roles in relation to the occupying powers. This context of meaning became the most important frame of reference for anyone considering the relationship between the victors and the losers. Since the occupation of the city, very different experiences and very different interpretations of these experiences existed side by side: on the one hand, there were rapes, thefts, plundering, and other forms of taking possession, and, on the other, there were experiences of being supplied food and presents; there were communal celebrations, and love relationships. As situations in which services and goods were traded, the bartering transactions in the Berlin black markets between Allied personnel and Germans lay somewhere between these two poles. Due to this, they were especially important both in the everyday experiences of the time as well as in the memories of the contemporaries. Whenever German observers spoke about black market trading with the occupying powers, they were simultaneously thematizing power relationships and experiences of power and powerlessness. The judgments of the new rulers fluctuated between thankfulness and reproach, between relief and horror.

The economic potency of the victors was immediately apparent to Berliners in postwar daily life. Although the victors did not exchange ivory for glass beads, their prosperity compared to Germans' dire need made unfair exchange a very important factor in many contemporary descriptions of black marketeering. The reports of German bartering partners who had had to exchange valuable goods for food articulated their sense of their partners having too many advantages: in contrast to the "primitives," to whom the "glass beads" had meant something, they saw simply that their exchange rates were unfavorable.

The peculiarity of trading between German participants and "foreign" soldiers becomes clear when one considers the initial situation. The precondition for trading was that "the weapons were silent." Independent of the conflicts that would later arise between the black marketeers on both sides, contemporaries viewed the bartering situation always also as the beginning of a new phase: the quiet after the battle and the newly acquired peace—irrespective of how insecure it might still have been.[100]

If, up to the last days of the war, many city-dwelling civilians had more or less perpetually had to take cover, they afterward found it safe to move about in a much larger area of the city, even though restrictions remained in place. Of course, many dangers persisted, such as curfews and controls and assaults by the "victors," so that they still could not use the full space of the city worry-free everywhere as in peacetime. It took some time for the severe trauma caused by the war to subside.[101] All the same, there were no more bombs falling and only sporadic shooting. In these circumstances, civilians still only went out into the streets when absolutely necessary, such as to stand in line for water, but it was also safer than before. In many respects, one can say that the city dwellers gradually began to reappropriate the urban space. Scenes in public space figure most prominently in the memories of contemporaries, suggesting that everyday life was getting back to normal; this meant primarily that the "inexorability of death in battle" as "the central primary experience, which all survivors had had" was receding into the background.[102]

Gertrud Heidelberg kept a very detailed, nearly daily diary, which captured the changes in everyday life from April 21 to July 28, 1945. Descriptions of the different spaces, which reflect the shifting possibilities of using them, appear in almost all her entries.[103] For Heidelberg, the cellar was synonymous with the "state of siege." In contrast, the street—the site of shootings and sexual assaults by soldiers—became the space that first signaled a fragile normalization. On May 8, she had written that "one doesn't want to go outside, the streets and the houses look so terrible," but this picture changed considerably in the following days. Clearing rubble, running errands, and meeting acquaintances took place in the streets. After the former retreat into the cellar, she perceived the first steps into public space as an idyll, even if a grotesque one: "everywhere these ugly ruins and in the chaos the blackbird sings its goodnight song." The street remained a site of "ugliness," but it also functioned as a space for resuming everyday routines interrupted by the war:

> life is starting once again to be normal. In the morning we go and get water. One attempts to prepare something to eat. From two to five in the afternoon there is street work, from which one becomes tired, and one comes home dirty. One washes up and—above all—rests.

These rhythms created a pattern to be seen and noted, a space between working during the day and relaxing in the evening, the first stages of normalization. The image of the blackbird singing its "goodnight song" already suggests this process.

Yet this process did not take place overnight. Rapes by members of the Red Army and other forms of assault caused many men and women to prefer to remain in hiding or to only dare "to go outside" for short periods[104]— at least until the fall of 1945. Only after the number of assaults had decreased considerably could one speak of a somewhat peaceful everyday urban life, even though it did not achieve the normalcy of previous or of later years; murders, abduction, et cetera, occurred fairly regularly up through the late 1940s.[105]

In this context, many observers regarded the public black markets as one of the greatest successes. Although some contemporaries, to be sure, described illegal trading as abnormal or even dangerous, many increasingly described the lively character of the marketplace, its hustle and bustle. Many city dwellers experienced the public black market primarily as a social event.[106] Eyewitness Rosa Baer recorded in her memoirs,

> it was once again a wonderful Sunday and I made my way down to "Unter den Linden". . . . one tried to take shortcuts whenever possible, so on this day I went diagonally across the Tiergarten and came out near the Reichstag. I had to go through thousands and thousands of people, a wonderful black market was thriving. . . . A raid began and I was right in the middle. . . . But it was no use, I was

> loaded onto a truck with many other people. First, we had to wait some hours. And then the most amusing thing happened. Everyone was eating; I just watched them. Noticing this many asked me: "Didn't ya score anything?" No, I said, I am passing through here by chance and still have to head on to "Unter den Linden."[107]

Rosa Baer surely remembered this excursion fondly because her "fellow passengers" then entreated her to help them "destroy" the evidence, that is, to help them eat all sorts of food. Her account depicts the illegal trading more as a social event and less as a truly unsettling and dangerous situation. She was not alone in feeling this way. Irmgard Chambalu, who in 1945 was 34 years old, remembered the black market as "a great pleasure." "Over time it became a sort of sport" to escape the police raids, she said, and one took pleasure in always meeting "someone you knew" and could feel a sense of accomplishment. Another probable factor in her experience of success was that, far from finding it difficult to meet new people face to face, she was able to experience her own individuality in a satisfying way within the crowds.[108] She was soon calling the illegal trading her "beloved black market."[109]

Whether Chambula bartered with occupying soldiers was not recorded. Such trading soon became especially challenging, in that they marked the winners and losers of the "total war" meeting to start up conversations, to negotiate goods and prices, and ultimately to trade.[110] These encounters took place in the context of a system of symbols wherein the distinction between victors and losers was rewritten or updated every day.[111] The Soviet flag on the Reichstag was only the best-known example of a new symbolic order reflecting the relationship between victor and loser—an order that extended far into the household, as well as the symbols and gestures of daily life. Other examples of this comprehensive reordering of signs and symbols of authority included signs in Russian, English, and French, the introduction of Moscow time in Berlin, and distributing hunting licenses for Allied soldiers. The new signs both expressed a change in power relations and helped to bring them about. In the tense quiet after battle, changes in symbols, representing the confusion in the status quo, became very important. Experiencing the defeat psychologically and fearing how the victors would treat them in the future made Berlin citizens especially sensitive to the different signs and customs of the "new masters."[112]

The physical presence and behavior of the Allied soldiers played a very prominent role in this.[113] Initially, Berliners perceived the soldiers as enemy combatants, plunderers, and rapists, but new encounters unfolded over time, for example, private conversations or meetings between citizens and Allied agencies. Of course, in these new situations, the victor-loser relationship was also significant. Depending on the attitude the opposite sides took and the gestures and signs they used, these encounters between Germans and members of the Allied forces could look very different. The victors had the advantage of having the power to take the initiative. The formula for determining the patterns of action and reaction between the parties was defined by the end of the war and shaped the relationships—at the level of the nation-states as well—far beyond the immediate postwar period.

Staging military marches and parades is one of the most important forms of symbolically portraying one's dominance. The entrance of the victorious generals into the defeated city, which stood *pars pro toto* for all of Germany, was part of a long tradition of well-established symbolic signs of authority. Red Army General Zhukov's ride through the ruins, in particular, adapted well-known symbolic patterns—the victory celebration as well as a claim to power—which demonstrated power and consolidated authority and was understood in this way by the citizens of the city.[114]

The right of the victor to carry arms was also a profound sign of the different power positions and thus the different negotiating positions. As combat operations ceased and both victors and losers had their hands literally "free" to check, to count, to pick up goods, to make themselves understood, and to trade, the pistols of the Allied soldiers marked a clear dividing line. The newly recruited German (auxiliary) policemen, deployed in order to fight the black market, soon faced the problem of their authority not being respected in the markets so that they could only stand around helplessly during violent disputes.[115]

German participants and observers paid very close attention to the signs and gestures of the victors while trading. For one thing, the illegal markets offered opportunities to meet the victors "eye to eye." Unlike the demonstrations of might such as one found, for example, in military parades, the losers und victors stood directly across from each other; they talked to each other, negotiated, and traded.

In a letter of August 21, 1946, Gerda Pfundt, who lived in Charlottenburg, came up with her own typology of the new rulers:

> a further feature of postwar Berlin is the Allied soldiers. With only a few exceptions, they don't really bother us. We have become accustomed to them, and we can hardly imagine the streets without them. The English are—as one would expect from their manner—reserved, polite, correct. The Americans, who are always chewing gum, are somewhat noisier, but essentially harmless with a few exceptions, then referred to as "Russians with creased trousers." I know nothing about the French because I haven't had any contact with them; indeed, I have scarcely seen any. One says, however, that they are also peaceful. And the Russians? Well yes—they are Russians. One has to have experienced them. I for one always have wobbly knees and put my watch and my bracelet into my handbag when they cross my path. One never knows.[116]

Bartering with members of the Red Army was considered especially precarious. Encountering the Russian victors was emotionally charged, generally with fear. In 1977, Margot Raedisch recalled a situation that had taken place at the black market in Tiergarten in the fall of 1945 when she was 30. Together with her four-year-old daughter, whom she, as she explains, could not leave alone by herself, and a "friend," whom she classified as more "spirited" than herself, she had made her way to the popular black market in order to get some food.

> On the edge of the Tiergarten there were Russian trucks; their soldiers were watching the scene in the black market. As we passed one such vehicle, a soldier who was no longer quite so young looked at us. Suddenly he ran up behind us and called loudly: "Little Kalinka, little Kalinka, you give me, I give you bacon and bread." While doing this he pointed excitedly at my daughter's doll. He continued yelling as he seemed to believe we had not understood him. That we had, but we did not want to trade the doll. The child had also understood what he wanted from us—distressed, she pressed the doll to her body and started to cry.[117]

After Raedisch had made the soldier understand that the girl did not want to part with the doll, he left them alone:

> He could not believe it and looked sadly at the doll and at my child. But then he stroked my daughter and said: "niet, niet!" He did not want to take it away. We were relieved; what could we have done if he had torn it away from us? His eyes told us that he very badly wanted the doll—certainly for his own child—but he had a good heart. And to recognize this in these times was very reassuring.[118]

Such accounts show the degree of mistrust of the Soviet soldiers that existed in the black markets. What Raedisch and Pfundt expressed openly can be found between the lines in other accounts. Karl Deutmann, for example, recorded a different trading situation in his diary:

> a Russian officer sat in an automobile. He had a knife in his hand, and in front of him there was a container with butter. A translator sat across from him. She handed him the watch so that he could examine it and conveyed to the Germans the number of kilos or the number of pounds of butter or bacon or canned meat. For gold pieces he gave fats; shoes, etc., were paid for in cash. There was, however, no deceit. What was agreed upon was adhered to. A G.P.U. (Soviet intelligence) officer, who suddenly appeared with a car, put an end to this. He was, however, not interested in how the Germans interacted among themselves. Later, after he had taken off, the business happily resumed.[119]

Deutmann's emphasis on the lack of deceit between the Russian officer and the German bartering partner points, first of all, to the basic problem of illegal markets: there was no legal framework. Yet beyond this, his account highlights practices that made the imbalance of power between unequal partners evident and reinforced it. The offering of goods, which Soviets then examined, impressively demonstrates whose market power was greater in such a bartering situation. The image of the individual Allied soldier surrounded by a cluster of German hustlers wanting to trade illustrated the economic power of these "foreigners," who had the scarce goods in demand at their disposal.

Multitudes of people hustlers clustering around one trader—this was a common, everyday scene in the black market. This phenomenon received special attention when, as Deutmann described in his example, Allied soldiers drove up in their cars and remained seated while trading. Already well before the war, as more and more cars came into the city, they had come to symbolize the unequal distribution of power. Since the 1920s, the automobile had played a prominent role in debates about luxury as well as in commentaries on social inequality in Berlin. As early as 1933, Berlin columnist Heinrich Hauser had noted in an article for the monthly, *Die Tat*, that "the difference in Germany between those who are transported in an automobile and those who are forced to walk is profound" and that the different forms of transport marked the "largest class differences."[120] This common picture, which characterized the social contrasts in Berlin according to the economic power of automobile drivers, had been an important part of the discourse on hustlers, as the story of Max Scheffler showed above. This picture was now transferred to the occupying soldiers sitting in automobiles.

In contemporary Germans' accounts, trading from within a car was a recurring theme,[121] which clearly showed the inequality between the "new masters" and the citizens of Berlin. The automobiles of the Allied soldiers also offered very practical advantages for illegal trading: mobility, means of transportation, and speed. The final point could be especially crucial as it enabled drivers to quickly obtain a general idea of the latest price developments in every market and to use them to their own advantage.[122]

On the other hand, German observers viewed cars as symbols of (trading) power. Allied traders' remaining seated symbolized their physical and economic strength, which the defeated regarded as equivalent to the victors parading "on a high horse." In contrast to these "new masters," German market participants as a rule came on foot, wandered down the individual market spots row by row, and afterward often had to make the arduous way home at least partly on foot. A contemporary poem captured this feeling of inferiority that Germans adopted toward the motorized soldiers:

> On the streets the cars whiz by/ fat Russians stretch out/ In the cushions of our carriages
> It seems they mock me/ That one there in front of me is drunk
> Vodka! He roars, all hail/ Oh how low we have sunk
> Poor Germany, are you still alive?/ (. . .) Wish they were all spooky spirits/ Passing me by
> But as I can't deny it/ This is "eastern Berlin."[123]

Yet Germans were wary of all the Allied soldiers, not just the members of the Red Army, which was particularly evident in regard to ongoing debate about German woman trading with Allied soldiers. "All the English correctness, American cheerfulness, and Russian brutishness," recalled one contemporary witness,

> do not prevent Berlin women from hooking up with the Allies. It begins with a Chesterfield or a "Hello, girlie" called out from a jeep and ends in true love and sometimes plans for marriage. The first Berlin girls have been granted permission to marry the English. The marriage announcements were even printed in newspapers. The Americans have not yet been given such permission. In general, there is

> nothing to be said against this activity. Were our soldiers always alone in France, Denmark, etc.? Less delightful is the variety of women who do not leave the meeting to chance but set up in front of their doorways and seize the initiative. Sadly, sadly, this does happen.[124]

In everyday situations "beneath" the level of official demonstrations of strength by the victors as well, Germans experienced the precarious dividing line between the winners and the losers. Although many contemporary accounts displayed an almost seismographic sensitivity to such experiences of inferiority, the accounts that stand out take as their subject the relationship between victors und losers in regard to gender relations. In an article titled "Social Passes—Popular After All: Keeping a Close Eye on the Berliners," the *Telegraf* informed its readers about the different types of German women who—in order to visit American clubs with their American partners—solicited so-called social passes.[125] The article expressly pointed out not only that most of the "girls" were already linked to Americans, but that the women were wearing make-up or "German stockings, knee-length socks" and also that some had already "discolored their German with one of those American accents" so "that it was difficult to understand them." The *Telegraf* described a scene for its readers as follows:

> Eight women had been invited. Three of them were dressed just like Americans . . . . With the others the signs of American resources confined itself to handbags, scarves, and the Camels they were smoking. Waiting made them all a little bit nervous. One girl had taken along her boyfriend, an American civil servant. She had a lavish, well-painted face, a costume trimmed with fur and red nail polish from the "land of boundless opportunity" on her neat fingers. As the waiting took too long for her boyfriend, he spoke a short but likely energetic word with the commission, and immediately it was the young lady's turn.

This article commented on the triangular configuration between German women, American soldiers, and German public opinion wherein humiliated men and disappointed women shaped a negative consensus. One motif for this perspective was the experience of powerlessness vis-à-vis the victors. The victors seemed to "take" the German women, and the inexperienced women appeared to be keen on securing their own advantage and youthful conspicuous consumption. Little was so clearly regarded as an item of outrage and revulsion as the figure of the "Fräulein" who in times of general defeat and hardship appeared to be a winner, standing beside the victors. The conscious knowledge that you belonged to the losers could always be reinforced through such small, daily defeats, in which the American "friend" reached his goal through pressure, and a German Fräulein who knew how to improve her situation through "American resources." But the knowledge could also be formulated or stylized as part of the German myth of being a nation of victims.[126]

That Allied soldiers took advantage of Germans was both a real experience and a part of this German myth. As the interpretations of illegal trading reveal, the image of the American soldiers in the occupation army was ambivalent. On the one hand, Germans (re-)gained a certain sovereignty when they successfully concluded business transactions. On the other hand, the history of the trades between Germans and members of the US Army was also narrated as a history of victimization; and German observers interpreted these soldiers' relationships with German women as manifestations of the victors collecting trophies or conducting raids.

Such victimization narratives reflect the widespread general perception that German society was humiliated and made up of losers in comparison to the victorious powers. This remained a familiar topos and was used to portray the black market as chaotic and as a symbol of social upheavals.

A Market of "Little People": The Black Market and the Social Question

Contemporaries' perceptions were shaped to a large degree by the picture of the German racketeers and the soldiers of the occupying forces participating in markets in the central squares of the city. This does not mean, however, that other circles of participants were forgotten. Just the opposite: the focus on the financially strong trading groups only obtained its significance from the contrasting characterizations that distinguished better market positions from worse ones and thus the powerful from the powerless.[127] When Karl Deutmann drove into the city on August 5, 1945, with his wife, he visited the black market at the Brandenburg Gate. What Deutmann discovered there was that the typology of the groups of participants and the goods they aimed to obtain reflected their different power positions. To be sure, there were clearly also Germans there who wanted to "indulge" themselves or who were looking for goods where the demand was elastic. Yet the vast majority of financially strong market participants were members of the occupying forces. As Deutmann pointed out, the German black marketeers he saw were trading mostly because they were poor. It was in no way the norm that they were seeking "small pleasures." At the same time, Deutmann evoked the future danger associated with trading valuables for such "luxury items": poverty.[128]

At one end of the scale, as contemporaries perceived it, were the financially strong German hustlers and the soldiers of the occupying forces. At the other end, there were the German participants with their impoverished misery. Observers particularly noticed the simple "normal consumers," as well as mothers, disabled persons—often veterans—and the elderly. Hille Ruegenberg recorded in her memoirs of the postwar Berlin period the worries of women who were "breadwinners" for family members:

> No one can rest for long when children, pale-faced, with hollow sockets, instill fear in a mother who is solely responsible for satisfying the hunger of their innocent mouths. . . . Amazing how in times of hardship strong forces are activated, whereas often the satiated are afflicted with phlegm. After the black market had begun, constantly looking, illegally, for additional food, I saw myself as a nervously fluttering

> mother bird, constantly scavenging instinctively for food—pitiful! Emotions, of any sort, were turned off—only cold rationality guaranteed chances of survival.[129]

The social division established when the regime divided the population into specific consumer groups at the beginning of the war was often criticized because it had prompted a "mentality of comparison" among the recipients.[130] This mentality continued after the war ended. After all, the allocation system had set forth a certain framework wherein, however unfair it might have been, one's social status was not linked to a seemingly arbitrary market mechanism, thus allowing every individual a horizontal classification. In contrast, the black market did not know such sociopolitical guidelines. In it, the allocation was a question of the price, one's decision over supply levels, and one's survival was in part purely a product of one's market power. At best, less capable participants could improve their starting position with their individual skill. Overall, however, the free play of market forces privileged those who had things to barter at their disposal, whether from access to goods in demand in their profession or from cash assets and unimpaired households from which single objects could be "converted to cash" on the market.

The black market played an important role in economic life on a whole. In early 1948 the Department of Trade and Industry of the Berlin municipal authorities estimated that a third of all goods traded in the city were traded on the black market.[131] Apart from particular trading segments, like the thriving art and drug segments, food and other commodities in very short supply were traded most often. The supply situation had worsened in the last months of the war. Both the loss of imports from the occupied territories and disruptions to transportation caused by the fighting contributed to this. Of course, immediately after the end of the war the Russian occupiers did everything they could to provide for the Berlin population. They fought the spread of epidemics, cleared the streets of rubble, and supplied the poverty-stricken population from their own military stocks in the beginning. According to Osmar White, an American war reporter, they benefited from the experiences they had had with their own destroyed cities. White came to the conclusion that "the Soviets in those early days did more to keep Berlin alive than the Anglo-Americans possibly could have done."[132] Still, because of the poor harvest in the summer of 1945, the situation worsened quickly. The winter of 1946/47, which became known as the "hunger winter," was the nadir.

Gerda Pfundt had perceived initial signs of the coming catastrophe as early as August 21, 1945, when she described the focus on food among the survivors in Berlin: "food is at present the most important problem, the one that we talk about the most, the problem behind which everything else fades. There is no encounter, no telephone conversation between Berliners in which one does not talk about food."[133] Then, after the catastrophic experiences of the winter, it was clear that they still resonated in June 1947 in the remarks of Berlin's mayor Louise Schroeder at the Minister Presidents' Conference in Munich. In her report on public health, she demanded "sufficient and correct nourishment for all Germans." She made an explicit reference to the "upcoming winter." Both the quantity and quality of food was important. All in all, the picture that Schroeder drew was quite dark. She referred above all to the high infant mortality rate as an indicator of the desperate situation.[134]

The misery burned deep into the collective memory. In 1946/47, 42-year-old Konrad Born reflected on the "hunger winter" in a poem, in which he described a black market in typical fashion under the mantle of the "moral economy" of the bartering era:

> Winter night cutting cold. Bombed out house.
> In the cellar the hustlers' dance hall
> "Hey, Max, give us another round of shots
> And come over here with a few cigarettes!"
> A woman lives in the temporary shelter on the mezzanine,
> Sick, lonely, driven out by the storm of war.
> "If Werner were still around, all would be well;
> And Heinz stayed in the East too!"
> "Hey waiter, twelve glasses—an' hurry;
> We can do the gasoline deal!"
> And glasses and plates clingin'.
> And prostitutes' tinny laughter.
> The walls torn open and the windows boarded up,
> A person coughing in the claws of the cold.
> Was that a hoarse, hungry dog
> Barking so consumptively just now?
> And as she screamed the last scream of death
> From the sinking, choking shadow:
> "Bella-bella-bella-Marie!"
> The rats bellowed in the cellar's hollow.[135]

The dichotomy between misery and luxury—and thus between the guilt and innocence associated with it—was typical for the problematic "moral economy" of the Berlin barter culture. This dichotomy placed the immorality of the hustlers, their practices, and their way of life in stark contrast to the misery of weaker persons. In Born's poem, moreover, the misery of the old woman is connected to her experiences of the war and the death of her men and set against the life of the hustlers in the cellar, which is described as a party centered on life in the present. The war and its consequences as described here offers hustlers the best conditions for living in luxury.

In 1945, in a "Morning Commentary" for Berlin Radio, editor Friedrich Flierl discussed a "director's cigar villa."[136] With this, Flierl was picking up on a lawsuit against the directors of the largest cigarette factory in the British zone, the August-Blase AG in Lübbecke, at which someone had claimed around 200,000 cigars for entertainment costs and used these as "trading materials for the building materials" for his villa. "We have, my listeners, all experienced some of these hustling practices," Flierl stated in his broadcast. "Alongside the cigar villa, there is most likely a cooking pot villa and a cheese villa.... Such adept 'personalities,' free of reservations towards the general public, are the ones who succeed in these areas." He went on to say that to business owners and managing directors who described bartering transactions as compensation, this was nothing more than a euphemism because compensation was in truth nothing more than "fraud, hustling, extortion and exploitation," which should be called "bluntly... by their real name." The result of such practices, he concluded, was an "economic anarchy" that dumped "all the burdens on the public economy, that is, on working people."[137]

Dichotomies such as these were characteristic of the debates over what constituted proper everyday morality in the state of emergency. They point to the complexity of a society in which moral security had become unstable. "One cannot treat industrious, hard-working people the same way one treats notorious foragers and hustlers," one "allotment owner Seybold" stated in outrage in a radio broadcast on the black market raids, noting that some of his "colleagues" had had their harvests taken away from them.[138] Such problems were discussed in innumerable letters to the editor, newspaper columns, and radio broadcasts. The *Telegraf* asked in a piece in January 1947, "Black market trading in these hard times—what is permitted?" The author had collected some examples:

> The dear mother who attempts on Brunnenstrasse to sell the old top hat of her dead husband for 25 or 30 marks in order to pay the rent; the diabetic who buys a small package of sweetener for 25 marks; the transportation worker who is not able to satiate his hungry flock of children and "obtained" a sack of potatoes from the farmers: have they committed a crime? Many would say: no. And yet it is so. This shows how wide the gap has become between what the law says is criminal and what in the minds of most people is just.[139]

Accounts such as these make clear that—in contrast to the impression one might get from Born's poem—"normal people" and the lower classes did participate in the black market. It was simply not true that there were active and successful hustlers, on the one hand, and poor and disadvantaged people, condemned to passivity, on the other. Indeed, the poor or disadvantaged were important participants in the illegal street trading. Of course, their starting position in negotiations was generally considerably worse than those they were trading with. Need or the hope to somewhat improve their situation was usually their motive for illegal trading, not opportunities for profit or the demand for goods of elastic demand.[140] The *Telegraf* wrote in an article from September 3, 1948, in this context of a "black market of the poor." In a "gray tenement" in Wedding, the reporter noted, there was a small market solely for the lower classes.

> Here, where there is need and worry, a black market for the poor has sprung up, murmuring and whispering on the billowing boulevard. Continuously, a steady

> stream of people fluctuates up and down the street.... A pregnant woman with a half-naked child on her arm, two skinny creatures pressed to her skirt, mumbled with monotonous pleading "powdered milk, nine D-Mark!" But no one bought it. Here they all have children and are themselves selling powdered milk.... Many old people are walking with their last bread from their last ration cards: 6 D-Mark at Rubelmaxe in the Lausepark gets you 20 Eastmark—that is the rent for a small apartment.... A young person on crutches, a loaf of bread in his jacket, limped back and forth. "I only have a pillow for it," whispers a woman. "Cash smiles," says the man. No one wants the pillow. The woman cries. She has not had bread for days.[141]

Such small neighborhood markets, often on street corners, in squares, and near train stations away from the large commercial centers remained visible in the city up to 1952. The police's efforts to curb these markets repeatedly ended in violence. For example, the *Telegraf* reported in May 1947 on an incident at Rosenthaler Platz in Berlin Mitte in which a policeman had pulled his weapon, threatened the crowd of black marketeers with it, and hit a young man "on the head with the butt of his gun ... so that he collapsed covered in blood." In response to the journalist's questions, the Press Office of the police stated that a "crowd that had gathered" had thrown stones at the policeman, and only then did he draw his weapon.[142] The site where this happened, the area around the Rosenthaler Platz, was one of the areas in Berlin where there were often violent conflicts with the police. The distribution of these areas of violent conflict corresponds broadly to the social-spatial division of the city.[143]

The records of Division 95 of the Berlin Special Court make it possible to draw a picture of those who traded in the black markets.[144] In this court's cases of offenses against consumer and market regulations, the black marketeers arrested on the streets were mostly sentenced to small punishments; there were no comprehensive investigations. Accordingly, it is not always possible to say exactly where the trading took place. The majority of the arrests were in smaller squares in the north, in the east, in the center of the city, and in the commercial area around the Silesian Gate in Kreuzberg. In some cases people were also arrested at Alexanderplatz or in the western parts of the city. The occupying power also noted that the individual illegal market areas reproduced the social divisions in the city that had developed over a long period of time. In their "Black Market & Price Control" report of April 1949, the British employees of the "Enforcement Department" recorded the following under the point "Details of Black Market": "In the richer districts the offer of all kinds of preserves has greatly increased, especially salmon in oil, sardines, etc."[145]

In short, the geography of the black market carried on the patterns of social inequality in the city. Still, with recourse to the seemingly rule-free and wild trading, tales of impoverishment could be told. Werner Grothge, who was 50 years old and unemployed when he was arrested, was typical of the less privileged circles of black marketeers. As was customary in black market cases related to need, the arresting officer noted in the documents that it was "not necessary" to search

Occupation group	*In%*
Small-income employees	33
Workers	28
Self-employed	16
Small trade	16
Other and non-identifiable	6

Figure 4.8 Occupation groups of male black marketeers, Superior Court of Justice, 1949–1952

for more evidence because it was clear that Grothge, who lived in Reinickendorf, was not a professional. As police trainee Wernicke noted in his report, Grothge was "discovered on 9 April 1949 at around 12:30 on Invalidenstrasse [a black market trading area] offering chocolate bars at 20 marks a piece." In the final report it stated, "Grothge was found in the area of the black market . . . standing around with two bars of chocolate in his hand." Like many other participants bartering because of their need, Grothge was no stranger to the 17th district where he was arrested: "Grothge had already been arrested by the 17th district police seven times for offenses pertaining to black market dealings," Wernicke wrote.[146] Such "small" repeat offenders were generally only verbally reprimanded for their first offenses: "although G. . . . was seriously cautioned, he continued the forbidden trade in restricted goods in the black market, without paying attention to the police's warnings. For this reason it is appropriate that G. finally be tried by the summary court." Accordingly, Grothge was "transferred for appropriate action" to criminal investigation unit 5 and, on April 11, 1949, only two days after his arrest, sentenced by the summary court to six months in prison. In his defense, Grothge pointed out that he was unemployed and therefore in a predicament. This made no impression on the court. The court's verdict referred to Grothge's previous convictions but abstained from any moral assessment. The final police report, by contrast, did make such an assessment, describing the accused as one "who lived solely from the black market."[147]

Focusing on a single case may distort the picture. It can no longer be ascertained whether Grothge acted out of poverty or simply to earn some easy, extra money. The picture becomes clearer if one compares his case with a sample of cases brought before the Berlin summary court. Evaluating the personal details of 200 people convicted by the summary court, we can see the social imbalance in the markets. Moreover, this market for the poor lasted a long time; similar numbers were recorded from 1949 until 1952 (see Figure 4.8).

If one compares this with the number of those convicted before the Berlin summary court during the war (see above, Chapter 2, section "Goods from all of Europe"), a number of things stand out. First, there is the relatively low percentage of self-employed persons. This was, above all, because these records reflected the new prosecution practices. In the round-ups and random checks of the known "black market areas," the police typically came into contact with a different clientele than when they were conducting their surveillance of regional businesses, where they had regularly arrested—apart from the guests—the owners of bars, cafés, and restaurants. Accordingly, the percentage of lower-level civil servants, lower-level clerical workers, and manual laborers was higher in the postwar period. The working class made up 29 percent, almost exactly the same share as the first two consumer groups (manual laborers and workers) comprised in Berlin's whole population in 1947.[148] This shift in numbers of convicted persons had an unambiguous social cause independent of the fact that the number of workers represented their share of the population. For what does not become apparent through the mere listing of the occupations is that a little more than half of all men convicted, although they had an occupation, were unemployed when they were arrested. The percentage of the people who were unemployed was therefore clearly around the percentage of the population, which in 1945 was 14.1 percent among men.[149] Thus, unemployment was the defining characteristic of those convicted of street trading across all occupations. Being unemployed meant that one was classified in the lowest card category, "V" ("various"). In order to be classified into a higher category one had to provide proof of a job.

In spite of the leveling brought about by the general chaos, that not a single member of the higher classes was caught in one of these public black market sites correlates both with the better economic starting position they enjoyed and with the social division of the city that kept middle-class citizens from visiting the "markets of the poor" in the poorer districts.

Unemployment was also an important characteristic of the social profile of the women convicted (see Figure 4.9). This shift was especially pronounced among lower-level civil servants and clerical workers. Whereas this group had made up 43 percent of all accused before the summary court during the war, this percentage decreased in the poor markets to about 10 percent. The group that saw the largest growth was women not registered as unemployed but as "without work"; indeed, this was the largest female group by a wide margin in the poor markets. These were women who were either dependent on their husbands' income or were widows. As they could not provide proof of employment, they also fell into the lowest categories of consumers. Many women in this group had been driven out of their wartime jobs in the course of men being reintegrated into the civil work force.[150] The decline in the number of lower-level civil servant jobs represented also hints at the increased difficulties women experienced, as

Occupation group	*In%*
Workers	24
Small-income employees	10
Self-employed	9
None	57

Figure 4.9 Occupation groups of female black marketeers, Superior Court of Justice, 1949–1952

this was the sort of job women had moved into. The percentage of women who came from the lower classes was even higher than among the men: it was 67 percent.[151]

That it was mostly the lower classes being tried in the cases before the summary court also becomes clear when one examines the goods traded. In 41 percent of the cases, food played the most important role in the trade; clothes in about 10 percent; 7.5 percent involved trading in other goods, above all fuel. A relatively large percentage concerned tobacco (29 percent) and foreign currencies (10.5 percent). Whereas tobacco and cigarettes were used above all as a currency for trading, in the foreign exchange transactions, it was significant that Berlin had two currencies. Although all of these commodity groups were also found in the other markets, the absence of a wide assortment of jewelry is especially interesting. Jewelry appeared in only 2.5 percent of the cases from the poor markets. This is another important piece of evidence pointing to these convictions arising from a market for the lower classes, whose participants did not have the trading equivalents especially sought after in other parts of Berlin.

Black Market Goods in the Postwar Years

A quantitative analysis of the flow of goods in the black markets of the postwar period is not possible. We lack the sources that would enable us to cover all areas of illegal trading. Contemporaries often estimated that a third or even 50 percent of the total turnover of some goods in Berlin took place on the black market. These contemporary estimates were themselves based on decreases in the urban income tax (down 27 percent) and corporation tax (down 21 percent) and the simultaneous increase in the income and sales taxes (both of which went up by 18 percent) in the first half of the tax year 1947/48. Of course, these indicators only took the goods produced and the services already provided in Berlin up to that point.[152] Nonetheless, these estimates give an impression of the huge importance of the black market for the postwar Berlin economy. Accordingly, the assortment available in the markets was quite diverse. Scarce goods typical of the time were traded just as often as the traditional goods of the underworld. Thus, food, weapons, and drugs appeared regularly in the markets alongside household objects, books, fake documents, and pictures of Hitler.[153]

Over time a spatial allocation evolved as indicated by descriptions that assigned certain groups of goods to certain marketplaces—for example, watches and jewelry to the central places (with the members of the occupying forces as buyers) or food to the market at Brunnenstrasse.[154] All in all, however, the illegal trading remained a relatively complex institution compared to legal consumer spaces. This confusing complexity also derived from postwar Berlin's increasing integration into an expanded network of international unofficial business relationships. The market thrived not only because of the goods and services produced in Berlin, but also because Berlin had become a hub of international trading after 1945, a site for transregional and transnational shipments.

International Flow of Goods

After the war, the assortment of goods available in the black market expanded considerably. Alongside the most important wartime black market goods, such as basic food items, clothing, and cigarettes, new and at times even exotic goods now began increasingly to turn up among the confiscations of the Berlin police and the employees at the Allied posts, including building materials, drugs, or Soviet automobiles.[155] The building materials were not too surprising. The editor of the *Neue Bauwelt*, Rudolf Weilbier, believed that the black market provided "the solid foundation for construction," without which nothing could "succeed" during the extensive work of rebuilding. The "object" of this "black construction," an article in the *Telegraf* explained, was "the so-called single-family homes, villas, boutiques, restaurants, pubs, and hustlers' apartments."[156]

In some specialized trading one could make substantial profits even with a relatively small quantity of goods. The 10.8 kg of opium confiscated from one woman on Varnhagenstrasse could have precluded her need for any further trading in the black market if she had been able to sell it.[157] The *Spiegel* reported in January 1947 that there were "fantastic possibilities for profit" in another market segment, the "diamond trade in Berlin":

> There top prices of 50,000 marks were paid for one flawless carat, almost one hundred times the peacetime price. At the same time one could acquire a one-carat diamond in Western Germany for 15,000 and in Hamburg for 22,000 marks. The Berlin buyers . . . it is assumed have their goods delivered directly "to the east." ("Beyond Warsaw all tracks disappear," the New York *Herald Tribune* wrote of this practice).[158]

This development was largely the result of the internationalization of trade advanced by the members of the occupying armies and other participants with contacts abroad; former prisoners of war and "foreign workers" or "forced laborers" also belonged to these groups. The flow of goods through Europe generally did not extend beyond Europe. It was, however, controlled by new actors and thus often changed direction. In the British "Black Market & Price Control" reports, there was a segment called "Main Source of Black Market Traffic." In August 1948, this segment listed the various provenances of black market goods: "Food from Russian and British zones. Food arriving by airlift at Gatow. Fruit, vegetables and potatoes from the Russian and Western zones. Gift parcels from Switzerland, Denmark, Sweden, Holland, and America, containing textiles and shoes. English, American, and Russian cigarettes."[159]

Berliners, too, used their contacts abroad to obtain foreign goods and to trade or sell these in the local market, most easily by mail. Participants who proved especially cunning were those for whom the illegal trade was merely an extension of their normal, "daytime" mail-order business. The case of Gertrud Gräber is exemplary. She had not started to trade illegally of her own volition but on someone else's behalf. Graber regularly received packages from an acquaintance named Münzer on Pearl Street in New York, who urged her to sell the goods on the black market for 4,000 marks a package and to deposit the proceeds into one of his bank accounts. He hoped to finance the reopening of his Berlin shop with them. Nothing came of this. The British informed the Public Safety Department of the American Military Administration as well as the relevant post office, thus putting an end to Münzer's personal financing of the reconstruction.[160]

This example of supplying products via mail was not unique. The *Tribüne*, which was close to the Soviet Military Administration, described the case of a lawyer who was unable to work because he had been "an active Nazi," yet he still had contact with his solvent clients. He got them black market goods through the mail. In this fashion, the well-educated black market trader said of himself, he had made far more money than he would have made had he just continued his lucrative law practice.[161] Repeatedly, the authorities involved in combating and controlling the black market discovered similarly structured transnational channels of supply that Germans had created.[162]

The vast majority of the international trade, however, was not done by Germans. Quite clearly, members of all the nations represented in Berlin tried to make money in the illegal business, much to the annoyance of the British investigators, who on September 29, 1948, noted:

> The black market has grown again this month. It is flooded with Allied property which includes cigarettes, tobacco, coffee, and all sorts of Allied foodstuffs. This is put down to the airlift pilots who are bringing the goods into Berlin and selling them on the black market to obtain Marks to enable them to have a night out in Berlin.[163]

The description of the most important trading sites in the British sector read like accounts from an international exchange: "The main three [black market centers] appear to be Bahnhof Charlottenburg, Bahnhof Zoo, and Schlüterstrasse. . . . At Schlüterstrasse the crowd consists mostly of Polish, Allied, and German nationals, while at Bahnhof Charlottenburg Polish, Yugoslav, Bulgarian, and other foreigners predominate."[164]

The Berlin black market was integrated into an international market through the foreign actors and the currencies they introduced. Displaced persons were considered, especially by the British offices, to be particularly active in using their international connections to benefit personally. The aforementioned report pointed out the profitable opportunities for such DPs and attributed the price reductions in the black market "to the steady reduction in the exchange rate of the dollar which results from the fact that larger amounts are brought to Berlin illegally from the Western zones where foreign exchange is cheaper." However, it also reported that the profit margins had decreased on account of the gradual assimilation of the dollar exchange rates and the concomitant drop in the price of gold. "At present it is 0.68 dollar for 1 gram of 5.85 carat gold. At the corner of Kurfürstendamm and Schlüterstrasse there is a new black stock exchange where hundreds of DP's meet daily in order to trade information about the latest development."[165] These observations fit the worldview of many an observer. In the August 26, 1948, edition, the reactionary *National-Zeitung* criticized "individuals, members of the Western allies, who are behind the black market" under the headline "Airlift Supplies the Black Marketeers: DPs say: 'One can always earn the most money in Berlin'. " The article blamed French and above all American sources for positively "flooding" the markets and the lax efforts of West Berlin police to combat and control the black market for its flourishing.

Fighting the trading, some of which was professionally organized, was a never-ending task. Successfully prosecuting these crimes required tremendous resources, so even the better equipped British posts could only watch the "hustle and bustle" helplessly. When there was a special interest, however, various agencies could coordinate and mobilize their forces. The case of fighting the trading of counterfeit Cadbury chocolates is worth detailing because it exemplifies both the characteristic structures of organized crime as well as the coordination and resources required for prosecution. Together with the Berlin police, members of the British Criminal Investigation Department (CID) came across numerous black marketeers trading primarily in chocolate in November 1948 in a routine raid around the Kurfürstendamm.[166] After initial arrests and confiscations, the investigators worked to discover who was involved and the source of the goods. The next raid was preceded by two days of surveillance of the scene on the Kurfürstendamm. On December 11 the policemen struck again, registering their campaign as "very successful." In 13 of the 16 arrests, they were able to secure Cadbury bars in small quantities. The actual success, however, was the arrest of two "small distributers" caught doling out their shipments to individual street traders. One of the two did this on bike but was still caught. After this, another raid was undertaken against—as it turned out—a larger chain of middlemen who not only tried to escape arrest but also threw stones at the arresting officers. The violent actions of the traders reinforced the suspicion that those arrested were not just small brokers in the Berlin black market.

What followed was classic police work. "All the persons arrested were closely and continuously interrogated with a view to ascertaining the main sources of supply." These interrogations led to the search of 30 houses and apartments. The largest (still modest) find came from a search in Wilmersdorf, where 142 bars of "Cadbury" chocolate were found. All in all, the investigators confiscated 432 bars of different sorts of chocolate and 8,800 American cigarettes. However, they still did not know where the goods actually came from. Only slowly, in the course of their investigations, did the picture both of the people involved and the flow of goods become clear. The British and Czech chocolate products originated from the American zone as well as from Switzerland. They were brought by truck through the Soviet zone to Berlin-Pankow, where they were temporarily stored before being transported in smaller amounts and in part with the assistance of members of Eastern European embassies into the Western sectors. The individual street traders on Kurfürstendamm in Charlottenburg were thus only the last link in a chain that included at least four middlemen.

The entire setup of the chocolate trade reminded the CID and the Berlin police of the well-known structures of organized crime: extensive distribution networks, a transnational setup, black marketeers who fought back, and—except for the street sales—payments being made in "cash." What most clearly indicated organized crime practices were the traders' methods for maintaining secrecy. Individual small traders worked independently of one another; they knew nothing about their "colleagues" and knew their contacts only by their nicknames: "almost invariably the names and addresses of the black marketeers are not known to one another, and they carry out black market business through pre-arranged meeting places or by nick-names."[167]

These professional security methods reduced risks to a minimum for organized networks. Such structures also made it easier to penalize the final, small distributors, because the suppliers had a large number of them. If one of the "small distributers" behaved disloyally, he or she could easily be replaced with someone else. This knowledge, as well as the awareness that they were integrated into a network of organized crime, made the middlemen compliant and submissive. The degree of organization also allowed the development of long-term trading relationships and secure (major) customer relations. In these long-term trading relationships, one could either terminate the business transaction or simply threaten to do so, and business partners knew the others had this option. This was a great advantage because it made it possible to "exchange" goods of lesser quality, in diluted form, or imitations. This path was not open to occasional, private traders who only traded with different people. Black market business transactions were thus a delicate question of trust; the degree of trust could decide which attitude the players would have in the future toward individuals as well as toward goods.

Significant Items: Black Market Goods as a Medium of Trust

The black market redirected the flow of goods. The market withdrew ever more goods from regular distribution channels. Due to the scarcity of provisions, large parts of the Berlin population attempted to purchase basic necessities on the black market. However, most contemporaries regarded black market goods as in the wrong place and at the wrong price. They were always ambivalent, being longed for or shady, objectionable products. The experience of scarcity and hardship advanced a fundamental distinction between elastic and inelastic demand. Even goods that had previously been something one could only occasionally afford were now considered "luxuries." There was a great yearning for such luxury goods. In his diary, Karl Deutmann remarked:

> an intoxication has come over the people, to barter, to trade, to enjoy once again something beautiful that one had long done without, indeed to own it at any price. Precious objects are parted with in order to once again eat bacon, to smoke a good cigarette, to wash oneself once again with good soap, to eat a piece of chocolate.[168]

The contact with such luxury goods was regularly described as an overpowering experience. One participant recalled how, when she came across a stranger by chance, she first noticed the breads he carried in his bag: "a curious, not immediately discernible smell suddenly filled my nose. I sniffed the unusually aromatic air right around me; it was, especially in contrast to the stuffy smell of the tattered clothes which most people were wearing back then, very pleasant—mmmmm!—simply intoxicating."[169]

Such descriptions of luxury items often compared two different types of goods as well as two different time references and two different value systems. In this perspective, the luxury came from the store. Someone who exchanged a cupboard, a library, or a picture for food (no matter how exhilarating it proved to be) was "hawking off" solid possessions for something fleeting, exchanging an item which might have signified security for "daily bread" and with it for a very limited future of perhaps the next 24 hours. This ambivalence of "euphoric" happiness in the moment and the bartering off of securities was a large problem, as indicated by the discernible frustration and resentment about unequal trades when a deal turned out to be clearly "fishy."

On the one hand, people associated delightful experiences—experiences they longed for—with the black market. On the other hand, the objects of these experiences were often disappointing, even when one could take possession of them as there were numerous imitations and low-quality products.[170] The trust in the quality of products had already been put to the test during the war as substitutes had replaced many products. This interrupted a long success story that had begun in the nineteenth century when modern product marketing and the professional depiction of actual and ascribed product characteristics gained an ever more crucial role. Brands proved to be especially competitive if consumers could trust them, if they stood for a standard of consistently high quality. Brand-name products offered a degree of security; they combined an unmistakable product physiognomy (price, packaging, and quantity) with reliable quality, always and everywhere. The 1930s brought the first stage of the history of brand communication to an end. Case studies indicate that "broad levels of the population" were already influenced by trust in brands during the "transition period of product communication" between the world wars during which brands continued to play an important role in the creation of trustworthiness within German consumer culture.[171]

In the rationing economy of World War II and especially on the black market, where goods of varying quality—whose quality was often difficult to verify—were traded, consumers persistently experienced insecurity instead of confidence in a familiar transaction. Trading in the black market tested one's trust in the product as well as in the respective trader. Karl Deutmann remembered exchanging,

> after a conversation at the hairdresser . . . a bottle of schnapps (a little under half a liter) for six to seven pounds of potatoes . . . . The man even brought them to the apartment and poured them into a basket for my wife. Later we found 2 large stones among them. The German is and remains a rascal.[172]

Another contemporary described an even more dramatic case of trading a dress for oil that turned out to be poisonous. A few hours after eating the oil on bread, "we all started feeling incredibly sick. . . . We thought this is the end! Many people died of it, for laboratory tests showed that it was Chinese wood oil, completely inedible for mankind! My urge to barter was finished!"[173]

In these two cases, the fact that those who were cheated had checked the goods for quality shows the prevalence of mistrust of goods and people and its influence on people's actions. Yet the measures had proved to be futile, which was very disappointing. The contemporary who bought the wood oil to eat concluded that "for these things I guess I was not talented enough."[174] But even less self-conscious participants more experienced in dealing with unfamiliar trading partners could never be completely certain. Ursula von Hanffstengel described the postwar years quite well in her memoirs, including among other things how she had withstood the pushy soldiers of the occupying forces and how she had "mastered" daily life. But she, too, was a victim of sellers of counterfeits. She had traded some watches for two pounds of butter that turned out to be "not butter, lard, reindeer oil or cart grease. Still the people finished it and strangely no one was worse off for using this 'Trojan horse'. "[175]

In the black market, goods became a means of verifying one's trust in people. As Deutmann's example shows, many participants associated disappointment not only with their particular case but also with the abuse of their trust and viewed these as symptoms of the times. Thus, the black market with its unsure terms of trade became synonymous with a culture of mistrust—a culture that had started in the breakup of stable sites and rules for doing business. Almost all accounts from these times refer to such experiences of disappointment, even if they were only secondhand.[176] The black market goods themselves, accurately remembered, formed the focal point of experiences that undermined trust. Thus, they were more than mere commodities: they were at the same time mediums of contact and items associated with different experiential contexts. Among these was, next to the question of trust, the question of the distribution of power between the bartering partners.

The cigarette was the most traded item that showed this relation. The handling of cigarettes and the vocabulary used to describe them reflected beliefs in the fragility of time as well as patterns of behavior. Above all, the discourse on cigarettes addressed different levels of sovereignty, and so it will be treated in detail below.

The Cigarette as a Collective Symbol of the Black Market Era

> A spring of comfort, an instrument against fear, a drug which procures relaxation, which makes hunger and boredom be forgotten, a medium for showing courtesy, a decision guidance, a stimulant, the arrow of cupid and a weapon against superiors—the cigarette which a soldier smokes gives him all that he needs. What would the soldier be without tobacco!
>
> (Richard Klein, *Cigarettes Are Sublime*)[177]

> The yellow coloration at the tips of his bloodless fingers gave away that he made less of an effort to sell cigarettes than to smoke them.
>
> (Phillip Kerr, Old Friends—*New Enemies*)[178]

It is part of the history of the "society in a state of complete disintegration" that cigarettes were more than a commodity in the black markets of the postwar era: they were a currency. The reasons for this were partly pragmatic. Cigarettes were convenient: "the cigarette is an internationally accepted unit; it is handy, easy to transport, practically packaged, rather durable and internationally 'standardized' for size and weight."[179] The cigarette took the place of money not only as an exchangeable currency. In its fleeting, evaporating materiality, it resembled the money of the inflation period, not because its value had decreased through a seemingly unstoppable multiplication, but because it could be consumed—cigarette by cigarette—and its worth literally evaporated into thin air. The cigarette was a product from the start, and a currency during the interim period, which made it a fitting equivalent for the black market since most observers assumed that the black market would also be only a passing phase. The elusiveness and temporary nature of the time thus found expression both in the illegal markets and in the tobacco currency.

Officially tobacco was considered more than a mere (fleeting) indulgence. Tobacco is, as the state council of the American zone asserted in a letter to military leaders, "today . . . not only an instrument for enjoyment, but more importantly an instrument for relaxation and a distraction from hunger and sorrow."[180] Consequently, the various powers endeavored to secure the supply of tobacco and to increase the size and acreage of the tobacco crops in Germany. The Soviet side had special success with a system that relied on premiums for deliveries of tobacco. In the Soviet occupation zone, within one year, between 1945 and 1946, the amount of acreage increased 60-fold. This tripled the previous high-level mark, yielding the Soviets a raw tobacco crop with a total value of 7.6 million marks. This was the equivalent of 27 percent of the total German harvest. In addition, all sides benefited from the tobacco-harvesting settlers, garden-plot holders, and smallholder farmers, whose combined revenues were estimated to be many millions of marks.[181]

Still, cigarettes—especially non-German ones—remained rare and especially desired, forming the top of the hierarchy of means of payment, with American brands at the very top. As an article in *Telegraf* in June 1946 explained,

> as [the Americans] in Germany can't pay in dollars, they have created the cigarette as an alternative currency. . . . For a package of "Ami [American cigarettes]," which over there costs 8 to 10 cents, one currently pays 130 marks, which means that one dollar corresponds to 1,200 to 1,500 marks. . . . This is most likely the reason General Clay has proclaimed an import prohibition. It is not exactly an uplifting spectacle to see the citizens of such a wealthy country, which has an excess of everything, take advantage of the poverty of a poor nation that is being bled dry to appropriate [that nation's] last fungible value almost without a service in return.[182]

This clearly articulated what the cigarette, as perhaps the most important collective symbol of the black market era, stood for: the different conditions of power that could be articulated through it.[183]

Under the title "Camel No Longer Attracts," a *Wirtschaftszeitung* reporter noticed shortly after the currency reform that cigarettes had forfeited their dominant market position:

> among the dethroned rivals of the old currency the cigarette is at the top, especially the American cigarette. The "Chesterfield," the "Lucky Strike," the "Camel" and the "Morris" . . . were for years not only the most noticeable items of exchange in the black market in these parts, they had also developed into another currency, into a modern edition of the "Kauri Shell." The American cigarette brought forth . . . goods, services and "favors" like a divining rod. The cigarette had become a vehicle of social change; it transported one closer to the top, and also let one go in the opposite direction. In addition, it became a measure of value for some of the trades in goods. . . . The German Mark took this cigarette-currency out of circulation. . . . The cigarette, even the American, "no longer attracts." . . . The cigarette is once again a cigarette, a stimulant, more or less desired. It is no longer a means of payment for which one can have anything and everything.[184]

In another *Telegraf* story, the cigarette symbolized the difference in power between Germans and Americans in a modern fairy tale. "The Girl with the 'American Cigs' " told the story of a four-year-old girl observed collecting cigarette stubs by "a large, broad-shouldered, white-haired man with a good-natured face." The American "bent over the little girl and discovered with difficulty—he didn't speak any German and the little girl of course did not understand English—that the twelve cigarette stubs were to be exchanged on the black market for food." The man was Mr. Warbington, a hard-working American farmer, who himself had a granddaughter and was so touched by the little girl's situation that he took matters into his own hands and started to organize aid packages from the United States to Germany. The article repeatedly stressed that he acted skillfully, obtaining the best possible terms with American producers, and arranged to send as many goods as possible at the lowest possible price to Berlin. When he told people of his action and how skillfully he had negotiated in the United States, "Mr. Warbington laughed loudly, with a roar."[185]

This tale made the difference in power between the American and the German side very clear by reversing the hustling situation. The aid of the American farmer, his self-confident bearing, could only be tolerated by resorting to the topic of family. His deftness in dealing with business partners in the United States formed the positive counterpart to the inconsiderate and "smart" hustlers in Berlin. Market mechanisms—this is the moral of the story—can also be used for a good cause. Nevertheless, there was something unsettling about the "loud laughter" of the benefactor, which brought the unequal distribution of power in the American-German relationship to mind and could only be captured with the metaphor of the "good uncle."

Such positive examples gave voice to the difficulties of the times just as much as descriptions of misery did. Collecting cigarette butts was humiliating. It belonged to the canon of practices circling around the cigarette. Other common practices were offering (or not offering) a cigarette as well as lighting, inhaling, extinguishing, or stepping on a cigarette. All of these actions—including how one inhaled, and especially how one extinguished a cigarette—had a wide range of forms, each of which articulated sovereignty. A cigarette could be flicked away, stubbed out by hand, thrown to the ground, or stamped out underfoot. In the eyes of many observers, these practices were an expression of carelessness or arrogance—albeit scarcely avoidable. At a time when city dwellers fought to "own" sections of the sidewalk for collecting discarded cigarette butts, every public gesture of this sort was also a demonstration of power. A Berlin woman remembered people "shadowing . . . smoking Americans to be able to bend down quickly and pick up the cigarette butt thrown away." Furthermore, she had seen how the contents of ash trays were regarded as "raw material" in some establishments and "would be picked apart and made into new cigarettes."[186]

Most importantly, the cigarette represented a hierarchy; it was possible to distinguish between the cigarette being used as a good and being used as a currency, which, in turn, distinguished between the powerful and the powerless. Whoever smoked cigarettes showed he did not need to see tobacco products as just a currency. To actually smoke cigarettes was a sign that one could afford to let what others used as currency go up in smoke, as is expressed in Philip Kerr's description of a Russian KGB officer. It was not by chance that one of the obvious images of splurging was to light cigarettes with paper money. Those who bent down to pick up cigarette butts regarded actually smoking them as the equivalent of burning money. At the same time, the sustained value of the cigarette currency depended on the number of cigarettes in circulation continually being reduced by consumption. This alleged "squandering" ensured that the monetary function remained and that cigarette butt collectors could continue to use the garbage for trading.

The cigarette became a collective symbol because the process of smoking expressed a multitude of meanings that thematized and boiled down some of the decisive conflicts of the black market era to their essence. Smoking (and especially its representation in contemporary reports, films, and stories) was never only a physical act but also a discursive one—in other words, "a silent, but eloquent way to express oneself." Smoking functioned as a "coded, rhetorically quite complex, narrative-like articulated discourse" through which far more could be conveyed than the mere fact of smoking (Figure 4.10). Likewise cigarettes presented "a subtle but efficient instrument . . . for regulating social interactions."[187]

Some people, most prominently "hustlers," used these possibilities to express their understanding of their roles. Thus, the cigarette became an attribute complementing the typical combination of male tranquility and sovereignty that had previously been suggested by gangsters and detectives. A hustler without cigarettes was not a hustler. Cigarettes were a part of hustlers' performance just like casual clothing and casual gestures; by smoking, they exhibited a certain nonchalance to the problems of the day. The casualness and coolness smoking conveyed, with its ostentatious indifference to the surrounding chaos, also found its way into contemporary youth discourse (Figure 4.11).[188]

Figure 4.10 Dress codes and typical postures in the black market, Berlin 1948
Source: LAB 1NK, Versorgung/Schwarzer Markt, Nr. 160976.

The hustler as a role model either had everything under control or could create control. Demonstrative smoking, smoking with nonchalance, even in seemingly precarious situations, became a symbol of the sovereign, unimpressed male. This symbolic constellation overlapped with fictional characters who kept calm even in the most dangerous situations. Keeping one's calm could best be illustrated through the obvious, deliberate lighting of a cigarette. If "normal" smokers regarded lighting a cigarette as a relaxing break, the same gesture in the face of great danger could only be understood as a sign of the highest attainable cool. Even in the (anti-)war movies produced long after the war, the smoker who seemingly always kept his cool—and remained free of any suspicion of ideological indoctrination—was a common motif. This was carried to the extreme in John Guillermin's "The Bridge at Remagen," in which a sergeant went about his work, even during a gun battle, with a cigar in his mouth.

The description of the cool smoker with everything under control conveyed power; being able to light a cigarette, preferably with a metal lighter, was more

Figure 4.11 Children selling cigarettes on the black market in Schöneberg, 1948
Source: LAB 1NK, Kinder, Nr. 1099.

than a gesture of mere serenity. Smoking a cigarette generally led to a pause in the conversation; it slowed down communication and therefore placed the person lighting the cigarette in the position of being the one who could continue the conversation whenever it pleased him. Whoever was smoking did not have to speak and, through this gesture, had established a hierarchy or reminded one of the existing one.

Even before cigarettes had taken on this symbolic meaning, they functioned as a means of establishing contact. This function increased in importance during the black market period. To offer someone a cigarette or to ask for one was an uncomplicated way of starting up a conversation, of becoming acquainted with someone, or even of initiating a trade. "Cigarettes often mediate democratic, international, and cosmopolitan traits. They overcome the barriers which the war had erected," Richard Klein realized in his book on smoking. The principle "that asking for a light cannot be rejected" opened up (and still opens up) chance acquaintances for smokers: "by entering into the magical circle of smokers the foreigner becomes an acquaintance or confidant."[189] On the other hand, one could not really turn down the offer of a cigarette, even if it was the last one because "accepting the last cigarette of a man who is in a miserable state and has nothing else left to give means restoring to him the gift of giving"; to do otherwise would deny him "the freedom . . . to act generously, discount his presents and insult him."[190]

The black market called this convention whereby the reciprocal service could be the acceptance of a one-sided gift into question and partly invalidated it. After all, what mattered concerning cigarettes in this context was the exchange of material assets; the once "harmless" gesture could be read as an offer to trade. As a medium of contact the cigarette remained effective. The fleetingness of the moment was of importance. Initially, the attempt at contact in these cases could be non-binding; it could be revoked. And even if a conversation or even a (trade) relationship developed from the request for a cigarette, such acquaintances had a different, less binding value than relationships that had developed over a long time. The fast pace of society and the superficiality in interpersonal relationships often criticized by contemporaries found an analogy in the cigarette as a way of making contact with people.

Cigarettes, well-known tools for initiating contact, were a part of the erotic game between sexual partners. Behind the outrage over the "new woman" who, equipped with a cigarette, flaunted her self-confidence, was the uncertainty over how a man should approach her. Whoever had mastered the new rules of the game could light her cigarette. But in this exchange, was one not perhaps entering into a (non-binding) agreement that could turn into a (dangerous) sexual one? With cigarettes in their hands, women not only started to smoke like men; they simultaneously opened up a public space for themselves. They stepped into a new communication situation, and male participants were not always certain how they were supposed to react.[191]

In the postwar period cigarettes were perceived in encounters between German women and soldiers of the occupying forces as a means of establishing contact and as a means of exchange. This reflected the power configurations. The subtext of the discourse on cigarettes was that German women yielded to the enemy—and the means of exchange were the enemy's cigarettes. There may have been rather pragmatic reasons behind the increase in female smoking during the war. A poll carried out by the Institute for Public Opinion Polling in Allensbach in 1949 on the female consumption of cigarettes found that 49 percent of the women surveyed claimed to have started smoking only during the war or in the postwar period. Yet this poll itself also conveyed a fixation on the possible meanings implicit in smoking.

The cigarette stood as a sign at an intersection of numerous lines of interpretation. In the end, the discourse on cigarettes enabled people to turn the disturbing experiences of the postwar era into describable—and thereby somewhat more graspable and explainable—experiences. This struggle to create order was behind all the talk connected with the black market. It was also characteristic of the practices of the participants on both sides. If the policies of the Allied forces and German security institutions to combat and control the black market could still be described as a mixture of inching ahead insecurely, of ideological rhetoric and pragmatic tranquility, the illegal marketplaces were sites that, on the one hand, appeared sociable and adventurous to Berliners, but which were also unsafe, and the chaos of the times clearly manifested itself in them. They stood for unreasonable demands of very different sorts: for unfamiliar practices and new players, for arbitrariness, for the loss of trust in goods, for social upheavals, and for misery, hunger, and the injustice of a market in which humans perceived one another as predators. Everywhere one could discern a desire for order, for rules that would make trust possible once again. This mistrusting and waiting for signals to create trust resulted from experiences of loss. For many, an everyday feeling of security had been lost in the chaos of the time. The black market was exactly in the middle. The black market was a realm of experience and the symbol for the absence of rules, an absence that was difficult to tolerate; and it was also a social event. The black market was the unjust redistributor who rewarded the "smart" and punished the weak. It was the site of creative development after the months of the "final battle." No matter how many single success stories described the market in the sense of a creative development, the black market stood above all for the desire for a new beginning.

CHAPTER 5

Stories of a New Beginning: The Economy of the Streets between the Currency Reform and the "Economic Miracle"

Contrary to what is generally believed, the black markets did not suddenly disappear in the summer of 1948. People continued to be indicted in Berlin for illegal street trading into the early 1950s.[1] All the same, the currency reform in East and West did represent the most significant break in the Berlin barter culture since the beginning of the war. With it, economic and currency decisions were made that—at least on the Western side—aimed to break with rationing and the controlled economy. As the restrictive measures were lifted, they gradually marginalized the illegal markets.

The first section of this chapter investigates this break and its significance for Berlin's bartering culture. The subsequent sections investigate how Berliners evaluated the attendant symptoms of black market trading and what role their experiences with the bartering culture played in the context of formulating a new economic order.

"High Politics" and New Currency Practices: The Effects of the Currency Reform on Berlin's Black Market

Berlin's black marketeers were accustomed to modifying their trading practices in rather varied temporal contexts. Even during the war, black marketeers had adapted to the political climate and planned for the possible end of the war. For example, they hoarded goods and oriented their trading to the continually changing cycles of the supply system, especially toward the end of the war. For example, Berlin police observed that trading was more intense after air raids, when special allocations were handed out.[2] When Germany began to lose the war in 1943, black marketeers started to hoard goods for the future. One of them stated in his interrogation that he wanted to build up a reserve for the period after the war; another remarked that he was expecting a "gas war" to come soon.[3] The testimony of arrested black marketeers repeatedly expressed their worries about the future and how these were strongly affected by their experiences during the hyperinflation period. One, for example, claimed that he wanted to put away some savings "for a rainy day" because he had "lost everything" at that time.[4] Generally, individual traders used these practices to secure their income only in a time of need. Brokers, by contrast, acted with much more foresight. One individual dealer explained in a letter that he was especially interested in soap and toiletries because he believed that these articles would be in short supply and high demand after the war.[5] Thus, black marketeers' time management practices always related to their individual strategies and were themselves derived from reactions to larger social and political developments, as well as microlevel organization.

The impending defeat made traders anticipate an uncertain future, which affected how they thought about time. People worried about their fate. How would the victors behave? What sort of repression could one expect? Of course, occasional, seasonal supply bottlenecks prompted some black marketeers to be on the lookout for "opportunities" and whatever was being offered at the moment.[6] However, alongside this, international politics and the actions of the victorious powers became increasingly important to the black marketeers. People expected Germany to lose; they expected the city to be occupied. What would that mean, and how would they get along with the new rulers? How would long-term political decisions impact them? Berlin, in particular, was becoming the center of an East-West confrontation that was gradually apparent even to the "simple man on the street." Such anxiety was only natural, as the international disputes would have rather serious consequences perceptible to all in their daily lives. The Red Army's seizure of the city, the first political and administrative measures of the Soviet rulers, the arrival of the Western Allies, the division of the city into four sectors, the coordination of the policies in the Allied military command, the work of the newly formed bodies for Berlin's self-government, and the beginning tension between the victorious powers, the Berlin blockade—most Berlin citizens followed these important political and military events very closely because they affected them directly. In this sense, everyday life in Berlin was extraordinarily politicized. Political developments and the everyday routines of the black market became closely intertwined and made it necessary for traders to stay up to date and analyze new information carefully. Although this was not a new phenomenon, the East-West confrontation increased traders' insecurity and their need for reliable information and direction on how to respond to new situations. The Berlin newspapers were full of articles on the advantages and disadvantages of certain developments and contained useful information such as the dollar exchange rate or prices on the black market.[7] For many, this constant need for information was a heavy burden. Some adapted professionally to the new conditions, and others passively resigned themselves to them. Yet even those who found the pressure of the uncertain circumstances intolerable began to adapt. The most prominent event that brought together the micro- and macro-elements of this development was the currency reform in July 1948.

The solution to the currency problem in Berlin shaped up as a race, with time playing a decisive role.[8] On July 22, 1948, the incumbent mayor, Louise Schröder, was ordered by the Chief of Staff of the Soviet Military Government to implement Order 111 of the currency reform. The regulations formulated in the order were to be put into effect the next day. The Western Allies were forced to take action. If they believed it was politically important to keep their own currency in their three sectors in the Western part of the city in order to maintain their claim to sovereignty, they would have to raise the money to pay for it. And how could West Berlin be supplied with its own currency? How could procurement and the markets be organized and safeguarded? Ultimately, these questions dealt with issues that extended far beyond the boundaries of Berlin; indeed, they pertained to the relationship to the West German state and to the political order in Europe. The Western city commanders decided not to adopt the currency reform and instead proclaimed that they were thinking of adopting the West German currency for West Berlin. Already one day later, on June 24, they laid the legal groundwork for this with the "Regulation for the Reform of the Monetary System." In the future the Deutsche Mark of the Bank Deutscher Länder (Bank of German States) was to be the official currency for the Western part of the city. One day later, the new currency was already circulating as legal payment.

With these steps, responsible parties on both sides had made "fundamental decisions in regard to currency policy." Something had started that had "its own dynamic" and led to both parts of the city being integrated into the Allies' respective legal and economic systems.[9] This development was completed by the middle of the 1950s. The currency reform was therefore an important step on the path to both the social market of the West and the planned economy of the East. In the days immediately before the reform the expectation of it had quite the opposite effect: it led to hoarding and to a flourishing black market. The fact that two parallel currencies existed side by side in a city that was more or less spatially intact, in which there were relatively free conditions for trading, ushered in amalgamations of the currency rates and traders trying to use the difference in value to generate extra profits.

In the weeks and months before the currency reform, Berliners were by no means only interested in questions of supply; often they paid more attention to the behavior of the Western powers toward Berlin and to the city's role in the emerging Cold War, as indicated in the thirteenth "Report on Berlin Morale" of the Public Opinion Research Office. The report of January 26, 1948, stated that currency reform continued "to occupy people's attention"[10] and that the public was exceptionally interested in the general political situation abroad and its impact on Berlin: "Not fuel, not food, not clothing nor currency reform but the pros and cons of the evacuation of the Western Allies from Berlin is the main consideration at the moment."[11] Large portions of the Berlin population in all four sectors feared that the Americans, British, and French could pull out of

Berlin, contrary to the assurances that General Clay, among others, had given. The failure of the London Conference (November/December 1947) to close the gap between the Western Allies and the Soviet Union and the militant demeanor of Cominform, in particular, had "conspired to give Berliners a bad attack of nerves." By contrast, Berliners' attitudes about the problem of the black market were reportedly laconic: "*Wer gut schmiert, der gut fährt*," noted the report, quoting a common German saying of the time along with an English translation ("he who bribes well fares well"). The report then concluded with a few words on a public opinion poll indicating that most Berliners considered the employees of the public administration to be corrupt.[12] All in all, the black market and its attendant symptoms took up exactly seven lines of a four-page report.

The belief that economic policy decisions were imminent had a tremendous impact on black market trading. Traders turned rapidly to foreign currencies and tangible assets, presumably because they were uncertain about the consequences the expected shift would have. The fourteenth "Report on Berlin Morale" commented on this:

> Fears of Currency Reform have led to increased trading. A veritable flight from the Mark took place at the beginning of the month when fears of Currency Reform were at their highest, with dealers trying to buy stable currency—chiefly British Pounds and US Dollars. Dollars were selling at RM 300–350, even rising in a few cases to RM 500. A gold 20 dollar piece is reported worth RM 20,000. Gold and silver and valuables generally have also risen in value. The Black Market in petrol is now deep rooted. . . . American filling stations are reported to be sources of Black Market petrol.[13]

The expectation of currency reform led, on the one hand, to a "flight into material assets." As these, however, could largely be exchanged only on the black market, illegal trading also "flourished" after the news of the imminent currency reform. A report of the British "Enforcement Department," which was responsible, among other things, for watching over the enforcement of Allied pricing policy, noted already in April 1948:

> The confidence in the currency has mostly vanished. The workman wants, if possible, to get a "payment in kind" besides his low actual salary, enabling him to get by barter the necessary goods for daily life. As to the entrepreneurs, the distrust in the currency is inducing them either to hold back their goods or to deliver them only against raw material. A large stock is considered to be the best guarantee for overcoming the currency reform.[14]

Thus, the same side effects could be observed in Berlin as had been observed in the Western zones of Germany before the D-Mark was introduced.[15] And, as in the Western zones, the first effect of the currency reform was a sharp rise in prices—sometimes over 300 percent.[16]

The further development of prices depended heavily on the fact that the Western Allies, following a recommendation of the municipal authorities, allowed payments in the Eastern currency. In the Western part of the city, important daily goods as well as rents for apartments were calculated for and paid for at a rate of 1:1.[17] On the one hand, the existence of the two currencies generated a great deal of uncertainty. A woman in Berlin reported:

> The new currency is making life much more difficult, as we have to get the currency from the Eastern sector. But I have no strength to do this. There are thousands of people there in front of the banks standing in line. There are accidents and even deaths. With East German money one can buy food. For textiles, thread, yarn, soap, shoes, or even fruit, however, Western money is required. Apartment rents and pensions and benefits are paid in East German money. There is a good deal of wild trading. Whereas people previously had whispered "gold, silver, chocolate, cigarettes," now they ask for Western money. These two currencies are going to kill us.[18]

This dark statement was only partly true because the two currencies also made many new forms of trading possible that allowed one to improve one's income. For example, as the currency was exchanged at different rates in East and West, it was possible to exchange money twice. A Berliner described the technique and the resulting chaos in detail:

> Since the first days of the currency reform the Berlin population has been in a state of high tension.... Previously lines had formed in front of the grocery stores and shops in order to get rid of the last old German money that one had. There are now lines in front of the currency exchange offices. These lines ultimately became the craziest black markets, such as we have not yet seen in Berlin in this concentration.... After hesitating in the beginning, clever Berliners in the Western sectors of the city now [after the currency reform] exchange the quota of 70 marks in the Eastern sector first because there they only have to show their rationing cards as identification. After this, they use their identity card to get the Western quota of 60 marks. When news of this spread by word of mouth, there was a genuine storm of the Eastern currency exchange offices by all West Berliners. The storm was even larger because the newspapers, too, began to write about this and called on Berliners to take advantage of it. What has taken place here in front of the currency exchange offices can scarcely be described, and certainly the West must be aware that there were serious incidents and even some deaths.[19]

Very quickly a value difference developed between the two currencies, with the real exchange rates showing different degrees of trust in them. One could certainly profit from this. As the Public Opinion Research Office pointed out in its "Notes on Currency Reform," which appeared regularly, many Berliners sought to profit from this value difference:

> The Eastmark is considered worthless in the three Western Sectors except for the buying of rationed foods, coupon articles... etc. If using the Eastmark in this connection the rate of the exchange is 1 Westmark to 1 Eastmark. This order allowing Berliners to spend Eastmarks in the Western Sectors was given by the Military

> Government. It is favoured by all Berliners as they can exchange on the Black Market 1 Westmark for 10 Eastmarks, thus buy their rations, pay their bills and rents etc. in Eastmark for 1/10th of the original cost.[20]

Clearly the British reporters suspected that not only the Berliners, who were directly confronted with the two currencies, but also their own supervisors were having difficulty staying on top of the complex and confusing situation. Thus, they illustrated the situation with two examples showing that some Berliners were adapting quite well. Different regulations for the use of the currencies in the East and the West had opened up a niche that East Berliners, especially, were able to exploit for profit. The first example concerned the (politically motivated) permission given to people living in the Eastern sector to pay for tickets for movie and theater performances in the Western sector with Eastern money. As a result, tickets were regularly bought with East German money and then sold on the black market for Western money. The traders could then exchange this Western money back into East German money on the black market at a rate of 1:10. Movie tickets thus quickly mutated into an equivalent currency that, even if only to a modest degree, compensated for the lower value of the East German money.

The second example illustrated a similar mechanism on a much smaller scale. The exchange equivalent that could be acquired in this case points to the everyday significance of even small trading advantages. This mechanism involved small coins. These had been devalued in the Western sectors at a rate of 1:10, making it possible to play the two currency systems off one another in everyday life: if one bought a newspaper that cost 15 cents in the West for two old marks, which now had a value of 20 cents, one might receive five old ten-cent pieces in change. Now one could not only go shopping in the East, where the money was worth 50 cents, but also buy two tickets for 20 cents for the S-Bahn, which was administered in the East: "So that one gets for 2 old Marks (20 Pfennige in Western money) a newspaper which is worth 15 Pfennige and furthermore 2 S-Bahn rides gratis."[21]

These were clearly conventional adaptation processes whose triviality indicates that people did not need to have professional experience with the black market in order to profit from it; the two currencies, in a sense, forced normal citizens to engage in practices that resembled those of the black market. That professional black marketeers responded to the new situation quite adeptly was openly admitted by the Berlin trade inspection service in a report translated into English:

> During the first days after the currency conversion professional Black Marketeers met in the well known Black Market centres to discuss, first of all, the new conditions, created by the currency reform and to exchange experiences. They refrain from offering Black Market goods until matters will have somewhat cleared up. In some cases small quantities of cigarettes were black-marketed.[22]

This exchange of information among black market brokers corresponded to everyday trading techniques such as those of the movie tickets described above, exploiting the two currencies in the city. Although such transactions did not generate large profits, they indicate that even occasional, private traders found ways to benefit. In the realm of black market trading, it was possibly much clearer than in the official markets what goods represented the equivalents of the new currencies.

However, speed was of the essence, because the value differences reflected in such bartering transactions evened out relatively quickly. One not only had to know where to get such goods for a comparatively favorable price but also had to react fast. In addition, the authorities did not just stand by and watch this activity but rather attempted to control practices that devalued the East German currency as a pure substitute currency. When black marketeers had automobiles and were thus able both to quickly change their place of business as well as to compare prices, the police did all they could to prevent this speed advantage, for example, by confiscating the automobiles.[23]

The weeks and months before and after the currency reform were thus perceived as fast-paced—a perception that combined with expectations and then assessments of the currency reform. Traders reckoned with the reform and thus attempted to anticipate its impact. Almost all black marketeers read about the "general political climate" and used the information to generate options for their trading and currency practices that, in turn, could often only be utilized within a narrow time frame. On top of this, difficulties in communication and transportation cut significantly into their trading time. Time turned out to be a determining factor not only in everyday life but also in shaping political processes.

Competitive conditions therefore not only shaped the introduction of the new currencies but also the internal order and supply of the city, and the establishment of the worldwide political framework. Everyday and "political" time frames became conceptualizations of scarcity that mutually reinforced one another. Under these conditions, a collective learning process took place in the streets that manifested itself in a whole series of adaptive practices typical of Berlin that were characterized by people trying to take advantage of the two currencies.

In addition, this practical level, so to speak, was continuously linked to efforts to provide and perceive order by applying moralistic categories to a reality experienced as contingent. Talking about market conditions thus always also expressed people's anxiety to reassure themselves in times of transition and change. Consequently, it fit into the moral discourse in which the critical economic conditions since the inflation era were the starting point for a heated debate concerning correct economic behavior. Many contemporaries smugly anticipated the changes the currency reform would cause to hustlers who had gotten rich in the black market. In this attitude, they did not consider that the little man, too, would be able to profit from the currency reform using similar practices.

When the currencies were introduced, those who had hoped that the market itself would punish the hustlers saw their hopes realized, albeit only after a transitional period, during which hustlers were able to conduct their business with special fervor. The idea that the new "honest" money would recreate "fair" exchange relationships contributed significantly to the moral legitimation of the reforms.

The Black Market as a Political Issue: The Debates Concerning the New Economic Order

Since its first large-scale appearance during World War I, the black market had been a political issue. The "hustler" debates during the 1920s, the changes in the semantics in the interwar era, and the National Socialist measures to combat and control the black market from 1939 on repeatedly reinforced this. The black market was associated not only with the malfunctioning of the economic system but also with important political questions concerning the economic order and its maintenance and questions on how quite varied groups could engage in morally proper behavior during and after World Wars I and II. Against the background of black market experiences during World War I and in the early 1920s, in particular, illegal trading came to have a significance that went far beyond purely administrative problems. The market, its protagonists, and their behavior became a prominent topic of debate after 1945, forming a polyvalent cipher for a part of the "moral economy" that negotiated social justice and decent behavior between World War I and the post-World War II era.

The experiences and the discursive configurations of the black market era helped to shape the moral implications of the social market economy. Yet the discourse formation was ambivalent. On the one hand, the discourse on the social market economy with its emphasis on commercial fairness was by definition far removed from the morality of the black market. On the other hand, the positive depiction of *homo oeconomicus* and his rationality, which up to then had been rather unpopular in Germany, led to a more sober evaluation of the rationality of the black market. In discussing this rationality, however, the representatives of the social market economy were careful to set themselves apart from the negative moral connotations of the discourse on hustlers that enjoyed broad support. The question of the economic rationality of the black market, in some cases, was even able to tie the social market economy to the negative reputation of hustlers.

After the end of the war, the morally charged discourse on the black market continued but took on a new significance against the backdrop of the competition between the systems in East and West. Starting with the assumption that the trading would cease one day, a first phase of historicization emerged during the black market era that took the everyday political controversies into account. Political elites as well as "common citizens" in East and West evaluated the black market, its contemporary forms, and the conditions that generated it in light of the contemporary controversies regarding future economic and political paths. This change in the direction of the discourse did not, however, clearly break with National Socialist discourse and patterns of interpretation but largely shifted them, emphasizing certain elements especially to influence public opinion. These elements took on a specific form in the context of the antagonism between East and West.

Urgent Problems: Prices and Justice

Black market trading, which triggered indignation, was to become both a topic and an argument in the debate about how to structure the new economy. Both sides—those in favor of a free market as well as those in favor of a regulated economy—found it relatively easy to interpret illegal trading in their discourse and to use it as an argument to illustrate the advantages and disadvantages of their respective economic concept. The supporters of a state-directed economy could count on widespread hostility toward black market trading. Their interpretation emphasized the "scandalous" aspects of illegal trading—above all, unequal access to the market, which rewarded some with unbelievable profits, whereas others had to part with all of their belongings just to survive. In this view, the "splurging" made possible by the dishonest business dealings that had made hustlers rich juxtaposed with the misery of people who had fallen on hard times through no fault of their own represented the clearest expression of "unbridled" market fundamentalism.

Dichotomies such as these formed components of an escalating rhetoric of apodictically driven debates about what constituted proper morality in "everyday life in a state of emergency." They make it all the more clear just how complex society was when moral certainties began to falter. Such problems were discussed in innumerable letters to editors, newspaper columns, and radio broadcasts, as well as in all sorts of guidebooks.

As early as August 19, 1945, a story on the station installed by the Soviets in Berlin decided to address the topic of "inappropriate price formation."[24] As a result of "extensive surveys," the editor explained, there could be no doubt that "the present untenable pricing policies in trade and commerce [had been] taken over without reflection from the Nazi era." His outrage was directed less at the officially fixed prices than at the "fantasy prices" that "war profiteers and Nazi big shots" supposedly had earlier and "easily" paid to businessmen "as one literally threw the money at them from our taxes and so-called voluntary duties and donations." "Of course," continued the commentator, there were also women to go along with this, "to participate in the lavish private parties, drinking champagne, in spite of the everyday worries and problems of the population," who were able "at a moment's notice to have special dresses sewn for them for a couple of hundred marks and to indulge in other forms of luxury." "We, however," he continued, "have at present no time and above all no reason to throw lavish parties; rather, we must concentrate on repairing or renewing our . . . badly damaged clothing," and this solely for the "sober purpose, in spite of all the difficulties, of going about our serious work in orderly and clean clothes." Ultimately, of course, both sides—buyers and sellers—were responsible for this intolerable situation: "Everyone who demands or pays such prices . . . is taking advantage of the people, as he is the initiator of an endless price spiral." At the end of the story, the commentator appealed urgently to his listeners to do what they could to stop this development:

> Free yourselves from all of your previous National Socialist customs and habits. Do not wait for the authorities to issue regulations or to take coercive measures. Do not wait until the trade unions become involved, which they certainly will one day because of the importance of this problem and because the working population has taken a stand, quite rightly, against the opportunists and hustlers.

To support, with "exemplary self-discipline," a "pricing policy that is appropriate for the time," he further argued, showed that one understood what was "necessary to build up a peaceful, democratic Germany," and, moreover, "contributed to doing away with one of the worst remnants of National Socialism."[25]

A radio program from February 1946 argued along similar lines of coming to grips with the past. The announcer asked rhetorically when it was that one could buy what one wanted and immediately answered, "It was before and in the first few years after 1933." As soon as it became clear that the slogan "cannons instead of butter" was meant seriously, the scarcity began. "And then," the speaker continued, "came the war with its ration coupons. [And] we are all acquainted with these." It was, however, important to remind people about the cause to "show whose fault it was that everything has become scarce, that maximum prices and rationing were introduced. It is the legacy of the National Socialist war leadership." One of the other legacies of the National Socialist years, he claimed, was the black market, and the story continued by reflecting on who the black marketeers were. On the one hand, he argued, the police "could tell you a thing or two" about "how many convicted criminals and well-known swindlers" were to be found among the black marketeers. On the other hand, he pointed out that black marketeering took place "not only in well-known streets and public squares but unfortunately also in many stores." Through their "old contacts," many businessmen were able again and again to obtain goods and to find buyers.[26]

The uncertainty about what did or did not constitute morally reprehensible behavior, and—more important in practice—what might have found its way into the regulations and ordinances, occupied both potential and actual black market traders. They were quite aware that there was something like a rationality of economic activity. Yet they wondered how individuals should orient their behavior to a "proper" collective morality. Advice programs like "You Ask—We Answer" of the Berlin station developed into an important source of information for Berliners unsure of themselves. In one edition a listener contacted the show in order to find out more about the "problem of bartering."[27] "For some time now," she wrote,

> I have been worried—as have many other national comrades (sic!)—about the problem of bartering. This bartering has taken on an alarming shape. Trading is certainly a good solution, so long as what is involved is a genuinely fair trade. Some of those who have been bombed out of their homes have been able to help

> themselves by trading one of their household items for another. What I am against is the trading—to cite only one example—of a valuable good for food. In this form of trading one of the trading partners will always be cheated.

As an example of the opposite opinion, the show presented a letter from a different woman who stated, "There are so many who are opposed to bartering. But this is none of their business. The only important thing is if the trading partners are satisfied with one another." The decisive question, the show asked, was who was right, and could the objects of trade really be a matter of indifference to others? The show then answered these questions with the typical propaganda of the official East Berlin agencies: one had to consider the source of the food being offered for bartering. The show then added apodictically: it "comes from the black market and can only have been brought into the black market by hustlers, thieves, dishonest civil servants, and deceitful businesspeople. These are parasites who live off our badly suffering public body (Volkskörper [sic!]), who embezzle goods in order to enrich themselves without a conscience. Whoever engages in such trading harms not only himself but also the general public." Therefore, he appealed to everyone, "Help remove these evils; put a stop to those harming the nation (Volksschädlinge [sic!])."

One important topic was the question of fair prices. Complaints about prices being too high accompanied the Berlin black market era as a never-ending lament. Letters to the editor of Berlin newspapers as well as to Berlin radio stations were full of outrage. Hans Feit, for example, complained in a letter of the "unbelievable prices in all the bars and restaurants on Motzstrasse." He was especially upset about the 24 marks "two pieces of potato pancakes" supposedly cost in the Marietta Bar there. The reporters exerted a good deal of effort investigating such complaints and calming the angry listeners. The reporters assured Mr. Feit that they had investigated "this matter" and that they had found out that in early August "indeed truly unacceptable prices were being asked." They were able to inform him, however, that the places he had mentioned were now "serving food at normal prices."[28]

What was a just punishment for black marketeers? This was also a highly controversial topic that exemplified the contradictions and intersections with the criminal prosecution policies of the occupying authorities. In a "commentary" from the summer of 1946 on Berlin radio, the reporter stated that the working population was demanding "the strongest possible measures against extortionists, hustlers, and freeloaders, who have become a genuine plague."[29] Although one needed to mention early successes by the police, it was still "not a secret that black market trading has moved from the streets and squares to the clip joints and other areas . . . where the underworld gathers." When, however, the police cracked down, the decisions of the courts often drove citizens to despair. "We are a long way from demanding that judges' decisions be dictated by the so-called 'public feeling', " the commentary stated. The Nazis used this phrase "public feeling" to provide legitimation for their breaches of the law. That did not mean, however, that the "new democratic justice can simply ignore the demands of broad sections of the hard-working population that there should be a harsh punishment for hustlers and of black marketeers."

The question of price monitoring was also being discussed by the trade unions according to a report of the same radio station in February 1946 with the title "Black Market and Productive Work." Workers were willing to accept a wage freeze in order to prevent inflation, it stated, yet they demanded in return "the ruthless suppression of any and every price speculation." As a result, a system of price controls was agreed to for the Neukölln district. The closing words of the broadcast repeated the idea that overcoming the black market was closely related to overcoming National Socialism:

> The quicker goods can be produced, the quicker the scarcity will be eliminated under which today all the people of Europe are suffering as a consequence of the Nazi war. And the quicker we will also reach a point where everyone can once again buy what he wants and the black market will only be remembered as a part of the dark atmosphere of the Nazi regime.

Old Problems in New Clothing: The Planned Economy

The connection between the black market and capitalism was highlighted and emphasized in East Berlin, where commentators repeatedly stated that illegal trading was an outgrowth of war and fascism, which itself was a product of capitalist imperialism. In this interpretation, black market trading resulted from the National Socialist war economy, which had robbed the working population of its livelihood. The unregulated market, representing the prototype of a "capitalist" economic system, without any security measures, "strangled" the "common worker" and privileged the hustler. The hustler did not work. Rather, he used all his time and energy to enrich himself at the expense of the "common man." Both in the general thrust as well as in the specific choice of concepts, this view represented a variation of National Socialist interpretations of the black market. Indeed, the antithesis between "work" and "trading" even employed a key point of interpretation of the old National Socialist economic ideology, distinguishing between "working and money grabbing capital."

The opposite poles, "working" and "hustling"—themselves a variation of the contradistinction of "working" and "money grabbing" capital—were reflected in the policy Soviet military leaders launched immediately after conquering the city: rather than subject those charged with black illegal trading to protracted trials, they instead put them to work immediately cleaning up the streets of Berlin.[30] The reasons for these measures were primarily pragmatic—to free the city of rubble and get it back into order. They were not expressly directed against black marketeers. It was quite easy to integrate such measures subsequently into anti-black market campaigns that sharply contrasted genuine reconstruction work for the new socialist Germany from black marketeering.

On September 4, 1945, the Berlin radio station ran a biased piece entitled "We See Black . . . ," which offered a somewhat elegiac interpretation of the immediate postwar situation by tracing the different meanings of the word "black" in various contemporary contexts.[31] This perspective, according to the commentators, was by no means "notoriously pessimistic." However, given the visible successes of the efforts to build up a new democratic state, which could be seen all around, the listeners "as responsible members of a Volksgemeinschaft [must also] see the shadows from the light of a situation that has been cleaned up; these shadows cannot be avoided, as shadows are the constant companions of light . . . We see black, indeed a great deal of black." They could no longer close their eyes to the problems associated with the color black that had moved into the foreground due to their common, everyday occurrence—such as the "black market" and "black marketeering." They referred to the "present situation" as "the legacy of a one-sided war economy and of a criminal, imperialistic war," both of which had themselves resulted from one of the defining characteristics of the times: scarcity. "Caught between the two poles of scarcity and people's needs," the responsible authorities had developed a "complicated and therefore very sensitive system" that "manifested" itself visibly in the rationing cards. This system regulated "the weak flow of goods between the producer and the distributor" and protected "value and price levels." This system contributed substantially to preserving value "against elements that would disrupt prices, leading to the devaluation of the money, which is known to all of us as . . . 'inflation' and which we remember with horror."

The piece emphasized collective morality and called on all citizens to refrain from participating in the black market, no matter how unimportant or insignificant their trading. Every "selfish behavior," manifested, for example, in small favors to keep up good relationships with tradesmen, had to be "repudiated with unchanged intensity." The black market was, it argued, not compatible with "our own greatest interest of guaranteeing the peace of the new German reality to be created."

There were clear anti-foreigner grumblings in the anti-black market discourse in East Berlin. Displaced persons were repeatedly targeted for attack, accused of the worst sort of black market transactions, together with members of the American army. *Neues Deutschland* reported in July 1948 that some members of a DP camp in Mariendorf that was about to be vacated were working openly with members of the American army to sell the goods in the warehouse.[32] The report stated that anything one could want was available there for D-Mark, from all sorts of cigarettes to the most elegant luxury cars. The purpose of this action was clear: "the last D-Mark of their share is to be taken out of the pockets" of the West Berliners. This tied the black market directly to the presence of the American troops, which itself was interpreted as predatory. Even members of the "Western police" were accused of working together with black marketeers.[33]

In the East, the currency reform was closely related to the black market. The new currency was seen as a black market currency that had been forced on the people for the purposes of speculation. With some satisfaction, a radio commentator claimed on July 7, 1948, that the Berlin city government had "capitulated." The decision "to carry out all public business only with the old German mark, with coupons glued on, which is valid in the Eastern zone" could safely be regarded as "officially taking back the mark dividing Berlin and retiring it from Berlin's economic life." The retreat of the mark had proceeded by "giant strides": "first it was 40%, then 25, then 10 and this evening it is already 0%." "This row of numbers" illustrated that the Western mark would soon "completely disappear from payment transactions in Berlin." With pleasure the reporter painted a picture of what was going to break loose that night in the editorial departments of the *Tagesspiegel* and of the *Telegraf* after the decision of the Berlin city government, "what a Hamburg paper had reported for the complete Eastern Zone: raving madness." Indicators of this were "the hangover atmosphere" that had dominated even before the decision was made "in the camp of those who were supporters of the Western mark." The commentator continued, "The *Tagesspiegel* writes today, in a desperate article, that this reorganization will turn the D-mark exclusively into an 'object of speculation.' 'Should you,' the *Tagesspiegel* asked in desperation, 'continue'—pay special attention to that word, my dear listeners—'to support the black market?' " With these remarks, the commentator believed that "the reactionary newspaper" had correctly described "the role of the Westmark as the black market currency."[34]

If one considers the shortages and the reactions of many Berliners to the economic chaos of the time, then it is not at all surprising that the ruling communist party of in the East, the SED, by no means stood alone in its belief that "given the present scarcity in regard to raw materials, transportation vehicles, fuels, and much more . . . the progress of the economy [could] only be secured by means of economic planning." Many political parties and groups shared this view,[35] including the SPD and large sections of the CDU in the West.[36]

The starting point for a planned economy was thus quite favorable. In a society that had become mistrustful because of economic crisis, the need for order was an ideal argument. "Planning," with its promise of security, could fill the gap left by the chaotic black market period. Most people considered the black market, even with all their individual positive experiences, very negative overall because of how it reordered the routines of everyday life, because of its irksome challenges and social upheavals. In this context, Walter Ulbricht, the general secretary of the Central Committee of the SED in East Germany from 1950, remarked that the GDR's economic plan was a "friend" that had brought about "something new and beautiful" everywhere in the streets. This statement made on the radio in the beginning of the 1950s and subsequently often quoted had two sides, however. On the one hand, it was justified in light of early, if modest, successes, but, on the other, it represented proverbial whistling in the dark.[37]

The reason it ignored dangers was that, although the plan prompted a reassuring return to well-ordered conditions in which the vast majority of goods could be purchased in shops, East Berliners (and East Germans in general) still lived "from plan to plan," with scarcity and "organizing"—or rationing—remaining common practices up through 1989. Although things were far different from before, bartering was still a part of everyday life. Of course, as one's very survival no longer depended on the black market, trading lost some importance, because the transition from "sustaining to shaping one's life" had opened up new chances. Nevertheless, the limits of these new opportunities were soon reached.[38] The claim of the East German state and party leadership that it "knew what the population" apparently needed "to satisfy its needs" did not fit the facts; the citizens of the GDR, to be sure, appreciated the level of security they had in regard to everyday things, yet they never gave up their claim of being sovereign consumers.[39]

A Successful Proposal for the Economic Order: The Social Market Economy

Forty years after the end of the war, in June 1985, the hustlers once again appeared in West German academic discourse—even if only on the margins. The setting for this "performance" pointed to what could be called classic examples of the success stories of West German postwar history. In the office towers of the Deutsche Bank in Frankfurt, at an event of the Gesellschaft für Unternehmensgeschichte (Business History Association), Tübingen economist Joachim Starbatty looked back at the social market economy from a historical-theoretical perspective.[40] Starbatty, the last academic assistant of Alfred Müller-Armack, who had coined the term "social market economy" and who had provided the theoretical substance behind the concept, discussed the so-called arbitrage phenomenon. Human behavior, he claimed, is often nothing more than "looking for time or profit differentials." In this, it resembles the movements in the stock markets that make use of exchange rate differences and interest rate differentials in order to level them. Analyzing the advantages and disadvantages of this approach in comparison with the "axiom of self-interest," Starbatty came to the conclusion that descriptive categories of economic behavior were especially useful as they avoided moral implications. At the same time, he emphasized the beneficial "macroeconomic" aspects of such behavior: people who organized collective compensatory movements were able to prevent misallocations and thus to slow down rising costs. Only dysfunctional institutions, Starbatty averred, clouded the picture: "if seeking profit differentials" produces "undesired macroeconomic results," one should "not address individual economic behavior but rather the institutional arrangements." He named "black markets, price gouging," and "hustling" as examples of such "undesired results." "Black markets," Starbatty concluded, are "a typical product of badly ordered or regulated production and trading relationships."[41]

Concepts such as "black market," "price gouging," and "hustling" may have sounded somewhat antiquated to Starbatty's audience, especially in a lecture that otherwise employed contemporary economic jargon and concentrated on current problems such as "the contribution of individuals to the production of collective goods." It would have made much more sense in the mid-1980s to discuss a different consequence of false institutional developments, one that Starbatty mentioned, namely, illegal employment (*Schwarzarbeit*). Yet the reference to the "black market" and those who had participated in it turned people's attention to the prologue of the economic new beginning. The reference was—besides being a part of the academic argument—reminiscent of the phase when the social market economy had been established, of the era of the currency reform and the implementation of "Rhineland" capitalism. Starbatty thus discussed in passing two topics whose correlation, as a rule, had been depicted quite one-dimensionally because this narrative was a part of the foundation myth of the Federal Republic. According to this myth, the social market economy was born in the summer of 1948 in the currency reform. The currency reform had brought about the end of the chaotic black market era and of the inadequate rationing system and laid the foundation for the West German "economic miracle."

The debates concerning economic systems and markets were at the heart of political discussions in West Berlin, in the Western zones, and in the Federal Republic in the early postwar period. The social market economy, a part of the success story of the West German state and one side of the debate, was not a natural law. Rather, the idea gradually prevailed over competing—in part diametrically opposed—proposals. The teleology formulated after these events, which linked the Federal Republic of Germany from the very beginning to this concept, does not do justice to the historical openness of the situation. This teleology is a part of the "invention of tradition," which itself significantly shaped the new state's set of beliefs.[42]

The tremendous importance attached to the question of the proper "moral economy," even in the Western contributions to this debate, can be illustrated by the outraged responses to a remark by Justice Minister Dehler of the Liberal Democratic Party (Freie Demokratische Partei, FDP) in December 1949. Dehler had suggested that "those who before the currency reform had violated economic provisions and regulations" had acted "economically quite rationally." Dehler made headlines with his recommendation for amnesty in cases of economic crime: " 'Black Market Was Rational': Dr. Dehler: Generous Amnesty for Economic Offenses," was the headline in *Die Welt*, while the *Sozialdemokrat* wrote with indignation, "Dr. Dehler Praises the Black Market."[43] "Some remarks of the minister in Bonn," reported the newspaper, had caused "a considerable sensation," because he had described the "black market as a 'market of economic rationality' . . . . Above all, the workers, who up to then had shown restraint, [would] not be surprised if the federal government proposed putting up a memorial for the unknown black marketeer."

This small debate quickly became a full-fledged controversy. Citizens, journalists, and experts expressed their outrage in numerous letters to the editor and commentaries. The justice minister had stated, pragmatically, that all black marketeers were "rational" people who had helped generate acceptance for the laws of the free market. These remarks, consistent with the model of *homo oeconomicus*, were an affront to contemporaries, who were attached to the idea of a moral economy and who thought largely in the categories of those who harmed the community (Gemeinschaftsschädlinge) and the welfare of the people. Dehler's interpretation not only contradicted National Socialist interpretations; it also broke with a widespread public opinion, supported by the National Socialist ideology, that black marketeering was an "evil" whereby a few people had enriched themselves at the expense of the vast majority because they had the necessary resources and a healthy dose of egotism. Rudolf Groß, who was 43 at the end of the war, formulated his disgust vis-à-vis the immoral hustle and bustle of the black marketplaces in Berlin (although he had participated in them), using language influenced by Christianity, "Now the black market, too, started to gain momentum with its charlatans and in that market people haggled and were cheated; it was worse here, I believe, than with the Pharisees in the temple at the time of Christ (!)."[44]

Such judgments, criticizing the "tricks," the imitations, the advantage-taking of the black markets, gave voice to a widespread attitude in Berlin. However, not only private individuals or those who had suffered personally from the black market spoke out. The moral discourse on the black market was centered in the Berlin newspapers. In the Berlin and business sections of the *Tagesspiegel*, commentators came out in favor of the currency reform and of ending most management of the economy. Yet although these articles did call for ending the command economy and for the greatest possible economic freedom, even the *Tagesspiegel* argued that the liberal economic system could not function without morality. "Success always depends on economic morality and on a determined administration, which especially after the currency reform should have the courage to crack down where guidance and steering are necessary."[45]

In these public debates, the black market was treated with disgust because it promoted—and reflected—a social morality interested only in profit, where people did not refrain from deceit, where they took advantage of the existential needs of others. A careful appraisal of this attitude toward the black market pointed out the difficulties of complete economic liberalization. A liberal economic order, one in which the invisible hand alone regulated supply and demand, was not conceivable in the German discourse. Commentators favorable to the market economy, as well, could not imagine a forward-looking economic system without economic morality—even if it was established and implemented with state power—and without the most individual economic activity being embedded in a set of collective values. The collective processing of black market experiences did not lead directly to affirmation of the social market economy. Rather, market liberalization, in particular, such as that promoted by later Economics Minister Ludwig Erhard, called forth associations with the hustler discourse.

The debates about the economic structures that should be established were quite controversial and diverse, even dividing political parties—for example, the CDU—and they also mobilized trade unions and representatives of the church.[46] From the very beginning, this was not solely a discourse among experts but also one of "the streets." Ludwig Aderbauer remarked on this phenomenon in his 1948 dissertation:

> the most important question is the frightening question: war or not. Alongside this, the public is interested in nothing so much as in currency reform and the black market. In the streets, in trains, in bars and restaurants . . . one repeatedly overhears such conversations. Any exchange of personal, quite private worries always leads to a discussion of these problems.[47]

The disputes and discussions concerning currency reform and the black market always circled around the same two sets of questions. First: how could the economic difficulties be overcome? And second: which economic system would best do this? Regardless of the starting point used to enter the debate, whether from the macroeconomic, theoretically informed perspective of the expert or from the perspective of a layman worried about his own rations, everyone participated in this broad discourse, which influenced public opinion regarding the future economic system. "Free market economy" or "planned economy," continuing "management measures" and the "price freeze" and thus the National Socialist "command economy" or "unleashing the market forces" and "currency reform"—broadly stated, these were the alternatives in the debate dominated by a majority that actually wanted both.

In the historiography, the patterns of interpretation are clear. The period after the currency reform is most often described as the beginning of a new economic success story. In this phase, Germany was committed to the idea of competition and free prices. The lifting of the price regulations under Economics Minister Erhard has a prominent place in the literature, although "political prices," housing, transportation, and the food market played an important role until far into the 1950s and approximately 30 percent of all private goods were subject to a closely supervised pricing policy.[48] "Government intervention in the setting of prices was repeatedly called for" both by the population and by interest groups and parts of the West German government and, as a consequence, also carried out. Researchers have recently described as "remarkable" the fact that even "in the phase of rapid growth after 1952 in spite of increasing incomes," the call for regulating prices "was made over and over again." The "pricing policy in the social market economy" had begun in the Basic Principles Act (Leitsätzegesetz) of 1948 with a "fundamental decision to secure the living standards of the population," because the planners working for Ludwig Erhard proceeded from the assumption that "in the short term the market mechanism would not create a sufficient supply, and as a result the prices would shoot up drastically." The "fundamental decision" aimed therefore to "protect the broadest sections of the population and was oriented toward the income of the working-class population."[49]

This policy turned out to be less successful than expected: "in spite of the high percentage of administered prices, which at first could be kept relatively stable," price levels continued to be "characterized by wild fluctuations" until 1952. The subjective impression in the population was correspondingly negative and was reflected in trade union protests and in public opinion polls. Because he saw the acceptance of the new economic system as endangered, Economics Minister Erhard relied on symbolic political gestures. His ministry "initiated . . . pricing policy measures such as the Everybody Program, the price comparison lists, the law against profiteering, the formation of a price council, and ultimately the *Konsumbrot* (consumption bread), whose symbolic importance was far greater than its actual economic significance."[50] This pricing strategy was successful and "remained in place throughout the 1950s." In the Adenauer administration, it was above all the chancellor himself who, in his desire for electoral successes, repeatedly criticized the fundamental free market course of his economics minister and attempted "to demonstrate the government's ability to act in the field of pricing policy." These public discussions contributed "to a sustained disagreement" between these two most prominent CDU politicians.[51]

The rival camps thus created were not overly apparent to those on the outside. The concept of the social market economy was so flexible that everyone was able to emphasize one or the other direction according to his needs. That is, the social market economy was an "ideologically pliable" construction: "some people emphasize the adjective, others the noun, and all are of the opinion that, above all, their interests are at stake."[52]

It was not at all surprising that even prominent representatives of the concept could change their image. Ludwig Erhard is certainly considered to be one of the liberal founders of West Germany's social market economy, but a radio address he gave on December 8, 1945, shows that he was not, in fact, so very liberal but worried about the dangers of an unrestricted market. Bavarian state economics minister at the time of the address, Erhard stated that although he was reluctant "to bring about economic order through police powers," the government could "no longer watch idly . . . while unscrupulous profiteers were taking advantage of unsettled legal relationships and shifts in competencies in order to squander public assets." Furthermore, while he was not opposed "to coming out in favor of a liberal economic model," conditions were not yet right for such a model: "in a fundamentally free market economy," such "personal freedom of movement" was "subject to requirements" that did not presently exist "given the shortages in all areas."[53] Although Erhard wished for economic conditions to be relaxed, he did not believe this could be achieved "through the chaos of arbitrariness, licentiousness, and brutal selfishness" but rather required that one take measures with all due severity against the "evil insects, parasites and grave robbers."[54] What is interesting, above all, in this address is that its title, "Economic Order Cannot Be Achieved through Police Power," suggested that it would have a more liberal slant.[55]

Can referring solely to the success of the social market economy sufficiently explain the history of its origins and establishment? The most prominent reference to contextualizing the beginning success story of the social market economy with an eye to the experiences of the black market era is found in the very writings of the scholar who coined the term, as mentioned above, Müller-Armack. In a much quoted textbook article on the subject, he referred explicitly to the difficulties of establishing and implementing the social market economy as he had defined the term. "If, after years of strict economic management, the concept of the Social Market Economy was successfully introduced to the German public," he wrote, "this was due to the negative experiences of an era in which economic management had not worked and in which there was ever greater currency disorder." At that time, it was only when the "malfunctions of economic planning" had been discussed that "a system based on freedom . . . could successfully claim to be able to solve the social problems [and find] support for this claim among broad sections of the population."[56] With this statement, one of the founders of the social market economy referred to the historical conditions that made the success of the concept possible, and at the same time he historicized his own contribution to the founding of the West German economic system. This 1956 article, therefore, already referred to the "black market era" as a necessary prologue to the very concept of the social market economy, and it recognized the experience of the "illegal" as an important backdrop to the actual realization of this concept.

The experiences of the 1940s were important for contemporary economists who had long been thinking about mixed economic systems and were attempting to reevaluate the role of the state in steering social and political tasks. Yet implementing an economic program required political support as well as convinced and convincing political decision-makers and sufficient support among the population.

One of the decisive advantages of the social market economy was that the concept was situated between the two poles of the general discussion that Erhard named in an article, "Free Market Economy and Planned Economy," in the *Neue Zeitung* on October 14, 1946. When it was reprinted in 1988, the editor wrote a short and pathos-filled introduction describing the contemporary context: "People were working like crazy, they were harassed by hunger, by the border between the zones, by corruption, and by the black market." The introduction also explained Erhard's aim "to make visible the diametrically opposite alternatives in regard to political order."[57] Erhard's statements in the article itself show the difference between the subsequent glorification of his program, which he himself had already started before his death and which continued thereafter, and the real program. In the article, without opening up a simple contradiction, Erhard stated that it was characteristic "that the differences in viewpoints find expression in extreme forms that appear to be irreconcilable—here the free market economy, there the planned economy, here socialism, there capitalism . . . whereas the actual economic development" led one to ask, "if there [are] not effective influences from both sides" suggesting "a convergence of the positions."[58] On the one hand, Erhard pointed out that a discussion marked by slogans and catchphrases was scarcely suited to finding a solution; on the other, his remarks expressed a thesis on polarization that the media took up and argued with great success, above all, in the election campaign for parliament in 1949. This thesis contrasted the free market economy and the planned economy, the CDU and SPD, and—always implied in the background and sometimes pointedly advanced—West and East.[59]

This staked out a framework of interpretation that would enable advocates of the social market economy, on the one hand, to propagate their concept in the following years as a persuasive compromise and, on the other, to address various fears and hopes by shifting the accents in one or the other direction. What Müller-Armack labeled a "vague usage" that occasionally hid its "intellectual demands" among the public turned out, on the contrary, to be one of the strengths of the concept. The combination of words in "social market economy," which some suggested had been "felt to be a contradiction in itself," constituted an attractive code for a new beginning; the "label" also profited from denoting the success of the economic policy. However, to explain its success one should look not only at the indices of (consumption goods) production, but also at the "softer" factor of a discourse element that was able to become established, especially since the "miracle" itself only very slowly took shape in everyday life. Consequently, the myth of the economic miracle unfolded—at least in part—in retrospective descriptions.

The unambiguous material success story that the concepts of "economic miracle" and "consumer society" suggest was by no means so clear at the "beginning of the consumer society." Michael Wildt described the first decade after the currency reform as "a good deal more frugal, more limited and more gray" than the myth of quick economic growth would have us believe.[60] The well-known motif of the shop windows filled with consumer goods once again concealed the fact that many were simply not able to immediately enjoy what they had "long done without." This does not negate the success story of the new economic beginning but does relativize it. Looking at the complete context of the social market economy's implementation requires this differentiation. The advocates of the new economic order were able to use the pliable concept of the social market economy successfully to deal with the problems of the chaotic era that preceded it.

The concept addressed a whole series of contemporary problems that every individual would have experienced daily. The central elements of the new economic order seemed to provide an answer to the existing "defects," or appeared at the very least promising in this regard, as indicated by Müller-Armack's observation in 1956: the "basic assumption of the social market economy—that it has to be possible to win trust among the broader spectrum of the population for the social accomplishments of the market economy—has been shown to be true."[61] The population trusted the new economic order because it promised stability and "social progress" alongside material success. Consumers' freedom formed the center of the public portrayal of the concept, as well as the promise of a higher standard of living for all German citizens. Within this conception, the market economy comprised a "system of social protection" that was guaranteed simply by the fact that "consumers guided the economy according to their needs" and were able to utilize the "price instrument" as "an essential apparatus for coordination and leveling out" for their own welfare. In contrast, "all central planning," in Müller-Armack's account, attempted "to steer the flow of goods" in a direction different from those of "the wishes of the consumers." This "orientation toward consumption" in itself already constituted "a social service of the market economy." Moreover, "the continual increase in productivity brought about and ensured by the system of competition" had a similar effect of fostering "social improvement," which was all the greater and more universal "to the degree that it is able to curb one-sided income formation, which has its origins in a special economic status."[62]

"One-sided income formation" and "special economic status": in common parlance these were "splurging" and "luxury." Popularly, those who enjoyed these traits were called "war profiteers" and "fat cats." During the war these terms had been used to refer, among other things, to party functionaries in prominent positions and to the system of an existing network of bartering relationships. According to Müller-Armack, the system of central planning combined with free market elements such as those that had existed in Germany in World War II produced above all blockades and obstacles that reduced Germany's economic performance. The social market economy, therefore, employed competition as "a coordinating principle," without falling back into a radical *laissez-faire* policy. The new social market economy comprised a "novel synthesis." "The concept of the social market economy can be defined as an idea concerning the political order whose goal is, on the basis of a competitive economy, to link free initiative with social progress that is secured precisely by the market's performance."[63] That a state social policy with its redistribution of wealth and its promises of security should come into being alongside this novel emphasis on the independent consumer made it that much easier for people to choose freedom, which represented not only a promise but also a danger.

Conclusion: Black Market Trading as a Radical Experience of a Free Market

Werner Abelshauser once remarked, "German history since 1945 has been above all economic history." According to Abelshauser, nothing "shaped the West German state more than its economic development." The East German state, too, linked "its fate from the very beginning to the promise of economic success." Prosperity became "one of the most important criteria of success in the East-West competition." For the contemporary history of the two German states, economic prosperity played the role of a "vehicle" of national identification and of the state's self-understanding. "The economic success of the early years," following this interpretation, served as the "material basis for the rich consensus that made balancing the interests of social groups possible."[1]

These narratives of economic growth and progress gained great significance because the successes—even the modest ones of the East German economy—stood out in comparison to the chaotic period that preceded them. The experiences of the black market era were thus incisive. Just as they overshadowed the era of relative stability during the 1930s, these experiences had an influence that can scarcely be overestimated for the two German societies in East and West. This development can, in part, be interpreted as deriving from quantifiable factors, but it also resulted from change in contemporaries' experiences—a turning away from the practices, risks, and culture of mistrust of the black market era. What does it mean in this context that the Federal Republic remained the only country in which an institution founded to protect consumers—the "Stiftung Warentest" (Foundation for Product Testing, established in 1964)—became a sort of state institution? What accounts for the fact that both the GDR and the Federal Republic experienced a "judicialization of [their] economic systems" on a scale unique to them in legal and economic history?[2] Is one of the explanations for this to be found in the radical market experiences of the 1940s? This can scarcely be quantified nor can it be unequivocally proven; it can, however, be made plausible.

For most people the black market—independent of all the adventurous success stories associated with it—was largely an imposition. Indeed, the very telling of black market experiences—generally described as successfully navigated adventures—points out how exceptional participants found the situation to be. But why was the market an imposition? Merely because it was illegal and turned decent citizens into criminals?

Taking a broader view, we can see that the observations made here in regard to Berlin's everyday trading can also be related to long-term social and cultural shifts that are more easily discerned by looking at the black market as an influential everyday space of consumer experience during the 1940s. This long decade then can be seen as a period of dissolution and reformulation of social norms. Consequently, the decade becomes an important point of reference for "economic histories as social histories" of the Federal Republic of Germany and the German Democratic Republic.

Insecurity and mistrust concerning ideas of everyday behavior became fundamental experiences that influenced how one evaluated roles and individual occupational groups. This was true for the GDR with its campaigns against private businessmen that built on such mistrust, thus discrediting whole occupations as hustling rabble. But this was also true for the Federal Republic. In his radio address in May 1948, Ludwig Erhard, above all, criticized retailers, whom he counted among those who had profited from the rationing. His statement was not completely wrong, but nor was it likely to help ease the poisoned atmosphere.[3]

Erhard was bound to find broad support for this view because of the black market's unequal distribution of power in favor of the sellers. When the black market ended, this unequal distribution continued, with those who had been financially strong retaining the most power in the new markets. Alongside the already much maligned "fat cats," other occupational groups were accused of having enriched themselves at the cost of the majority, including retailers, restaurant owners, waiters, farmers, and city employees. The limited access to scarce goods privileged occupational groups that had such access, giving them the advantages of a supply oligopoly. Those unhappy with this situation could do little about it.

Under the conditions of the bartering culture, there were directly perceivable shifts in social life, especially in the social relationships in the workplace and in the private life of the market participants. Relationships to acquaintances, neighbors, and colleagues were among those affected as they became subject to the imperative of trading, thereby becoming components of monetary or exchange relationships. It was difficult for those who had seen how quite literally everything was for sale on the black market not to think of love or family relationships in terms of product categories. Additionally, the black market undermined the traditional relationship to goods and to bartering or shopping as well-known fixtures of everyday life; the black market thus promoted a culture of mistrust as well as a longing for "normal" forms of interaction and business. Customers immediately had to identify fakes, imitations, or even the diluting of goods and mention them in the price negotiations to avoid getting swindled. They bore all the risk and all the costs for testing the quality of the goods. They had no enforceable rights, like those guaranteed by the state in legal markets. Consequently, both personal relationships as well as one's relationships to goods were exposed to a fundamental culture of mistrust.

Outraged observers responded to these uncertainties and disadvantages by casting the hustler as the ideal type that profited from crisis. This profile of the hustler had a long tradition filled with experiences, beginning with World War I and its aftermath. Against the backdrop of changed historical conditions as well as the plurality of forms of hustling, this discourse reduced the complexity of social reality. Although the image of the hustler it presented did refer to events people had observed, it also reduced the true complexity of rather varied trading practices and groups of participants, which ranged from the occasional, private traders to the large brokers of illegal trade. In the black market era, hustlers were the protagonists of a moral economy that sought to order a reality experienced as contingent and disadvantageous and to recreate a sense of security by means of a simple moral pattern. Anyone could be accused of being a hustler—from neighbors to complete strangers, assumed to be dark powers operating in the background. In fact, of course, primarily fringe groups were so accused, so the accusation fit into that broader discourse that supported the inclusive connotations of the Volksgemeinschaft by defaming those who were not supposed to belong to it.

At the same time, this hustler discourse also thematized the central problem of the experiences of power and powerlessness in this moral economy. After the war, these experiences became intertwined with people's perceptions of a precarious relationship between the victors and the losers. Different interpretations of hierarchies of signs flowed into the descriptions of the bartering activity in the Berlin black markets, expressing both feelings of power and humiliation (in the markets) and articulating both disappointment and insecurity in a discourse of victimization. New patterns of explanation picked up on this discourse in part, for example, by construing support and assistance as evidence of friendship or partnership and using it as a means of taking sides with one or the other of the occupying powers.

The space where new and experienced black market traders encountered one another was the public black marketplaces that began to spread out in the winter of 1944/45 and had become fixed parts of the everyday life of Berlin consumers by the summer of 1945. The public squares upset many observers, although others perceived them as a space of a new and peaceful sociability after the war. Those who were upset saw the social relationships cultivated in them as immoral because they damaged the community. It is characteristic that these relationships were expressed in market categories because the black market—at least as soon as it was a visible public phenomenon—quickly became known as the black "*Börse*" (or stock market). The frequently observed phenomenon of haggling over prices caused a great deal of irritation. Given their experience with set rations and "frozen" prices, many Berliners responded with skeptical astonishment to the visible practices of the trading, especially as, because of the scarcity, the traders named prices that seemed to be "fantasy prices" yet represented an observable everyday reality, generating an extraordinary sense of the unreal.

Stock exchanges are institutions in which one can observe how prices are formed. The reference to black markets as black stock exchanges thus points to the shifting and threatening economic contexts in which contemporaries found themselves, where they became more aware of the "free play" of market forces. The provocative fact, visible in the public squares, that prices—which, on the one hand, resulted from supply and demand, and, on the other hand, from observed prices—were fluid phenomena that no longer had anything to do with the familiar price schemes resulting from invisible price-structuring processes generated uncertainty. In the exchanges, one could observe "how that enigmatic economic product, the price, comes about."[4]

The use of the term "stock exchange" for the public black markets pointed to two things: it expressed people's irritation with their newness, but it also suggested an attempt to reduce their complexity; giving them a name suggested that one at least partly understood them. The crux of this analogy, however, was that although it enabled a classification, this could not fully explain the complex events in the exchanges and thus had to become more an expression of helplessness. Most participants perceived what happened in these "stock exchanges" as impenetrable. The concept thus primarily captured their feelings of powerlessness, their sense of becoming the plaything of anonymous powers—or of powers reduced to a clearly defined group of people: German hustlers, displaced persons, and Allied soldiers. One attributed the processes one had observed to these groups in order to satisfy a need for security and for scapegoats. What was obscene about this became clear in the comparison of the hustler as a gambler in a dangerous economy to the powerless market subjects with no way to actively intervene and affect what was going on.

Against this background, the experiences of the black market era were influential in two ways. For one thing, they shaped the history of experiences with a market economy. Some of the most important threads of the discourse in the negotiations about self-concepts on both sides of the internal German border were the developments of both domestic economies and their market forms (often in comparison to one other), the limits and possibilities of consumption, and questions of "social security." Consumers' economic (i.e., trading) potency and security became core elements of collective desires as well as of self-images. Whereas in the GDR the transition "from plan to plan" limited the extent to which people were confronted daily with unsettling market mechanisms, the Federal Republic aimed to fence in the market economy to limit consumers' experience of fluctuations.[5] "Rhineland capitalism" was very different from its Anglo-American equivalent. Although this development had a long history of predecessors, people's black market experiences profoundly strengthened it. Free price formation, especially, met with mistrust, which was oriented around the discourse on hustlers, leading to appeals for market ethics and state control.

An interpretation of the "chaotic new beginning amidst the rubble" that made the black market and everything associated with it appear to be a transitional phenomenon like a ghost that suddenly appeared and would disappear just as quickly became characteristic in this period. It marked a way of dealing with experiences of insecurity, chaos, social disorder, allegedly perpetual advantages for some—in short, with all that constituted the overwhelmingly suspicious atmosphere of the black market era. Indeed, on posters, the black market was portrayed as a spirit, a nightmare that had to be banished. It was generally believed that the currency reform had, in fact, successfully banished it.

This reading of the black market resulted in part from widely shared experiences. At the same time, it aligned the participants and their illegal practices in a row of descriptions that characterized the great chaos of the time as only a short episode that could be historicized through individual perspectives and took on a discourse life of its own. In a way, this resembled the contemporary attitude of focusing only on the immediate future, yet such a reading reduced even "incomprehensible" events to an allegedly manageable size that could ultimately be overcome.

This interpretation served to exonerate people in two regards. On the one hand, it enabled both big- and small-time black marketeers to put their illegal past behind them by invoking the discursively constructed caesura of before and after the currency reform. Similar to the myth of the "zero hour" in 1945, this perspective formulated a second, economic "zero hour" that primarily distinguished two daily areas of practice from one another. This touches on the second level of exoneration because it was crucial to the public acceptance of the new political and economic systems that this intervening period of illegal practices be characterized as overcome.

Accordingly, research into the history of consumption needs to be more precise because the success story "at the beginning of consumer society" was by no means as smooth as the terms "economic miracle" and "consumer society" suggest. The first decade after the currency reform was more complex than the myth of rapid economic recovery would have us believe. The well-known motif of shop windows filled with goods did not mean that everyone was suddenly able to enjoy what they had "long missed." Rather, what was important about the shop window motif lay on a different level of meaning that cannot be found by analyzing budgets. The image *also* expresses relief at things once again being in their place. "Normalization" was unfolding in the reestablishment of stable, daily areas of practice in which goods were in shop windows, roles were clearly distributed and understood, role patterns and interactions were clear, and established social relations were not endangered by the trading. Instead of having to barter, one could once again go shopping.

On the macro level, the dominant, semi-official economic histories of the two German states functioned as integrating narratives; the success stories provided a form of (substitute) national legitimation. Underlying a good portion of this specific "rhetoric of economics" were the experiences with the chaotic bartering era and its most irritating institution: the black market. The black market was a photo negative, the opposite of what was desired. Both German states could describe the goal of economic "normalization" in the sense of turning one's back on a society of scarcity and avoiding social upheavals by pointing to the black market as a symbol of a period of misery and to the hustler as the one who had profited from the general economic and social chaos, from the society of insecurity and suspicion. Norbert Frei suggested that the West German federal government's "Amnesty Law" of 1949, in referring to the "years of hardship, of moral degeneration, and the legal aberrations" of the black market, aimed to cover up the political aspect of the law as amnesty for Nazi criminals. Nonetheless, that it did so indicates that the consensus view among the population was that turning away from the chaotic "economic conditions" was necessary.

The black market era thus formed a consensus-generating reference point for public interpretations of the new economic beginning that helped as a subtext until recently to shape many fields of discourse in the postwar period—even in the two states' perceptions of one another. For example, the discourse in the Federal Republic spoke of the "backwardness" of East Germany's state socialism and its consumer culture by referring to bartering practices and rationing, which many GDR citizens remained familiar with up to 1989. On East German television, the "Black Channel"—propaganda broadcast each week—described life in the "capitalist metropolis" as a juxtaposition of misery and luxury, of begging, speculating, and economic crime, employing a pattern of interpretation that had helped to forge the basic consensus regarding the state form by aiming to secure the opposite of the black market era.

The short but intensive epoch of German history marked by black market trading in the 1940s gave citizens radical experiences with markets. These coincided with their experience of rapid social mobility, which for most of them, under the conditions of the time, led to a radical social decline. There is much to suggest that Germans' specific reservations concerning uncontrolled, liberal markets can be traced back to these experiences.

Notes

Introduction

1. Thomas Pynchon, *Gravity's Rainbow* (1973; New York, 2000), 107.
2. LAB (Landesarchiv Berlin), F Rep. 240 (Zeitgeschichtliche Sammlung), Acc. 2651, 5, 504/1.
3. Max Brinkmann, *Kleiner Knigge für Schieber* (Berlin, 1921), 85.
4. See, for example, Edgar Wolfrum, *Die geglückte Demokratie: Geschichte der Bundesrepublik Deutschland von ihren Anfängen bis zur Gegenwart* (Stuttgart, 2006), 33; and Manfred Görtemaker, *Geschichte der Bundesrepublik Deutschland* (Munich, 2003), 29. There is a more extensive treatment in Christoph Kleßmann, *Die doppelte Staatsgründung: Deutsche Geschichte 1945–1955*, 5th ed. (Göttingen, 1991), 46–50. For East Germany, see Ulrich Mählert, *Kleine Geschichte der DDR* (Munich, 1998), 27; and Dietrich Staritz, *Geschichte der DDR*, rev. ed. (Frankfurt am Main, 1996), 55. There is no reference at all to the black market period in Hermann Weber, *Die DDR 1945–1990*, 3rd ed. (Munich, 2003).
5. Michael Wildt notes that the bartering and black markets belong to the "blind spots in our historical knowledge"; see Wildt, *Am Beginn der Konsumgesellschaft: Mangelerfahrung, Lebenshaltung, Wohlstandshoffnung in Westdeutschland in den fünfziger Jahren*, 2nd ed. (Hamburg, 1995), 278. This circumstance has begun to change as case studies emerge. For Berlin we now have Paul Steege, *Black Market, Cold War: Everyday Life in Berlin, 1946–1949* (Cambridge, UK, 2007); however, this comprehensive study is limited to the postwar years, and it analyzes the Berlin black markets as sites of the Cold War conflict. There is also Stefan Mörchen, *Schwarzer Markt: Kriminalität, Ordnung und Moral in Bremen 1939–1949* (Frankfurt am Main, 2011), which reads the conflicts over the illegal markets first and foremost as indicators of changing concepts of crime and order. Individual aspects of the black markets are treated in the following: Wildt, *Am Beginn der Konsumgesellschaft*; Wildt, *Der Traum vom Sattwerden: Hunger und Protest, Schwarzmarkt und Selbsthilfe* (Hamburg, 1986); Rainer Hudemann, *Sozialpolitik im deutschen Südwesten zwischen Tradition und Neuordnung 1945–1953: Sozialversicherung und Kriegsopferversorgung im Rahmen französischer Besatzungspolitik* (Mainz, 1988), 75–77; Paul Erker, *Ernährungskrise und Nachkriegsgesellschaft: Bauern und Arbeiterschaft in Bayern 1943–1953* (Stuttgart, 1990); Werner Bührer, "Schwarzer Markt," in *Deutschland unter alliierter Besatzung 1945–1949/55: Ein Handbuch*, ed. Wolfgang Benz, 365–66 (Berlin, 1999); Werner Haeser, "Vom Schwarzmarkt und Tauschhandel

zur Deutschen Mark," *Schmallenberger Heimatblätter* 62 (1995/96): 75–81; Rainer Gries, *Die Rationengesellschaft: Versorgungskampf und Vergleichsmentalität: Leipzig, München und Köln nach dem Kriege* (Münster, 1991); and Alexander Link, *"Schrottelzeit": Nachkriegsalltag in Mainz* (Mainz, 1990). On efforts in Berlin to fight the black market, see Jörg Roesler, "The Black Market in Post-War Berlin and the Methods Used to Counteract It," *German History* 7 (1989): 92–107. The black markets are also discussed briefly in the historiography on Berlin; see, for example, David Clay Large, *Berlin: A Modern History* (New York, 2001), 146. For the Ruhr, see Lutz Niethammer, "Privat-Wirtschaft: Erinnerungsfragmente einer anderen Umerziehung," in *"Hinterher merkt man, dass es richtig war, dass es schiefgegangen ist." Nachkriegs-Erfahrungen im Ruhrgebiet*, ed. Niethammer, 61–62 (Berlin, 1983). See also the following contemporary works: Ludwig Aderbauer, "Der Schwarze Markt als Folge der Geldunordnung" (PhD diss., Ludwig-Maximilian University of Munich, 1948); Paul Werner Meyer, "Über das Phänomen des deutschen Schwarzen Marktes" (PhD diss., Friedrich-Alexander University of Erlangen-Nürnberg, 1949); and Karl Kromer, *Schwarzmarkt, Tausch- und Schleichhandel* (Schloß Bleckede an der Elbe, 1947). Karl Bader, *Soziologie der deutschen Nachkriegskriminalität* (Tübingen, 1949), does not treat the black market per se but refers to its importance repeatedly in the context of "female crime," malfeasance, and receiving stolen goods. See also Hilde Thurnwald, *Gegenwartsprobleme Berliner Familien* (Berlin, 1948); and Josef Schouz, "Volkskundliche Studie über das Bandenwesen des 'Schwarzen Marktes' " (PhD diss., University of Göttingen, 1953). Contemporary studies that paid greater attention to the complexity of the markets include Horst Mendershausen, "Prices, Money and the Distribution of Goods in Postwar Germany," *American Economic Review* 39 (1949): 647–72; and Mendershausen, *Two Postwar Recoveries of the German Economy* (Amsterdam, 1955).

6. See the summary of the debate concerning a "structuralist" versus a "historicist" interpretation of the economic upswing in Hans-Ulrich Wehler, *Gesellschaftsgeschichte*, vol. 4, *Vom Beginn des Ersten Weltkriegs bis zur Gründung der beiden deutschen Staaten 1914–1949* (Munich, 2003), 966–67.
7. Martin Broszat, Klaus-Dietmar Henke, and Hans Woller, eds., *Von Stalingrad zur Währungsreform: Zur Sozialgeschichte des Umbruchs in Deutschland*, 3rd ed. (Munich, 1990), quotes xxvi and xxv.
8. LAB F Rep. 240, Acc. 2651.
9. Ursula Weber, *Der Polenmarkt in Berlin: Zur Rekonstruktion eines kulturellen Kontakts im Prozess der politischen Transformation Mittel- und Osteuropas* (Neuried, 2002), 110–17.
10. Broszat, Henke, and Woller, eds., *Von Stalingrad zur Währungsreform.*
11. See Hartmut Berghoff and Jakob Vogel, "Wirtschaftsgeschichte als Kulturgeschichte: Ansätze zur Bergung transdisziplinärer Synergiepotentiale," in *Wirtschaftsgeschichte als Kulturgeschichte: Dimensionen eines Perspektivenwechsels*, ed. Berghoff and Vogel, 9–41 (Frankfurt am Main, 2004).
12. Hubert Schmitz, *Die Bewirtschaftung der Nahrungsmittel und Verbrauchsgüter 1939–1950: Dargestellt am Beispiel der Stadt Essen* (Essen, 1956), 41–42.
13. Gries, *Die Rationengesellschaft.*
14. Belinda Davis, *Home Fires Burning: Food, Politics, and Everyday Life in World War I Berlin* (Chapel Hill, NC, 2000).
15. Ernst Reuß, *Berliner Justizgeschichte* (Berlin, 2000), 127–28.
16. "Die Wirtschaft," no. 4 (1948): 120. See also Roesler, "Black Market," 92.

17. See here Wildt, *Am Beginn der Konsumgesellschaft.*
18. See Uwe Spiekermann, *Basis der Konsumgesellschaft: Entstehung und Entwicklung des modernen Kleinhandels in Deutschland* (Munich, 1999); and idem, "From Neighbor to Consumer: The Transformation of Retailer-Consumer Relationships in Twentieth-Century Germany," in *The Making of the Consumer: Knowledge, Power and Identity in the Modern World*, ed. Frank Trentmann, 147–74 (Oxford, UK, 2006).
19. Hans-Ulrich Wehler, *Die Herausforderung der Kulturgeschichte* (Munich, 1998), 138. See also Thomas Sokoll, "Kulturanthropologie und Historische Sozialwissenschaft," in *Geschichte zwischen Kultur und Gesellschaft: Beiträge zur Theoriedebatte*, ed. Thomas Mergel and Thomas Welskopp, 232–72 (Munich, 1997).
20. See especially Martin H. Geyer, *Verkehrte Welt: Revolution, Inflation und Moderne, München 1914–1924* (Göttingen, 1998), 13–14, who sees the "city as . . . synecdoche"; and Davis, *Home Fires Burning.*
21. Quote from Max Weber, *Wirtschaft und Gesellschaft: Grundriss der verstehenden Soziologie*, ed. Johannes Winckelmann, 5th ed. (Tübingen, 1980), 385.
22. On economic anthropological approaches, see Susana Narotzky, "Economic Anthropology," in *International Encyclopedia of the Social and Behavioral Sciences*, ed. Neil J. Smelser and Paul B. Baltes (Oxford, UK, 2001), 8:4069; and the relevant groundwork: Narotzky, *New Directions in Economic Anthropology* (London, 1997); Stuart Plattner, "Economic Behavior in Markets," in *Economic Anthropology*, ed. Plattner, 209–21 (Stanford, CA, 1989). The classic ethnological approach: Clifford Geertz, "The Bazaar Economy: Information and Search in Peasant Marketing," *American Economic Review* 68, no. 2 (1978): 28–32; and Clifford Geertz, "Suq: The Bazaar Economy in Sefrou," in *Meaning and Order in Moroccan Society: Three Essays in Cultural Analysis*, ed. Clifford Geertz, Hildred Geertz, and Lawrence Orsen, 123–264 (Cambridge, UK, 1979). On NIE, see Stefan Voigt, *Institutionenökonomik* (Munich, 2002); Rudolf Richter and Eirik Furubotn, *Neue Institutionenökonomik: Eine Einführung und kritische Würdigung*, trans. Monika Streissler, 3rd ed. (Tübingen, 2003).
23. Jens Beckert, "Vertrauen und die performative Konstruktion von Märkten," *Zeitschrift für Soziologie* 31, no. 1 (2002): 27–43; Mark Granovetter, "Economic Action and Social Structure: The Problem of Embeddedness," *Amercian Journal of Sociology* 91 (1985): 481–510.
24. Harrison White, "Varieties of Markets," in *Social Structures: A Network Approach*, ed. Barry Wellman and S. D. Berkowitz (New York, 1987), 232.
25. Religious questions, on the other hand, played a less important role in Berlin's black market than they did in Mauss's analysis. Marcel Mauss, *Die Gabe: Form und Funktion des Austauschs in archaischen Gesellschaften*, trans. Eva Moldenhauer (Frankfurt am Main, 1984). On the central concept of reciprocity as the foundation of the social in Mauss and Simmel, see Christian Papilloud, *Le Don de Relation: Georg Simmel—Marcel Mauss* (Paris, 2002). For the context, see Malte Zierenberg, "Tauschen und Vertrauen: Zur Kulturgeschichte des Schwarzhandels im Berlin der 1940er Jahre," in *Wirtschaftsgeschichte als Kulturgeschichte*, ed. Berghoff and Vogel *Wirtschaftsgeschichte als Kulturgeschichte: Dimensionen eines Perspektivenwechsels*, 169–94 (Frankfurt am Main, 2004).
26. On trust as a fundamental sociological problem, see Niklas Luhmann, *Vertrauen: Ein Mechanismus der Reduktion sozialer Komplexität*, 4th ed. (Stuttgart, 2000). For historical research on trust, see Ute Frevert, "Vertrauen in historischer Perspektive," in *Politisches Vertrauen: Soziale Grundlagen reflexiver Kooperation*, ed.

Rainer Schmalz-Bruns and Reinhard Zintl, 39–60 (Baden-Baden, 2002); Martin Fiedler, "Vertrauen ist gut, Kontrolle ist teuer: Vertrauen als Schlüsselkategorie wirtschaftliches Handelns," *Geschichte und Gesellschaft* 27 (2001): 576–92; Hartmut Berghoff, "Vertrauen als ökonomische Schlüsselvariable: Zur Theorie des Vertrauens und der marktwirtschaftlichen Produktion von Sozialkapital," in *Die Wirtschaftsgeschichte vor der Herausforderung der New Institutional Economics*, ed. Karl-Peter Ellerbrock and Clemens Wischermann, 58–71 (Dortmund, 2003); and Zierenberg, "Tauschen und Vertrauen."

27. Luhmann, *Vertrauen*; Luhmann, *Soziale Systeme: Grundriß einer allgemeinen Theorie*, 7th ed. (Frankfurt am Main, 1999). From an ethnological perspective: Geertz, "Bazaar Economy"; and Geertz, "Suq." For the extensive literature on institutional economics, see pars pro toto Douglass C. North, *Institutions, Institutional Change and Economic Performance* (Cambridge, UK, 1990).
28. Luhmann, *Vertrauen*, 39.
29. See Frevert, "Vertrauen in historischer Perspektive," 41; Frevert refers to Simmel.
30. See Berghoff and Vogel, "Wirtschaftsgeschichte als Kulturgeschichte"; and Zierenberg, "Tauschen und Vertrauen."
31. Weber, *Wirtschaft und Gesellschaft*, 37.
32. Geertz, "Bazaar Economy," 32; Zierenberg, "Tauschen und Vertrauen."
33. On the significance of heirlooms in identity formation, see Ulrike Langbein, *Geerbte Dinge: Soziale Praxis und symbolische Bedeutung des Erbens* (Cologne, 2002).
34. Consider, too, the influence of goods fed into the Berlin market by occupation troops after the war; Steege, *Black Market, Cold War*, 35.
35. André Steiner, ed., *Preispolitik und Lebensstandard: Nationalsozialismus, DDR und Bundesrepublik im Vergleich* (Cologne, 2006).
36. On these sites, see Malte Zierenberg, "The Trading City: Black Markets in Berlin during World War II," in *Endangered Cities: European Cities in the Era of the World Wars*, ed. Roger Chickering and Marcus Funck, 145–58 (Leiden, 2004).
37. Roesler, "Black Market."
38. On networks and research in this field, see Dorothea Jansen, *Einführung in die Netzwerkanalyse: Grundlagen, Methoden, Forschungsbeispiele* (Opladen, 1999).
39. Zierenberg, "Trading City"; Irene Bandhauer-Schöffmann, "Women's Fight for Food: A Gendered View of Hunger, Hoarding, and Blackmarketing in Vienna after World War II," in *Women in Towns: The Social Position of European Urban Women in a Historical Context*, ed. Marjatta Hietala, 158–79 (Stockholm, 1999).
40. See especially Norman M. Naimark, *The Russians in Germany: The History of the Soviet Zone of Occupation, 1945–1949* (Cambridge, MA, 1995).
41. Georg Simmel, *Philosophie des Geldes*, 4th ed. (Frankfurt am Main, 1996 [Leipzig, 1900]), 319.
42. Viviana A. Zelizer, "Economic Sociology," in *International Encyclopedia of the Social and Behavioral Sciences*, ed. Neil J. Smelser and Paul B. Baltes, 8:4131 (Oxford, UK, 2001).
43. Luhmann, *Vertrauen*, 9.
44. The phrase "everyday life in a state of emergency" comes from Susanne zur Nieden, *Alltag im Ausnahmezustand: Frauentagebücher im zerstörten Deutschland 1943 bis 1945* (Berlin, 1993).
45. On the public sphere, see Jürgen Gerhards and Friedhelm Neidhardt. "Strukturen und Funktionen moderner Öffentlichkeit: Fragestellungen und Ansätze," in *Öffentlichkeit, Kultur, Massenkommunikation: Beiträge zur Medien- und*

Kommunikationssoziologie, ed. Stefan Müller-Doohm, 31–88 (Oldenburg, 1991). See also Jörg Requate, "Öffentlichkeit und Medien als Gegenstände historischer Analyse," *Geschichte und Gesellschaft* 25 (1999): 5–31; and Zierenberg, "Tauschen und Vertrauen."

46. See Anthony Giddens, *The Consequences of Modernity* (Cambridge, 1990), 79; Geertz, "Suq"; Fiedler, "Vertrauen ist gut," esp. 584.
47. On the effects of the "final battle," see Anthony Beevor, *Berlin: The Downfall 1945* (London, 2007).
48. See Zierenberg, "Tauschen und Vertrauen."
49. In this way, lawmakers created a market for a new kind of how-to literature, and manuals arose to help police and consumers make their way through the jungle of black market regulations. See Kromer, *Schwarzmarkt.*
50. On the various approaches to understanding discourses in terms of power, see Achim Landwehr, *Geschichte des Sagbaren: Einführung in die historische Diskursanalyse* (Tübingen, 2001).
51. Frank Bajohr, *Parvenüs und Profiteure: Korruption in der NS-Zeit* (Frankfurt am Main, 2001), 62.
52. On the concept of the public sphere, which is important to this study, see Gerhards and Neidhardt, "Strukturen und Funktionen moderner Öffentlichkeit."
53. On the "moral economy," see Edward P. Thompson, "The Moral Economy of the English Crowd in the 18th Century," *Past and Present* 50 (1971): 76–136. In the present study, Thompson's concept is used broadly to designate primarily moral interpretations of economic issues and the resulting defensive postures that economic actors assume.

Chapter 1

1. Belinda Davis, *Home Fires Burning: Food, Politics, and Everyday Life in World War I Berlin* (Chapel Hill, NC, 2000).
2. LAB A Rep. 358–02 (Staatsanwaltschaft bei dem Landgericht), 89667, indictment, not paginated.
3. In light of such sentences, it is problematic to speak of "peccadilloes" as Mark Spoerer does in "Die soziale Differenzierung der ausländischen Zivilarbeiter, Kriegsgefangenen und Häftlinge im Deutschen Reich," in *Das Deutsche Reich und der Zeite Weltkrieg*, vol. 9, pt. 2, *Die deutsche Kriegsgesellschaft 1939 bis 1945: Ausbeutung, Deutungen, Ausgrenzung*, ed. Jörg Echternkamp (Munich, 2005), 562. The fact that not even close to all cases could be prosecuted does not belie the rigorous sentencing policy. In the trials before the Berlin Special Court, jail terms were the rule, and the death penalty was imposed in some cases. For examples of the latter for "War Economy Crimes," see LAB, A, Rep. 358–02, 89703, 89770, and 87805. Spoerer's broad generalization that "the German authorities" allowed black marketeers to be active "as long as the business transactions only served [their] personal needs" is incorrect. For some examples from the Cologne Special Court, see Malte Zierenberg, "Zwischen Herrschaftsfragen und Verbraucherinteressen: 'Kriegswirtschaftsverbrechen' vor dem Sondergericht Köln im Zweiten Weltkrieg," *Geschichte in Köln* 50 (2003): 175–95.
4. One must take chronology into account (which Spoerer does not). As Mark Thornton observes in *The Economics of Prohibition* (Salt Lake City, 1991), 75–77, prohibition can at first be efficient because it is relatively easy to apply the

appropriate sanctions to a weakly developed market structure with few participants. As prohibition continues, however, costs increase and the efficiency of sanctions decreases in proportion to the development of alternative market infrastructures and increasing numbers of participants. The result: "The marginal cost of increased prohibition . . . increases." Ibid., 77.

5. Ian Kershaw, *Hitler 1889–1936*, trans. Jürgen Peter Krause and Jörg W. Rademacher, 4th ed. (Stuttgart, 1998), 663–744. On the *Machtübergabe*, "transfer of power," see Hans-Ulrich Wehler, *Gesellschaftsgeschichte,* vol. 4, *Vom Beginn des Ersten Weltkriegs bis zur Gründung der beiden deutschen Staaten 1914–1949* (Munich, 2003), 580–85. On the history of the NSDAP's rise in general, see Richard J. Evans, *The Coming of the Third Reich* (London, 2003).
6. Gottfried Feder, *Das Programm der NSDAP und seine weltanschaulichen Grundgedanken*, 13th ed. (Munich, 1930), 9.
7. Mark Spoerer, "Die soziale Differenzierung der ausländischen Zivilarbeiter, Kriegsgefangenen und Häftlinge im Deutschen Reich," in *Das Deutsche Reich und der Zweite Weltkrieg*, vol. 9, pt. 2, *Die deutsche Kriegsgesellschaft 1939 bis 1945: Ausbeutung, Deutungen, Ausgrenzung*, ed. Jörg Echternkamp (Munich, 2005), 485–576; Wehler, *Gesellschaftsgeschichte*, 4:770.
8. This is the "Volksschädlingsverordnung," September 5, 1939, *Reichsgesetzblatt* 1: 1679.
9. September 26, 1920, *Reichsgesetzblatt* 1: 4.
10. Quoted in Cornelia Schmitz-Berning, *Vokabular des Nationalsozialismus* (Berlin, 1998), 671.
11. Bajohr notes aptly that "the harshest critics of the Weimar Republic's alleged fat-cat economy [*Bonzenwirtschaft*] . . . established a real fat cat economy to a theretofore unknown degree"; see Frank Bajohr, *Parvenüs und Profiteure* 49–97, quote 67. For the debates over Berlin's corruption cases, see Cordula Ludwig, *Korruption und Nationalsozialismus in Berlin 1924–1934* (Berlin, 1998).
12. See, however, the modifications to the crisis paradigm in Moritz Föllmer and Rüdiger Graf, *Die "Krise" der Weimarer Republik: Zur Kritik eines Deutungsmusters* (Frankfurt am Main, 2005).
13. See, for example, Detlef Lehnert and Klaus Megerle, "Identitäts- und Konsensprobleme in einer fragmentierten Gesellschaft: Zur politischen Kultur in der Weimarer Republik," in *Politische Kultur in Deutschland*, ed. Dirk Berg-Schlosser and Jakob Schissler, special issue of *Politische Vierteljahresschrift* 18 (1987): 80–95; and Andreas Wirsching, *Die Weimarer Republik. Politik und Gesellschaft* (Munich, 2000), 84–95. Thomas Mergel notes in *Parlamentarische Kultur in der Weimarer Republik* (Düsseldorf, 2002), 27–29, that fragmented societies were more the rule than the exception in Europe before 1945; however, see Andreas Wirsching, *Vom Weltkrieg zum Bürgerkrieg. Politischer Extremismus in Deutschland und Frankreich 1918–1933/39. Berlin und Paris im Vergleich* (Munich, 1999), on the special situation of the development of extreme political antagonisms under the mantle of a "civil war" in Berlin during Weimar. Dirk Schumann argues in a different direction, using the example of Saxony in his *Politische Gewalt in der Weimarer Republik: Kampf um die Straße und Furcht vor dem Bürgerkrieg* (Essen, 2001).
14. Schumann, *Politische Gewalt*, 376.
15. Martin H. Geyer, *Verkehrte Welt: Revolution, Inflation und Moderne, Munich 1914–1924* (Göttingen, 1998), 396.

16. For the basic outlines of this interpretation, see Detlev J. K. Peukert, *Die Weimarer Republik Krisenjahre der klassischen Moderne* (Frankfurt am Main, 1987), 13–25, 213–42. On the differences compared to the situation in 1949, see Christoph Gusy, "Einleitung—Weimar: Geschichte als Argument," in *Weimars lange Schatten: "Weimar" als Argument nach 1945*, ed. Gusy, 16–21 (Baden-Baden, 2003); and the remarks by Theodor Heuss, *Aufzeichnungen 1945–1947*, ed. and with introduction by Eberhard Pikart (Tübingen, 1966), 128, quoted in Ulrich Baumgärtner, "Von einer Republik zur anderen: Theodor Heuss' Wahrnehmung und Deutung der Weimarer Republik nach 1945," in *Weimars lange Schatten*, ed. Gusy, 92–117.
17. See Wolfgang Hardtwig, "Einleitung: Politische Kulturgeschichte der Zwischenkriegszeit," and Thomas Mergel, "Führer, Volksgemeinschaft und Maschine: Politische Erwartungsstrukturen in der Weimarer Republik und dem Nationalsozialismus 1918–1936," both in *Politische Kulturgeschichte der Zwischenkriegszeit 1918–1936*, ed. Wolfgang Hartwig, 7–22, 91–128 (Göttingen, 2005).
18. See Stefan Malinowski, "Politische Skandale als Zerrspiegel der Demokratie: Die Fälle Barmat und Sklarek im Kalkül der Weimarer Rechten," *Jahrbuch für Antisemitismusforschung* 5 (1996): 46–65; and Frank Bösch, "Historische Skandalforschung als Schnittstelle zwischen Medien-, Kommunikantions- und Geschichtswissenschaft," in *Die Medien der Geschichte: Historizität und Medialität in interdisziplinärer Perspektive*, ed. Fabio Crivellari, Kay Kirchmann, Marcus Sandl, and Rudolf Schlögl, 445–64 (Konstanz, 2004). On the sequels to such forms of political instrumentalization in the two German dictatorships, see Martin Sabrow, ed., *Skandal und Diktatur: Formen öffentlicher Empörung im NS-Staat und in der DDR* (Göttingen, 2004).
19. Mergel, *Parlamentarische Kultur*, 378–79.
20. See Peukert, *Die Weimarer Republik*, 85–87.
21. *Der Montag: Jahrgedächtnis* von Friedrich Hussong, no. 43, November 9, 1925, 1.
22. *Vorwärts*, no. 100, from February 28, 1925, 2nd suppl., 1.
23. See Geyer, *Verkehrte Welt*, 167–95.
24. On the "legal uncertainty in the bourgeois legal relationships," see ibid., 209; and the introduction to Bernd Widdig, *Culture and Inflation in Weimar Germany* (Berkeley, 2001), 3–30.
25. Geyer, *Verkehrte Welt*, 383; see also Martin Geyer, "Die Sprache des Rechts, die Sprache des Antisemitismus: 'Wucher' und soziale Ordnungsvorstellungen im Kaiserreich und der Weimarer Republik," in *Europäische Sozialgeschichte: Festschrift für Professor Schieder*, ed. Christoph Dipper, Lutz Klinkhammer, and Alexander Nützenadel, 413–29 (Berlin, 2000).
26. Geyer, *Verkehrte Welt*, 239–40.
27. Robert Scholtz, "Die Auswirkungen der Inflation auf das Sozial- und Wohlfahrtswesen der neuen Stadtgemeinde Berlin," in *Konsequenzen der Inflation*, ed. Gerald Feldman and J. Th. M. Houwink ten Cate, 45–75 (Berlin, 1989). For a contemporary description, see Gustav Böß, *Die Not in Berlin: Tatsachen und Zahlen* (Berlin, 1923).
28. Robert Scholz, "Die Auswirkungen der Inflation," 55–58.
29. Ibid., 64–65; Molly Loberg, "Berlin Streets: Politics, Commerce, and Crowds, 1918–1938" (PhD diss., Princeton University, 2006).

30. Geyer, *Verkehrte Welt*, 243.
31. Detlev J. K. Peukert, *Volksgenossen und Gemeinschaftsfremde: Anpassung, Ausmerze und Aufbegehren unter dem Nationalsozialismus* (Opladen, 1982), 233. See Geyer, *Verkehrte Welt*, 396, on the Nazis' *völkisch* (national and racialist) strategy to commingle "extortion," "Versailles," the 1918 revolution, and anti-Semitic sentiments in their propaganda. Anti-Semitic stereotypes of Jews as "extortionists" and as disturbers of the public order could, however, also be found in Social Democratic magazines; see Julia Schäfer, *Vermessen—gezeichnet—verlacht: Judenbilder in populären Zeitschriften 1918–1933* (Frankfurt am Main, 2005).
32. Geyer, *Verkehrte Welt*, 244–46.
33.

> Look at the long row of luxury autos that the heavy industrialists, wholesale merchants, and bankers use to drive through the city . . . They were bought at a time when the common people had to face terrible poverty. Look at the increase in the number of luxury and gourmet restaurants in which the bourgeoisie squanders its loot.
>
> *Vorwärts*, no. 548, November 20, 1924, 1

34. Wolfgang Schivelbusch, *Kultur der Niederlage* (Berlin, 2001).
35. In this regard, Geyer, *Verkehrte Welt*, analyzes the hyperinflation as the devaluation of a medium of communication, which complicated social action. For a similar argument, see Hansjörg Siegenthaler, *Regelvertrauen, Prosperität und Krisen: Die Ungleichmäßigkeit wirtschaftlicher und sozialer Entwicklungen als Ergebnis individuellen Handelns* (Tübingen, 1993), 16; Siegenthaler sees the economic crisis as a catalyst for communicative processes of self-analysis. Regarding Versailles, see Gerhard Krumeich, ed., *Versailles 1919: Ziele—Wirkung—Wahrnehmung* (Essen, 2001); Manfred Franz Boemeke, ed., *The Treaty of Versailles: A Reassessment after 75 Years* (Cambridge, UK, 1998); and Eberhard Kolb, *Der Friede von Versailles* (Munich, 2005). On the "weight of the past," see Ulrich Heinemann, "Die Last der Vergangenheit. Zur politischen Bedeutung der Kriegsschuld- und Dolchstoßdiskussion," in *Die Weimarer Republik 1918–1933. Politik, Wirtschaft, Gesellschaft*, ed. Karl Dietrich Bracher, Manfred Funke, and Hans-Adolf Jacobsen, 371–86 (Düsseldorf, 1987), 371. Speaking with absolute certainty has been interpreted as a rhetorically vital feature in what was actually an insecure society and was perhaps most strongly present in the stab-in-the-back legend; see Boris Barth, *Dolchstoßlegenden und politische Desintegration: Das Trauma der deutschen Niederlage im Ersten Weltkrieg 1914–1933* (Düsseldorf, 2003).
36. Quoted in *Berliner Tageblatt*, no. 215, May 13, 1919.
37. Gottfried Niedhardt, "Der Erste Weltkrieg: Von der Gewalt im Krieg zu den Konflikten im Frieden," in *Wie Kriege enden: Wege zum Frieden von der Antike bis zur Gegenwart*, ed. Bernd Wegner (Paderborn, 2002), 205.
38. Adolf Weber, *Reparationen, Youngplan, Volkswirtschaft* (Berlin, 1929), 9.
39. See Geyer, *Verkehrte Welt*, 294. This transfer of the stereotypical image of the enemy took a specific direction. Again and again, indignant rhetoric of defeat painted a propagandistic caricature in which "internal" and "external" enemies alike were defined by their dishonest economic practices. This rhetoric did not abate but rather outlived the Weimar Republic. It became an important motif in World War II, too, especially in the propaganda against England. "Perfidious Albion" remained for the National Socialist propaganda a hotbed of "warmongers" and "war profiteers." See

the *Parole der Woche*, no. 44, 1940, which was distributed in leaflets. Reprinted in *SOPADE, 1940, p. 31. Deutschland-Berichte der Sozialdemokratischen Partei Deutschlands (SOPADE) 1934–1949*, ed. Klaus Behnken (Salzhausen/Frankfurt am Main, 1980).

40. Quoted in *Berliner Tageblatt*, no. 217, May 14, 1919.
41. All parties wanted to reduce reparations, but they differed over the best way to achieve this goal; Wehler, *Gesellschaftsgeschichte*, 244.
42. Such economic terms formed an essential strand of the anti-Semitic discourse, which included talk of the "stock market Jews," "the bank Jews," and "the money Jews"; Othmar Plöckinger, *Reden um die Macht? Wirkung und Strategie der Reden Adolf Hitlers im Wahlkampf zu den Reichstagswahlen am 6. November 1932* (Vienna, 1999), 115.
43. Hanne Bergius, "Berlin als Hure Babylon," in *Die Metropole: Industriestruktur in Berlin im 20. Jahrhundert*, ed. Jochen Boberg (Munich, 1988), 82.
44. Geyer, *Verkehrte Welt*, 273.
45. Hanne Bergius, "Berlin als Hure Babylon," 107–108. See also Katharina von Ankum, ed., *Women in the Metropolis: Gender and Modernity in Weimar Culture* (Berkeley, CA, 1997).
46. Ankum, *Women in the Metropolis*, 104.
47. Nevertheless, encounters with the criminal milieu remained problematic and had to be brought about by "fate"—for example, love for a weak, young girl. In the end, everything had to come out all right. See, for instance, the informative plot of the film *Asphalt*, directed by Joe May, which played in the movie houses in 1929. Already the film poster made clear what was involved: the young protagonist was exposed to the dangers of the modern asphalt city, Berlin. The poster, in blue and gray, showed the lettering "ASPHALT" on a slanted surface, smooth as glass, as the letters themselves start to slip and slide. See Gottfried Korff and Reinhard Rürup, eds., *Berlin, Berlin: Die Ausstellung zur Geschichte der Stadt* (Berlin, 1987), 471–73, which includes revealing set designs.
48. On the image of the criminal in media, see Sheila Brown, *Crime and Law in Media Culture* (Buckingham, 2003).
49. The original German:

> Am Kurfürstendamm da hocken zusammen
> die Leute von heute mit großem Tamtam.
> Brillianten wie Tanten, ein Frack mit was drin,
> Ein Nerzpelz, ein Steinherz, ein Doppelkinn.
> Perlen perlen, es perlt der Champagner.
> Kokotten spotten: Wer will, der kann ja
> Fünf Braune für mich auf das Tischtuch zählen.
> Na, Schieber, mein Lieber?—Nee, uns kann's nicht fehlen.
> Und wenn Millionen vor Hunger krepieren:
> Wir wolln uns mal wieder amüsieren.
>
> Quoted in Bergius, "Berlin als Hure Babylon," 113

50. Ibid.
51. *Vorwärts*, no. 548, November 20, 1924, 1; *Berliner Lokal-Anzeiger*, no. 208, May 3, 1925, 7, Beiblatt 1 (letter to the editor).
52. Schmitz-Berning, *Vokabular des Nationalsozialismus*, 637.

53. This desire also appeared, in a weaker form, in academic discourses, for example, in economics. In the contemporary discussion of Joseph Schumpeter's *Theorie der wirtschaftlichen Entwicklung* (1911), at the center of which stands the capitalist entrepreneur as the agent of "new combinations" and thus the source of economic development, Walter Eucken asked if there had been enough entrepreneurs since 1918 who "possessed the will and the ability to be leaders of the [economic] development." Even though Eucken answered yes, his formulation of the question in this manner pointed out how skeptical many were, and how many saw the search for personalities capable of making decisions as a manifestation of a comprehensive crisis. Furthermore, Eucken saw the cause of the crisis in the "state-societal organization," thus implicitly shifting the "leadership" problem into the realm of the political. See Walter Eucken, "Staatliche Strukturwandlungen und die Krise des Kapitalismus," *Weltwirtschaftliches Archiv* 36 (1932): 298. Dieter Haselbach, "Die Lehren aus Weimar in den Wirtschaftswissenschaften nach 1945: Der Ordoliberalismus," in *Weimars lange Schatten Weimars Lange Schatten: "Weimar" als Argument nach 1945*, ed. Christoph Gusy, 118–47 (Baden-Baden, 2003), might impute to the economist too much of a critical distance when he suggests that Eucken's argumentation was based on long-term developments and scarcely made reference to the Weimar period. At the very least, Eucken's word choices evinced a semantic alignment with the contemporary discourse of crisis, despite his having criticized widespread faith in the "total state" and only for this reason finding himself strictly opposed to National Socialist ideas about "leadership." See Haselbach, 125–26, and on the proximity of his ideas to those of Carl Schmitt, 129–30.
54. Quoted in Christian Schottmann, *Politische Schlagwörter in Deutschland zwischen 1929 und 1934* (Stuttgart, 1997), 514.
55. Ibid., 518.
56. Peukert, *Volksgenossen und Gemeinschaftsfremde*, 233.
57. Ian Kershaw, *Hitlers Macht: Das Profil der NS-Herrschaft* (Munich, 2000), 248.
58. The regime made this change quite explicitly, for example, in 1934, when the party congress utilized the slogan "Party Convention of Loyalty."
59. Large sections of the population thus responded with more restraint when new accusations of corruption undermined their confidence in the collection campaigns of the National Socialist People's Welfare Organization (NSV); see Bajohr, *Parvenüs und Profititeure*, 179.
60. It therefore seems questionable to speak in this context of an "accommodating dictatorship," as Götz Aly does in *Hitlers Volksstaat: Raub, Rassenkrieg und nationaler Sozialismus* (Frankfurt am Main, 2005), even independently of the transfers that were actually provided.
61. Ian Kershaw, *Der Hitler-Mythos: Führerkult und Volksmeinung* (Stuttgart, 1999); Klaus Schreiner, "'Wann kommt der Retter Deutschlands?' Formen und Funktionen von politischen Messianismus in der Weimarer Republik," *Saeculum* 49 (1998): 107–60; Mergel, "Führer, Volksgemeinschaft und Maschine."
62. On the difference between trust and hope, see Harald Wenzel, "Vertrauen und die Integration moderner Gesellschaften," in *Politisches Vertrauen: Grundlagen reflexiver Kooperation*, ed. Rainer Schmalz-Bruns and Reinhard Zintl, 61–76 (Baden-Baden, 2002). On Hitler's special position, which was not affected by the criticism of "fat cats," see Bajohr, *Parvenüs und Profititeure*, 180, who quotes the Berlin Police President chief of police: "In this context, the population refers continually to the modest and reserved demeanor of the Führer."

63. Ute Frevert, "Vertrauen in historischer Perspektive," in *Politisches Vertrauen: Soziale Grundlagen reflexiver Kooperation*, ed. Rainer Schmalz-Bruns and Reinhard Zintl (Baden-Baden, 2002), 54–55.
64. Wenzel, "Vertrauen," 65.
65. Ibid., 71.
66. Victor Klemperer, *LTI: Notizbuch eines Philologen* (Leipzig, 1999), 129.
67. Mergel, "Führer, Volksgemeinschaft und Maschine," 126, points to examples from everyday usage, such as when renters and landlords were described as a housing community. Since the German Jurists' Conference in 1936, lawyers were supposed to bear the title Guardian of the Law (*Rechtswahrer*). This change was "the expression of a complete metamorphosis," claimed the state secretary in the German justice ministry, Roland Freisler: "*Rechtswahrer* . . . the very word suggests someone who is deployed for a special task, and this special task, this occupation, is to guard the law. And whoever calls himself a Rechtswahrer is thus also taking an oath to actually fulfill this task"; Roland Freisler, *Nationalsozialistisches Recht und Rechtsdenken* (Berlin, 1938), 86–88.
68. This shift also found expression in a preference for partnerships over incorporation. To be sure, the original ideological radicalism gave way after 1939 to second thoughts about the configuration of a so-called *volkstümliche GmbH* or "racial inc." All in all, however, the partnership remained "the preferred legal form in the National Socialist economy"; see Matthias Stupp, *GmbH-Recht im Nationalsozialismus: Anschauungen des Nationalsozialismus zur Haftungsbeschränkung, Juristischen Person, Kapitalgesellschaft und Treupflicht: Untersuchungen zum Referentenentwurf 1939 zu einem neuen GmbH-Gesetz* (Berlin, 2002), 350.
69. Michael Burleigh, *The Third Reich: A New History* (London, 2001), 12.
70. Uwe Spiekermann, "From Neighbour to Consumer: The Transformation of Retailer-Consumer Relationships in Twentieth-Century Germany," in *The Making of the Consumer: Knowledge, Power and Identity in the Modern World*, ed. Frank Trentmann, 147–74 (Oxford, 2006).
71. Deutsches Historisches Museum (DHM), Rep. I, 2. Weltkrieg, F1, M, Tagebuch Deutmann, June 24, 1945.
72. David Clay Large, *Berlin: A Modern History* (New York, 2001), 48–50. On the history of department stores in Imperial Germany, see Hans-Peter Ullmann, " 'Der Kaiser bei Wertheim'—Warenhäuser im wilhelminischen Deutschland," in *Europäische Sozialgeschichte*, ed. Christoph Dipper, Lutz Klinkhammer, and Alexander Nützenadel, 223–36.
73. See Jochen Boberg, "Reklamwelten," in *Die Metropole: Industriestruktur in Berlin im 20: Jahrhundert*, ed. Jochen Boberg, 184–89 (Munich, 1988).
74. For an impressive description of a "flying" exchange at the Volksbühne in the center of Berlin, see Joseph Roth's report, "Der Orient in der Hirtenstraße: Besuch in der fliegenden Börse," reprinted in *Joseph Roth in Berlin: Ein Lesebuch für Spaziergänger*, ed. Michael Bienert (Cologne, 1996). There is also a photograph here, p. 84, from 1934 of the hustle and bustle of the marketplace in the Grenadierstrasse (Scheunenviertel).
75. Davis, *Home Fires Burning*; Anne Roehrkohl, *Hungerblockade und Heimatfront: Die kommunale Lebensmittelversorgung in Westfalen während des Ersten Weltkrieges* (Stuttgart, 1991).

76. LAB A Rep. 001–02 (Stadtverordnetenversammlung von Berlin), no. 2310, 54. In the city council meeting on June 26, 1921, the councilman Merten from the Democratic Party estimated the number of street traders at between 20,000 and 25,000. See ibid., 139.
77. Ibid., p. 42.
78. LAB A Rep. 037–08 (Bezirksamt Charlottenburg), 51.
79. See the letter signed by nine retail business owners to the municipal government from April 23, 1921, in LAB A Rep. 001–02, no. 2310, 116–17. See also the letter from the Association for Trade and Commerce from May 12, 1921, in ibid., 122–23.
80. LAB A Rep. 001–02, no. 2310, 54.
81. Thomas Lindenberger, *Straßenpolitik. Zur Sozialgeschichte der öffentlichen Ordnung in Berlin 1900–1914* (Bonn, 1995).
82. LAB A Rep. 001–02, no. 2310, 59.
83. Ibid., 84.
84. Ibid. The Bezirksamt Mitte was also of this opinion. See ibid, pp. 153–54.
85. See LAB A Rep. 001–02 Nr. 2310, pp. 141–42.
86. Ibid.
87. Uwe Spiekermann, *Basis der Konsumgesellschaft: Entstehung und Entwicklung des modernen Kleinhandels in Deutschland* (Munich, 1999), 202.
88. See Gideon Reuveni, "Wohlstand durch Konsum: Straßenhandel und Versicherungszeitschriften in den zwanziger Jahren," in *Die "Krise" der Weimarer Republik: Zur Kritik eines Deutungsmusters*, ed. Moritz Föllmer and Rüdiger Graf (Frankfurt am Main, 2005), 274–75.
89. Statistisches Landesamt der Stadt Berlin, ed., *Berlin in Zahlen* (Berlin, 1947), 360.
90. Reuveni, "Wohlstand durch Konsum," 275.
91. On the importance of the market halls, see Erich Rindt, "Die Markthallen als Faktor des Berliner Wirtschaftslebens" (PhD diss., Friedrich-Wilhelms-Universität Berlin, 1928).
92. Otto Büsch, *Geschichte der Berliner Kommunalwirtschaft in der Weimarer Epoche* (Berlin, 1960), 126.
93. See ibid., 127; and *Statistisches Jahrbuch der Stadt Berlin* 5 (1929): 56.
94. Ibid., 56.
95. Ibid.
96. Spiekermann, *Basis der Konsumgesellschaft.*
97. LAB A Rep. 001–02, no. 2310, p. 142.
98. Spiekermann, "From Neighbour to Consumer," 153.
99. Statistisches Landesamt der Stadt Berlin, ed., *Berlin in Zahlen*, 167.
100. Ibid.
101. Spiekermann, "From Neighbour to Consumer," 149.
102. Ibid., 156.
103. See ibid., 138.
104. See the urban renewal program for the capital developed by Albert Speer for the Generalbauinspektor (GBI) für die Reichshauptstadt„ which was accelerated in 1937. At first, it was supposed to be carried out without any financial constraints. By 1941, however, it had become increasingly problematic because of labor and material shortages. The actual expenditures of the GBI never reached the amount planned. See Harald Engler, *Die Finanzierung der Reichshauptstadt: Untersuchungen zu den hauptstadtbedingten staatlichen Ausgaben Preußens und des Deutschen Reiches*

in Berlin vom Kaiserreich bis zum Dritten Reich (1871–1945) (Berlin, 2004), 387–430.

105. On the concept of "the masses," see George L. Mosse, *The Nationalization of the Masses: Political Symbolism and Mass Movements in Germany from the Napoleonic Wars through the Third Reich* (New York, 1975).
106. Large, *Berlin*, 255.
107. Quoted Robert Gellately, *Backing Hitler: Consent and Coercion in Nazi Germany* (Oxford, UK, 2001), 36.
108. Large, *Berlin*, 295.
109. Spiekermann, "From Neighbour to Consumer," 157.
110. See Statistisches Landesamt der Stadt Berlin, ed., *Berlin in Zahlen*, 183. By containing street trading, the responsible agencies could calm down enraged retail business owners. In March 1936, complaints from such businessmen even reached the state chancellery. In an "urgent appeal," the proprietor of a stand in the Central Market Hall I in the Neue Friedrichstrasse expressed his displeasure. He had "attempted since 1933 here in the Berlin market to keep his house . . . in order," without noticing "any changes hav[ing] occurred to contain or to prohibit the street trading." LAB A Pr. Br., Rep. 57 (Stadtpräsident der Reichshauptstadt Berlin), no. 511, letter to State Secretary Lummers, March 30, 1936.
111. Kershaw, *Hitler 1889–1936*, 724–28.
112. See ibid. The officially mandated levels of meat consumption sank from 71.6 kg per capita in 1934 to 55.2 kg per capita in 1936. See Statistisches Landesamt der Stadt Berlin, ed., *Berlin in Zahlen*, 206.
113. SOPADE, 1934, pp. 179.
114. SOPADE, 1936, pp. 1405.
115. SOPADE, 1938, pp. 637.
116. Spiekermann, "From Neighbour to Consumer," 158.
117. This was a "special case" because the rationing did not aim at a general prohibition of the trade in certain goods but rather was merely supposed to organize a reduced, controlled release of goods, that is, a "supply-reduction policy"; Thornton, *Economics*, 73–77.
118. See Wilhelm Henrichsmeyer, Oskar Gans, and Ingo Evers, *Einführung in die Volkswirtschaftslehre*, 10th ed. (Stuttgart, 1993), 202–203.
119. Gustavo Corni and Horst Gies, *Brot, Butter, Kanonen: Die Ernährungswirtschaft in Deutschland unter der Diktatur Hitlers* (Berlin, 1997), 558.
120. Ibid., 562.
121. Jost Dülffer, *Deutsche Geschichte 1933–1945: Führerglaube und Vernichtungskrieg* (Stuttgart, 1992), 139.
122. Corni and Gies, *Brot, Butter, Kanonen*, 581.
123. A Rep. 001–02, no. 1552, 118–19.
124. All quotes in ibid., 128.
125. Ibid., 134.
126. Davis, *Home Fires Burning*; Roehrkohl, *Hungerblockade und Heimatfront.*
127. Karl-Heinz Klüber, *Gesetzliche Grundlagen zur Schwarzmarktbekämpfung*, 3rd ed. (Hamburg, 1948).
128. Ibid., 5.
129. Ibid. The list of regulations which were related at least indirectly to black marketeering offenses included a prohibition on raising prices (1936), as well as a "prohibition of tying arrangements (*Kopplungsverbot*) and of price gouging by middlemen"

(1937). There were also regulations on pricing (1944) and on the maximum price allowed for used goods (1942). On top of this there was an older regulation on the obligation to provide information (1923) as well as seven regulations issued by the Allied Military Government; among these were the Allied Control Council Act No. 50 from 18 December 1947.

130. See the War Economy Regulations from 4 September 1939 in the last revised version of 25 March 1942. *Reichsgesetzblatt* 1: 147.
131. LAB A Rep. 358–02, 89673, 45.
132. Henry Picker, *Hitlers Tischgespräche im Führerhauptquartier* (Munich, 1979), 541.
133. Zierenberg, "Zwischen Herrschaftsfragen und Verbraucherinteressen."
134. *Deutsche Justiz* (1939): 1753.
135. Ibid., 1754.
136. Ibid.
137. *Deutsche Justiz* (1940): 256.
138. Ibid., 1271.

Chapter 2

1. See the short introduction in Willi Boelcke, *Der Schwarzmarkt: Vom Überleben nach dem Kriege* (Stuttgart, 1986); and Rainer Gries, *Die Rationen-Gesellschaft: Versorgungskampf und Vergleichsmentalität: Leipzig, München und Köln nach dem Kriege* (Münster, 1991), as well as Frank Bajohr, *Parvenüs und Profiteure: Korruption in der NS-Zeit* (Frankfurt am Main, 2001). Bajohr, however, concentrates on corruption cases.
2. On the following analysis, see LAB A Rep. 358–02 89667.
3. Ibid., indictment from March 31, 1945 (unpaginated).
4. See Dorothea Jansen, *Einführung in die Netzwerkanalyse: Grundlagen, Methoden, Forschungsbeispiele* (Opladen, 1999), 127–62 and 193–236, on the logic behind this.
5. LAB A Rep. 358–02 89667, pp. 45ff.
6. Ibid.
7. Ibid., p. 86.
8. See Statistisches Landesamt der Stadt Berlin, ed., *Berlin in Zahlen*, 83.
9. LAB A Rep. 358–02 89667, p. 59.
10. Ibid., p. 46.
11. Ibid., interrogation Kuschy (unpaginated).
12. See Niklas Luhmann, *Vertrauen: Ein Mechanismus der Reduktion sozialer Komplexität*, 4th ed. (Stuttgart, 2000), 23–24.
13. See Jansen, *Einführung*, 65.
14. For the following, see LAB A Rep. 358–02 89667, pp. 25ff.
15. Ibid., p. 32.
16. Ibid.
17. Ibid., p. 57.
18. On Wiggers's professional life, see ibid., pp. 24ff.
19. A Rep. 358–02 79976.
20. Ibid., 89667, pp. 6ff.
21. The following is based on LAB A Rep. 358–02 89667, pp. 25ff.
22. The records of the Gestapo contain references to problems the police had in organizing their work. As the "police informer" (*nachrichtenmäßige Verbindung*) Erna

Kuschy had also reported on the "political character" of activities taking place in Franz Seidemann's and Martha Rebbien's residences (listening to "enemy radio stations" and "agitation against political institutions and personalities"), the Gestapo took over the case. However, the Gestapo soon complained about the "inability of the police to provide enough policemen." (LAB A Rep. 358–02 89667, unpaginated, Schreiben der Geheimen Staatspolizei, Staatspolizeileitstelle Berlin, from November 11, 1944.)

23. Jansen, *Einführung*, 173–75.
24. All quotes ibid., p. 175.
25. LAB A Rep. 358–02, p. 49.
26. That these groups of people were overrepresented was only in part because of their privileged access to goods in demand and their ability to establish contacts. The fact that the trade inspection service (Gewerbeaußendienst or GAD) of the Berlin police, whose task was to supervise stores, bars, and restaurants, did a large part of the investigative work, contributed to this result. See above in the section, "Bartering Spaces and Movement Patterns."
27. The War Economy Regulations did not formulate any concrete details. See the War Economy Regulations from September 4, 1939 (RGBl. I. p. 1609).
28. See the example of Hermann Weese below.
29. LAB A Rep. 358–02 8443, p. 20. The market in Neukölln was so small that one witness, while visiting a restaurant, recognized a ring that had previously been offered to her for sale on the finger of an acquaintance. See ibid., p. 28.
30. Ibid.
31. Ibid., p. 31.
32. See Ruth Federspiel, *Soziale Mobilität im Berlin des zwanzigsten Jahrhunderts. Frauen und Männer in Berlin-Neukölln* (Berlin, 1999), on the difficulties in analyzing social profiles in Berlin.
33. LAB A Pr. Br. Rep. 030, Tit. 90 Nr. 7619/2, Der Leiter des GAD, Tagesbefehl Nr. 13 from July 6, 1943.
34. Statistisches Landesamt der Stadt Berlin, ed., *Berlin in Zahlen*, 16.
35. Ibid., 96.
36. Ibid., 16.
37. This is a factor that black market researchers all too often accept as given, without reflecting sufficiently on it. See, for example, Boelcke, *Schwarzmarkt*, 47ff.
38. Anthony Giddens, *The Consequences of Modernity* (Cambridge, UK, 1990), 21–25.
39. See Moritz Föllmer, ed., *Sehnsucht nach Nähe. Interpersonale Kommunikation in Deutschland seit dem 19. Jahrhundert* (Stuttgart, 2004), 14–15.
40. Clifford Geertz, "The Bazaar Economy: Information and Search in Peasant Marketing," *American Economic Review* 68, no. 2 (1978): 32.
41. See Hans Joas, "Rollen- und Interaktionstheorien in der Sozialisationsforschung," in *Neues Handbuch der Sozialisationsforschung*, ed. Klaus Hurrelmann and Dieter Ulich, 137–52 (Weinheim, 1991), as well as Jens Asendorpf and Rainer Banse, *Psychologie der Beziehung* (Bern, 2001), 7–9.
42. Ibid.
43. See here as well Erving Goffman, *Relations in Public: Microstudies of the Public Order* (Brunswick and London, 2010).
44. Asendorpf and Banse, *Psychologie*, 7.
45. Only after they had reached a significant degree of professionalization were brokers able to maintain a relatively stable stock of goods and thus stabilize the supply situation, even if it was still quite restricted.

46. LAB A Rep. 358–02 80961, p. 34.
47. That is what happened in the case of the former German wrestling champion Werner Seelenbinder, who was caught while attempting to get some food through "communist contacts" and handed over to the Volksgerichtshof. See LAB A Rep 358–02 91164. Jewish black market participants faced the same problem. See ibid., 80408, p. 20.
48. See Wilhelm Henrichsmeyer, Oskar Gans, and Ingo Evers, *Einführung in die Volkswirtschaftslehre*, 10th ed. (Stuttgart, 1993), 52–54.
49. Quoted in Elke Kupschinsky, "Die vernünftige Nephertete. Die Neue Frau der 20er Jahre in Berlin," in *Die Metropole: Industriestruktur in Berlin im 20: Jahrhundert*, ed. Jochen Boberg, 164–73 (Munich, 1988), 165.
50. Viviana A. Zelizer, "Economic Sociology," in *International Encyclopedia of the Social and Behavioral* Sciences, ed. Neil J. Smelser and Paul B. Baltes, 8:4131 (Oxford, UK, 2001), argues similarly against a popular myth that suggests that business relationships have a negative impact on "private" relationships.
51. See Susanne zur Nieden, "Erotische Fraternisierung. Der Mythos von der schnellen Kapitulation der deutschen Frauen im Mai 1945," in *Heimat—Front. Militär und Geschlechterverhältnisse im Zeitalter der Weltkriege*, ed. Karen Hagemann and Stefanie Schüler-Springorum, 313–25 (Frankfurt am Main, 2002).
52. "The marriage market," according to Merith Niehuss, looking at the nineteenth century, "at least of the bourgeoisie, was . . . influenced by a materialistic way of thinking; what counted most was the market value of the future marriage partner." In the time frame under investigation here, choosing a partner followed a pattern that did not exclude marrying for love but set limits on this practice. In general, one can observe above all a "strong tendency to marry within the same social group." See Merith Niehuss, *Familie, Frau und Gesellschaft. Studien zur Strukturgeschichte der Familie in Westdeutschland 1945–1960* (Göttingen, 2001), 302–303, as well as Peter Borscheid, "Geld und Liebe. Zu den Auswirkungen des Romantischen auf die Partnerwahl im 19. Jahrhundert," in *Ehe, Liebe, Tod. Zum Wandel der Familie, der Geschlechts- und Generationsbeziehungen in der Neuzeit*, ed. idem and Hans-Jürgen Teuteberg, 112–34 (Münster, 1983).
53. See Pierre Bourdieu, "Gabe und do ut des," in *Praktische Vernunft*, 94–103 (Frankfurt am Main, 1998), on veiling trades by a delay in time.
54. Elizabeth Heineman, *What Difference Does a Husband Make?: Women and Marital Status in Nazi and Postwar Germany* (Berkeley, 1999), 46.
55. Ibid.
56. Ibid.
57. This calls into question Heineman's assertion based on the lack of success of the state's efforts that women were not "worried enough" and thus hesitated to enter into new partnerships. See ibid., 50.
58. Heterosexual trading networks were the rule. See, however, LAB A Rep 358–02, 89841, pp. 21ff., for an example of a homosexual trading network.
59. As a rule, the phrase "friendly relations" (*freundschaftlicher Verkehr*) suggests sexual contacts. See ibid.
60. LAB A Rep. 358–02 80384, p. 3.
61. LAB A Rep. 358–02, 80004, p. 44.
62. Ibid., p. 42.
63. Ibid.
64. Ibid., p. 41.

65. Ibid., written judgment, p. 3.
66. See Heineman, *Difference*, 55.
67. LAB A Rep 358–02, 80004, p. 45.
68. Ibid., pp. 44ff.
69. Ibid., p. 81.
70. Ibid., p. 45.
71. This exceptional situation ultimately disproves Luhmann's observation that two-person relationships "on the basis of their own terms and conditions . . . without social networking are rare and problematic." The demonstrative, emphatic disentanglement from the social network points to the fundamental relationship to one's environment. See Niklas Luhmann, *Liebe als Passion. Zur Codierung von Intimität* (Frankfurt am Main, 1992), 39.
72. A Rep. 358–02 80692.
73. Ibid., Report of the "Privat-Auskunftei und Detektei Herbert K. Krause" of May 12, 1943.
74. Ibid., p. 55.
75. Ibid., p. 20.
76. Ibid., p. 54.
77. On the East Prussian transactions, see ibid., pp. 101ff.; on his going into hiding, p. 18.
78. Ibid., pp. 43–44.
79. Max Weber, *Wirtschaft und Gesellschaft: Grundriss der verstehenden Soziologie*, ed. Johannes Winckelmann, 5th ed. (Tübingen, 1980), 214.
80. Ibid.
81. Ibid., 216.
82. See Robert Gellately and Nathan Stoltzfus, eds., *Social Outsiders in Nazi Germany* (Princeton, 2001); and Robert Gellately, *Backing Hitler: Consent and Coercion in Nazi Germany* (Oxford, UK), 2001.
83. See for example LAB A Rep. 358–02 79555.
84. LAB A Rep 358–02 89841, p. 20.
85. Ibid., p. 41. See for a further example of the acknowledged taboo ibid., 80384, p. 8.
86. See for example ibid., 89842, pp. 17–18, as well as 80067, p. 34.
87. Ibid., 80006, pp. 26–27.
88. LAB A Rep 358–02 80354–55.
89. Ibid., 80004, p. 9.
90. Ibid., 87593, p. 35.
91. Ibid., 80139, p. 47.
92. Ibid., p. 13.
93. See Jürgen Gerhards and Friedhelm Neidhardt, "Strukturen und Funktionen moderner Öffentlichkeit: Fragestellungen und Ansätze," in *Öffentlichkeit, Kultur, Massenkommunikation: Beiträge zur Medien- und Kommunikationssoziologie*, ed. Stefan Müller-Doohm, 31–88 (Oldenburg, 1991).
94. The police viewed spaces where a limited "meeting public" came together with mistrust. See the interesting reference to a store as a "substitute public sphere" in the verdict against a person accused (and later convicted) of offenses against War Economy Regulations, who in this case was also accused of making "malicious remarks." The judges explained: "To be sure, he did not make his remarks publicly. However, he did make them in front of people he had to know did not agree with these remarks. Therefore, he had to assume that these people would bring his remarks

into the substitute public sphere (*Ersatzöffentlichkeit*)." LAB A Rep. 358–02 89673, p. 45. Businesses and restaurants were thus especially suspicious "substitute public spheres," attracting the attention not only of prosecuting authorities. Such businesses and restaurants could also become the subject of broad generalizations; certain occupations such as waiting on tables and retailing were broadly discredited as spheres of "hustling." See Malte Zierenberg, "Berlin tauscht. Schwarzmärkte in Berlin 1939–1950," *Informationen zur modernen Stadtgeschichte* 2 (2004): 45–53; Adelheid von Saldern, "Stadt und Öffentlichkeit in urbanisierten Gesellschaften. Neue Zugänge zu einem alten Thema," *Informationen zur modernen Stadtgeschichte* 2 (2000): 3–15, has suggested the term "informal public spheres" for such spaces, which—as she herself admits—would exclude a broad range of rather different sorts of public spheres.

95. Statistisches Landesamt der Stadt Berlin, ed., *Berlin in Zahlen*, 222.
96. Erich Giese, *Das zukünftige Schnellbahnnetz für Groß-Berlin* (Berlin, 1919), 71–75. See Thomas Lindenberger, *Straßenpolitik: Zur Sozialgeschichte der öffentlichen Ordnung in Berlin 1900–1914* (Bonn, 1995), 43–45.
97. See, for example, the interrogation on November 18, 1944, LAB A Rep. 358–02 89667, pp. 45ff. Even after the end of the war people walked to the vast majority of their black market sites. This had to do above all with the destruction of the transportation infrastructure and the need to reappropriate the city after the "bunker era.". See below, Chapter 3.
98. LAB A Rep. 358–02 89667, p. 10 and unpaginated, interrogation by the Geheime Staatspolizei on December 12, 1944. The Berlin telephone network remained relatively insignificant in the everyday life of Berliners for a long time. To be sure, the number of public phones within the city more than doubled between 1925 and 1930 from around 234,395–524,627. However, most of the new phones were intended for the public authorities. After this infrastructure had been created, the further expansion of the telephone network was slow. Between 1930 and 1940 only about 100,000 new public phones were added. The number of local calls increased within the same period of time by only about 10 percent. Public telephones remained rare. If in 1930 there were only 5,586 public telephones, ten years later their number had increased by only 30. Statistisches Landesamt der Stadt Berlin, ed., *Berlin in Zahlen*, 243.
99. See for example LAB A Rep. 358–02 89667, pp. 57, 70.
100. Viviana A. Zelizer, *The Social Meaning of Money: Pin Money, Paychecks, Poor Relief, and Other Currencies* (London, 1994).
101. For one of the few exceptions, see LAB A Rep. 358–02 79783. It seems that long-term, successful, and stable network relationships depended especially on the familiarity of the participants and spatial considerations.
102. Andreas Gestrich, "Neuzeit," in *Geschichte der Familie*, ed. Andreas Gestrich, Jens-Uwe Krause, and Michael Mitterauer, 364–652 (Stuttgart: Kröner, 2003), 643.
103. Ibid., 644.
104. LAB A Rep. 358–02 80139, p. 8. See also ibid., 89659, p. 18.
105. Gestrich, "Neuzeit," 463.
106. Ibid.
107. Ibid., 469.
108. Ibid., 472.
109. Walter Benjamin, *Das Passagen-Werk. Gesammelte Schriften* (Frankfurt am Main: Suhrkamp, 1991), 6.1:53. On the "need for closure," see Gert Selle, *Die*

eigenen vier Wände. Zur verborgenen Geschichte des Wohnens (Frankfurt am Main, 1993), 13.

110. Ibid., 21.
111. See Ralf Blank, "Kriegsalltag und Luftkrieg an der Heimatfront," in *Das Deutsche Reich und der Zweite Weltkrieg*, vol. 9/2, *Die Deutsche Kriegsgesellschaft 1939 bis 1945. Ausbeutung, Deutungen, Ausgrenzung*, ed. Jörg Echternkamp, 357–461 (Munich, 2005), 419.
112. Richard Bessel, " 'Leben nach dem Tod'. Vom Zweiten Weltkrieg zur zweiten Nachkriegszeit," in *Wie Kriege enden*, ed. Wegner, 239–58 (Paderborn, 2002), 252.
113. Statistisches Landesamt der Stadt Berlin, ed., *Berlin in Zahlen*, 145.
114. Ibid., 137.
115. Ibid., 139.
116. Bodenschatz, Harald. "Altstadt und Mietskasernenstadt. Felder der Stadterneuerung zwischen den beiden Weltkriegen am Beispiel Berlin," in *Stadterneuerung in der Weimarer Republik und im Nationalsozialismus*, ed. Christian Kopetzki, 252–43 (Kassel, 1987); and SOPADE, 1938, p. 1109.
117. David Clay Large, *Berlin: A Modern History* (New York, 2001), 313. The buildings erected in the second "construction boom" between 1937 and 1940 often had significant defects. There were repeated complaints concerning the quality of the buildings, which were too quickly built and badly conceived. Furthermore, the rents were too high. For a one-room apartment in the suburbs one paid 75 marks in 1938; for an apartment in a new building in Lichtenberg in an area that shortly before had still been garden allotments, one still paid 40 marks a month. See SOPADE, 1938, pp. 1126–28.
118. LAB A Rep. 358–02 8933, copy of the verdict (January 3, 1945), p. 5.
119. Adelheid von Saldern, *Häuserleben: zur Geschichte städtischen Arbeiterwohnens vom Kaiserreich bis heute* (Bonn, 1995). See also the works of Schmiechen-Ackermann on the significance of the block warden.
120. This could include hanging up portraits of Hitler in one's apartment to assuage a suspicious block warden. See SOPADE, 1940, 16.
121. See Gellately, *Backing Hitler*, 256–57.
122. Ibid., 261.
123. Von Saldern, *Häuserleben*, 252.
124. See ibid.
125. Trading also took place in air-raid shelters. See LAB A Rep. 358–02 80562, p. 15. However, there is little archival evidence of such trading, which suggests that the lack of the necessary trust and privacy in them inhibited trading. Traders probably feared that "unreliable elements" would inform on them.
126. LAB A Rep. 358–02 89667, p. 46.
127. Ibid., 79932, p. 1.
128. Ibid., 89667, pp. 12–13.
129. Ibid., 80099, p. 6.
130. See, for example, ibid., 79946, p. 13.
131. See LAB A Rep. 358–02 89842, p. 17; ibid., 80067, p. 34.
132. See, for example, LAB A Rep. 358–02 79946, p. 30; ibid., 87908, p. 1.
133. LAB A Rep. 358–02 79946, p. 1.
134. LAB A Rep. 358–02 80067, p. 1.
135. Ibid., p. 28.
136. Ibid., p. 62.

137. Ibid., p. 63.
138. LAB A Rep358–02 79946, p. 5.
139. LAB ARep358–02 80408, p. 27.
140. See for an example of a description of the Alexanderplatz LAB A Rep. 358–02 79813, p. 1.
141. LAB ARep358–02 80407, p. 9.
142. Statistisches Landesamt der Stadt Berlin, ed., *Berlin in Zahlen*, 180–83.
143. Ibid., p. 245. Aschinger provides an example of a firm that profited from this development. Aschinger had started in 1892 as a bar in the Leipziger Straße. In the 1930s, the business had grown into one of Europe's largest hotel and restaurant concerns. The government supported the business with orders for the May 1 celebrations and the Olympic Games. In 1937, as a result of the "Aryanization" of its competitor Kempinski, Aschinger took over Kempinski and integrated it. As the firm was able, with the approval of the National Socialist leadership, to continue to offer its "basic meal without a ration card" in its restaurants and snack bars in the center of the city during the war, Aschinger must have profited considerably from the rationing. See Allen, pp. 107ff. At any rate, given the number of customers at Aschinger, it is not at all surprising that the Aschinger branches soon developed into prominent sites for black market trading. See LAB A Rep. 358–02 3016; 79976; 80099, p. 11; 80408, p. 28.
144. Ibid., p. 169.
145. See Christian Engeli and Wolfgang Ribbe, "Berlin in der NS-Zeit," in *Geschichte Berlins*, vol. 2, *Von der Märzrevolution bis zur Gegenwart*, ed. idem (Berlin, 1989), 24–44, 982; as well as Alfred Zimm, *Die Entwicklung des Industriestandortes Berlin. Tendenzen der geographischen Lokalisation bei den Berliner Industriezweigen von überörtlicher Bedeutung sowie die territoriale Stadtentwicklung bis 1945* (Berlin, 1959).
146. Bodenschatz, *Altstadt*, 67.
147. Gustav Böß, *Die Not in Berlin: Tatsachen und Zahlen* (Berlin, 1923), 115.
148. LAB A Pr. Br. Rep. 030, Tit. 90 Nr. 7619/2, Der Leiter des GAD, Entwurf Sonderbefehl, July 1942.
149. See, for example, ibid., Tagesbefehl Nr. 3, January 20, 1943, as well as Tagesbefehl Nr. 13, July 6, 1943.
150. LAB A Pr. Br. Rep. 030, Tit. 90 Nr. 7619/2, Der Leiter des GAD, Tagesbefehl Nr. 13, July 6, 1943.
151. Lindenberger, *Straßenpolitik*, 105–106. On ethnomethodology, see Sacks, *Notes*. See Annette F. Timm, "The Ambivalent Outsider: Prostitution, Promiscuity, and VD Control in Nazi Berlin," in *Social Outsiders in Nazi Germany*, ed. Robert Gellately and Nathan Stoltzfus, 192–211 (Princeton, 2001), 200, for the distribution of the prostitute milieu in certain bars in the "problem districts."
152. Since the middle of the nineteenth century, Berlin Jews had settled in the northern section of the district Mitte. In 1866 the huge New Synagogue was built here in the Oranienburger Strasse. In 1925, 30,000 Jews lived in Mitte. See Richarz, Monika. "Jüdisches Berlin und seine Vernichtung," in *Die Metropole. Industriekultur in Berlin im 20. Jahrhundert*, ed. Boberg, 216–25.
153. Bodenschatz, *Altstadt*, 73.
154. Grüneberg, Ernst. *Die Reichshauptstadt Berlin. Eine Heimatkunde für Berliner Schulen* (Breslau, 1938).
155. See Large, *Berlin*, 103–105.

156. Ernst Engelbrecht and Leo Heller, *Berliner Razzien* (Neu-Finkenkrug, 1924).
157. Ibid., 43–46.
158. Even if there were no exact information, the Berlin police adopted the hint from a "confidential source" that goods were being "delivered to the Kurfürstendamm." See LAB A Rep. 358–02 89798, p. 1.
159. Edition from November 9, 1947.
160. Alfred Kerr, Mein Berlin. *Schauplätze einer Metropole* (Berlin, 1999).
161. Richarz, *Jüdisches Berlin*, 217–18.
162. This was one way that the space of possible consumption was limited; aspects of this limitation remained in place until 1951. See Thomas Scholze, "Zur Ernährungssituation der Berliner nach dem Zweiten Weltkrieg. Ein Beitrag zur Erfahrung des Großstadtalltags (1945–1952)," *Jahrbuch für Geschichte* 35 (1987): 539–64.
163. See, for example, LAB PR. Br. Rep. 57, Nr. 365, transcript from January 21, 1942, "Regelung über Versand und Mitnahme von Waren aus den besetzten französischen, belgischen und niederländischen Gebieten durch Wehrmachtangehörige usw."
164. Ibid.
165. All quotes ibid.
166. Bajohr, *Parvenüs und Profiteure*, 88–90.
167. See, for example, LAB A Rep 358–02 89962; ibid., 79932, 79809, 79946, 87970, as well as 80164, p. 3, 80429, p. 3, 80342, p. 10.
168. Ibid., 89667, p. 59.
169. Ibid., 88234, p. 22.
170. Especially at the beginning of Nazi rule in 1933, just before the opening of the Olympic Games in 1936, and at the beginning of the war, prostitutes fell victim to ideologically motivated campaigns. See Gisela Bock, *Zwangssterilisation im Nationalsozialismus. Studien zur Rassenpolitik und Frauenpolitik* (Opladen, 1986), 417.
171. Timm, "Outsider," 192.
172. LAB Pr. Br. Rep 57, Nr. 365, p. 6.
173. Timm, "Outsider," 201.
174. LAB A Rep. 358–02 80384, 7/2.
175. "Being served"(*Bedienung*) was the customary euphemism for sex. See ibid., 15/2. The term "monitor girls"(*Kontrollmädchen*) was used to designate prostitutes who were registered and who underwent a regular health check. See Timm, "Outsider." The term was already common during the Weimar era. The Statistisches Jahrbuch der Stadt Berlin noted in volume 5 in 1929 (257) for the period from December 1926 to August 1927 that there was a slight decrease in the number of women registered as *Kontrollmädchen*, from 7,113 to 6,267. In September 1927, the law to combat the spread of STDs was modified (the law was passed on February 18, 1927), and this changed the way the data was collected. See ibid.
176. LAB A Rep. 358–02 80384, p. 21.
177. See Bajohr, *Parvenüs und Profiteure*.
178. For an example of discrimination, see the case of Elisabeth Hanke, LAB A Rep. 358–02 80004.
179. Saldern, *Stadt*.
180. Karl Marx, *The Power of Money: Economic and Philosophic Manuscripts of 1844*, trans. Martin Mulligan (Moscow, 1959), 42.

181. Georg Simmel, *The Philosophy of Money*, 3rd exp. ed., ed. David Frisby, trans. Tom Bottomore and David Frisby (New York, 2004), 178.
182. Zelizer, *Meaning*, 3, speaks, for example, of "divided economies" and "moral earmarking" when amounts of money are kept separate according to their source of income and are used for different expenses.
183. Simmel, *Philosophy*, 126.
184. Ibid., 87908, 95.
185. See, for example, LAB A Rep 358–02 80067, p. 3.
186. See Willi Boelcke, *Die Kosten von Hitlers Krieg. Kriegsfinanzierung und finanzielles Kriegserbe in Deutschland 1933–1948* (Paderborn, 1985), 112.
187. See LAB A Rep 80139, p. 60.
188. Ibid., 80099, p. 33.
189. Ibid., 79809, p. 53.
190. This phenomenon has been observed, for example, in the earnings of "young male prostitutes." One young man described his earnings as being "like a hot stone that burns a hole in your pocket." Zelizer, *Meaning*, 70.
191. See, for example, LAB A Rep 358–02 80139, p. 4.
192. See F Rep 240 Acc. 2651 Nr. 4, p. 402/4. See also ibid., p. 412/4: "Christmas and no tree . . . but a small child. What to do?" For an example of the preparations for a marriage, see ibid., p. 364/4: "For the meal we put in front of our best man and bridesmaid asparagus and eggs that cost 200 RM; I got that much for my old tennis shoes." A further postwar "festive occasion" that often prompted black market trading was "celebrating seeing one another again." See ibid., Nr. 3, p. 193/2.
193. LAB A Rep 358–02 80398, p. 4. See also LAB A Rep 358–02 80164, p. 5–6. It is not clear where Martha Rebbien got her "seed money." It is, however, very likely that she invested a large part of the profits she made into maintaining her trading.
194. LAB A Rep 358–02 80004.
195. Ibid.
196. For a case that describes this creeping transition, see LAB A Rep. 358–02 80067, p. 8. See also ibid., 80099, pp. 5–7 and 30–32.
197. See ibid., 80375, p. 8.
198. Ibid., 89781, p. 19.
199. The German original reads "gewissenloser Kriegshyänen," or "unscrupulous war hyenas."
200. LAB A Rep 358–02 80067, p. 36.
201. LAB A Rep 358–02 80384, p. 22. See further ibid., 89717, p. 10/2.
202. LAB A Rep 358–02 80164, pp. 40–41.
203. See the extensive interrogation that Martha Rebbien's trading partner, Wiggers, was required to undergo because of his detailed notes, LAB A Rep 358–02 89667, pp. 62–65.
204. LAB A Rep 358–02 89667, pp. 62/2–3.
205. See LAB A Rep. 358–02 8443.
206. LAB A Rep. 358–02 89667, unpaginated, interrogation record of the Geheime Staatspolizei, Staatspolizeileitstelle Berlin, of December 12, 1944.
207. See the section below, in Chapter 4, "A Market of 'Little People': The Black Market and the Social Question."
208. Alfred Müller-Förster, *Aufgewärmte Kartoffeln. Ein Büchlein für Politiker, Schieber und Schornsteinfeger, für Reichspräsidenten, Schuster, Minister, Jungfrauen und solche, die es werden wollen* (Hamburg, 1926).

209. Max Brinkmann, *Kleiner Knigge für Schieber* (Berlin, 1921).
210. See Achim Landwehr, *Geschichte des Sagbaren: Einführung in die historische Diskursanalyse* (Tübingen, 2001), 103–106 and 130–33. Quote: Reinhart Koselleck, "Erinnerungsschleusen und Erfahrungsschichten. Der Einfluss der beiden Weltkriege auf das soziale Bewusstsein," reprinted in *Zeitschichten. Studien zur Historik*, idem, 265–84 (Frankfurt am Main, 2000), 267.
211. LAB A Rep. 358–02, 80128, p. 77.
212. That legal terms were adapted to fit social reality was not a new phenomenon. Martin H. Geyer, *Verkehrte Welt: Revolution, Inflation und Moderne, Munich 1914–1924* (Göttingen, 1998), 220, has pointed out that in the "extortion issue" of the early 1920s, a semantic shift in the vocabulary used by judges occurred that reflected contemporary discomfort about the divergence between the popular sense of justice and the administration of the law.
213. Robert Gellately and Nathan Stoltzfus, eds., *Social Outsiders in Nazi Germany* (Princeton, 2001).
214. Geyer, *Verkehrte Welt*, 180.
215. Henry Picker, *Hitlers Tischgespräche im Führerhauptquartier* (Munich, 1979), 213.
216. LAB A Rep. 358–02, 89506, p. 2.
217. All quotes from LAB A Rep. 358–02, 88105, p. 2.
218. LAB A Rep. 358–02, 88069, p. 4.
219. Ibid., 8723, copy of the judgments (unpaginated).
220. Ibid., 88446, p. 14.
221. LAB A Rep. 358–02, 88580, p. 2.
222. Perceptions have been distorted by the black market being a topic in work on "foreign laborers," "forced laborers," and "displaced persons," although, on the whole, historians have given it little attention. These non-historical works cannot be criticized for this, but this focus highlights foreigners when the talk is of the black markets so that the authors only restate (involuntarily) the incorrect picture of the black market that contemporaries had. See Mark Spoerer, "Die soziale Differenzierung der ausländischen Zivilarbeiter, Kriegsgefangenen und Häftlinge im Deutschen Reich," in *Das Deutsche Reich und der Zweite Weltkrieg*, vol. 9, pt. 2, *Die deutsche Kriegsgesellschaft 1939 bis 1945: Ausbeutung, Deutungen, Ausgrenzung*, ed. Jörg Echternkamp, 485–576 (Munich, 2005); Ulrich Herbert, *Fremdarbeiter. Politik und Praxis des 'Ausländer-Einsatzes' in der Kriegswirtschaft des Dritten Reiches* (Bonn, 1985); Boelcke, *Schwarzmarkt*.
223. Hans-Ulrich Wehler, *Gesellschaftsgeschichte*, vol. 4, *Vom Beginn des Ersten Weltkriegs bis zur Gründung der beiden deutschen Staaten 1914–1949* (Munich, 2003), 769; Herbert, *Fremdarbeiter*.
224. See above in this chapter, "Bartering Culture and the Transformation of Social Relationships." Networks composed of foreigners formed one segment of the Berlin black market; they functioned as "ethnic economies" yet were also intertwined with other "native" networks. For an example of a network of Italian black marketeers who organized their bartering networks as "paesani," see LAB A Rep. 358–02, 80099. On the phenomenon of the "paesani," see William Foote Whyte, *Street Corner Society: Die Sozialstruktur eines Italienerviertels* (Berlin, 1996); on the Italians in Germany, see Ralf Lang, *Italienische "Fremdarbeiter" im nationalsozialistischen Deutschland 1937–1945* (Frankfurt am Main, 1996).
225. On the following: LAB A Rep. 341–02 9792. Knowing quite well that being labeled a "half-Jew" would negatively impact their sentence, individual suspects

attempted to change this classification even after their arrest. One can see this in Ernst Abrahamson's notes handwritten in detention awaiting trial: "1. Aryan question. I request that I be allowed to raise the topic once again." He further noted that it was not fully clear who his father was and that he had already submitted a request to the Interior Ministry to "change his name and to be rehabilitated in the Aryan question to at least 25%." See LAB A Rep. 358–02 89717, p. 23. Yet these same notes sealed his fate, as they contained information on numerous black market transactions, which prosecutors introduced as evidence. See ibid., p. 85.

226. Ibid., p. 1.
227. Ibid.
228. Ibid., p. 65.
229. LAB A Rep. 358–02, 89778, p. 3.
230. See Dorothea Schmidt, *Zeitgeschichte im Mikrokosmos. Ein Gebäude in Berlin-Schöneberg* (Berlin, 2004), 11–14.
231. LAB A Rep. 358–02, 89778, p. 8.
232. Ibid., p. 9.
233. Ibid., p. 26.
234. LAB A Rep. 358–02, 80477, pp. 29, 86, 94.
235. Ibid., p. 100. The official in charge of the case spoke of Scheffler's girlfriend as his paramour. Ibid.
236. Street trading had been associated with fancy automobiles as early as the 1920s. At the meeting of the Berlin City Council on May 26, 1921, the representative of the German National People's Party, Linke, noted,

> if you look at the picture of the present street trading, you can see from the manner in which it is conducted that many people of means are involved in it, as the street trading is conducted from buses, cabs, etc., and you all know exactly how much an automobile or a cab costs for half a day.

LAB A Rep. 001–02, Nr. 2310, p. 141. See Geyer, *Verkehrte Welt*, 244. On the ambivalence of the concept of the "Roaring Twenties," which also had violent and ecstatic, orgiastic connotations, see Helmut Lethen, "Chicago und Moskau," in *Die Metropole*, ed. Boberg, 190–213 (Munich, 1988).

237. Ibid., 198. Hans-Ulrich Gumbrecht, *In 1926: Living on the Edge of Time* (Cambridge, MA, 1998), 28, points out that driving an automobile, glamorous in and of itself, was always simultaneously viewed as a "potentially criminal act." This is evident from how quickly the police arrested drivers after accidents. In a Berlin example Gumbrecht cites, the police were barely able to stop a mob of people from lynching a driver responsible for an accident that had killed a number of people at the scene. In one case, which had a number of parallels to Scheffler's example, the interrogator noted that although the suspect had claimed to have no previous convictions, he had been involved in an automobile accident in 1937 and that he had had to pay four fines for driving a "car without a light." See LAB A Rep. 358–02, 89778, p. 3. As early as the 1930s in the "battle against asocial people," Berlin police had included "obstinate traffic offenders" in fringe groups that needed to be combated by preventive action in the interest of the Volksgemeinschaft. "Traffic offenders" were thus a focus of surveillance, like beggars, prostitutes, pimps, homosexuals, psychopaths, and even "price cutters and hustlers." See Wolfgang Dreßen,

"Modernität und innerer Feind," in *Die Metropole*, ed. Boberg, 262–81 (Munich, 1988).

238. Despite steady increases in the numbers of people driving since the 1920s, cars remained relatively rare in Berlin. In 1929, there were 42,844 registered automobiles. The highest number of registered cars in Berlin before the war was 122,326 in 1939, yielding a ratio of cars to citizens of 1:35. See Hans Stimmann"Weltstadtplätze und Massenverkehr," in *Die Metropole*, ed. Boberg, 138–43 (Munich, 1988).
239. Thomas Mann, *Unordnung und Frühes Leid: Die Erzählungen* (Frankfurt am Main, 2005), 679.
240. Hachenburg, quoted in Geyer, *Verkehrte Welt*, 207.
241. Ibid., 385.
242. Ibid., 107.
243. Ibid.
244. Ibid., 107–108.
245. On the stigmatization of and discrimination against promiscuous people during the war, see Timm, "Outsider," 202–205.
246. Ursula von Kardorff, *Berliner Aufzeichnungen: 1942–1945*, ed. Peter Hartl (Munich, 1992), 137.

Chapter 3

1. Daniel Libeskind, *Radix—Matrix: Architecture and Writing* (Munich, 1997), 113.
2. References can be found in the reports of the Wehrmachtpropaganda (see Wolfram Wette, ed., *Das letzte halbe Jahr. Stimmungsberichte der Wehrmachtpropaganda 1944/45* [Essen, 2001], 151–55), as well as in individual police reports and court records. See LAB A Rep. 358–02 123725; 79979, pp. 12ff.; LAB Pr. Br. Rep. 030–01 Nr. 1095, p. 5. See Adam Kendon, *Conducting Interaction: Patterns of Behavior in Focused Encounters* (Cambridge, UK, 1990), on the concept of "focused gatherings."
3. See Susanne zur Nieden, *Alltag im Ausnahmezustand: Frauentagebücher im zerstörten Deutschland 1943 bis 1945* (Berlin, 1993). On the collapse of "normal" everyday life in Berlin during the "final battle," see also Anthony Beevor, *Berlin: The Downfall 1945* (London, 2007).
4. On the acts of violence by the Gestapo and the criminal justice system, see Ralf Blank, "Kriegsalltag und Luftkrieg an der Heimatfront," in *Das Deutsche Reich und der Zweite* Weltkrieg, vol. 9/2, *Die Deutsche Kriegsgesellschaft 1939 bis 1945. Ausbeutung, Deutungen, Ausgrenzung*, ed. Jörg Echternkamp, 386–90 (Munich, 2005).
5. On how city space and forms of consumption mutually influence each other, see Paul Glennie, "Consumption, Consumerism and Urban Form: Historical Perspectives," *Urban Studies* 35 (1998): 927–51, 944.
6. Nobuo, 70.
7. PRO HWI/3607, Japanese Ambassador Reports on Life in Berlin, March 15, 1945. All of the following quotations are also from ibid.
8. See Bernd Martin, "Der Schein des Bündnisses. Deutschland und Japan im Krieg 1940–1945," in *Formierung und Fall der Achse Berlin—Tokio*, ed. Gerhard Krebs and Bernd Martin, 27–53 (Munich, 1994), 31.
9. On the building's history, see Jost Dülffer, "Die japanische Botschaft im Tiergarten im Rahmen der nationalsozialistischen Umgestaltung der Reichshauptstadt Berlin," in *Formierung und Fall*, ed. Krebs and Martin, 75–92.

10. LAB 358–02 89781, p. 21.
11. Victor Klemperer, *LTI: Notizbuch eines Philologen* (Leipzig, 1999), 322.
12. Martin Broszat, Klaus-Dietmar Henke, and Hans Woller, *Von Stalingrad zur Währungsreform: Zur Sozialgeschichte des Umbruchs in Deutschland*, 3rd ed. (Munich, 1990).
13. This increased need for mobility is reflected in the continual increases in the use of public transportation in the city from 1933. Indeed, between 1933 and 1943 the number of people transported nearly doubled, to 2.27 million. In 1944, because of the destruction, the number declined to 1.82 million. See Statistisches Landesamt der Stadt Berlin, ed. *Berlin in Zahlen* (Berlin, 1947), 216–17. On the harm done to industrial and transportation enterprises in the "last half year" of the war in Germany as a whole, see Blank, "Kriegsalltag," 446–48.
14. Thomas Neumann, "Der Bombenkrieg. Zur ungeschriebenen Geschichte einer kollektiven Verletzung," in *Nachkrieg in Deutschland*, ed. Klaus Naumann 319–42 (Hamburg, 2001), 324.
15. See Anthony Giddens, *The Constitution of Society: Outline of the Theory of Structuration* (Cambridge, UK, 1984), 111–12.
16. Ibid., 66.
17. See the film clips that had been stored in archives in Moscow, which Irmgard von zur Mühlen edited and made available to the public with the titles *Bomben auf Berlin. Leben zwischen Furcht und Hoffnung* (Chronos Film GmbH, Kleinmachnow). One can see the disintegration of everyday routines quite clearly in them. Goebbels kept the film clips, which were sometimes recorded immediately after the air raids, under wraps. The images from the second half of the war contrast sharply with the images of largely peaceful everyday life at the beginning of the war.
18. The significance of these everyday routines for achieving stabilization has been proven in experiments conducted by Harold Garfinkel, "A Conception of, and Experiments with, 'Trust' as a Condition of Stable Concerted Actions," in *Motivation and Social Interaction*, ed. O. J. Harvey, 187–238 (New York, 1963), 198: "The critical phenomenon is . . . the perceived normality of environmental events as this normality is a function of the presuppositions that define the possible events." This confirms the finding in Bernd Wegner, ed., *Wie Kriege enden: Wege zum Frieden von der Antike bis zur Gegenwart* (Paderborn, 2002), xxii, that "even in times of war one can find over and over islands of peace." Accordingly, we need to recognize that the apparent dichotomy of war and peace, spatially and temporally, is not always so clear.
19. For example, 222 and 226 people, respectively, died in the air raids in 1940 and 1941. David Clay Large, *Berlin: A Modern History* (New York, 2001), 311. By contrast, 3,758 people died, according to the official statistics, in the air raid on November 23, 1943, which lasted barely two hours. See Sven Felix Kellerhoff and Wieland Giebel, eds., *Als die Tage zu Nächten wurden. Berliner Schicksale im Luftkrieg* (Berlin, 2003), 221.
20. Ursula von Kardorff, *Berliner Aufzeichnungen: 1942–1945*, ed. Peter Hartl (Munich, 1992), 88–89.
21. Ibid., 93.
22. Ibid., 130.
23. Deutsches Historisches Museum (DHM), Rep. I/ 2. Weltkrieg/ F1/ M, Deutmann's diary entry from September 1, 1943, No. 122 (numbered by the author). (Hereafter cited as DHM, Deutmann diary). Deutmann's diary is one of the best sources for the history of everyday life in Berlin during and immediately after the war. Deutmann exhaustively and largely objectively chronicled his observations on the effects of the

air war on everyday life in the city. The reports are not only extraordinarily detailed, but they also corroborate the information, such as the sites, the times, and the intensity of the air raids, found in official sources, such as official statistics. See Laurenz Demps, "Die Luftangriffe auf Berlin. Ein dokumentarischer Bericht I/II," *Jahrbuch des Märkischen Museums* 4 and 7 (1978): 27–68 and 7–44. Reprinted as a table in Kellerhoff and Giebel, *Tage zu Nächten*, 216–30.

24. DHM, Deutmann diary, February 10, 1944, No. 182.
25. The War Damages Offices were increasingly overextended. Often they did not have enough material resources, and they had no interest in providing financial compensation in part because of the danger of inflation. See Blank, "Kriegsalltag," 425. Many tried to circumvent the system through bribes, favors, and attractive bartering offers. See the case of a construction manager responsible for repairing damage done by the bombs who accepted bribes a number of times; for example, he gave preferential treatment to repairing the "bomb damage in butcher shops." LAB A Rep. 341–02 6475.
26. See Gert Selle, *Die eigenen vier Wände. Zur verborgenen Geschichte des Wohnens* (Frankfurt am Main, 1993), 23.
27. Kardorff, *Aufzeichnungen*, 119–20. Even the difficulties in organizing the special allocations after air raids were a sign of disintegration. Beginning in the middle of September 1943, the cards, whose printing was centralized in Berlin, could no longer be distributed immediately after air raids in Ruhr cities, for example, because of transportation difficulties. This undermined the purpose of these special allocation cards, namely, to alleviate the supply difficulties caused by the air raids and above all to strengthen the "morale" of the urban population. To guarantee the psychologically important effect of the "coffee or schnapps to calm one's nerves," the printing had to be decentralized. See Dorothea Schmidt, *Zeitgeschichte im Mikrokosmos: Ein Gebäude in Berlin-Schöneberg* (Berlin, 2004).
28. See Blank, "Kriegsalltag," 385, and 417–32.
29. Kardorff, *Aufzeichnungen*, 160.
30. Ibid., 122–23. Moreover, the structure of the events of the two World Wars "created a crack in the traditions of intimacy . . . so that the sexual behavior patterns of bourgeois society were broken down." Reinhart Koselleck, "Erinnerungsschleusen und Erfahrungsschichten: Der Einfluss der beiden Weltkriege auf das soziale Bewusstsein," Reprinted in *Zeitschichten. Studien zur Historik* (Frankfurt am Main, 2000), idem, 265–84.
31. On the background, see Julia S. Torrie, "Preservation by Dispersion: Civilian Evacuations and the City in Germany and France 1939–1945," in *Endangered Cities: Military Power and Urban Societies in the Era of the World Wars*, ed. Marcus Funck and Roger Chickering, 47–62 (Boston, 2004). The consequences of the evacuation often fell on the shoulders of family fathers who earned their money combating black market trading. For example, the policemen working for the trade inspection service of the Berlin police were informed in March 1944 that their "holiday for 1944/45," including "holidays for the purpose of visiting the family that had been evacuated," could only be granted if the number taking leave remained beneath 15 percent of the total force because of the tense situation. Exceptions would not be considered "under any circumstances." LAB A Pr. Br. Rep. 030, Tit. 90 Nr. 7619/2, Der Leiter des GAD, Tagesbefehl Nr. 4 from March 2, 1944.
32. Statistisches Landesamt der Stadt Berlin, ed., *Berlin in Zahlen*, 58; Large, *Berlin* 327.
33. LAB APrBr Rep 030–01, Nr. 1095, paragraph 4.
34. Ibid., paragraph 3.

35. Ibid., paragraph 3/2.
36. Ibid., paragraph 5, report from April 9, 1945.
37. Ibid.
38. On the criminality among the youth during and immediately after the war, see Frank Kebbedies, *Außer Kontrolle. Jugendkriminalität in der NS-Zeit und der frühen Nachkriegszeit* (Essen, 2000).
39. See Patrick Wagner, *Volksgemeinschaft ohne Verbrecher. Konzeption und Praxis der Kriminalpolizei in der Weimarer Republik und des Nationalsozialismus* (Hamburg, 1996), 316.
40. Hans von Hentig, "Die Kriminalität des Zusammenbruchs," *Schweizerische Zeitschrift für Strafrecht* 63 (1947): 337–41, 337.
41. Karl Bader, *Soziologie der deutschen Nachkriegskriminalität* (Tübingen, 1949), 1. Numerous publications were dedicated to legal as well as sociological research into the "steadily spreading" problem of criminality. See the bibliography in ibid.
42. Ibid., 2.
43. Statistisches Landesamt der Stadt Berlin, ed., *Berlin in Zahlen*, 144.
44. Kardorff, *Aufzeichnungen*, 94.
45. See Werner Schöllgen, *Grenzmoral: Soziale Krisis und neuer Aufbau* (Düsseldorf, 1946).
46. On this interdependence, see Jennifer Evans, *Life among the Ruins: Cityscape and Sexuality in Cold War Berlin* (New York, 2011).
47. See Blank, "Kriegsalltag," 377.
48. Ibid., 110–11.
49. Ibid., 396–97.
50. At the beginning of the war, cards assigned people to a certain bunker, seat, or cot. On this and for the quote: ibid., 410–11.
51. Everyday life, in a sense, "ducked away" during the war. The camouflage practices developed to confuse incoming bombers also illustrate this development: for example, the important east-west axis along the Charlottenburger Chaussee, which bombers used for orientation, was covered over. See the pictures in Christian Engeli and Wolfgang Ribbe, "Berlin in der NS-Zeit," in *Geschichte Berlins*, vol. 2, *Von der Märzrevolution bis zur Gegenwart*, ed. idem (Berlin, 1989), 999, as well as Davide Deriu, "Between Veiling and Unveiling: Modern Camouflage and the City as a Theater of War," in *Endangered Cities*, ed. Funck and Chickering, 15–34, on the competition between bombing and camouflage technologies.
52. See Schöllgen, *Grenzmoral*, 260–65.
53. See Maren Löw, *Raumsoziologie* (Frankfurt am Main, 2001), 161–63, referring to Giddens, on the significance of the environment for constituting a feeling of everyday security.
54. Kardorff, *Aufzeichnungen*, 122 and 133. See also ibid., 110, where she speaks of "a herd of human animals." The comparison of humans to animals commonly coded the disintegration of normal life. Ruth Andreas-Friedrich wrote shortly after the end of the war on May 12, 1945, in her diary: "We turn onto Wilhelmstrasse. Ruins and dust. Dust and ruins. Where a basement still remained, there the collectors romp about, wriggling up and down the steps, just like maggots on a piece of cheese." Ruth Andreas-Friedrich, *Schauplatz Berlin* (Frankfurt am Main, 1984), 30.
55. Such descriptions resemble discourses of orienting oneself, in which, for example, after (natural) catastrophes, urban dwellers, as "therapeutic communities," develop mechanisms of "survival" and of "carrying on." See Andreas Ranft and Stefan Selzer,

eds., *Städte aus Trümmern. Katastrophenbewältigung zwischen Antike und Moderne* (Göttingen, 2004).

56. Kardorff, *Aufzeichnungen*, 309.
57. DHM, Deutmann diary, entry from March 4, 1945.
58. Ibid., entry from June 24, 1945.
59. Ibid.
60. Wette, *Das letzte halbe Jahr*, 127–355.
61. On such agreement even in the last phases of the war, see Robert Gellately, *Backing Hitler: Consent and Coercion in Nazi Germany* (Oxford, UK, 2001), 15 and 311.
62. See Malte Zierenberg, "The Trading City: Black Markets in Berlin During World War II," in *Endangered Cities*, ed. Funck and Chickering, 145–58.
63. They anticipated the comparison of the origins of the Weimar Republic to the origins of the Federal Republic. Probably one of the most famous examples is the statement by Theodor Heuss, *Aufzeichnungen 1945–1947*, ed. and with introduction by Eberhard Pikart (Tübingen, 1966), 50, who noted in 1945 that Germans had registered their recent defeat in their consciousness "as one of the most terrible days in German history; however, we are in a completely different moral situation than that in which we experienced the political-military collapse of November 1918."
64. See Zierenberg, "Trading City."
65. Wette, *Das letzte halbe Jahr*, 217–18.
66. Ibid., 151 and 156.
67. Ibid.
68. Statistisches Landesamt der Stadt Berlin, ed., *Berlin in Zahlen*, 25. The official statistics for 1947 give the same percentages. Given the immense destruction and the only partly successful rebuilding measures, this seems unlikely. See "Zahlen zeigen Zeitgeschehen: Berlin 1945–1947," Berliner Statistik 3. special issue 1 (1947): 5. The cleanup operations after the end of the war were among the first measures the Soviet occupiers took up. The operations were systematically planned on "derubbling maps" (*Enttrümmerungskarten*) (LAB LAZ Nr. 5648). Numerous photos from the time give an idea of how much difficulty the rubble caused. See, for example, Hans J. Reichardt, *Raus aus den Trümmern. Vom Beginn des Wiederaufbaus in Berlin 1945* (Berlin, 1988); and Reinhard Rürup, ed., *Berlin 1945. Eine Dokumentation* (Berlin, 1995); as well as Reinhard Rürup and Gottfried Korff, *Berlin: Die Ausstellung zur Geschichte der Stadt* (Berlin, 1987), 577 and 595.
69. Large, *Berlin*, 348.
70. DHM, Deutmann diary, entry from February 3, 1945 (No. 314).
71. Ibid., entry from August 23, 1943 (No. 118).
72. Kardorff, *Aufzeichnungen*, 78.
73. Ibid., 122.
74. DHM, Deutmann diary, entry from August 23, 1943 (No. 118).
75. Ibid., entry from February 3, 1945 (No. 314).
76. Ibid., entry from March 3, 1945 (no number).
77. The attacks in November caused considerable property damage and fundamentally changed the appearance of the city. The city "remained the main target in the winter 1943/44." At the end of the "Battle of Berlin" more than 812,000 people were homeless and more than 9,000 were either dead or missing. See Blank, "Kriegsalltag," 373–74.
78. Joseph Goebbels, Die Tagebücher. Sämtliche Fragmente, 15 vols., ed. Elke Fröhlich (Munich, 1987–98), 10:238.

79. LAB A Rep 005-03-01, Nr. 149, p. 55.
80. Ibid., p. 59.
81. Train stations were particularly favored among these. See Chapter 4: "New Spaces: Public Black Markets."
82. "To be flexible meant everything!" Hille Ruegenberg wrote this in her memoirs of 1976. F Rep 240 Acc 2651 Nr. 2, p. 111/5.
83. According to contemporary legal experts, this was a problem because punishments no longer were perceived as proportional to their respective crimes, especially in comparison with the draconian punishments of the National Socialist era. See Bader, *Soziologie*, 2–3.
84. Elisabeth Noelle and Erich-Peter Neumann, eds., *Jahrbuch der öffentlichen Meinung* 3 (1975): 150.

Chapter 4

1. This phenomenon has been investigated for social and revolutionary movements with the rational choice approach method. For a case study, see Klaus-Dieter Opp, "DDR '89: Zu den Ursachen einer spontanen Revolution," in Der Zusammenbruch der DDR, ed. Hans Joas and Martin Kohli (Frankfurt, 1994), 194–221, and the problematization of an approach influenced by Mancur Olson in Hans Joas and Wolfgang Knöbl, *Sozialtheorie: Zwanzig einführende Vorlesungen* (Frankfurt am Main, 2004), 162–64.
2. The hesitant attitude of the British agencies in the campaign against black marketeering contributed to the Tiergarten remaining a popular black market trading center. The measures to combat black marketeering remained controversial among the occupying Allied powers, especially in the inner-city trading areas. The British and Soviets accused each other of fostering trading in their respective zones by failing to control it vigilantly. See PRO FO 1012/175 Blackmarkets, 66. In July 1948, the conflict came to a head, becoming the topic of a heated debate concerning police force management within Berlin. See Norbert Steinborn and Hilmar Krüger, eds. *Die Berliner Polizei 1945–1992* (Berlin, 1993), 57–59.
3. Archiv des Deutschen Historischen Museums, Rep. I/ 2. Weltkrieg/ F1/ M, Tagebuch Deutmann, entry from August 5, 1945.
4. LAB F Rep. 240 2651 Nr. 4, p. 370/1.
5. For an example of the application of these models to partial entities like inner-city areas, see Michael Porter, "The Competitive Advantage of the Inner City," *Harvard Business Review* 74 (1995): 55–71, as well as idem, *Competitive Advantage* (New York, 1985).
6. See Eric Sheppard, "Competition in Space and between Places," in *A Companion to Economic Geography*, ed. idem and Trevor J. Barnes, 169–86 (Oxford, 2000).
7. LAB F Rep 240 Acc. 2651, Nr. 6, p. 614/4.
8. Compare LAB F Rep. 240 Acc. 2651 Nr. 4, p. 396/3.
9. See, for example, *Times* [London], Thursday, April 18, 1946, p. 5; Friday, August 20, 1948, p. 4; Wednesday, March 26, 1952, p. 5.
10. See "Black Markets Boom in Berlin," *Life*, September 10, 1945, pp. 51–54, in which there are numerous photos.
11. See Jörg Roesler, "The Black Market in Post-War Berlin and the Methods Used to Counteract It," *German History* 7 (1989): 92–107, as well as PRO FO 1012/176 Economics/Black Market, pp. 114.

12. On the concept of the "mental map," see *Geschichte and Gesellschaft*, Sonderheft 28 (2002). See, above all, the foreword by Conrad and the article by Schenk. Fritjof B. Schenk, "Mental Maps. Die Konstruktion von geographischen Räumen in Europa seit der Aufklärung," *Geschichte und Gesellschaft* 28 (2002): 493–514, outlines some theoretical positions before presenting his remarks on the "Konstruktion von geographischen Räumen in Europa seit der Aufklärung," 493–95. See further Maren Löw, *Raumsoziologie* (Frankfurt am Main, 2001), 254–62.
13. See F Rep 240 Acc 2651 Nr. 5, p. 504/4; PRO FO 1012/174 Economics/Black Market, pp. 105 and 116. Warm rooms had already been set up in the Weimar period "for the needy." In November 1927, there were 62 warm rooms throughout the city, providing beds for 4,627 people. *Statistisches Jahrbuch der Stadt Berlin* 5 (1929): 219.
14. LAB F Rep 240 Acc. 2651, Nr. 5, p. 578/1. Names changed.
15. Schenk, *Mental Maps*, 494, hereafter and in the following.
16. LAB F Rep. 240 Acc. 2651 Nr. 5, p. 578/1.
17. Ibid.
18. Ibid., 578/2.
19. This structure of goods had its own tradition, which built on both legal and illegal precursors. On illegal foodstuff markets during the war, for example, see LAB A Rep 358–02 80407.
20. On the regulations of the Charlottenburg district municipality, see LAB A Rep 037–08 Nr. 515b, pp. 279–80.
21. Ibid., p. 285.
22. See "Raid at Potsdamer Platz," *Telegraph*, July 23, 1948.
23. "Christmas Market or Hustler's Bazaar?," *Berlin at Midday*, December 15, 1947, p. 3. On seasonal trade overall, see LAB F Rep 240 Acc. 2651 Nr. 4, p. 402, as well as PRO FO 1012/175, p. 53, 112, 110; and FO 1012/176, pp. 13, 119, 148, 178, 179, 187, 188.
24. LAB C Rep 303/9 81, p. 169/2, report from October 22, 1945.
25. See PRO FO 1012/175 Black Market, p. 114.
26. For an introduction to this, see Maren Lorenz, *Leibhaftige Vergangenheit. Einführung in die Körpergeschichte* (Tübingen, 2000).
27. The "hunger winter" of 1946/47 provides a sad and notorious example of this. For more on survival strategies to combat the food shortage, see Sylvia Robeck and Gabriela Wachter, eds., *Kalter Krieg und warme Küche. 200 Berliner Rezepte im Kontext der Stadtgeschichte* (Berlin, 2007).
28. Erving Goffman, *Relations in Public: Microstudies of the Public Order* (New York, 1971), 28–60.
29. LAB F Rep 240, Nr. 5, p. 503/1.
30. Ibid., p. 94.
31. LAB F Rep 240, Nr. 5 p. 503/1.
32. See for example LAB A Rep 358–02, 8443.
33. LAB F Rep 240, Nr. 4, p. 302/1.
34. See LAB F Rep 240, Nr. 5, p. 504/4.
35. Goffman, *Relations*, 29–35.
36. On interaction theory, see Adam Kendon, "Spatial Organization in Social Encounters: The F-formation System," in *Conducting Interaction: Patterns of Behavior in Focused Encounters*, 209–37 (Cambridge, UK, 1990), who investigates "focused encounters" in the tradition of Erving Goffman's interaction patterns.
37. Ibid., 209.

38. For a countertrend in modernity, see Moritz Föllmer, *Sehnsucht nach Nähe: Interpersonale Kommunikation in Deutschland seit dem 19. Jahrhundert* (Stuttgart, 2004).
39. F Rep 240 Acc 2651, Nr. 4, p. 402/2.
40. Kendon, "Spatial Organization in Social Encounters: The F-formation System," 233–34.
41. Irwin Altman, *The Environment and Social Behavior: Privacy, Personal Space, Territory, and Crowding* (Monterey, 1975).
42. LAB F Rep 240, Nr. 5, p. 503/1.
43. Ibid., Nr. 6, p. 689/2.
44. See, for example, ibid., Nr. 5, pp. 581/2.
45. Archiv des Deutschen Historischen Museums, Rep. I/ 2. Weltkrieg/ F1/ M, Tagebuch Deutmann (unpaginated).
46. On the following, in general, see Jens Beckert, "Vertrauen und die performative Konstruktion von Märkten," *Zeitschrift für Soziologie* 31, no. 1 (2002): 27–43.
47. Niklas Luhmann, *Vertrauen: Ein Mechanismus der Reduktion sozialer Komplexität*, 4th ed. (Stuttgart, 2000), 37–40, already discussed this.
48. Beckert, "Vertrauen", 27, convincingly argues that the payoff situation in trust games can motivate the trust-recipient (the buyer) to invest in the presentation of his or her own credibility since these are "sequentially predetermined" vis-à-vis the trust-donor (the seller), who, in turn, faces the binary decision to accept/reject the offered good. This in turns depends on the way the trading partner presents himself or herself.
49. On the limitations of economic trade theories, see ibid., 28.
50. Ibid., 34.
51. Ibid., 37–38.
52. See, for example, LAB F Rep 240, Nr. 5.
53. See LAB F Rep. 240 Acc 2651 Nr. 2, p. 111/2.
54. The following is based on LAB A Rep 358–02 87905, prosecutor at the regional court, ruling of the first criminal division of the Appeals Court in Berlin of October 6, 1959 (notarized copy) (unpaginated).
55. DRA B 203-01-01/0263.
56. On the Soviet Union, see Julie Hessler, *A Social History of Soviet Trade: Trade Policy, Retail Practices, and Consumption, 1917–1953* (Princeton, 2004); on the United States, see Thomas Welskopp, "Bis an die Grenzen des Gesetzes. Die Reaktion der legalen Alkoholwirtschaft auf die National Prohibition in den USA, 1920–1933," *Zeitschrift für Unternehmensgeschichte* 52 (2007): 3–32; on Great Britain, Ina Zweiniger-Bargielowska, *Austerity in Britain: Rationing, Controls, and Consumption 1939–1955* (Oxford, 2000); and on France, Paul Sanders, *Histoire du Marché Noir 1940–1946* (Paris, 2001).
57. On this, see Paul Steege, *Black Market, Cold War: Everyday Life in Berlin, 1946–1949* (Cambridge, UK, 2007), 105–47.
58. On the Soviet policy of seeing work as a form of reparation payment, see Sergej Mironenko, Lutz Niethammer, and Alexander von Plato, eds. *Sowjetische Speziallager in Deutschland 1945–1950*, vol. 2, *Sowjetische Dokumente zur Lagerpolitik* (Berlin, 1998), 30–36. This policy was adapted quickly after the Soviets conquered Berlin.
59. See http://www.loc.gov/rr/frd/Military_Law/Enactments/06LAW49.pdf.

60. See Petra Weber, *Justiz und Diktatur. Justizverwaltung und politische Strafjustiz in Thüringen 1945–1961* (Munich, 2000), 79–90.
61. See Roesler, "Black Market." According to British observers, Control Council Law No. 50 was as inefficient as the German laws. Concerning the law and the difficulties in applying it, one report said that it was "primarily directed against major offenses and, if literally interpreted, might well lead to injustices in the case of petty offenders." PRO FO 1012/175, p. 6.
62. LAB C Rep. 303–09 222, pp. 270–71, Der Polizeipräsident in Berlin, note from September 18, 1945.
63. DRA, B 203-01-01/0130.
64. PRO Fo 1012/175, p. 6.
65. See below, Chapter 4, "A Market of 'Little People': The Black Market and the Social Question."
66. See ibid., as well as PRO FO 1012/175 Black Market, p. 114, and the article, "Razzia am Potsdamer Platz," *Telegraf*, July 23, 1948.
67. On the failures of criminal prosecution, among other things, see Roesler, "Black Market."
68. LAB C Rep. 303–09 222, p. 294, Der Polizeipräsident in Berlin, Leitworte, May 16, 1946.
69. Ibid., p. 295.
70. The following is based on DRA, B 203-01-01/0129.
71. *Der Morgen*, edition of January 9, 1946, p. 6. Similar events were by no means rare. For an example, see LAB C Rep. 303–09 223, Der Polizeipräsident in Berlin, p. 113.
72. LAB C Rep. 303–09 223, p. 201, Der Polizeipräsident in Berlin, Internes Schreiben an die Abteilung K. of January 11, 1946.
73. *Der Morgen*, January 9, 1946, p. 6.
74. LAB C Rep. 303–09 223, p. 174.
75. DRA, B 202-00-07/0053.
76. DRA, B 202-00-07/0063.
77. LAB C Rep. 303–09, Der Polizeipräsident in Berlin, no. 223, p. 187.
78. See Jennifer Schevardo, *Vom Wert des Notwendigen. Preispolitik und Lebensstandard in der DDR der fünfziger Jahre* (Stuttgart, 2006), and Ingo-Sascha Kowalczuk, "Opfer der eigenen Politik? Zu den Hintergründen der Verhaftung von Minister Karl Hamann (LDPD)," In *Jahrbuch zur Liberalismusforschung* 16 (2004): 221–271, as well as, especially, Ina Merkel, *Utopie und Bedürfnis. Die Geschichte der Konsumkultur in der DDR* (Cologne, 1999), 248, who speaks of the HO shops as promoting a "policy of two classes of goods."
79. On the debates concerning the intensity of the efforts to control and combat the black market, see PRO FO 1012/175 Blackmarkets, p. 66.
80. LAB C Rep. 303–09, Der Polizeipräsident in Berlin, no. 223, p. 199. See Weber, *Justiz*, 90–97.
81. See Steege, *Black Market*, 1–17.
82. LAB C Rep. 303/9 223, p. 209.
83. See Siegfried Heimann, "Karl Heinrich und die Berliner SPD, die sowjetische Militäradministration und die SED," *Gesprächskreis Geschichte der Friedrich-Ebert-Stiftung* 70 (2007): 1–65, on the history of the division of Berlin.
84. PRO FO 1012/175, p. 71.
85. Ibid.

86. Ibid.
87. Andreas Daum, *Kennedy in Berlin. Politik, Kultur und Emotionen im Kalten Krieg* (Paderborn, 2003), 147 and 149.
88. Ibid., 39. See Gerhard Keiderling, *'Rosinenbomber' über Berlin. Währungsreform, Blockade, Luftbrücke, Teilung: Die schicksalsvollen Jahre 1948/49* (Berlin, 1998), 238–55, on "everyday life in the besieged fortress" and on campaigns such as dropping chocolates via parachutes to the children of the city during the blockade.
89. Daum, *Kennedy*, 162–70.
90. On the image of the United States and of Russia in National Socialism as well as on the propaganda during wartime, see Philipp Gassert, *Amerika im Dritten Reich. Ideologie, Propaganda und Volksmeinung 1933–1945* (Stuttgart, 1997); Norman M. Naimark, *The Russians in Germany: The History of the Soviet Zone of Occupation, 1945–1949* (Cambridge, MA, 1995), 1–8; and Hans-Erich Volkmann, ed., *Das Russlandbild im Dritten Reich* (Cologne, 1994).
91. See, for example, Wolfram Wette, ed., *Das letzte halbe Jahr: Stimmungsberichte der Wehrmachtpropaganda 1944/45* (Essen, 2001), 334.
92. David Clay Large, *Berlin: A Modern History* (New York, 2001), 359.
93. Richard Bessel, " 'Leben nach dem Tod'. Vom Zweiten Weltkrieg zur zweiten Nachkriegszeit," in *Wie Kriege enden. Wege zum Frieden von der Antike bis zur Gegenwart*, ed. Bernd Wegner, 239–58 (Paderborn, 2002) correctly notes that the mass rapes are an "essential starting point for a serious discussion and analysis of the history of the GDR."
94. *Telegraf*, March 8, 1947, 4.
95. See Götz Aly, *Hitlers Volksstaat: Raub, Rassenkrieg und nationaler Sozialismus* (Frankfurt am Main, 2005), on plundering as one of the key characteristics of German war society.
96. Quoted in Frank Bajohr, *Parvenüs und Profiteure: Korruption in der NS-Zeit* (Frankfurt am Main, 2001), 86.
97. Quoted in ibid., 87.
98. Ibid., 85.
99. LAB F Rep 240 Acc 2651 Nr. 6, 748/5.
100. See Horst Carl, "Krieg und Kriegsniederlage—historische Erfahrung und Erinnerung," in *Kriegsniederlagen. Erfahrungen und Erinnerungen*, ed. idem, Hans-Henning Kortüm, Dieter Langewiesche, and Friedrich Lenger (Berlin, 2004), 1–11 on the history of experiencing defeat.
101. See Bessel, "Leben."
102. Reinhart Koselleck, "Erinnerungsschleusen und Erfahrungsschichten. Der Einfluss der beiden Weltkriege auf das soziale Bewusstsein," reprinted in *Zeitschichten. Studien zur Historik*, idem (Frankfurt am Main, 2000), 275.
103. The following is quoted in LAB F Rep 240 Acc 2651 Nr. 6, pp. 748xff.
104. On the rapes, see Naimark, *Russians*, 69–140.
105. On the increase in criminality as a characteristic of German postwar society, see Hans-Ulrich Wehler, *Gesellschaftsgeschichte*, vol. 4, *Vom Beginn des Ersten Weltkriegs bis zur Gründung der beiden deutschen Staaten 1914–1949* (Munich, 2003), 953.
106. Descriptions of the black market primarily as a social and somehow entertaining phenomenon picked up on the discourse of the Weimar years that characterized the illegal "hustle and bustle" as part of modernity—at times with fatalistic cheerfulness. See the development of the black market motif in cabaret, for example, in Günter Neumann's "Revue of the Zero Hour," which advertised with the headline "Black Market Fair."

107. LAB F Rep 240 Acc 2651 Nr. 6, p. 370/1.
108. See Richard Sennet, *Flesh and Stone: The Body and the City in Western Civilization* (London, 2002), 349–54.
109. LAB F Rep 240 Acc 2651 Nr. 6, p. 689/2.
110. A compromise peace was ruled out from the very beginning because of the imperialistic expansion and destructive policies of the Germans. See Jost Dülffer, "Frieden nach dem Zweiten Weltkrieg? Der Friedensschluss im Zeichen des Kalten Krieges," in *Wie Kriege enden*, ed. Wegner, 213–37, 214.
111. On the significance of everyday interaction for the relationship between Germans and their occupiers, see the remarks in Stefan-Ludwig Hoffmann, "Das Dilemma der Besatzer. Alliierte Deutschlandpolitik nach 1945: Pragmatismus vor Rigorismus," *WZB-Mitteilungen* 114 (2006): 15–17. On the occupation policies of the US, see Uta Gerhardt, *Soziologie der Stunde Null. Zur Gesellschaftskonzeption des amerikanischen Besatzungsregimes in Deutschland 1944–1945/46* (Frankfurt am Main, 2005).
112. Large, *Berlin*, 350.
113. This topic, which expressed itself in the descriptions of the Russian soldiers, can be found, for example, in the entries in the diary of the famous "Anonyma." See Anonyma, Eine Frau in Berlin. Tagebuch–Aufzeichnungen vom 20. April bis 22. Juni 1945 (Frankfurt, 2003).
114. This gesture—ultimately modified to the modern form of entering the city on a tank—became a part of the visual imagery of Russian propaganda. See http://www.dhm.de/ausstellungen/mythen-der-nationen/popups/bilder/h_09.jpg (last accessed on July 20, 2007).
115. See LAB C Rep. 303/9 222, p. 270 for an overview of the problems German (auxiliary) policemen encountered in combating and controlling the black market.
116. LAB F Rep 240 Acc 2651 Nr. 5, 462/5–6.
117. LAB F Rep 240 Acc. 2651 Nr. 4, 420.
118. Ibid.
119. DHM, Deutmann diary, June 24, 1945.
120. Quoted in Michael Bienert, *Berlin wird Metropole: Fotografien aus dem Kaiser-Panorama* (Berlin, 2000), 187.
121. See the pictures in "Black Markets Boom in Berlin," *Life*, September 10, 1945, 54.
122. See "Schwarze Börse entmotorisiert," *Telegraf*, October 23, 1948, 6.
123. LAB F Rep 240 Acc 2651 Nr. 2, 119/2.

> Auf der Straße flitzen Autos/ Fette Russen räkeln sich/ In den Polstern uns'rer Wagen
> Mir scheint sie verhöhnen mich,/ Der da vor mir geht ist trunken
> Wodka! Brüllt er, lebe hoch/ Ach wie tief sind wir gesunken/
> Armes Deutschland, lebst du noch?/ (. . .) Wünscht es wären Spukgestalten
> Die an mir vorüberziehn/ Aber ach ich kanns nicht leugnen
> Das ist "östliches Berlin."

124. LAB F Rep 240 Acc 2651 Nr. 5, 462/5–6.
125. All of the following quotes are from the *Telegraf*, January 24, 1947.
126. See Annette Brauerhoch, *Fräuleins und GIs* (Frankfurt am Main, 2006); Maria Höhn, *GIs and Fräuleins: The German-American Encounter in 1950s West Germany* (Chapel Hill, 2002); Elizabeth Heineman, "The Hour of the Woman: Memories

of Germany's 'Crisis Years' and West German National Identity," in *The Miracle Years: A Cultural History of West Germany 1949–1968*, ed. Hanna Schissler, 21–56 (Princeton, 2001), on women between "*Trümmerfrau*" and "*Amiliebchen*" in postwar Germany.

127. The topic of power and helplessness played a role even in cases concerning prominent traders. See the *Telegraf* from July 10, 1947, 5.
128. DHM, Deutmann diary, entry from August 5, 1945.
129. LAB F Rep 240 Nr. 2, 111/1.
130. Rainer Gries, *Die Rationengesellschaft: Versorgungskampf und Vergleichsmentalität: Leipzig, München und Köln nach dem Kriege* (Münster, 1991), see subtitle.
131. *Die Wirtschaft* 3 (1948/4), 120. See Roesler, "Black Market," 92.
132. Osmar White, *The Conquerors' Road* (Cambridge, UK, 1996), 126.
133. LAB F Rep. 240 Acc. 2651 Nr. 5, p. 462/4.
134. See the report in the *Telegraf*, June 7, 1947, 3.
135. LAB F Rep. 240 Acc. 2651 Zeitgeschichtliche Sammlung Nr. 5, p. 489. The German original reads as follows: Winternacht schneidende Kälte. Zerbombtes Haus./Im Keller die Tanzbar der Schieber/"Mensch, Maxe, jieb noch paar Doppelte aus/und komm mit paar Chesterfield rieba!"/In der Notwohnung Hochparterre haust eine Frau,/krank, einsam, vom Kriegssturm vertrieben./"Wenn mein Werner noch wäre, ja dann wär't jut;/auch Heinz ist im Osten jeblieben!"/"Och, Oba, zwölf Alkolat aba fix;/det Jeschäft mit'n Sprit kenn wa machen!"/Und Gläserklingen, Tellergeklirr/Und blechernes Dirnenlachen./Die Wände zerklafft und die Fenster verpappt,/keucht ein Mensch in den Klauen der Kälte./War das eben ein heiserer, hungriger Hund,/der dort oben so schwindsüchtig bellte?/Und als sie den letzten Todesschrei schrie/aus den sinkenden, würgenden Schatten:/"Bella-Bella-Bella-Marie!"/grölten unten im Keller die Ratten.
136. DRA, B 204-02-01/0371.
137. All quotes ibid.
138. DRA, B 204-03-02/0163.
139. *Telegraf*, January 5, 1947, 8.
140. See Andreas Dinter, *Berlin in Trümmern. Ernährungslage und medizinische Versorgung der Bevölkerung Berlins nach dem Zweiten Weltkrieg* (Berlin, 1999). The whole book is dedicated to this topic on the catastrophic living conditions, above all in regard to the food situation and the provision of medical care.
141. "Der Schwarze Markt der Armen," *Telegraf*, September 3, 1948, 4.
142. *Telegraf*, May 1, 1947, 6. The newspaper did not describe any connection to the May Day celebrations.
143. See Thomas Lindenberger, *Straßenpolitik: Zur Sozialgeschichte der öffentlichen Ordnung in Berlin 1900–1914* (Bonn, 1995), 114–15.
144. These records in the Berlin archive consist of a couple of hundred cartons that have not yet been catalogued.
145. PRO FO 1012/177, Economics—Black Market, 36.
146. LAB [o. Rep.] 95 Ds 414/49, pp. 1–3.
147. Ibid., p. 11.
148. "Zahlen zeigen Zeitgeschehen," Special issue 3, *Berliner Statistik* 1 (1947): 29. This does not contradict Niethammer's observation that the industrial workers of the Ruhr had a comparatively good position in the black markets because of their additional allowances. The percentage of manual workers was much higher in the Ruhr than in Berlin, where it was on average only 3 percent.

See Lutz Niethammer, "Privat-Wirtschaft: Erinnerungsfragmente einer anderen Umerziehung," in *"Hinterher merkt man, dass es richtig war, dass es schiefgegangen ist." Nachkriegs-Erfahrungen im Ruhrgebiet*, ed. idem (Berlin, 1983), 94.

149. Statistisches Landesamt der Stadt Berlin, ed., *Berlin in Zahlen*, 13.
150. Wehler, *Gesellschaftsgeschichte*, 756.
151. See Klaus-Jörg Ruhl, *Verordnete Unterordnung. Berufstätige Frauen zwischen Wirtschaftswachstum und konservativer Ideologie in der Nachkriegszeit 1945–1963* (Munich, 1994), as well as Anita Pfaff, *Typische Lebensläufe von Frauen der Geburtsjahrgänge 1910–1975* (Stuttgart, 1979), and for West Berlin Edith Hinze, *Lage und Leistung erwerbstätiger Mütter: Ergebnisse einer Untersuchung in West-Berlin* (Berlin, 1960), on the "prescribed subordination" of West German women in working society.
152. *Die Wirtschaft*, 1948/4, 53.
153. See LAB F Rep. 240 Acc 2651 Nr. 3, p. 237.
154. Thomas Scholze, "Zur Ernährungssituation der Berliner nach dem Zweiten Weltkrieg. Ein Beitrag zur Erfahrung des Großstadtalltags (1945–1952)," *Jahrbuch für Geschichte* 35 (1987): 522, refers to "a street in Charlottenburg . . . [where] there was a black market only for egg yolk powder, which could only be obtained with children's ration cards."
155. See PRO FO 1012/175 Economics/Black Market, pp. 20 and 67.
156. "Die 'schwarze' Bauwirtschaft," *Telegraf*, January 23, 1948, 3.
157. See the report, "Schwarzhandelsware Opium," *Telegraf*, February 25, 1948, 6.
158. *New York Herald Tribune*, January 4, 1947, 15.
159. Ibid., 114.
160. Ibid., 15.
161. "Schwarzhandel per Post," *Tribüne*, November 10, 1947, 12.
162. See, for example, ibid., 177, 21, for an example of such a shipment from Sweden.
163. Ibid., 175, 119.
164. Ibid.
165. Ibid.
166. On the following, see PRO FO 1012/176, pp. 162–65. The manufacturers of the (imitation) brand-name goods were also interested in the imitations. In a letter from September 9, 1949, Cadbury Brothers Ltd. wrote to the British Military Administration in Berlin that the firm was interested in intensifying the prosecution of the criminals: "We are most anxious that the sale of this chocolate be stopped." PRO 1012/177, p. 82.
167. Ibid., p. 161.
168. DMH, Deutmann diary, entry from August 5, 1945.
169. LAB F Rep. 240 Acc. 2651 Nr. 2, p. 111/2.
170. See LAB A Rep. 358–02 89681 for examples of professional counterfeit techniques (with photographs of the tools and of the counterfeit ration cards).
171. See Rainer Gries, *Produkte als Medien. Kulturgeschichte der Produktkommunikation in der Bundesrepublik und der DDR* (Leipzig, 2003), 135–38, and 570–74.
172. DHM, Deutmann diary, entry from August 6, 1945.
173. LAB F Rep. 240 Acc. 2651 Nr. 4, p. 402/2.
174. Ibid.
175. Ibid. Nr. 6, p. 698/2.
176. See the complete collection of files, LAB F Rep. 240 Acc. 2651.

177. The original poem reads as follows:

> Eine Quelle des Trostes, ein Mittel gegen die Angst, eine Droge, die Entspannung verschafft, den Hunger und die Langeweile vergessen macht, ein Mittel, Höflichkeit zu bezeigen, eine Entscheidungshilfe, ein Wachmacher, der Pfeil Cupidos und eine Waffe gegen die Vorgesetzten—die Zigarette, die ein Soldat raucht, gibt ihm alles, was er braucht. Was wäre der Soldat ohne Tabak! (Richard Klein, *Schöner blauer Dunst. Ein Lob der Zigarette.*
>
> (Munich, 1992)

178. The original quotation reads as follows: "Die Gelbfärbung an den Spitzen seiner blutleeren Finger verriet, dass er sich nicht so viel Mühe machte, Zigaretten zu verkaufen wie zu rauchen." Philip Kerr, *Alte Freunde—neue Feinde* (Reinbek, 2000), 155.
179. Günter Schmölders, "Die Zigarettenwährung," in *Sozialökonomische Verhaltensforschung. Festschrift für Günter Schmölders zum 70. Geburtstag*, ed. Gerhard Brinkmann, 166–71 (Berlin, 1973), 166. See as well Christoph Merki, "Die amerikanische Zigarette, das Maß aller Dinge. Rauchen in Deutschland zur Zeit der Zigarettenwährung 1945–1948," in *Tabakfragen: Rauchen aus kulturwissenschaftlicher Sicht*, ed. Thomas Hengartner and Christoph Merki, 57–82 (Zurich, 1996); and Gerhard Stoltmann, "Die Zigarettenwährung," *Deutsche Tabak Zeitung* 5 (1982): 10.
180. Quoted in Merki, "Die amerikanische Zigarette," 57.
181. See "Das Tabakjahr 1946," *Telegraf*, January 28, 1947, 4.
182. "Umstrittenen 'Tabakregie'," *Telegraf*, June 10, 1947, 2.
183. See Jürgen Link,"Literaturanalyse als Interdiskursanalyse: Am Beispiel des Ursprungs literarischer Symbolik in der Kollektivsymbolik," in *Diskurstheorien und Literaturwissenschaft*, ed. Jürgen Fohrmann and Harro Müller, 284–307 (Frankfurt am Main, 1988), for a definition of the concept of "collective symbols."
184. "Camel zieht nicht mehr," *Telegraf*, July 2, 1948, 5.
185. "Das Mädchen mit den 'Ami-Kippen'," *Telegraf*, August 31, 1948, 4.
186. LAB F Rep. 240 Acc. 2651 Nr. 4, pp. 396/2–4.
187. Klein, *Schöner blauer Dunst*, 283 and 285.
188. See Kaspar Maase, " 'Lässig' kontra 'zackig'—Nachkriegsjugend und Männlichkeiten in geschlechtergeschichtlicher Perspektive," in *Sag mir, wo die Mädchen sind.... Beiträge zur Geschlechtergeschichte der Jugend*, ed. Christina Benninghaus and Kerstin Kohtz, 79–101 (Cologne, 1999).
189. Klein, *Schöner blauer Dunst*, 234.
190. Ibid., 237–38.
191. See Elke Kupschinsky, "Die vernünftige Nephertete. Die Neue Frau der 20er Jahre in Berlin," in *Die Metropole: Industriestruktur in Berlin im 20: Jahrhundert*, ed. Jochen Boberg, 167–69 (Munich, 1988).

Chapter 5

1. [No repository number] 95 Ds Akten der Abteilung 95 des Berliner Kammergerichts.
2. LAB A Rep. 358–02 80196, p. 3.
3. Ibid., 89781, pp. 20, as well as 80384, p. 8.
4. Ibid., 79809, pp. 85 and 93.

5. LAB A Rep. 341–02 9792, letter from March 10, 1943 (unpaginated).
6. Ibid., p. 17.
7. See, for example, "Dollar und Schwarzmarkt, mit Grafiken," *Der Tag*, March 20, 1949.
8. For the following, see Frank Zschaler, "Die Lösung der Währungsfrage in Berlin 1948/49. Weichenstellungen für die Nachkriegsentwicklung der deutschen Hauptstadt," in *Sterben für Berlin? Die Berliner Krisen 1948:1958*, ed. Burghard Ciesla, Michael Lemke, and Thomas Lindenberger, 47–58 (Berlin, 2000), as well as idem, *Öffentliche Finanzen und Finanzpolitik in Berlin 1945–1961: Eine vergleichende Untersuchung von Ost- und West-Berlin mit Datenanhang 1945–1989* (Berlin, 1995), 15–24. For the developments in West Berlin, see Michael Wolff, *Die Währungsreform in Berlin 1948/49* (Berlin, 1991).
9. Zschaler, "Währungsfrage," 53.
10. PRO FO 1005/862, p. 2.
11. Ibid.
12. Ibid., p. 4.
13. Ibid., p. 9.
14. PRO FO 1012/175, p. 138 (4).
15. See Wolfgang Benz, *Geschichte des Dritten Reiches* (Munich, 2000), 190–94.
16. An overview of prices is available in the Price Office of the City of Berlin, Abt. Ernährung, Aufstellung über die Wirkung der Einführung der Westmark auf die Preise. FO 1012/326, Allied Commandantura, Trade and Industry Committee, Economics—Currency and Prices, unpaginated.
17. See Zschaler, "Währungsfrage," 49–52.
18. LAB F Rep 240, Nr. 6, pp. 748x4.
19. LAB F Rep 240, Nr. 6, pp. 753x1 ff. Emphasis/italics in the original.
20. PRO FO 1056/565 Public Opinion Research Office, Notes on Currency Reform No. 1, June 30, 48 (unpaginated.).
21. Ibid.
22. PRO FO 1012/176, p. 67.
23. See "Schwarze Börse entmotorisiert," *Telegraf*, October 23, 1948, 4.
24. On the history of the radio and its political role in the Soviet zone and in the GDR, see Klaus Arnold and Christoph Classen, eds., *Zwischen Pop und Propaganda. Radio in der DDR* (Berlin, 2004); and Christoph Classen, *Faschismus und Antifaschismus. Geschichte im Radio der SBZ/DDR 1945–1953* (Cologne, 2004).
25. All quotes: DRA, B 202-00-01/0015.
26. All quotes: DRA, B 203-01-01/0261.
27. All quotes: DRA, B 202-00-07/0053.
28. All quotes: DRA, B 202-00-07/0051.
29. All quotes: DRA, B 203-01-01/0025.
30. See above, Chapter 4, the section "Criminal Prosecution and Symbolic Politics."
31. All quotes: DRA, B 202-00-06/0347.
32. "Das UNRRA-Lager wird geräumt," *Neues Deutschland*, July 23, 1948.
33. "Westpolizei schützt Schieber," *Tägliche Rundschau*, August 15, 1945.
34. All quotes: DRA, B 204-02-01/321.
35. Quoted in Jörg Roesler, *Die Wirtschaft der DDR. Publikation der Landeszentrale für politische Bildung Thüringen* (Erfurt, 2002), 7.
36. See André Steiner, *Von Plan zu Plan: Eine Wirtschaftsgeschichte der DDR* (Munich, 2004), 41.
37. On the lack of success, see ibid., 56–92.

38. Ina Merkel, *Utopie und Bedürfnis: Die Geschichte der Konsumkultur in der DDR* (Cologne, 1999), 329. It was possible to have "normal" shopping experiences after 1953 in the flourishing stores of the commission-retail trade. See Heinz Hoffmann, *Der Kommissionshandel im planwirtschaftlichen System der DDR: Eine besondere Eigentums- und Handelsform* (Leipzig, 2001). On the displacements in consumer shopping brought about by 1989, see Annett Schultz, "Privathaushalte und Haushalten in Ostdeutschland," Discussion Paper FS III 97–405, WZB (Berlin, 1997).
39. Merkel, *Utopie und Bedürfnis*, 88. See also Philipp Heldmann, *Herrschaft—Wirtschaft—Anoraks. Konsumpolitik in der DDR der Sechzigerjahre* (Göttingen, 2004), as well as Steiner, *Plan*, 7–17.
40. Joachim Starbatty, "Die Soziale Marktwirtschaft aus historisch-theoretischer Sicht," in *Entstehung und Entwicklung der Sozialen Marktwirtschaft. Im Auftrag der Gesellschaft für Unternehmensgeschichte*, ed. Hans Pohl, 7–26 (Wiesbaden, 1986).
41. All quotes ibid., 20–22.
42. See Eric Hobsbawm, "Introduction: Inventing Tradition," in *The Invention of Tradition*, ed. idem and Terence Ranger, 11–14 (Cambridge, 2003)
43. All editions from December 1, 1949.
44. LAB F Rep 240, Nr. 3, p. 237/2.
45. "Bewirtschaftung," *Der Tagesspiegel*, August 14, 1945, 5.
46. The Ahlen Program of the CDU stated:

> the capitalist economic system did not do justice to the vital interests of the German people in regard to their state and their social order.... The content and the goal (of) social and economic restructuring can no longer be the capitalist pursuit of profit and power, but rather only the well-being of our people. Through a communal design the German people are to receive an economic and social constitution that befits the law and the dignity of man, that serves the intellectual and material development of our people, and that establishes a secure foundation for internal and external peace.
>
> (Konrad Adenauer Foundation)

47. Ludwig Aderbauer, "Der Schwarze Markt als Folge der Geldunordnung" (PhD diss., Ludwig-Maximilian University of Munich, 1948), 1.
48. Irmgard Zündorf, *Der Preis der Marktwirtschaft. Staatliche Preispolitik und Lebensstandard in Westdeutschland 1948 bis 1963* (Stuttgart, 2006), 9.
49. Ibid., 305.
50. The so-called *Konsumbrot* was a cheap brown bread heavily subsidized by the West German state until 1953 and in West Berlin until 1958. See the cabinet minutes of the federal government on the issue (online): http://www.bundesarchiv.de/cocoon/barch/11/k/k1951k/kap1_2/kap2_10/para3_18.html.
51. Zündorf, *Preis der Marktwirtschaft*, 306.
52. Karl Georg Zinn, *Soziale Marktwirtschaft. Idee, Entwicklung und Politik der bundesdeutschen Wirtschaftsordnung* (Mannheim, 1992), 44.
53. Ludwig Erhard, *Gedanken aus fünf Jahrzehnten. Reden und Schriften*, ed. Karl Hohmann (Düsseldorf, 1988), 57.
54. Ibid., 58.
55. Ibid., 55.

56. Müller-Armack, "Soziale Marktwirtschaft," *Handwörterbuch der Sozialwissenschaften* (Stuttgart, 1956), 9:390–92.
57. Erhard, *Gedanken aus fünf Jahrzehnten*, 69.
58. Ibid.
59. See Jürgen Niemann, *Auftakt zur Demokratie: Der Bundeswahlkampf 1949 zwischen Improvisation und Ideologie* (Bochum, 1994).
60. Michael Wildt, *Am Beginn der Konsumgesellschaft: Mangelerfahrung, Lebenshaltung, Wohlstandshoffnung in Westdeutschland in den fünfziger Jahren*, 2nd ed. (Hamburg, 1995), 256. Wildt relativizes an interpretation that otherwise is still very much in the forefront and apparently is still employed—as needed—to provide the context for some arguments. See, for example Christoph Gusy, "Einleitung—Weimar: Geschichte als Argument," in *Weimars lange Schatten*, ed. idem (Baden-Baden, 2003), 16–18: Although he presents the "young Bonn Republic" as a "site of economic growth and of stability," thus hinting at an expansion of the paradigm of the economic miracle, he also emphasizes the material development from which "large sections of the population palpably profited."
61. Müller-Armack, "Soziale Marktwirtschaft," 392.
62. Ibid., 390.
63. Ibid.

Conclusion

1. Werner Abelshauser, *Deutsche Wirtschaftsgeschichte seit 1945* (Munich, 2004), 11–12.
2. Gerold Ambrosius, " 'Sozialistische Planwirtschaft' als Alternative und Variante in der Industriegesellschaft—die Wirtschaftsordnung," in *Überholen ohne einzuholen: Die DDR-Wirtschaft als Fußnote der deutschen Geschichte?*, ed. André Steiner, 11–31 (Berlin, 2006), 26.
3. Alfred C. Mierzejewski, *Erhard: A Biography* (Princeton, 2005), 70.
4. Dirk Baecker, "Die Preisbildung an der Börse," *Soziale Systeme* 5 (1999): 287–312, 287.
5. See André Steiner, *Plan*. The German title referred to here is slightly different from that of the English translation: *The Plans That Failed: An Economic History of the GDR* (New York, 2010).

Bibliography

Archival Sources

Archiv des Deutsches Historisches Museum (DHM)
Rep. I, 2. Weltkrieg, F1, M Tagebuch Deutmann
Landesarchiv Berlin (LAB)
A, Rep. 001–02, Stadtverordnetenversammlung von Berlin
A, Rep. 037–08, Bezirksamt Charlottenburg
A, Rep. 358–02, Staatsanwaltschaft bei dem Landgericht
A Pr. Br. Rep. 57, Stadtpräsident der Reichshauptstadt Berlin
F, Rep. 240, Acc. 2651, Zeitgeschichtliche Sammlung

Deutsches Rundfunkarchiv Potsdam (DRA)

Newspaper Collections
DRA, B 202-00-01/0015
DRA, B 202-00-07/0053
DRA, B 202-00-07/0051
DRA, B 203-01-01/0025
DRA, B 203-01-01/0261
DRA, B 204-03-02/0163

Public Record Office (Kew/London) (PRO)

Foreign Office (FO)
936/741 Control Office for Germany and Austria/Operation ≪Sparkler≫ and Large-Scale Black Market Activities
936/744 Control Office for Germany and Austria/Services of Police CID Men to Detect Large-Scale Black Market Dealings
1005/862 Hq. Mil. Gvm. Troops Berlin/Price Control
1009/862 Hq. Mil. Gvm. Troops Berlin/Public Opinion Research Office. Special Reports on Morale 326
1012/52 Hq. Mil. Gvm. Troops Berlin/Police Orders
1012/174-177 Hq. Mil. Gvm. Troops Berlin/Economics/Black Market
1012/326 Hq. Mil. Gvm. Troops Berlin Allied Kommandatura Trade and Industry Committee

1012/483 Hq. Mil. Gvm. Troops Berlin/Routine Reports and Returns/Burgermeisters Monthly Reports
1012/594 Hq. Mil. Gvm. Troops Berlin/Public Safety Branch
1012/651 Hq. Mil. Gvm. Troops Berlin/Preisamt Contribution
1012/683 Hq. Mil. Gvm. Troops Berlin/Legal/Prisons/Juveniles
1051/449 Hq. Mil. Gvm. Troops Berlin/Control Commission for Germany (British Element) Manpower Division
1056/565 Public Opinion Research Office, Notes on Currency Reform
1090/684 Hq. Mil. Gvm. Troops Berlin/Public Safety Branch/Monthly Reports
HWI/3607 Japanese Ambassador Reports on Life in Berlin, 15th March, 1945

Periodicals

Berliner Tageblatt
Berliner Zeitung
Der Montag
Der Spiegel
Der Tag
Der Tagesspiegel
Der Telegraf
Die Neue Zeitung
Die Welt
Die Wirtschaft
Herald Tribune
National-Zeitung
Tägliche Rundschau
The Times (London)
Tribüne
Vorwärts

Published Primary Sources and Contemporary Literature

Aderbauer, Ludwig. "Der Schwarze Markt als Folge der Geldunordnung." PhD diss., Ludwig-Maximilian University of Munich, 1948.
Andreas-Friedrich, Ruth. *Schauplatz Berlin.* Frankfurt am Main, 1984.
Anonyma. *Eine Frau in Berlin.* Tagebuchaufzeichnungen vom 20. April bis 22. Juni 1945. Frankfurt am Main, 2003.
Bader, Karl. *Soziologie der deutschen Nachkriegskriminalität.* Tübingen, 1949.
Bienert, Michael, ed. *Joseph Roth in Berlin: Ein Lesebuch für Spaziergänger.* Cologne, 1996.
Böß, Gustav. *Die Not in Berlin: Tatsachen und Zahlen.* Berlin, 1923.
Brinkmann, Max. *Kleiner Knigge für Schieber.* Berlin, 1921.
Engelbrecht, Ernst and Leo Heller. *Berliner Razzien.* Neu-Finkenkrug, 1924.
Erhard, Ludwig. *Gedanken aus fünf Jahrzehnten: Reden und Schriften*, ed. Karl Hohmann. Düsseldorf, 1988.
Feder, Gottfried. *Das Programm der NSDAP und seine weltanschaulichen Grundgedanken*, 13th ed. Munich, 1930.
Freisler, Roland. *Nationalsozialistisches Recht und Rechtsdenken.* Berlin, 1938.
Giese, Erich. *Das zukünftige Schnellbahnnetz Groß-Berlin.* Berlin, 1919.
Grüneberg, Ernst. *Die Reichshauptstadt Berlin. Eine Heimatkunde für Berliner Schulen.* Breslau, 1938.

Hentig, Hans von. "Die Kriminalität des Zusammenbruchs." *Schweizerische Zeitschrift für Strafrecht* 63 (1947): 337–41.

Heuss, Theodor, *Aufzeichnungen 1945–1947*, ed. and with introduction by Eberhard Pikart. Tübingen, 1966.

Kardorff, Ursula von. *Berliner Aufzeichnungen: 1942–1945*, ed. Peter Hartl. Munich, 1992.

Klemperer, Victor. *LTI: Notizbuch eines Philologen*. Leipzig, 1999.

Klüber, Karl-Heinz. *Gesetzliche Grundlagen zur Schwarzmarktbekämpfung*, 3rd ed. Hamburg, 1948.

Kromer, Karl. *Schwarzmarkt, Tausch- und Schleichhandel*. Schloß Bleckede an der Elbe, 1947.

Lang, Ralf. *Italienische "Fremdarbeiter" im nationalsozialistischen Deutschland 1937–1945*. Frankfurt am Main, 1996.

Lethen, Helmuth. "Chicago und Moskau." In *Die Metropole. Industriekultur in Berlin im 20. Jahrhundert*, ed. Boberg, 190–213. Munich, 1988.

Mendershausen, Horst. "Prices, Money and the Distribution of Goods in Postwar Germany." *American Economic Review* 39 (1949): 647–72.

——. *Two Postwar Recoveries of the German Economy*. Amsterdam, 1955.

Meyer, Paul Werner. "Über das Phänomen des deutschen Schwarzen Marktes." PhD diss., Friedrich-Alexander University of Erlangen-Nürnberg, 1949.

Müller-Armack, Alfred. "Soziale Marktwirtschaft." *Handwörterbuch der Sozialwissenschaften*, Vol. 9, 390–92. Stuttgart, 1956.

Müller-Förster, Alfred. *Aufgewärmte Kartoffeln. Ein Büchlein für Politiker, Schieber und Schornsteinfeger, für Reichspräsidenten, Schuster, Minister, Jungfrauen und solche, die es werden wollen*. Hamburg, 1926.

Noelle, Elisabeth and Erich-Peter Neumann, ed. *Jahrbuch der öffentlichen Meinung* 3 (1975).

Picker, Henry. *Hitlers Tischgespräche im Führerhauptquartier*. Munich, 1979.

Rindt, Erich. "Die Markthallen als Faktor des Berliner Wirtschaftslebens." PhD diss., Berlin, 1928.

Roth, Joseph. "Der Orient in der Hirtenstraße: Besuch in der fliegenden Börse." In *Joseph Roth in Berlin: Ein Lesebuch für Spaziergänger*, ed. Michael Bienert, 72–75. Cologne, 1996.

Schmitz, Hubert. *Die Bewirtschaftung der Nahrungsmittel und Verbrauchsgüter 1939–1950: Dargestellt am Beispiel der Stadt Essen*. Essen, 1956.

Schöllgen, Werner. *Grenzmoral. Soziale Krisis und neuer Aufbau*. Düsseldorf, 1946.

Schouz, Josef. "Volkskundliche Studie über das Bandenwesen des 'Schwarzen Marktes'." PhD diss., University of Göttingen, 1953.

Statistisches Landesamt der Stadt Berlin, ed. *Berlin in Zahlen*. Berlin, 1947.

Thurnwald, Hilde. *Gegenwartsprobleme Berliner Familien*. Berlin, 1948.

Weber, Adolf. *Reparationen, Youngplan, Volkswirtschaft*. Berlin, 1929.

White, Osmar. *The Conquerors' Road*. Cambridge, UK, 1996.

"Zahlen zeigen Zeitgeschehen." Special issue 3, *Berliner Statistik* 1 (1947).

Secondary Sources and Other Literature

Abelshauser, Werner. *Deutsche Wirtschaftsgeschichte seit 1945*. Munich, 2004.

Altman, Irwin. *The Environment and Social Behavior: Privacy, Personal Space, Territory, and Crowding*. Monterey, CA, 1975.

Aly, Götz. *Hitlers Volksstaat: Raub, Rassenkrieg und nationaler Sozialismus*. Frankfurt am Main, 2005.

Ambrosius, Gerold. "'Sozialistische Planwirtschaft' als Alternative und Variante in der Industriegesellschaft—die Wirtschaftsordnung." In *Überholen ohne einzuholen. Die DDR-Wirtschaft als Fußnote der deutschen Geschichte?*, ed. André Steiner, 11–31. Berlin, 2006.

Ankum, Katharina von, ed. *Women in the Metropolis: Gender and Modernity in Weimar Culture*. Berkeley, CA, 1997.

Arnold, Klaus and Christoph Classen, eds. *Zwischen Pop und Propaganda: Radio in der DDR*. Berlin, 2004.

Asendorpf, Jens and Rainer Banse. *Psychologie der Beziehung*. Bern, 2001.

Baecker, Dirk. "Die Preisbildung an der Börse." *Soziale Systeme* 5 (1999): 287–312.

Bajohr, Frank. *Parvenüs und Profiteure: Korruption in der NS-Zeit*. Frankfurt am Main, 2001.

Bandhauer-Schöffmann, Irene. "Women's Fight for Food: A Gendered View of Hunger, Hoarding, and Black Marketing in Vienna after World War II." In *Women in Towns: The Social Position of European Urban Women in a Historical Context*, ed. Marjatta Hietala, 158–79. Stockholm, 1999.

Barth, Boris. *Dolchstoßlegenden und politische Desintegration: Das Trauma der deutschen Niederlage im Ersten Weltkrieg 1914–1933*. Düsseldorf, 2003.

Baumgärtner, Andreas. "Von einer Republik zur anderen: Theodor Heuss' Wahrnehmung und Deutung der Weimarer Republik nach 1945." In *Weimars lange Schatten*, ed. Gusy, 92–117.

Beckert, Jens. "Vertrauen und die performative Konstruktion von Märkten." *Zeitschrift für Soziologie* 31, no. 1 (2002): 27–43.

Beevor, Anthony. *Berlin: The Downfall 1945*. London, 2007.

Benz, Wolfgang. *Geschichte des Dritten Reichs*. Munich, 2000.

Berghoff, Hartmut. "Vertrauen als ökonomische Schlüsselvariable: Zur Theorie des Vertrauens und der marktwirtschaftlichen Produktion von Sozialkapital." In *Die Wirtschaftsgeschichte vor der Herausforderung der New Institutional Economics*, ed. Karl-Peter Ellerbrock and Clemens Wischermann, 58–71. Dortmund, 2003.

Berghoff, Hartmut and Jakob Vogel, eds. *Wirtschaftsgeschichte als Kulturgeschichte: Dimensionen eines Perspektivenwechsels*. Frankfurt am Main, 2004.

——. "Wirtschaftsgeschichte als Kulturgeschichte: Vom Versuch der Bergung transdisziplinärer Synergiepotentiale." In *Wirtschaftsgeschichte als Kulturgeschichte*, ed. Berghoff and Vogel, 9–41.

Bergius, Hanne. "Berlin als Hure Babylon." In *Die Metropole*, ed. Boberg, 102–19.

Bessel, Richard. "'Leben nach dem Tod'. Vom Zweiten Weltkrieg zur zweiten Nachkriegszeit." In *Wie Kriege enden*, ed. Wegner, 239–58.

Bienert, Michael. *Berlin wird Metropole: Fotografien aus dem Kaiser-Panorama*. Berlin, 2000.

Blank, Ralf. "Kriegsalltag und Luftkrieg an der Heimatfront." In *Das Deutsche Reich und der Zweite Weltkrieg*. Vol. 9/2, *Die Deutsche Kriegsgesellschaft 1939 bis 1945. Ausbeutung, Deutungen, Ausgrenzung*, ed. Jörg Echternkamp, 357–461. Munich, 2005.

Boberg, Jochen, ed. *Die Metropole: Industriestruktur in Berlin im 20: Jahrhundert*. Munich, 1988.

——. "Reklamwelten." In *Die Metropole*, ed. Boberg, 184–89.

Bock, Gisela. *Zwangssterilisation im Nationalsozialismus: Studien zur Rassenpolitik und Frauenpolitik*. Opladen, 1986.

Bodenschatz, Harald. "Altstadt und Mietskasernenstadt. Felder der Stadterneuerung zwischen den beiden Weltkriegen am Beispiel Berlin." In *Stadterneuerung in der Weimarer Republik und im Nationalsozialismus*, ed. Christian Kopetzki, 252–43. Kassel, 1987.

Boelcke, Willi A. *Der Schwarzmarkt: Vom Überleben nach dem Kriege*. Stuttgart, 1986.

——. *Die Kosten von Hitlers Krieg: Kriegsfinanzierung und finanzielles Kriegserbe in Deutschland 1933–1948*. Paderborn, 1985.

Boemeke, Manfred Franz, ed. *The Treaty of Versailles: A Reassessment after 75 Years*. Cambridge, UK, 1998.

Borscheid, Peter. "Geld und Liebe. Zu den Auswirkungen des Romantischen auf die Partnerwahl im 19. Jahrhundert." In *Ehe, Liebe, Tod. Zum Wandel der Familie, der Geschlechts- und Generationsbeziehungen in der Neuzeit*, ed. idem and Hans-Jürgen Teuteberg, 112–34. Münster, 1983.

Bösch, Frank. "Historische Skandalforschung als Schnittstelle zwischen Medien-, Kommunikations- und Geschichtswissenschaft." In *Die Medien der Geschichte: Historizität und Medialität in interdisziplinärer Perspektive*, ed. Fabio Crivellari, Kay Kirchmann, Marcus Sandl, and Rudolf Schlögl, 445–64. Konstanz, 2004.

Bourdieu, Pierre. "Gabe und do ut des." In *Praktische Vernunft*, 94–103. Frankfurt am Main, 1998.

Brauerhoch, Annette. *Fräuleins und GIs*. Frankfurt am Main, 2006.

Brinkmann, Gerhard, ed. *Sozialökonomische Verhaltensforschung. Festschrift für Günter Schmölders zum 70. Geburtstag*. Berlin, 1973.

Broszat, Martin, Klaus-Dietmar Henke, and Hans Woller. *Von Stalingrad zur Währungsreform: Zur Sozialgeschichte des Umbruchs in Deutschland*, 3rd ed. Munich, 1990.

Brown, Sheila. *Crime and Law in Media Culture*. Buckingham, 2003.

Bührer, Werner. "Schwarzer Markt." In *Deutschland unter alliierter Besatzung 1945–1949/55: Ein Handbuch*, ed. Wolfgang Benz, 365–67. Berlin, 1999.

Burleigh, Michael. *The Third Reich: A New History*. London, 2001.

Büsch, Otto. *Geschichte der Berliner Kommunalwirtschaft in der Weimarer Epoche*. Berlin, 1960.

Carl, Horst. "Krieg und Kriegsniederlage—historische Erfahrung und Erinnerung." In *Kriegsniederlagen: Erfahrungen und Erinnerungen*, ed. idem, Hans-Henning Kortüm, Dieter Langewiesche, and Friedrich Lenger, 1–11. Berlin, 2004.

Ciesla, Burghard, Michael Lemke, and Thomas Lindenberger, eds. *Sterben für Berlin? Die Berliner Krisen 1948:1958*. Berlin, 2000.

Classen, Christoph. *Faschismus und Antifaschismus: Geschichte im Radio der SBZ/DDR 1945–1953*. Cologne, 2004.

Corni, Gustavo and Horst Gies. *Brot, Butter, Kanonen: Die Ernährungswirtschaft in Deutschland unter der Diktatur Hitlers*. Berlin, 1997.

Daum, Andreas. *Kennedy in Berlin: Politik, Kultur und Emotionen im Kalten Krieg*. Paderborn, 2003.

Davis, Belinda. *Home Fires Burning: Food, Politics, and Everyday Life in World War I Berlin*. Chapel Hill, NC, 2000.

Demps, Laurenz. "Die Luftangriffe auf Berlin. Ein dokumentarischer Bericht I/II." *Jahrbuch des Märkischen Museums* 4 and 7 (1978): 27–68 and 7–44.

Deriu, Davide. "Between Veiling and Unveiling: Modern Camouflage and the City as a Theater of War." In *Endangered Cities*, ed. Funck and Chickering, 15–34.

Dinter, Andreas. *Berlin in Trümmern: Ernährungslage und medizinische Versorgung der Bevölkerung Berlins nach dem Zweiten Weltkrieg.* Berlin, 1999.

Dipper, Christoph, Lutz Klinkhammer, and Alexander Nützenadel, eds. *Europäische Sozialgeschichte: Festschrift für Professor Schieder.* Berlin, 2000.

Dreßen, Wolfgang. "Modernität und innerer Feind." In *Die Metropole*, ed. Boberg, 262–81.

Dülffer, Jost. *Deutsche Geschichte 1933–1945: Führerglaube und Vernichtungskrieg.* Stuttgart, 1992.

——. "Die japanische Botschaft im Tiergarten im Rahmen der nationalsozialistischen Umgestaltung der Reichshauptstadt Berlin." In *Formierung und Fall der Achse Berlin-Tokio*, ed. Krebs and Martin, 75–92.

——. "Frieden nach dem Zweiten Weltkrieg? Der Friedensschluss im Zeichen des Kalten Krieges." In *Wie Kriege enden*, ed. Wegner, 213–37.

Engeli, Christian and Wolfgang Ribbe. "Berlin in der NS-Zeit." In *Geschichte Berlins*, Vol 2, *Von der Märzrevolution bis zur Gegenwart*, ed. idem, 24–44. Berlin, 1989.

——. "Krieg und Kriegsfolgen in Berlin im Vergleich zu anderen Großstädten." In *Berlin im Europa der Neuzeit. Ein Tagungsbericht*, ed. Wolfgang Ribbe and Jürgen Schmädeke, 399–416. Berlin, 1990.

Engler, Harald. *Die Finanzierung der Reichshauptstadt: Untersuchungen zu den hauptstadtbedingten staatlichen Ausgaben Preußens und des Deutschen Reiches in Berlin vom Kaiserreich bis zum Dritten Reich (1871–1945).* Berlin, 2004.

Erker, Paul. *Ernährungskrise und Nachkriegsgesellschaft: Bauern und Arbeiterschaft in Bayern 1943–1953.* Stuttgart, 1990.

Eucken, Walter. "Staatliche Strukturwandlungen und die Krise des Kapitalismus." *Weltwirtschaftliches Archiv* 36 (1932): 297–321.

Evans, Jennifer. *Life among the Ruins: Cityscape and Sexuality in Cold War Berlin.* New York, 2011.

Evans, Richard J. *The Coming of the Third Reich.* London, 2003.

Federspiel, Ruth. *Soziale Mobilität im Berlin des zwanzigsten Jahrhunderts: Frauen und Männer in Berlin-Neukölln.* Berlin, 1999.

Fiedler, Martin. "Vertrauen ist gut, Kontrolle ist teuer: Vertrauen als Schlüsselkategorie wirtschaftlichen Handelns." *Geschichte und Gesellschaft* 27 (2001): 576–92.

Föllmer, Moritz, ed. *Sehnsucht nach Nähe. Interpersonale Kommunikation in Deutschland seit dem 19. Jahrhundert.* Stuttgart, 2004.

——, and Rüdiger Graf. *Die "Krise" der Weimarer Republik: Zur Kritik eines Deutungsmusters.* Frankfurt am Main, 2005.

Foote Whyte, William. *Street Corner Society: Die Sozialstruktur eines Italienerviertels.* Berlin, 1996.

Frevert, Ute. "Vertrauen in historischer Perspektive." In *Politisches Vertrauen: Soziale Grundlagen reflexiver Kooperation*, ed. Rainer Schmalz-Bruns and Reinhard Zintl, 39–60. Baden-Baden, 2002.

Funck, Marcus and Roger Chickering, eds. *Endangered Cities: Military Power and Urban Societies in the Era of the World Wars.* Boston, 2004.

Garfinkel, Harold. "A Conception of, and Experiments with, 'Trust' as a Condition of Stable Concerted Actions." In *Motivation and Social Interaction*, ed. O. J. Harvey, 187–238. New York, 1963.

Gassert, Philipp. *Amerika im Dritten Reich: Ideologie, Propaganda und Volksmeinung 1933–1945.* Stuttgart, 1997.

Geertz, Clifford. "Suq: The Bazaar Economy in Sefrou." In *Meaning and Order in Moroccan Society: Three Essays in Cultural Analysis*, ed. Clifford Geertz, Hildred Geertz, and Lawrence Orsen, 123–264. Cambridge, UK, 1979.

——. "The Bazaar Economy: Information and Search in Peasant Marketing." *American Economic Review* 68, no. 2 (1978): 28–32.

Gellately, Robert. *Backing Hitler: Consent and Coercion in Nazi Germany.* Oxford, UK, 2001.

Gellately, Robert and Nathan Stoltzfus, eds. *Social Outsiders in Nazi Germany.* Princeton, 2001.

Gerhards, Jürgen and Friedhelm Neidhardt. "Strukturen und Funktionen moderner Öffentlichkeit: Fragestellungen und Ansätze." In *Öffentlichkeit, Kultur, Massenkommunikation: Beiträge zur Medien- und Kommunikationssoziologie*, ed. Stefan Müller-Doohm, 31–88. Oldenburg, 1991.

Gerhardt, Uta. *Soziologie der Stunde Null. Zur Gesellschaftskonzeption des amerikanischen Besatzungsregimes in Deutschland 1944–1945/46.* Frankfurt am Main, 2005.

Gestrich, Andreas. "Neuzeit." In *Geschichte der Familie*, ed. Gestrich, Krause, and Mitterauer, 364–652.

Gestrich, Andreas, Jens Krause, and Michael Mitterauer. *Geschichte der Familie.* Stuttgart, 2003.

Geyer, Martin H. "Die Sprache des Rechts, die Sprache des Antisemitismus: 'Wucher' und soziale Ordnungsvorstellungen im Kaiserreich und der Weimarer Republik." In *Europäische Sozialgeschichte*, ed. Dipper, Klinkhammer, and Nützenadel, 413–29.

——. *Verkehrte Welt: Revolution, Inflation und Moderne, Munich 1914–1924.* Göttingen, 1998.

Giddens, Anthony. *The Consequences of Modernity.* Cambridge, UK, 1990.

——. *The Constitution of Society: Outline of the Theory of Structuration.* Cambridge, UK, 1984.

Glennie, Paul. "Consumption, Consumerism and Urban Form: Historical Perspectives." *Urban Studies* 35 (1998): 927–51.

Glennie, Paul. "Consumption within Historical Studies." In *Acknowledging Consumption*, ed. Daniel Miller, 164–202. London, 1995.

Goebbels, Joseph. Die Tagebücher. Sämtliche Fragmente. 15 vols. Edited by Elke Fröhlich. Munich, 1987–1999.

Goffman, Erving. *Interaction Ritual: Essays on Face-to-Face Behavior.* New York, 1967.

——. *The Presentation of the Self in Everyday Life.* New York, 1959.

——. *Relations in Public: Microstudies of the Public Order.* New York 1971.

Görtemaker, Manfred. *Geschichte der Bundesrepublik Deutschland.* Munich, 2003.

Granovetter, Mark. "Economic Action and Social Structure: The Problem of Embeddedness." *American Journal of Sociology* 91 (1985): 481–510.

Gries, Rainer. *Die Rationengesellschaft: Versorgungskampf und Vergleichsmentalität: Leipzig, München und Köln nach dem Kriege.* Münster, 1991.

——. *Produkte als Medien: Kulturgeschichte der Produktkommunikation in der Bundesrepublik und der DDR.* Leipzig, 2003.

Gumbrecht, Hans-Ulrich. *In 1926: Living on the Edge of Time.* Cambridge, MA, 1998.

Gusy, Christoph. "Einleitung—Weimar: Geschichte als Argument." In *Weimars Lange Schatten: "Weimar" als Argument nach 1945*, ed. idem, 1–22. Baden-Baden, 2003.

Haeser, Werner. "Vom Schwarzmarkt und Tauschhandel zur Deutschen Mark." *Schmallenberger Heimatblätter* 62 (1995/96): 75–81.

Hagemann, Karen and Stefanie Schüler-Springorum, eds. *Heimat—Front. Militär und Geschlechterverhältnisse im Zeitalter der Weltkriege*. Frankfurt am Main, 2002.

Hardtwig, Wolfgang. *Politische Kulturgeschichte der Zwischenkriegszeit 1918–1936*. Göttingen, 2005.

Haselbach, Dieter. "Die Lehren aus Weimar in den Wirtschaftswissenschaften nach 1945: Der Ordoliberalismus." In *Weimars lange Schatten*, ed. Gusy, 118–47.

Heimann, Siegfried. "Karl Heinrich und die Berliner SPD, die sowjetische Militäradministration und die SED." *Gesprächskreis Geschichte der Friedrich-Ebert-Stiftung* 70 (2007): 1–65.

Heineman, Elizabeth. "The Hour of the Woman: Memories of Germany's 'Crisis Years' and West German National Identity." In *The Miracle Years: A Cultural History of West Germany 1949–1968*, ed. Hanna Schissler, 21–56. Princeton, 2001.

——. *What Difference Does a Husband Make: Women and Marital Status in Nazi and Postwar Germany*. Berkeley, 1999.

Heinemann, Ulrich. "Die Last der Vergangenheit: Zur politischen Bedeutung der Kriegsschuld- und Dolchstoßdiskussion." In *Die Weimarer Republik 1918–1933: Politik, Wirtschaft, Gesellschaft*, ed. Karl Dietrich Bracher, Manfred Funke, and Hans-Adolf Jacobsen, 371–86. Düsseldorf, 1987.

Heldmann, Philipp. *Herrschaft—Wirtschaft—Anoraks. Konsumpolitik in der DDR der Sechzigerjahre*. Göttingen, 2004.

Hengartner, Thomas and Christoph Merki, eds. *Tabakfragen: Rauchen aus kulturwissenschaftlicher Sicht*. Zurich, 1996.

Henrichsmeyer, Wilhelm, Oskar Gans, and Ingo Evers. *Einführung in die Volkswirtschaftslehre*, 10th ed. Stuttgart, 1993.

Herbert, Ulrich. *Fremdarbeiter: Politik und Praxis des "Ausländer-Einsatzes" in der Kriegswirtschaft des Dritten Reiches*. Bonn, 1985.

Hessler, Julie. *A Social History of Soviet Trade: Trade Policy, Retail Practices, and Consumption, 1917–1953*. Princeton, 2004.

Hinze, Edith. *Lage und Leistung erwerbstätiger Mütter: Ergebnisse einer Untersuchung in West-Berlin*. Berlin, 1960.

Hobsbawm, Eric. "Introduction: Inventing Tradition." In *The Invention of Tradition*, ed. idem and Terence Ranger, 11–14. Cambridge, 2003.

Hoffmann, Heinz. *Der Kommissionshandel im planwirtschaftlichen System der DDR: Eine besondere Eigentums- und Handelsform*. Leipzig, 2001.

Hoffmann, Stefan-Ludwig. "Das Dilemma der Besatzer. Alliierte Deutschlandpolitik nach 1945: Pragmatismus vor Rigorismus." *WZB-Mitteilungen* 114 (2006): 15–17.

Höhn, Maria. *GIs and Fräuleins: The German-American Encounter in 1950s West Germany*. Chapel Hill, 2002.

Hudemann, Rainer. *Sozialpolitik im deutschen Südwesten zwischen Tradition und Neuordnung 1945–1953: Sozialversicherung und Kriegsopferversorgung im Rahmen französischer Besatzungspolitik*. Mainz, 1988.

Jansen, Dorothea. *Einführung in die Netzwerkanalyse: Grundlagen, Methoden, Forschungsbeispiele*. Opladen, 1999.

Joas, Hans. "Rollen- und Interaktionstheorien in der Sozialisationsforschung." In *Neues Handbuch der Sozialisationsforschung*, ed. Klaus Hurrelmann and Dieter Ulich, 137–52. Weinheim, 1991.

Joas, Hans and Wolfang Knöbl. *Sozialtheorie: Zwanzig einführende Vorlesungen*. Frankfurt am Main, 2004.

Kebbedies, Frank. *Außer Kontrolle: Jugendkriminalität in der NS-Zeit und der frühen Nachkriegszeit*. Essen, 2000.

Keiderling, Gerhard. *'Rosinenbomber' über Berlin. Währungsreform, Blockade, Luftbrücke, Teilung. Die schicksalsvollen Jahre 1948/49*. Berlin, 1998.

Kellerhoff, Sven Felix and Wieland Giebel, eds. *Als die Tage zu Nächten wurden: Berliner Schicksale im Luftkrieg*. Berlin, 2003.

Kendon, Adam. *Conducting Interaction: Patterns of Behavior in Focused Encounters*. Cambridge, UK, 1990.

Kerr, Philip. *Alte Freunde—neue Feinde*. Reinbek, 2000.

Kershaw, Ian. *Der Hitler-Mythos: Führerkult und Volksmeinung*. Stuttgart, 1999.

——. *Hitler 1889–1936*, trans. Jürgen Peter Krause, 4th ed. Stuttgart, 1998.

——. *Hitlers Macht: Das Profil der NS-Herrschaft*. Munich, 2000.

Klein, Richard. *Schöner blauer Dunst: Ein Lob der Zigarette*. Munich, 1992.

Kleßmann, Christoph. *Die doppelte Staatsgründung: Deutsche Geschichte 1945–1955*, 5th ed. Göttingen, 1991.

Kolb, Eberhard. *Der Friede von Versailles*. Munich, 2005.

Korff, Gottfried and Reinhard Rürup, eds. *Berlin, Berlin: Die Ausstellung zur Geschichte der Stadt*. Berlin, 1987.

Koselleck, Reinhart. "Erinnerungsschleusen und Erfahrungsschichten. Der Einfluss der beiden Weltkriege auf das soziale Bewusstsein." Reprinted in *Zeitschichten. Studien zur Historik*, ed. idem, 265–84. Frankfurt am Main, 2000.

Kowalczuk, Ingo-Sascha. "Opfer der eigenen Politik? Zu den Hintergründen der Verhaftung von Minister Karl Hamann (LDPD)." *Jahrbuch zur Liberalismusforschung* 16 (2004): 221–71.

Krebs, Gerhard and Bernd Martin, eds. *Formierung und Fall der Achse Berlin-Tokio*. Munich, 1994.

Krumeich, Gerhard, ed. *Versailles 1919: Ziele—Wirkung—Wahrnehmung*. Essen, 2001.

Kupschinsky, Elke. "Die vernünftige Nephertete. Die Neue Frau der 20er Jahre in Berlin." In *Die Metropole*, ed. Boberg, 164–73.

Landwehr, Achim. *Geschichte des Sagbaren: Einführung in die historische Diskursanalyse*. Tübingen, 2001.

Langbein, Ulrike. *Geerbte Dinge: Soziale Praxis und symbolische Bedeutung des Erbens*. Cologne, 2002.

Large, David Clay. *Berlin: A Modern History*. New York, 2001.

Lehnert, Detlef and Klaus Megerle. "Identitäts- und Konsensprobleme in einer fragmentierten Gesellschaft: Zur politischen Kultur in der Weimarer Republik." In "Politische Kultur in Deutschland," ed. Dirk Berg-Schlosser and Jakob Schissler. Special issue of *Politische Vierteljahresschrift* 18 (1987): 80–95.

Lethen, Helmut. "Chicago und Moskau." In *Die Metropole*, ed. Boberg, 190–213.

Libeskind, Daniel. *Radix–Matrix: Architecture and Writing*. Munich, 1997.

Lindenberger, Thomas. *Straßenpolitik. Zur Sozialgeschichte der öffentlichen Ordnung in Berlin 1900–1914*. Bonn, 1995.

Link, Alexander. *'Schrottelzeit': Nachkriegsalltag in Mainz*. Mainz, 1990.

Link, Jürgen. "Literaturanalyse als Interdiskursanalyse. Am Beispiel des Ursprungs literarischer Symbolik in der Kollektivsymbolik." In *Diskurstheorien und Literaturwissenschaft*, ed. Jürgen Fohrmann and Harro Müller, 284–307. Frankfurt am Main, 1988.

Loberg, Molly. "Berlin Streets: Politics, Commerce, and Crowds, 1918–1938." PhD diss., Princeton University, 2006.

Lorenz, Maren. *Leibhaftige Vergangenheit. Einführung in die Körpergeschichte.* Tübingen, 2000.

Löw, Maren. *Raumsoziologie.* Frankfurt am Main, 2001.

Ludwig, Cordula. *Korruption und Nationalsozialismus in Berlin 1924–1934.* Berlin, 1998.

Luhmann, Niklas. *Liebe als Passion. Zur Codierung von Intimität.* Frankfurt am Main, 1992.

——. *Soziale Systeme: Grundriß einer allgemeinen Theorie,* 7th ed. Frankfurt am Main, 1999.

——. *Vertrauen: Ein Mechanismus der Reduktion sozialer Komplexität,* 4th ed. Stuttgart, 2000.

Maase, Kaspar. " 'Lässig' kontra 'zackig'—Nachkriegsjugend und Männlichkeiten in geschlechtergeschichtlicher Perspektive." In *Sag mir, wo die Mädchen sind. . . . Beiträge zur Geschlechtergeschichte der Jugend,* ed. Christina Benninghaus and Kerstin Kohtz, 79–101. Cologne, 1999.

Mählert, Ulrich. *Kleine Geschichte der DDR.* Munich, 1998.

Malinowski, Stefan. "Politische Skandale als Zerrspiegel der Demokratie: Die Fälle Barmat und Sklarek im Kalkül der Weimarer Rechten." *Jahrbuch für Antisemitismusforschung* 5 (1996): 46–65.

Mann, Thomas. *Unordnung und Frühes Leid: Die Erzählungen.* Frankfurt am Main, 2005.

Martin, Bernd. "Der Schein des Bündnisses: Deutschland und Japan im Krieg 1940–1945." In *Formierung und Fall der Achse Berlin—Tokyo,* ed. idem and Gerhard Krebs, 27–53. Munich, 1994.

Marx, Karl. *The Power of Money: Economic and Philosophic Manuscripts of 1844,* trans. Martin Mulligan. Moscow, 1959.

Mauss, Marcel. *Die Gabe: Form und Funktion des Austauschs in archaischen Gesellschaften,* trans. Eva Moldenhauer. Frankfurt am Main, 1984.

Mergel, Thomas and Thomas Welskopp. "Führer, Volksgemeinschaft und Maschine: Politische Erwartungsstrukturen in der Weimarer Republik und dem Nationalsozialismus 1918–1936." In *Politische Kulturgeschichte der Zwischenkriegszeit 1918–1936,* ed. Hardtwig, 91–128.

——, eds. *Geschichte zwischen Kultur und Gesellschaft: Beiträge zur Theoriedebatte.* Munich, 1997.

——. *Parlamentarische Kultur in der Weimarer Republik.* Düsseldorf, 2002.

Merkel, Ina. *Utopie und Bedürfnis: Die Geschichte der Konsumkultur in der DDR.* Cologne, 1999.

Merki, Christoph. "Die amerikanische Zigarette, das Maß aller Dinge. Rauchen in Deutschland zur Zeit der Zigarettenwährung 1945–1948." In *Tabakfragen. Rauchen aus kulturwissenschaftlicher Sicht,* ed. Thomas Hengartner and Christoph Merki, 57–82. Zurich, 1996.

Mierzejewski, Alfred C. *Erhard: A Biography.* Princeton, 2005.

Mironenko, Sergej, Lutz Niethammer, and Alexander von Plato, eds. *Sowjetische Speziallager in Deutschland 1945–1950.* Vol. 2, *Sowjetische Dokumente zur Lagerpolitik.* Berlin, 1998.

Moeller, Robert G. *West Germany under Construction: Politics, Society, and Culture in the Adenauer Era.* Ann Arbor, MI, 1997.

Mörchen, Stefan. " 'Echte Kriminelle' und 'zeitbedingte Rechtsbrecher': Schwarzer Markt und Konstruktionen des Kriminellen in der Nachkriegszeit." *Werkstatt Geschichte* 15 (2006): 57–76.

——. *Schwarzer Markt: Kriminalität, Ordnung und Moral in Bremen 1939–1949*. Frankfurt am Main, 2011.

Mosse, George L. *Die Nationalisierung der Massen: Von den Befreiungskriegen bis zum Dritten Reich*, trans. Otto Weith. Frankfurt am Main, 1976.

Naimark, Norman M. *The Russians in Germany: The History of the Soviet Zone of Occupation, 1945–1949*. Cambridge, MA, 1995.

Narotzky, Susana. "Economic Anthropology." In *International Encyclopedia of the Social and Behavioral* Sciences, ed. Neil J. Smelser and Paul B. Baltes, 8:4069. Oxford, UK, 2001.

——. *New Directions in Economic Anthropology*. London, 1997.

Neumann, Thomas. "Der Bombenkrieg. Zur ungeschriebenen Geschichte einer kollektiven Verletzung." In *Nachkrieg in Deutschland*, ed. Klaus Naumann, 319–42. Hamburg, 2001.

Nieden, Susanne zur. *Alltag im Ausnahmezustand: Frauentagebücher im zerstörten Deutschland 1943 bis 1945*. Berlin, 1993.

——. "Erotische Fraternisierung: Der Mythos von der schnellen Kapitulation der deutschen Frauen im Mai 1945." In *Heimat—Front. Militär und Geschlechterverhältnisse im Zeitalter der Weltkriege*, ed. Hagemann and Schüler-Springorum, 313–25.

Niedhardt, Gottfried. "Der Erste Weltkrieg: Von der Gewalt im Krieg zu den Konflikten im Frieden." In *Wie Kriege enden*, ed. Wegner, 188–211.

Niehuss, Merith. *Familie, Frau und Gesellschaft: Studien zur Strukturgeschichte der Familie in Westdeutschland 1945–1960*. Göttingen, 2001.

Niemann, Jürgen. *Auftakt zur Demokratie: Der Bundeswahlkampf 1949 zwischen Improvisation und Ideologie*. Bochum, 1994.

Niethammer, Lutz. "Privat-Wirtschaft: Erinnerungsfragmente einer anderen Umerziehung." In *"Hinterher merkt man, dass es richtig war, dass es schiefgegangen ist." Nachkriegs-Erfahrungen im Ruhrgebiet*, ed. idem, 17–105. Berlin, 1983.

North, Douglass C. *Institutions, Institutional Change and Economic Performance*. Cambridge, UK, 1990.

Opp, Klaus-Dieter. "DDR '89. Zu den Ursachen einer spontanen Revolution." In *Der Zusammenbruch der DDR*, ed. Hans Joas and Martin Kohli, 194–221. Frankfurt am Main, 1994.

Papilloud, Christian. *Le Don de Relation: Georg Simmel—Marcel Mauss*. Paris, 2002.

Peukert, Detlev J. K. *Die Weimarer Republik: Krisenjahre der klassischen Moderne*. Frankfurt am Main, 1987.

——. *Volksgenossen und Gemeinschaftsfremde: Anpassung, Ausmerze und Aufbegehren unter dem Nationalsozialismus*. Opladen, 1982.

Pfaff, Anita. *Typische Lebensläufe von Frauen der Geburtsjahrgänge 1910–1975*. Stuttgart, 1979.

Plattner, Stuart, ed. *Economic Anthropology*. Stanford, CA, 1989.

——. "Economic Behavior in Markets." In *Economic Anthropology*, ed. idem, 209–21. Stanford, CA, 1989.

Plöckinger, Othmar. *Reden um die Macht? Wirkung und Strategie der Reden Adolf Hitlers im Wahlkampf zu den Reichstagswahlen am 6. November 1932*. Vienna, 1999.

Porter, Michael. *Competitive Advantage*. New York, 1985.

——. "The Competitive Advantage of the Inner City." *Harvard Business Review* 74 (1995): 55–71.

Pynchon, Thomas. *Gravity's Rainbow*. 1973. New York, 2000.

Ranft, Andreas and Stefan Selzer, eds. *Städte aus Trümmern. Katastrophenbewältigung zwischen Antike und Moderne*. Göttingen, 2004.

Reichardt, Hans J. *Raus aus den Trümmern. Vom Beginn des Wiederaufbaus in Berlin 1945*. Berlin, 1988.

Requate, Jörg. "Öffentlichkeit und Medien als Gegenstände historischer Analyse." *Geschichte und Gesellschaft* 25 (1999): 5–31.

Reuß, Ernst. *Berliner Justizgeschichte*. Berlin, 2000.

Reuveni, Gideon. "Wohlstand durch Konsum: Straßenhandel und Versicherungszeitschriften in den zwanziger Jahren." In *Die "Krise" der Weimarer Republik*, ed. Föllmer and Graf, 267–86.

Richarz, Monika. "Jüdisches Berlin und seine Vernichtung." In *Die Metropole. Industriekultur in Berlin im 20. Jahrhundert*, ed. Boberg, 216–25.

Richter, Rudolf and Eirik Furubotn. *Neue Institutionenökonomik: Eine Einführung und kritische Würdigung*, trans. Monika Streissler, 3rd ed. Tübingen, 2003.

Robeck, Sylvia and Gabriela Wachter, eds. *Kalter Krieg und warme Küche: 200 Berliner Rezepte im Kontext der Stadtgeschichte*. Berlin, 2007.

Roehrkohl, Anne. *Hungerblockade und Heimatfront: Die kommunale Lebensmittelversorgung in Westfalen während des Ersten Weltkrieges*. Stuttgart, 1991.

Roesler, Jörg. "The Black Market in Post-War Berlin and the Methods Used to Counteract It." *German History* 7 (1989): 92–107.

——. *Die Wirtschaft der DDR. Publikation der Landeszentrale für politische Bildung Thüringen*. Erfurt, 2002.

Rürup, Reinhard, ed. *Berlin 1945. Eine Dokumentation*. Berlin, 1995.

—— and Gottfried Korff, eds. *Berlin. Die Ausstellung zur Geschichte der Stadt*. Berlin, 1987.

Ruhl, Klaus-Jörg. *Verordnete Unterordnung. Berufstätige Frauen zwischen Wirtschaftswachstum und konservativer Ideologie in der Nachkriegszeit 1945–1963*. Munich, 1994.

Sabrow, Martin, ed. *Skandal und Diktatur: Formen öffentlicher Empörung im NS-Staat und in der DDR*. Göttingen, 2004.

Saldern, Adelheid von. "Stadt und Öffentlichkeit in urbanisierten Gesellschaften: Neue Zugänge zu einem alten Thema." *Informationen zur modernen Stadtgeschichte* 2 (2000): 3–15.

——. *Häuserleben: zur Geschichte städtischen Arbeiterwohnens vom Kaiserreich bis heute*. Bonn, 1995.

Sanders, Paul. *Histoire du Marché Noir 1940–1946*. Paris, 2001.

Schäfer, Julia. *Vermessen—gezeichnet—verlacht: Judenbilder in populären Zeitschriften 1918–1933*. Frankfurt am Main, 2005.

Schenk, Fritjof B. "Mental Maps. Die Konstruktion von geographischen Räumen in Europa seit der Aufklärung." *Geschichte und Gesellschaft* 28 (2002): 493–514.

Schevardo, Jennifer. *Vom Wert des Notwendigen. Preispolitik und Lebensstandard in der DDR der fünfziger Jahre*. Stuttgart, 2006.

Schissler, Hanna, ed. *The Miracle Years: A Cultural History of West Germany, 1949–1968*. Princeton, NJ, 2001.

Schivelbusch, Wolfgang. *Kultur der Niederlage*. Berlin, 2001.

Schmidt, Dorothea. *Zeitgeschichte im Mikrokosmos: Ein Gebäude in Berlin-Schöneberg*. Berlin, 2004.

Schmitz-Berning, Cornelia. *Vokabular des Nationalsozialismus*. Berlin, 1998.

Schmölders, Günter. "Die Zigarettenwährung." In *Sozialökonomische Verhaltensforschung. Festschrift für Günter Schmölders zum 70. Geburtstag*, ed. Gerhard Brinkmann, 166–71. Berlin, 1973.

Scholz, Robert. "Die Auswirkungen der Inflation auf das Sozial- und Wohlfahrtswesen der neuen Stadtgemeinde Berlin." In *Konsequenzen der Inflation*, ed. Gerald Feldman and J. Th. M. Houwink ten Cate, 45–75. Berlin, 1989.

Scholze, Thomas. "Zur Ernährungssituation der Berliner nach dem Zweiten Weltkrieg. Ein Beitrag zur Erfahrung des Großstadtalltags (1945–1952)." *Jahrbuch für Geschichte* 35 (1987): 539–64.

Schottmann, Christian. *Politische Schlagwörter in Deutschland zwischen 1929 und 1934*. Stuttgart, 1997.

Schreiner, Klaus. " 'Wann kommt der Retter Deutschlands?' Formen und Funktionen von politischen Messianismus in der Weimarer Republik." *Saeculum* 49 (1998): 107–60.

Schultz, Annett. "Privathaushalte und Haushalten in Ostdeutschland." Discussion Paper FS III 97–405, WZB. Berlin, 1997.

Schumann, Dirk. *Politische Gewalt in der Weimarer Republik: Kampf um die Straße und Furcht vor dem Bürgerkrieg*. Essen, 2001.

Selle, Gert. *Die eigenen vier Wände. Zur verborgenen Geschichte des Wohnens*. Frankfurt am Main, 1993.

Sennet, Richard. *Flesh and Stone: The Body and the City in Western Civilization*. London, 2002.

Sheppard, Eric. "Competition in Space and between Places." In *A Companion to Economic Geography*, ed. idem and Trevor J. Barnes, 169–86. Oxford, 2000.

Siegenthaler, Hansjörg. *Regelvertrauen, Prosperität und Krisen: Die Ungleichmäßigkeit wirtschaftlicher und sozialer Entwicklungen als Ergebnis individuellen Handelns*. Tübingen, 1993.

Simmel, Georg. *Philosophie des Geldes*, 4th ed. Frankfurt am Main, 1996.

——. *The Philosophy of Money*, ed. David Frisby, trans. Tom Bottomore and David Frisby, 3rd exp. ed. New York, 2004.

Sokoll, Thomas. "Kulturanthropologie und Historische Sozialwissenschaft." In *Geschichte zwischen Kultur und Gesellschaft*, ed. Mergel and Welskopp, 232–72.

Spiekermann, Uwe. *Basis der Konsumgesellschaft: Entstehung und Entwicklung des modernen Kleinhandels in Deutschland*. Munich, 1999.

——. "From Neighbour to Consumer: The Transformation of Retailer-Consumer Relationships in Twentieth-Century Germany." In *The Making of the Consumer: Knowledge, Power and Identity in the Modern* World, ed. Frank Trentmann, 147–74. Oxford, 2006.

Spoerer, Mark. "Die soziale Differenzierung der ausländischen Zivilarbeiter, Kriegsgefangenen und Häftlinge im Deutschen Reich." In *Das Deutsche Reich und der Zweite Weltkrieg*. Vol. 9, Pt. 2, *Die deutsche Kriegsgesellschaft 1939 bis 1945: Ausbeutung, Deutungen, Ausgrenzung*, ed. Jörg Echternkamp, 485–576. Munich, 2005.

Starbatty, Joachim. "Die Soziale Marktwirtschaft aus historisch-theoretischer Sicht." In *Entstehung und Entwicklung der Sozialen Marktwirtschaft. Im Auftrag der Gesellschaft für Unternehmensgeschichte*, ed. Hans Pohl, 7–26. Wiesbaden, 1986.

Staritz, Dietrich. *Geschichte der DDR*, rev. ed. Frankfurt am Main, 1996.

Steege, Paul. *Black Market, Cold War: Everyday Life in Berlin, 1946–1949*. Cambridge, UK, 2007.

Steinborn, Norbert and Hilmar Krüger, eds. *Die Berliner Polizei 1945–1992*. Berlin, 1993.

Steiner, André. *The Plans That Failed: An Economic History of the GDR*. New York, 2010.

——, ed. *Preispolitik und Lebensstandard: Nationalsozialismus, DDR und Bundesrepublik im Vergleich*. Cologne, 2006.

——, ed. *Überholen ohne einzuholen. Die DDR-Wirtschaft als Fußnote der deutschen Geschichte?* Berlin, 2006.

——. *Von Plan zu Plan: Eine Wirtschaftsgeschichte der DDR*. Munich, 2004.

Stimmann, Hans. "Weltstadtplätze und Massenverkehr." In *Die Metropole*, ed. Boberg, 138–43.

Stoltmann, Gerd. "Die Zigarettenwährung." *Deutsche Tabak Zeitung* 5 (1982): 10.

Stupp, Matthias. *GmbH-Recht im Nationalsozialismus: Anschauungen des Nationalsozialismus zur Haftungsbeschränkung, Juristischen Person, Kapitalgesellschaft und Treupflicht: Untersuchungen zum Referentenentwurf 1939 zu einem neuen GmbH-Gesetz*. Berlin, 2002.

Thompson, Edward P. "The Moral Economy of the English Crowd in the 18th Century." *Past and Present* 50 (1971): 76–136.

Thornton, Mark. *The Economics of Prohibition*. Salt Lake City, 1991.

Timm, Annette F. "The Ambivalent Outsider: Prostitution, Promiscuity, and VD Control in Nazi Berlin." In *Social Outsiders in Nazi Germany*, ed. Robert Gellately and Nathan Stoltzfus, 192–211. Princeton, 2001.

Torrie, Julia S. "Preservation by Dispersion: Civilian Evacuations and the City in Germany and France 1939–1945." In *Endangered Cities*, ed. Funck and Chickering, 47–62.

Ullmann, Hans-Peter. "'Der Kaiser bei Wertheim'—Warenhäuser im wilhelminischen Deutschland." In *Europäische Sozialgeschichte*, ed. Dipper, Klinkhammer, and Nützenadel, 223–36.

Voigt, Stefan. *Institutionenökonomik*. Munich, 2002.

Volkmann, Hans-Erich, ed. *Das Russlandbild im Dritten Reich*. Cologne, 1994.

——. *Ökonomie und Expansion: Grundzüge der NS-Wirtschaftspolitik*. Munich, 2003.

Wagner, Patrick. *Volksgemeinschaft ohne Verbrecher: Konzeption und Praxis der Kriminalpolizei in der Weimarer Republik und des Nationalsozialismus*. Hamburg, 1996.

Weber, Hermann. *Die DDR 1945–1990*, 3rd ed. Munich, 2003.

Weber, Max. *Wirtschaft und Gesellschaft: Grundriss der verstehenden Soziologie*, ed. Johannes Winckelmann, 5th ed. Tübingen, 1980.

Weber, Petra. *Justiz und Diktatur: Justizverwaltung und politische Strafjustiz in Thüringen 1945–1961*. Munich, 2000.

Weber, Ursula. *Der Polenmarkt in Berlin: Zur Rekonstruktion eines kulturellen Kontakts im Prozess der politischen Transformation Mittel- und Osteuropas*. Neuried, 2002.

Wegner, Bernd, ed. *Wie Kriege enden. Wege zum Frieden von der Antike bis zur Gegenwart*. Paderborn, 2002.

Wehler, Hans-Ulrich. *Die Herausforderung der Kulturgeschichte*. Munich, 1998.

——. *Gesellschaftsgeschichte*. Vol. 4, *Vom Beginn des Ersten Weltkriegs bis zur Gründung der beiden deutschen Staaten 1914–1949*. Munich, 2003.

——. "Kommentar." In *Geschichte zwischen Kultur und Gesellschaft*, ed. Welskopp, 351–66.

Welskopp, Thomas. "Bis an die Grenzen des Gesetzes. Die Reaktion der legalen Alkoholwirtschaft auf die National Prohibition in den USA, 1920–1933." *Zeitschrift für Unternehmensgeschichte* 52 (2007): 3–32.

Wenzel, Harald. "Vertrauen und die Integration moderner Gesellschaften." In *Politisches Vertrauen: Grundlagen reflexiver Kooperation*, ed. Rainer Schmalz-Bruns and Reinhard Zintl, 61–76. Baden-Baden, 2002.

Wette, Wolfram, ed. *Das letzte halbe Jahr. Stimmungsberichte der Wehrmachtpropaganda 1944/45*. Essen, 2001.

White, Harrison. "Varieties of Markets." In *Social Structures: A Network Approach*, ed. Barry Wellman and S. D. Berkowitz, 226–60. New York, 1987.

Widdig, Bernd. *Culture and Inflation in Weimar Germany*. Berkeley, 2001.

Wildt, Michael. *Am Beginn der Konsumgesellschaft: Mangelerfahrung, Lebenshaltung, Wohlstandshoffnung in Westdeutschland in den fünfziger Jahren*, 2nd ed. Hamburg, 1995.

——. *Der Traum vom Sattwerden: Hunger und Protest, Schwarzmarkt und Selbsthilfe*. Hamburg, 1986.

Wirsching, Andreas. *Die Weimarer Republik: Politik und Gesellschaft*. Munich, 2000.

——. *Vom Weltkrieg zum Bürgerkrieg. Politischer Extremismus in Deutschland und Frankreich 1918–1933/39. Berlin und Paris im Vergleich*. Munich, 1999.

Wolff, Michael. *Die Währungsreform in Berlin 1948/49*. Berlin, 1991.

Wolfrum, Edgar. *Die geglückte Demokratie: Geschichte der Bundesrepublik Deutschland von ihren Anfängen bis zur Gegenwart*. Stuttgart, 2006.

Zelizer, Viviana A. "Economic Sociology." In *International Encyclopedia of the Social and Behavioral Sciences*, ed. Neil J. Smelser and Paul B. Baltes, 8:4131. Oxford, UK, 2001.

——. *The Social Meaning of Money: Pin Money, Paychecks, Poor Relief, and Other Currencies*. London 1994.

Zierenberg, Malte. "Berlin tauscht. Schwarzmärkte in Berlin 1939–1950." *Informationen zur modernen Stadtgeschichte* 2 (2004): 45–53.

——. "Tauschen und Vertrauen: Zur Kulturgeschichte des Schwarzhandels im Berlin der 1940er Jahre." In *Wirtschaftsgeschichte als Kulturgeschichte*, ed. Berghoff and Vogel, 169–94.

——. "The Trading City: Black Markets in Berlin during World War II." In *Endangered Cities*, ed. Funck and Chickering, 145–58.

——."Zwischen Herrschaftsfragen und Verbraucherinteressen: 'Kriegswirtschaftsverbrechen' vor dem Sondergericht Köln im Zweiten Weltkrieg." *Geschichte in Köln* 50 (2003): 175–95.

Zimm, Alfred. *Die Entwicklung des Industriestandortes Berlin. Tendenzen der geographischen Lokalisation bei den Berliner Industriezweigen von überörtlicher Bedeutung sowie die territoriale Stadtentwicklung bis 1945*. Berlin, 1959.

Zinn, Karl Georg. *Soziale Marktwirtschaft. Idee, Entwicklung und Politik der bundesdeutschen Wirtschaftsordnung*. Mannheim, 1992.

Zschaler, Frank. "Die Lösung der Währungsfrage in Berlin 1948/49. Weichenstellungen für die Nachkriegsentwicklung der deutschen Hauptstadt." In *Sterben für Berlin? Die Berliner Krisen 1948:1958*, ed. Burghard Ciesla, Michael Lemke, and Thomas Lindenberger, 47–58. Berlin, 2000.

——. *Öffentliche Finanzen und Finanzpolitik in Berlin 1945–1961: Eine vergleichende Untersuchung von Ost- und West-Berlin mit Datenanhang 1945–1989*. Berlin, 1995.

Zündorf, Irmgard. *Der Preis der Marktwirtschaft: Staatliche Preispolitik und Lebensstandard in Westdeutschland 1948 bis 1963*. Stuttgart, 2006.

Zweiniger-Bargielowska, Ina. *Austerity in Britain: Rationing, Controls, and Consumption 1939–1955*. Oxford, 2000.

Index

Note: The letter 'n' following locators refers to notes.

Lightning Source UK Ltd.
Milton Keynes UK
UKHW050219181121
394037UK00025B/502

9 781137 017741